Dreamland

Dreamland

America's Immigration Lottery in an Age of Restriction

CARLY GOODMAN

The University of North Carolina Press Chapel Hill

Library of Congress Cataloging-in-Publication Data *to come*
ISBN 978-1-4696-7304-2 (cloth: alk. paper)
ISBN 978-1-4696-7305-9 (ebook)

Cover illustration: [[*to come*]]

For Sylvia and Rose

And for the people who move

Contents

Part III

Illustrations

Dreamland

Introduction

· ·

On eBay I bought an envelope for $3.99. It had been mailed on October 13, 1995, from Tamale in northern Ghana to an office suite in Los Angeles. It was likely for sale because of the affixed stamps, four of them, each worth 100 cedis. The featured image on the stamps is Cape Coast Castle, a former European outpost on the coast of the Gulf of Guinea through which hundreds of thousands of African people were moved before being shuffled onto ships, bound for the Americas.

The envelope is addressed to a rather official name: "New U.S. Government Lottery," a reference to the United States diversity visa, or green card, lottery. Through this program, the United States makes immigrant visas available to people around the world who would like to make lives in America. A person in Ghana mailed this envelope, presumably to enter the lottery, spinning fortune's merry wheel and hoping for good luck and a green card. The green card lottery has come to play a powerful role as one of very few channels for African immigration to the United States in a new era of immigration restriction.

The Cape Coast Castle stamps on the envelope are a visual reminder that places like Ghana and the United States have long been linked together through a history made by trade, exchange, and migration—most prominently the forced migration of enslaved people. The fading images of the castle remind us of the roots of today's global inequality, of processes that shape the directions of migrations even now. A symbol of conquest, theft, and oppression, made into a national attraction and stamp, was casually affixed to a dispatch that would trace a new route across the Atlantic.

The thin paper of the envelope is an artifact of the tremendous flurry of global lottery-related activity that began in the summer of 1994. Unlike most other immigration policies, the lottery offered a chance of immigration to people without ties to the United States. These immigrants would not be selected because of family connections, particularly valued skills, or special humanitarian need. Rather, the lottery was run to enable people from "underrepresented" countries to gain the opportunity to migrate legally, a prospect otherwise all but denied them. The early advocates for this kind of program hoped it would benefit Europeans whose experiences

Envelope from Ghana to Los Angeles, postmarked October 13, 1995. Photograph by author.

of immigration restriction showed white policymakers how harmful such restrictions could be. Offering immigrant visas by lottery would then allow for a flow of white immigrants to the United States in an age of largely Asian and Latin American immigration.

The diversity visa lottery did that. But it also opened doors, long blocked, to Black immigrants from Africa. When the lottery was introduced to African countries, it arrived in a context of austerity, with many other emigration possibilities hindered, and it therefore fueled a cottage industry of migration-related services and a festive annual tradition. Banners, posters, flyers, and signs announced the lottery's annual start, and with it, a signal of American openness and welcome. The lottery painted America as a dreamland. It was a gesture that people understood as targeting African people specifically. It went against the restrictionist grain, allowing Africans a rare alternative to a long-standing sense of global marginalization.

In the 1995 lottery, 6.5 million entries from around the world vied for just 55,000 available visas. After having their names drawn as winners, lottery registrants could then apply for an immigrant visa. Running an immigration admissions program as a lottery traded its ordinary bureaucratic sobriety for a sense of whimsy. Rather than a set of criteria written by powerful gate-keepers, the lottery placed luck front and center, as if to acknowledge the randomness that shapes our lives: where we are born, what rights we are afforded, whether we have the power to come and go as we please. These depend on happenstance and contingency, rather than something earned—why pretend otherwise? More than 20,000 diversity visas would be issued to people from Africa in that first year, including more than 2,000 to Ghanaians.

The envelope I found on eBay wasn't sent to a government agency—even if the address line suggested otherwise. I recognized the recipient's address as the private offices of an American attorney at a suite on Wilshire Boulevard in Los Angeles. I had seen the address printed with photos of the lawyer David L. Amkraut's face, on advertisements in Ghanaian newspapers from the 1990s. Amkraut, I learned after googling him, was sanctioned by the Federal Trade Commission in 1997 for deceptive practices around the green card lottery. He was accused of inflating his success record, sending multiple entries for his clients (which disqualified them), and then withholding from clients their identifying case numbers to coerce them to retain his legal services for the next step of the process.[1] Intermediaries like Amkraut, along with an array of local actors in Africa, sought to make a profit, or a living, in an era that tended to elevate entrepreneurial daring. Such practices reflected the rising value of migration services in this era of globalization, especially those that tapped into and alleviated people's anxieties about approaching increasingly fortified U.S. borders. Amkraut denied the charges but agreed to certain steps of redress, including offering free lottery services to past clients for the next upcoming lottery.[2]

We don't know if the envelope's sender got lucky and won, or if they availed themself of the opportunity to work with Amkraut again for free. Maybe they received a visa, flew to the United States, landed a job, and found an apartment. Went back to school, met a spouse, started a family. Wrote themselves into the American story. Over more than a quarter century of the lottery's operation, half a million people from Africa have received diversity visas to the United States. Altogether 1.2 million people have been issued these visas, adding to the diversity of American society, and bringing their talents and aspirations to these shores.

In the 2020s, this object is a relic. This paper envelope contains a story of duplicity and profit seeking. It is adorned with a historical symbol of the slavery, plunder, and anti-Blackness that patterned the modern world. And it nevertheless testifies to the sender's hope for the promise of the American dream. Today, the lottery is conducted online. Indeed, its history is intertwined with the internet's history and the internet has shaped its spread through African countries. And the lottery has continued to bring people in, even as the United States has moved away from the immigration generosity that the lottery signaled, to embrace more punitive and harsh policies of restriction.

Poster showing President Barack Obama holding a green card, advertising the American lottery, Yaoundé, Cameroon, 2015. Photograph by author.

This shift in our politics of immigration has come even as the lottery has been an enormous boon to the United States. It has been extremely popular globally, even when the United States and Americans have not rated particularly highly in public opinion. Despite its legislative origins in racist logics about the value of white immigration to American society, the lottery has both targeted broader diversity and delivered it. It has been a surprisingly successful program of major significance that points toward what good, inclusive migration policy might look like.

The lottery's story helps us recognize that immigration includes but is not limited to what happens at the U.S.-Mexico border. And when we think about immigration, it isn't enough to identify anti-immigration policies as cruel and harmful, though they are. Instead, here is a positive example of immigration's potential gifts. The United States and Americans stand to benefit if we embrace broad, forward-looking policies that create conditions of welcome and that challenge white supremacy.

This is even more clear to me now than when I first learned about the lottery in 2011. I was traveling in West Africa and observed that a U.S. policy with almost no public profile in the United States was the subject of tremendous energy in countries like Ghana and Togo. The same was true in Ethiopia, Sudan, Kenya, and elsewhere. Its appeal was buoyed by shifts in people's attitudes toward migration in a context of economic reconfiguration, austerity policies, and persistent marginalization. Subsequent research trips to Africa, to Ghana and Cameroon, affirmed the power of this program to shape people's ideas and expectations about migration to the United States.

But I also soon learned in archives in the United States how the lottery's legislative roots reflected serious limits on the dazzling picture of American generosity conjured in cyber cafés across Africa. The debate that produced the program was largely unconcerned with creating a path to citizenship for African people. Instead, the lottery's origins were framed as a form of restitution to be made to the Irish, especially Irish immigrants living without legal status in the United States. Advocates and sympathizers touted the contributions made by Irish immigrants throughout U.S. history and decried recent policy changes that had removed their former advantage in a system that once explicitly privileged whiteness.[3]

Empathy infused the debate, as policymakers imagined their own forebears, who might also have been shut out had they come in the late twentieth century. Such exclusions would have denied the United States key stories about its unique place in the world. Celebrations of immigration as a historical driver of American progress, especially when imagined as primarily white, framed the visa lottery's genesis. Because of the necessity of crafting policy that appeared fair and nonracist, proponents of a program that would enable more white immigration couched it as serving America's "diversity," borrowing a term then much in vogue. It worked, and the visa lottery became part of the law.

It happened because policymakers at the time recognized not only that restrictions caused harms but also that adding people to America was a good thing. With new people came new workers, caregivers, thinkers, energy, and dreams. They didn't see the prospect of migration to the United States as a crisis. As the Cold War waned, America's future seemed abundant. Many imagined that a future with more immigrants would be even brighter. As a result, the program widened the doors just a bit more than its strongest advocates expected. It wasn't that its legislators were antiracists—far from it. But they didn't doubt that American democracy would be strengthened by the presence of immigrants, and that included people of color. That sliver ultimately created genuine access and opportunities for people whose aspirations to emigrate were all but invisible at the time in Washington.

As African people used the lottery to come to the United States, to bring their talents and their family members, to gain skills and experiences here, the program has revealed itself to be a beneficial one. Newcomers often arrive with strongly held beliefs about America's opportunities and promise. Immigration drives American economic growth, revives neighborhoods, allows for new families and communities to thrive, for people to encounter each other, to grow, and to learn. Extending opportunities for migration allows people from outside the United States to use their skills to earn more money than they could at home. Some have argued that these benefits redound not only to local U.S. communities and workplaces but to families and others back home, when immigrants send remittances and share the skills and experiences they have gained.

In the United States, growing African immigration has helped to fulfill the stated goal of the lottery program by fostering greater diversity. But it has done more. A rapidly increasing proportion of Black Americans is foreign born. The presence of Black immigrants may help foster new conversations about global Black history and solidarities across borders. Already Black immigrant advocacy groups have focused attention on the fact and rallying cry that immigration is a Black issue, and they have added their voices to movements fighting structural racism within and beyond the immigration system. Black immigrants and their experiences in the United States may help shape how the country reckons with anti-Blackness and immigration restriction, together. Recognizing the connections and inter-sections between struggles for immigrant rights and Black lives may yield a richer vision of freedom for all.[4]

The lottery represents a relatively small portion of our large and complex immigration admissions system, but it has been vulnerable to criticism nevertheless. That it has remained intact is as unexpected as the circumstances of its creation, and an outcome of congressional inaction and deadlock. Detractors have charged that it makes no sense given the rationale of the immigration system, that it poses a security risk, that its goal of diversity undermines unity, and that the United States cannot afford to be generous in its immigration policies. It is remarkable that it has persisted, especially given dramatic changes to the immigration system since the 1990s, including the rise of militarized immigration enforcement, detention, deportations, and violence targeting undocumented immigrants and immigrants of color. Strengthened institutional anti-immigration and an increasingly vocal restrictionist movement are just two components of a resurgent nativist force that plays a growing role in American politics, constituting a formidable backlash to the pluralist politics that created the lottery.

The conditions of austerity and economic reconfiguration that made dreams of leaving Africa more potent for those who play the green card lottery were not unique to Africa, of course. In the United States, the gutting of the social safety net, rising inequality, and an atmosphere of insecurity provided context for spikes of anti-immigration politics since the 1990s, helping create this new era of immigration restriction. Our uneven and combined world has become connected after all, and truly understanding restriction here and hope there demands we look more closely at the lottery.

Welcoming immigrants based on luck alone has an absurd quality that reflects deeper truths about the prominent place of luck and chance in our world. Indeed, a system based around luck is uncomfortably apt for a world that has increasingly given up on collective capacities for change. Access to a dignified life seems to depend on individuals' good fortune to be born in the right time and place, or to win a chance at a green card with vanishingly long odds. Luck defines winners and losers. In place of choices about how to live good lives and build futures for our children, we have chance. In place of the very idea of the public good, we have hardening borders.

It is impossible to ignore how immigrant exclusion and restriction, and how even facially neutral and inclusive policies for immigrant admissions, are driven by a conception of America as a primarily white country. This concept is deeply rooted in American history, but the presidency of Donald

Trump recently brought much to the surface. His birtherism, attacks on legal immigration, vitriol for the diversity visa lottery, and derisive comments about immigrants from majority-Black countries exposed deep truths about immigration gatekeeping as profoundly anti-Black. In the entire history of the lottery's operation, it was only during the Trump administration and the coronavirus pandemic that the program was ever seriously scaled back, an effort that the lottery's defenders have identified as part of the politics of white grievance.

The president's adviser Stephen Miller, defending a legislative effort to curtail legal immigration from Africa and elsewhere, sneered in a television interview that the Statue of Liberty wasn't really a beacon of hope for immigrants. Instead, he argued, echoing talking points from the Far Right, "the Statue of Liberty is a symbol of American liberty lighting the world. The poem that you're referring to was added later (and) is not actually part of the original Statue of Liberty."[5]

It is true that the poem was not an original part of the statue. During the 1880s, Emma Lazarus wrote the poem, "The New Colossus," with its famous lines "Give me your tired, your poor, your huddled masses yearning to breathe free." She was inspired by the stories of Jewish refugees being held on Wards Island in New York.[6] The poem was only inscribed on a plaque and added to the base in 1903, seventeen years after the statue's dedication. The subsequent symbolism of the "Mother of Exiles" that became so widely accepted in the mid-twentieth century promoted a very narrow conception of the nation of immigrants, one that privileged the experiences of European migrants and their descendants.[7] The story had its limits.

But Miller and Trump weren't all that interested in the statue's other meanings, either, including Édouard de Laboulaye's intention to use the gift to commemorate the emancipation of 4 million enslaved people in America after the Civil War. An early model showed the statue illuminating the world with her torch, as we recognize today. In her other hand, the statue held broken shackles, marking the end of slavery.[8] In the final version, chains still lay by her feet.[9] But by the time of her dedication in 1886, Reconstruction was over, and African Americans who had fought for freedom were "moved back again toward slavery," as W. E. B. Du Bois described, when Jim Crow descended. The idea that the United States could be "enlightening" the world with its version of "liberty" was clearly incongruous.[10] Later, when she became a symbol for the U.S. admission of refugees and for celebrating the legacies of European immigration, Black Americans were forced to wonder again why America's promises to them went unfulfilled.

Poster advertising visa lottery services and showing the Statue of Liberty, Yaoundé, Cameroon, 2015. Photograph by author.

There is power in these two stories we tell about the statue—that she stands for ours as a nation of immigrants, and that she stands as a symbol of liberty and the end of slavery. But both stories are incomplete.

There is no symbol more associated with the visa lottery than the iconic statue. She adorned the materials of the Irish advocates who sought the program. She hovered over the immigration hearings of the late 1980s, receiving a massive makeover and party for her hundredth birthday in 1986. She was emblazoned on the posters and banners outside uncountable internet cafés and travel agencies across Africa advertising the annual lottery. And she became a key site for a protest, by Patricia Okoumou, an African immigrant, against Trump administration immigration policies. In light of America's unresolved histories, the statue is an ambivalent symbol. But perhaps in the visa lottery we can see that ambivalence reconciled. For the statue to stand for welcoming and embracing migrants, it must also embody the liberation of Black Americans.

What has become clearer over time is that those who seek to eliminate the diversity visa lottery do so because it represents a threat to white power in America. As a result, the lottery's champions not only have recognized the pragmatic benefits of the program and how it serves U.S. interests but have seen it as a bulwark against the collapse of multiracial, pluralistic democracy. The elimination of the lottery can be understood as part of the backlash against advancements and freedoms of African Americans in recent decades. This context makes the lottery more than a quirky holdover from the 1990s. Indeed, it makes an urgent case that the United States must commit to a future of immigration generosity that ensures ongoing immigration from African countries that have long been blocked and have been made less stable and less livable over the past decades by U.S. economic and foreign policies. As migration scholar Harsha Walia says, "It's those same fault lines of plunder around the world that are the fault lines of migration."[11] A more just world would allow more people to stay home and thrive. But if such massive and deepening disparities continue to exist across borders, then a more just and equitable world is one with more migration opportunities, fewer obstacles and restrictions, robust protections of people's dignity, and less rigid gatekeeping. This is even more pressing as it becomes clear that existing methods of categorizing migration—labor, family, refugee, climate—fail to recognize people's lived experiences, and borders further limit mobility. Why not a lottery? Enabling a future with Black migration, through the lottery and other channels, allows us to see the lottery as a form of repair. Our fates are linked together, and our future depends on the strengths of the communities we build together.

Part I

1 Undocumented and Irish

· ·

The first time Sean Benson landed in New York, he came as a student from Ireland, on an exchange trip to see the country that loomed so large in the Irish imagination. The second time, he took a gamble.[1] It was the same flight, just a few years later—EI #105 from Dublin to JFK—but this time was different. After finishing his degree in management at Trinity College, he had struck out in the job market in Ireland. Many others suffered the same fate. Benson was part of a postwar Irish baby boom reaching adulthood only to find that good jobs and opportunities weren't keeping pace with their numbers.

Leaving home wasn't easy. In fact, the idea that he would ever have to leave his home and his family had been the furthest thing from his mind. His parents never thought they'd have to say goodbye to their children. But by 1985, with degree in hand and no job, he felt he had no choice—not if he was going to live the kind of life he'd dreamed of and planned for. There were simply no options for him in Ireland. Reluctantly, he entered a kind of exile. Even so, he was ambitious, ready to begin his life as an adult, to earn a living, and to put his education and skills to use.

Benson had worked briefly on Wall Street when he was first in New York on a J-1 exchange visa, so he was ready to pick up where he'd left off. Wall Street in the 1980s was dazzling—the stuff of Hollywood glamor in films like *Wall Street* (1987) and *Working Girl* (1988). New York, city of possibilities, was where he would start his life. He talked his way into a tourist visa at the U.S. consulate in Dublin, packed his bags, and soon found himself sharing a city with the Statue of Liberty—and millions of dreamers and strivers. There was nobody to greet him at the airport when he arrived, but a friend had a place in Woodside, Queens, where he could crash. He and about ten other guys, all of them undocumented, stayed there. Within a couple of days, he had landed a job at a restaurant on the east side of Manhattan.

Six months later when his visa expired, Benson stayed.

As an immigrant without legal status or work authorization in the United States, Benson joined a growing cohort. Between 1982 and 1986, hundreds of thousands of Irish people—as much as 10 percent of Ireland's population—fled a cratering economy at home.[2] Nearly 150,000, like Benson, sought a new life in New York.[3]

In 1987 alone some 105,000 Irish people entered the United States as temporary visitors, with 81,000 listing "pleasure" as their reason for travel. That unemployment in Ireland stood at 19 percent at the time hinted that many of these tourists intended to stay in the United States and seek work.[4] Overstaying nonimmigrant visas was hardly unique to the Irish. A government commission that studied immigration had recommended in its 1981 report that the United States devote more resources to investigating people who overstayed temporary visas (and "student visa abusers"). Though they entered the country with permission, those who continued to live and work here beyond the terms of their visa did so without authorization.

By the mid-1980s, several million noncitizens were living without status in America, some of them Irish, but many more hailing from Mexico, Central America, and elsewhere. People who couldn't secure immigrant visas often came anyway, drawn by the promise of better opportunities and work, dreams of a more stable life, or driven away from unlivable conditions at home. The reason that people migrated without permission was that the United States strictly limited legal immigration. Even those who resided for a long time in the United States, who felt fully enmeshed in their American communities, struggled to access legal status because of the limitations set on immigration. But people did what they had to do to survive—crossing the border without permission, overstaying temporary visas, working without authorization, sometimes using random digits as their Social Security numbers. Benson happened to have received a Social Security card in his name during his previous, temporary stint in New York, which made getting a job easier this time around. But he observed that employers typically hired undocumented people in his circle with a "wink and a nod" in those days.

After work every night, Benson and his mates would go out, enjoy the city, soak up its lights, mingle, and flirt with the Irish girls coming off their shifts as Upper East Side nannies. Wall Street money was driving the opening of shiny new restaurants and sophisticated clubs, while downtown artists kept the city loose and hip. The city was gritty, bustling, and dense: the opposite of staid, green, old-fashioned Ireland.

But New York felt familiar too. For generations, Irish immigrants had made new lives in New York, worked hard, raised their families, and left their mark. And while they'd historically known hardships, encountered discrimination for being Irish or Catholic, and even been targets for xenophobic violence, they had also thrived over the years, transforming blocks and whole neighborhoods of the Bronx, Queens, and Manhattan, setting their kids up for white, middle-class suburban lives and upward mobility. Telltale Irish pubs dotted the city. Each March witnessed parades and parties for St. Patrick's Day. The actual, and mythic, roles played by Irish immigrants in building New York and making the city what it was now fed the imaginations of the young Irish immigrants carving space for themselves in the 1980s, even though they were generations removed from those previous, storied migrations. Just as their predecessors had, the Irish immigrants of the 1980s would leave a lasting impact on America and its relationship to immigration.

· · · · · ·

In the mid-nineteenth century, Irish immigrants came by the millions. In some years they constituted a third or even half of *all* immigrants to the United States, particularly during the Irish Famine beginning in 1845.[5] While they often were able to find work and survive, Irish immigrants were not quite welcomed with open arms. Violent mobs of nativists targeted them.[6] Cartoonists portrayed them as apes. As if in anticipation of the future waves of xenophobia that would accompany each new era of immigration, New York City and state officials fretted then about Irish newcomers' purported inability to assimilate, arguing that Irish poverty, Catholicism, and drinking made them irrevocably un-American. These local practices and policies of immigrant exclusion, designed to exclude the Irish, who were deemed undesirable, formed the foundation for later federal policies of immigration restriction and regulations that would increasingly police categories of race and gender and reinforce America's hierarchies.[7]

When the United States slammed the gates on almost all immigration in the 1920s—in deference to eugenics and ideas about "race betterment" then in vogue—almost all immigrant visas would go to people from countries such as Great Britain, Germany, and Sweden, in northern and western Europe. The aim of this framework of immigration admissions was to "preserve" the existing racial "stock" of the United States—which policymakers intentionally defined as white and primarily Protestant. They pointedly ignored populations of African Americans, Indigenous people, Asian Americans, and Latinos who resided in the United States in their calculations of the country's existing demographics. They thought the racial character of the United States could be preserved as white by encouraging more white, European immigration, from only the most racially desirable countries, while formally blocking nearly all others.

Overall, migration fell after the enactment of these 1920s national origins quotas. But Ireland enjoyed a relatively generous quota of 28,000 visas annually. That decade 200,000 Irish immigrated to the United States. Although a visa was now required, Irish people would have experienced almost no limits on who could come. Within each country's set quota, the United States set priorities for who should be admitted—for example, the family members of U.S. citizens and those workers with skills needed by U.S. employers. But the Irish quota was so generous that most people came through the "nonpreference" category, which received any unused "preference" visas if not enough family members or skilled workers came in a given year.

During the Great Depression and World War II, immigration plummeted. The economic crisis reshaped people's calculations of risk and depleted the savings people needed to fund their migrations—money for travel, rent, and to hold one over until a new job or income could be secured. Wartime further complicated migration; it displaced many people while countries simultaneously erected new barriers to migration. This historic dip in immigration reminds us that while immigration patterns are shaped profoundly by U.S. policies—what countries are favored, how many visas are on offer—events and shifts beyond the United States also affect how and why people move.

Only 15,000 Irish immigrants came in the 1940s, during and after the war.[8] The numbers ticked up again in the 1950s. Half a million people fled Ireland during what was deemed a "lost decade," before the economy began to rebound there and the flow of Irish immigrants slowed.[9] They barely constituted a trickle by the mid-1960s and 1970s, as things improved at home.[10] More than 70,000 Irish immigrants had arrived in the United States between 1956 and 1965—during that lost decade—but only 10,000 arrived between 1976 and 1985.[11]

In the 1980s, the United States admitted more than 6 million immigrants. Only 10 percent came from European countries—a huge change from just a few decades earlier. Half came from the Americas—over a million people from Mexico alone. Almost 40 percent came from Asian countries. A minuscule 2 percent came from the entire continent of Africa.[12]

Irish immigration to the United States slowed because opportunities improved at home. Many in Benson's generation, born in the decades after World War II, had access to high-quality education that had never been widely available before. The country made an investment in young people and the future, in part to prepare the nation for its 1973 entry into the

European Economic Community. Nevertheless, mismanagement and global economic problems in the 1970s caused the Irish economy to stagnate.

The decline of the Irish economy in the late 1970s and early 1980s coincided with the coming of age of the post–World War II generation, people who had been raised with high hopes for themselves and high expectations for their place in the world. Having worked hard and accessed education their parents hadn't been able to, they expected to be able to build lives for themselves in Ireland among friends and family. The idea that they would have no choice but to leave—as so many Irish exiles had done before them— was a bitter one.

Yet just as those in his grandfather's generation had done, Benson and his cohort were pushed to go abroad—to the United Kingdom, Europe, and the United States—in search of opportunity. Despite resistance among Benson and his contemporaries, exit seemed wired in. Many went to nearby London for work, but the United States remained a viable destination too, in part because of strong cultural memory of its history as a sanctuary for Irish exiles. As immigrants in America, the Irish had faced harassment, grinding exploitative work, and abuse, yes—but they had eventually been welcomed into the fold of the American story, foundational to its history and identity, when they had been accepted as white.[13] The Irish formed a core part of the American story—and thus a place for Irish exiles remained.[14]

But the New Irish, as those who, like Benson, immigrated in the 1980s called themselves, faced distinct challenges as they set out to make America home. That's because they belonged to a new category of immigrant and encountered restrictions that their nineteenth-century predecessors hadn't had to worry about.

They were undocumented—and vulnerable. As a *Philadelphia Inquirer* article put it in 1987, "Raised on Irish-American success stories and convinced that Ireland has a special relationship with America, the new immigrants are often surprised to find they are treated much like other illegal aliens. They, too, are underpaid, overworked and subject to arrest and deportation."[15]

"We were all undocumented. We were all afraid to have a bill arrive in our name," Benson later explained.[16] Another Irish immigrant told the *Boston Globe*, "It's just a constant fear at work. You don't know. Is it the IRS, is it Immigration, is it Social Security? . . . It never leaves you; you never forget."[17] Insecurity due to immigration status touched every part of life.

Why were the Irish who arrived in the 1980s considered undocumented, whereas their counterparts a half century earlier had been easily absorbed, welcomed as white and desirable?

The answer, Benson and his colleagues would soon discover, was rooted in the history of immigration restriction.

· · · · · ·

Since the nineteenth century the U.S. federal government had taken on an increasingly robust role in gatekeeping migration, imposing limits and restrictions on some, like the Chinese in the 1880s, while encouraging the arrival of others, like western Europeans.[18] In the twentieth century, eugenic theorists placed white, northern and western Europeans near the top of their ethnic hierarchies. They brought Irish Americans into the category of whiteness while castigating others—Africans, Asians, Jews, and eastern Europeans—as degenerate and biologically harmful to the polity.[19] The Irish were among those encouraged because immigration restriction was a tool for constructing whiteness. "America must be kept American," Calvin Coolidge declared in 1923. The Irish belonged, in his definition, while people with ethnicities and races deemed undesirable did not. Xenophobia simultaneously reinforced inclusion for some immigrants and exclusion for others.[20]

Through immigration restrictions, the destruction of Indigenous communities, and enslavement and postslavery disfranchisement of African Americans, the United States government aimed to define American identity as white. But this project was always contested, if not downright contradicted, by the presence of people who weren't white, and in particular by the fight for equality by Black Americans. After fighting for freedom in the Civil War and gaining formal citizenship through the Fourteenth Amendment, African Americans continued into the twentieth century to defend and expand upon these gains and to make the promises of American democracy truer. Nowhere was this struggle more successful and prominent than during the civil rights movement of the 1950s and 1960s, when Congress adopted the most sweeping legislation since Reconstruction to expand citizenship and rights to Black Americans and other people of color.

This spirit of reform extended to the nation's immigration policies, and legislators were moved to strip overtly racist language out of immigration policy. Building on decades of reformers' work pushing for changes, Congress tossed the explicitly eugenicist national origins quotas of the 1920s into the dustbin of history. What they adopted in their place retained a restrictionist framework, setting numerical limits on immigration by country. The assumptions that the United States should have control over migration, and that migration should adhere to strict limits, endured.

With the adoption of the Hart-Celler Act in 1965, however, Congress signaled that the United States would no longer discriminate against immigrants based on their national origin, a stand-in for ethnic and racial identity. "The American nation today stands as eloquent proof that there is no inherent contradiction between unity and diversity," Peter Rodino, a congressman from New Jersey, said in a 1964 hearing.[21] The racist quotas on the books were a blight on America's reputation abroad. They always had been, as many critics had pointed out at the time, with calls for change intensifying after World War II exposed the devastating violence of Nazi racism and antisemitism.[22] But the issue became newly urgent in an era when so many African and Asian nations were undergoing decolonization and shaking off European rulers. At the time, the United States was waging the global Cold War, in which it sought to win people's hearts and minds and demonstrate its superiority to communism.[23] Telling people from countries of nonwhite people that they would be excluded from migrating because of their race undermined the most basic promise of American democracy.

To signal the strengths and benefits of U.S. liberalism, the United States ended formal exclusions based on nationality. Instead, it would prioritize and admit immigrants on the basis of family ties to the United States. American citizens would be able to petition for their family members to join them, and this way newcomers would be joining already settled relatives, reinforcing the importance of the "nuclear family." Other immigrants could come to fill specific types of jobs, typically those requiring specific skills and training. While liberalizing immigration in some ways, the new system also imposed *new* limits, creating restrictions on immigration from the Western Hemisphere, and generating new pressures for unauthorized immigration from Mexico, Caribbean countries, and elsewhere in the Americas.

Stripping away formal racist restrictions was important to a coalition of policymakers. But few cared about making immigration admissions fairer. Few even considered immigrants from regions outside of Europe. The ambitions of 1960s liberal policymakers didn't extend far beyond undoing a mistake of the past.[24] Many even hoped that centering family unity would perpetuate the ethnic composition of immigration for some time and encourage further European immigration, albeit on a less eugenic basis than in the past. Some were hoping to return to what they imagined of the nineteenth and early twentieth centuries, when their own families had migrated.[25]

But that idealized past of largely European immigration wasn't coming back. After 1965, immigrants from previously excluded regions like Asia began to come in greater numbers, sometimes as refugees, other times as students or high-wage workers. Once established in the United States, people could become citizens and petition for their family members to join them, creating a pattern described sometimes derisively as "chain migration." Legal immigration would become increasingly nonwhite after 1965. Simultaneously, immigration from Mexico and the rest of the Western Hemisphere, not previously limited by numbers, continued. Now facing new numerical limits that didn't reflect existing migration patterns or U.S. labor needs, many came without authorization. As the number of immigrants of color, both unauthorized and authorized, ticked up in the following years, the politics of immigration became more fraught, and questions about who really belonged and who could integrate into American society became pressing.[26]

Additionally, after the 1965 reform, the Irish faced immigration restrictions where there had been none before. Once favored as serving the main goal of U.S. immigration policy—to keep America "American"—young Irish immigrants of the 1980s no longer had access to a generous visa quota. The new system valued the appearance of race neutrality, sought to serve U.S. foreign policy goals in the Cold War, and served a labor market far different from nineteenth-century industrialization. As a result, being Irish was no longer grounds for an immigrant visa.

That's why Benson and others like him came as students or visitors and overstayed their visas. They couldn't qualify for an immigrant visa ahead of time because without a U.S. citizen spouse, child, parent, or sibling to sponsor them, they were out of luck. The system also permitted lawful permanent residents to petition for their spouses and children, and U.S. citizens for their siblings. It was a tight, circumscribed definition of family. People without close family ties to the United States could still apply if they had specific skills needed by the U.S. economy, but a new certification required affirmatively and prior to entry by the secretary of labor made this path inaccessible to most. Since Irish immigration had dwindled after 1965, those coming in the 1980s were unlikely to have close family members to sponsor them.

• • • • • •

Although this cohort of Irish immigrants was following a path well worn by millions of Irish immigrants before them, they faced new legal hurdles. And soon, with the passage of another immigration reform in 1986, public scrutiny of immigrants' legal statuses would increase. This made the situation for undocumented immigrants ever starker and riskier—even among white immigrants, like Benson, who did not face racial discrimination on the job or easy visual racial profiling as an "undocumented immigrant," a category understood as comprising mostly Mexican people.

Overstaying visitor visas and acquiring housing and employment was possible for the Irish—especially as the U.S. consulate continued to issue temporary visas—but precarious. Many people lived in substandard and crowded housing. Employment, too, was uncertain, and often people worked at jobs that didn't take full advantage of their training and talents.

In other words, they lived as other undocumented immigrants did.

Irish immigrants weren't going to stand for that. "I couldn't believe that Irish people were living like this," Benson said. "In America of all countries."[27] They had come of age in a time and place that made them feel empowered. When they had to go into exile despite the promise of a growing, modern Ireland, it made them resentful, even radical. Now many Irish were living underground, unfree, in fear.

"We weren't brought up to dig potatoes," Benson said. "We were brought up to do something better."[28]

2 Getting Legal

· ·

"Like, white Europeans? Illegal? Can't be." Living without status in New York in 1985, Patrick Hurley pointed out that there was something off about the Irish being among the undocumented. It didn't make sense to him or to the Irish Americans he talked to.

Migration was in his blood. His parents left Ireland in the early 1950s in search of better opportunities in New Zealand, and that's where Pat was born. But even before his Irish parents, his grandparents had also been emigrants—his maternal grandfather had migrated to America in 1910, to Boston, served in World War I for the United States on the western front, and naturalized as an American citizen. His maternal grandmother, an Irish Republican, escaped to Canada after the Irish civil war, before crossing the border into the United States—another "illegal immigrant," Patrick would say wryly. Together, his grandparents moved back to Ireland in the late 1920s, where his mom was born. She'd gone to New Zealand. Now Hurley had joined the family tradition and arrived in the United States. And he too was "illegal."

He worked removing asbestos along with a workforce of other undocumented Irish and Polish laborers—not the work he'd envisioned, given his talent for writing. He saw the potential talent of his cohort being squandered. People lived scared, and this made them vulnerable. Hanging out in the bars with a bunch of twenty-somethings was fun. But what would their futures look like if the Irish couldn't regularize their status? "What's going to happen to all these people? Nobody really seemed to care," Hurley ruminated.[1] The situation felt untenable.

Hurley and the other young Irish had followed in the footsteps of their forebears, but rather than being welcomed, they'd encountered this newly restrictive, post-1965 system that denied them legal status. Not only were they no longer a favored group, but the United States in the 1980s was building its capacity to track and punish immigrants without status, which made their situations feel especially precarious.

Being undocumented was more than an administrative or legal category, although these elements burdened Hurley and his cohort—unfairly and unnecessarily, Hurley thought. The contradiction was that white people weren't supposed to have to navigate such burdens. That's because being labeled "illegal" was as much a racial category as an immigration status.

· · · · · ·

Hurley's assessment reflected more than a century of policy. The United States had long encouraged the entry of white Europeans for their labor and roles as settlers as the United States expanded westward. Freedom and mobility went hand in hand and tended to be preserved for white people. The United States also blocked the entry of foreign-born people on the basis of race and ethnicity—beginning in federal law with the Chinese Exclusion Acts and later through restrictions based on eugenicist standards about the relative racial "purity" of various European ethnicities. Borders became tools that further restricted the mobility and freedom of nonwhite people—think of the redrawing of the U.S.-Mexico border with the 1848 Treaty of Guadalupe Hidalgo, which made Mexican and Indigenous people strangers in their native lands, or the use of hardening interstate borders to block the mobility of free Black people and to facilitate the entry of enslaved African Americans. Through such border practices, the United States had systematically defined who belonged and who didn't along racial lines.[2]

Not only did white Europeans enjoy privileged status at ports of entry, but they could also access forms of relief and legal status unavailable to others within the United States. In the era of restriction between the 1920s and 1960s, generally Europeans without legal status could *become* legal with relative ease, through the Registry Act or other mechanisms.[3] Access to such bureaucratic processes made life livable for these individuals and their families, but they were typically not available to members of groups formally excluded by the law. Consequently, policies of inclusion reinforced the same ideas about belonging as policies of exclusion.

White Americans often say that new immigrants should "get in line" and "come legally" because that is what they think their own ancestors did. But they don't necessarily recognize the policy framework that made it easy for white immigrants to come or to adjust their status before 1965, not least because such avenues have all but been foreclosed for today's undocumented immigrants, particularly for people of color. Family secrets of unlawful entries, illicit border crossings, and forged documents were also forgotten, buried, or never known. And people like Hurley's grandmother who came in the early part of the twentieth century didn't face the kind of immigration enforcement bureaucracy that existed by the 1980s. For these reasons, white European immigration tended to be remembered as orderly and legal, even if it wasn't, while the migration of nonwhite people invited scrutiny and suspicion, even when it was authorized.

That many immigrants in the 1970s, both with and without legal status, were people of color played a key role in generating anxiety about immigration and its perceived threats to the existing racial order. Debate about immigration increasingly focused on the figure of the "illegal alien," who was imagined as a single, Mexican man crossing the border to work in agriculture. As historians have pointed out, it was U.S. policies that restricted the legal immigration of Mexicans and their mismatch with the labor market that produced undocumented immigration in the first place. If Americans expressed concern about unauthorized immigration, it tended to be locally concentrated in places like California and southern Texas, where many agricultural workers lived and labored.

But soon other events provoked broader speculation that the immigration system was "out of control" and disorderly. Focusing the debate on migrants' formal legal status and border insecurity helped frame the issue as one of "law and order" without using expressly racist language, even when racism clearly played a role.

When U.S. policies unleashed unrest and violence in Central America, more than a million people fled El Salvador and Guatemala, many of them to the United States to seek asylum. But because they had escaped regimes that the United States supported, they were denied en masse.[4] In the 1970s and 1980s, scores of Haitians fled their island's dictatorship, but the U.S. classified these "boat people" as economic migrants, not refugees deserving of protection. The Reagan administration began aggressively intercepting their boats and turning them back, preventing safe passage to the United States. Those who landed were denied legal status. One African American newspaper editorialized that the policy was clearly racist. "If you're Black, get back," went the headline.[5] The Immigration and Naturalization Service had made an administrative decision to render the Statue of Liberty's welcome message invalid for Haitians. "The Statue of Liberty is a beckon of welcome to immigrants, white, but, a Statue of limitation to Haitians, black," Jesse Jackson was quoted saying.[6]

People arriving at U.S. borders to claim asylum were not undocumented; they were following what the law required. But they, along with the unauthorized migration of agricultural workers and others, became associated with a system out of control.[7] In refugee resettlement, too, many Americans expressed hostility to newcomers who were not white. For example, the United States resettled refugees from Vietnam, Laos, and Cambodia in the aftermath of the U.S. war in Southeast Asia, in part to answer the humanitarian crisis, atone for American violence, and fulfill Cold War foreign policy aims.[8] More than a million people came to the United States, mostly in the late 1970s, and some became targets of white supremacist violence when communities bristled at the idea of welcoming Asian refugees.[9] The public's perception of a disorderly migration system coincided with the post-1965 shift to a legal admissions system that was no longer primarily geared toward admitting white immigrants.

· · · · · ·

By the 1980s, policymakers were motivated to address a system that, in their view failed to control migration and wasn't serving U.S. labor needs. The end of the Bracero guest worker program in 1964 and the imposition of limits on Western Hemisphere migration had reduced the number of workers allowed to cross the U.S.-Mexico border, who, as a seasonal labor force, had long formed the backbone of the U.S. agricultural industry. While employers would learn that an undocumented labor force could be a cheap, malleable labor force, reformers believed that legalizing undocumented people was a good way to ensure adequate workers.

Others were concerned about the exploitation of undocumented people and supported reforms that would grant them legal status to protect them from unscrupulous employers. Among those leading the push for reform were immigrants themselves and Chicano activists, who saw the immigration system as deeply entwined with racial discrimination.[10]

Policymakers could see that the system unfairly kept a large number of people in a perpetual state of "illegal" status, something that didn't reflect on a person's character but that showed the flaws and limitations of a restrictive system. They were also motivated to create legal status for immigrant workers whose labor was understood as essential.[11] Policymakers of both parties talked about this as "amnesty"—forgiveness for being in violation of immigration statute—for the undocumented residing in the United States. As Ronald Reagan said in 1984, "I believe in the idea of amnesty for those who have put down roots and lived here, even though some time back they may have entered illegally."[12]

After trying and failing to pass legislation for years, Congress finally passed a major bill in 1986, the Immigration Reform and Control Act (IRCA). It provided a mechanism for the legalization of undocumented people, but its main thrust was to address and curtail further unauthorized immigration across the U.S.-Mexico border.[13] Policymakers took a punitive approach, implementing increased security measures to intercede migrants at the border along with a system of sanctions to punish employers who hired the undocumented. Such measures, policymakers argued, would deter unauthorized migration. Their solution to a problem caused by restriction, then, was more restriction.

Policymakers of color criticized the bill, recognizing which communities these forms of enforcement would fall most heavily upon. Members of the Congressional Hispanic Caucus voted against various iterations of the bill. Concerned that the employer sanctions provisions would unfairly target and punish Mexican Americans and others who might be profiled as undocumented, the liberal senator Ted Kennedy (D-MA) declined to support the bill.

So, too, did the Congressional Black Caucus (CBC). Activist Jesse Jackson decried pejorative talk of "illegal aliens." He said, "Undocumented workers are people. We must not continue the U.S. policy of taking their productive years and then blaming them for all the economic ills of our nation." He worried that the Simpson-Mazzoli bill, as IRCA was known, "would force undocumented workers to carry passbooks," and abridge their civil liberties.[14] While immigration restrictionists had long argued that liberal immigration policies harmed Black Americans, members of the CBC didn't necessarily see the issue in those terms. Rep. Shirley Chisholm (D-NY), for example, protested "there are some who believe that I and my colleagues in the Congressional Black Caucus should worry more about the socioeconomic problems of Black Americans and forget about Haitians and Ethiopians. . . . We shall continue to oppose discrimination against those who are only separated from us by their arrival in the Americas in different times."[15] Because of IRCA's inclusion of employer sanctions, both the Hispanic and Black Caucuses split their votes, torn between wanting to prevent the harms of the law's punitive elements and wanting to see measures implemented that would help immigrant communities.

When IRCA is remembered today, it is often recalled as the last time that Congress passed a mass legalization program for people out of status. This "amnesty," endorsed by Reagan, ultimately enabled 2.7 million undocumented people to gain legal status, the majority of whom were Mexican nationals. Even conservative politicians accepted this component of the bill because they recognized that it was needed proverbially to wipe the slate clean: the law would regularize the status of people here, while purportedly sealing the border and preventing further unauthorized migration.

Whether the 1986 law is remembered as successful varies depending on who you talk to. But for people who were able to gain legal status as a result, as the historian Eladio Bobadilla writes, "life changed tangibly and totally . . . as they suddenly found themselves with newfound freedoms and newfound rights." For one Mexican man, it felt "like a blindfold was taken off my eyes."[16]

· · · · · ·

But IRCA's legalization programs would not help the Irish very much. Fewer than a thousand Irish people qualified due to the timing of their arrivals—most came *after* the 1982 cutoff date.[17] This felt unfair, given that they *too* were living undocumented lives largely because of policy changes made in the mid-1960s. Hurley said, "an amnesty is something that you give to some-one who has done wrong. As far as I was concerned, my grandfather fought with the U.S. army on the western front and was wounded and received the Purple Heart. I had intimate links with this country. Familial links with this country. I had done nothing wrong."[18]

This consequence of the 1965 act had been apparent to Irish Americans immediately at the time. Knowing that the law would restrict Irish migra-tion, they pushed for fixes. One late 1960s ad in the *New York Times* likened the restriction of Irish immigration to the treatment of the Irish a century before: "No Irish Need Apply"—for visas in this case, rather than jobs. Ken-nedy's role in forging the Hart-Celler Act felt like a particular betrayal. As Hurley later remarked, "It was Ted Kennedy who did something wrong, not me. He should be getting the amnesty, you know."

Bills to "correct this injustice," framed in the language of civil rights and repair, were introduced but didn't amount to anything.[19] The chair of the Senate Judiciary Committee, James O. Eastland (D-MS), a segregationist who lamented the end of the national origins quotas, held no hearings on immigration, killing any legislation that came his way.

But opportunity came in the 1980s to do something.

A congressman from Massachusetts, Brian Donnelly, introduced legisla-tion in 1985 to make visas available to his undocumented Irish constituents. Donnelly represented the Eleventh District of Massachusetts, which included lower Boston, Quincy, and the South Shore, areas with numbers of Irish and Irish American residents so substantial that collectively they made up the most Irish district in the country.[20] He considered himself an "Irish kid from Dorchester."[21] He seized the language of "injustice" to argue for immigrant visas for the Irish, who he thought were unfairly excluded.

The plight of Irish people like Benson or Hurley affected him on a gut level. But how could he argue that the admission of Irish people served an urgent humanitarian need? Refugees and asylum seekers fled life-threatening persecution. Maybe some Irish people faced persecution, but most Irish immigrants spoke about seeking brighter economic opportunities than they could find in Ireland.

Likewise, some Irish immigrants had sought-after professional skills (skills they were typically unable to use without legal work authorization), but others didn't. Many worked in bars and restaurants or in then-booming building trades. But the immigration system didn't recognize or prioritize their broad economic contributions. Few could claim to be able to fill jobs Americans wouldn't. While the counterargument that they, like other immigrants, constituted a drain on the economy was baseless, one couldn't really make a persuasive, affirmative, solely economic argument for their admission, beyond the fact that adding more workers, taxpayers, consumers, and users of services generally contributes to the strength of the economy.

The question became: How would admitting Irish immigrants, and legalizing those already here, serve the national interest of the United States?

Some summoned the imagery of past Irish immigration to answer this question, as Hurley did, linking his entitlement to legal status to the contributions of his grandparents. But advocates also framed the need in broader terms.

What had made nineteenth- and twentieth-century European immigrants so crucial to the American story, they argued, was the process of migrating. People had uprooted their lives, worked hard, and become American through the crucible of the migration experience. And *shouldn't* a person without existing ties to the United States be able to come, work hard, and make good? That was the promise of the American dream and core to the country's identity as a "nation of immigrants," wasn't it? Deploying this narrative elided how immigration was a tool of American settler colonialism and the displacement of Indigenous people, while masking limits on social mobility. But it did resonate with those Americans whose own families' migration stories were central to their sense of themselves.

To make his proposal appealing, Donnelly broadened his view, seeking a policy solution not just for the Irish but for people from *other* countries that had seen their visa numbers diminished after 1965.[22] They were, of course, primarily European, since European nations had been most privileged previously. On paper, African countries now had a much higher visa limit (although few ways to acquire a visa), while Latin American countries had gone from having no quota at all to having access to the same number of visas as any other country in the world. Donnelly's bill gleaned support from local Massachusetts-area groups representing Italian, Greek, German, and Canadian immigrants, as well as Irish immigrants.[23] The strategy of reaching beyond the Irish helped broaden the appeal of Donnelly's proposed visa program, or at least dampened criticism by other immigrant and other ethnic groups.[24] Sen. John Kerry (D-MA) introduced companion legislation in the Senate. "The migration of large numbers of people from Ireland over the many years has been of great benefit to our nation-building process," he said.[25] Those bills didn't pass.

But they managed to get a tiny program, based on Donnelly's failed stand-alone bill, passed as part of IRCA.[26]

They succeeded by critiquing the harms of restriction and the narrowness of immigration admissions, which since 1965 emphasized family unity above other values. Prioritizing family ties served a clear interest for the American people and offered built-in stability to new arrivals while reinforcing rigid understandings of gender and family.[27] But it also shut out entirely those aspiring emigrants abroad without such connections. Immigrants from Latin American and Asian countries, who came through the family system, now constituted the majority of immigration. But Europeans without close family members to sponsor them, in part because Europe's postwar economic recovery made staying home more appealing, had limited access to visas.

The federal government had commissioned a study of the issue beginning in 1979. The Select Commission's 1981 report recommended that Congress expand the category of "independent" immigrants to allow for the admission of more people outside of the family system. In a clear echo of the advocacy of the Irish in the 1960s, the commission wrote, "Persons who cannot now qualify because they come from countries without an immigration base in the United States such as many African nations, or from countries from which immigration was historic rather than recent, as in the case of many European nations, will have an immigration channel opened to them."[28] The commission linked twin appeals to fairness, bringing in countries long shut out, and nostalgia, including those once welcomed but more recently shut out.

That the report came amid an immigration debate largely focused on addressing unauthorized immigration reflected broader American ambivalence about the issue. Even as the country rejected and excluded immigrants, it continued to valorize the idea of immigration. The "independent" immigrant embraced by the Select Commission recalled certain images of who that person was: most likely white and, in any case, exceptional. People dismissed as "economic migrants" from Mexico and those fleeing for their lives from Haiti and El Salvador—people who were seeking to come to the United States at the very moment that the Select Commission did its work—didn't belong to this category.

The idea that "independent" immigrants should be encouraged also emerged in the context of a culture that venerated the plucky upstart individual during the "me" decade of the 1970s, as Americans abandoned communitarian thinking and embraced atomistic individualism. In the 1980s (especially in New York City) yuppiedom reigned, as the Reagan administration pursued deregulation, tax cuts, and antigovernment rhetoric. The kind of entrepreneurialism admired in mythologies of past immigration was revived to weave the 1980s' Wall Street boom into the American narrative. Who better to grow the economy than hardworking individuals betting on themselves?

Today's restrictions that *stifled* European immigration were described as no more just than those that had previously favored Europeans. Only 537 Irish immigrants were admitted in 1984 through the preference system—a tiny number compared with the past.[29] Rev. Joseph A. Cogo, testifying before Congress for the American Committee on Italian Migration, called the results of 1965 "discrimination in reverse." He criticized "the theoretically ideal system of one world ceiling on a first-come, first-served basis" as having "resulted in the traditional European immigration being drastically disadvantaged."[30]

To open a channel for independent immigrants, then, Congress adopted Donnelly's idea and created a program within IRCA known as NP-5, which authorized 5,000 "non-preference" visas per year for two years, 1987 and 1988, to go to nationals of countries "adversely affected" by the Immigration Act of 1965. They were called "non-preference" because they were outside the family preference system and employment visas—the types of visas the Irish had tended to use when they had an ample visa quota before 1965.

The State Department developed a formula to determine whether a country was "adversely affected" by the Immigration Act of 1965, comparing immigration in the years between 1966 and 1985 with the period from 1953 to 1965.[31] When the State Department produced a list of thirty-six adversely affected countries, it included Ireland and Northern Ireland. The whole idea was to reverse-engineer a list that would enable Irish access to visas.[32] Most of the thirty-six countries on the list were European, because Ireland, Great

Britain, France, and Germany (now divided into two nations), among others, had enjoyed a relative advantage before 1965. Because so few legal immigrants from Africa or Asia had been admitted previously, few countries from those regions were included.

Framing the reform that had ended those previous advantages as a kind of "harm" to be redressed, however unintentional, worked. Donnelly visas were to be distributed on a first-come, first-served basis, through an open application system, with white people heavily favored. Others excluded from the U.S. legal immigration system who didn't have the same clout with policymakers, including people of color castigated as "illegal," were largely ineligible because their countries of origin weren't considered to be adversely affected.

· · · · · ·

On Christmas Eve in 1986 Irish newspapers announced the Donnelly visas. While the impetus for the program had come from undocumented immigrants already living in the United States, the program was also open to people abroad. The U.S. embassy in Dublin was immediately overwhelmed with calls. *Irish America* reported that "an overnight cottage industry sprung up with courier services offering to mail the applications in the U.S.—for a fee."[33] In Canada, U.S. consular offices were also flooded with thousands of calls and inquiries.[34]

The application period lasted just one week, from January 21 through January 27, 1987, a Wednesday through the following Tuesday. Registrants could mail applications to a special post office box in Washington, DC, through the U.S. Postal Service (USPS).[35] The open registration system was designed to be simple for users and for administrators alike.

Collectively, applicants sent in over 1 million applications.[36] The program's entry format offered an advantage to those living in or close to the United States, where they had better access to the USPS system and could expect prompt delivery to the target post office box. Benson, who had been in New York for more than a year and a half already, sent in over 400 applications for himself, staggering them in the mail on different days and slipping them in different mailboxes to maximize his chances of being among the lucky first few picked.[37] Some applicants drove to Washington, DC, to drop their entries in mailboxes as close as possible to the destination. Canadian applicants reportedly spent weeks sending in multiple forms leading up to the one-week entry period. "You have to," one man said. "Sometimes it takes 2½ weeks to get a letter to Albany." Another Canadian man drove to Plattsburgh, just over the New York border, to post his application, "this being far too important a project to trust to Canada Post. 'You know what they say about our 34-cent stamps,' he said. 'Seventeen cents for storage, 17 for service.'"[38]

When Benson checked his mailbox in early spring, he learned that he was among the lucky winners. He received his green card in July 1987.[39] Over a quarter of a million Irish people applied for Donnelly visas—more than 7 percent of the population of the Republic of Ireland.[40] Of the 10,000 visas issued in 1987 and 1988, the Irish won a plurality—3,112 of them—more than nationals of any of the other adversely affected nations included in the program. A 1989 *Irish America* article marveled, "Now the Donnelly visa is as indelibly imprinted in the Irish psyche as the issue of illegal emigration" itself.[41] A quarter century later in 2011, Donnelly was recognized in Dublin for having made an outstanding contribution to the American experience.[42]

· · · · · ·

The Donnelly visa program served as both a stopgap measure and a test run. In Washington, it demonstrated the feasibility of making visas available to "independent" immigrants.[43] It revealed enthusiasm for nonpreference visas both within the United States and at U.S. consulates in eligible countries. Seeing the high demand, officials concluded that they should have limited applications to one per person and lengthened the application period to cut down on the frenzy—even if witnessing people's enthusiasm to apply to move permanently to the United States was edifying. The program hadn't set off alarm bells in the growing anti-immigration movement, in part because it involved only a small number of migrants, most of whom were white Europeans. Donnelly visa immigrants closely resembled mid-twentieth-century immigrants—an era that inspired nostalgia on the right and that fed the popularity of the "nation of immigrants" mythology.

But further action would be needed. Tens of thousands of Irish immigrants remained "illegal." They recognized that the imposition of employer sanctions as part of IRCA would threaten livelihoods, and the risk of deportation loomed. As Hurley wrote to the editor at *Irish America*, "The hour of decision approaches, before the full force of the recently-passed immigration act is brought to bear. . . . There is no future for us back in the 'old country.'"[44] The Donnelly visa's success helped convince the Irish in America that much more could be done for the undocumented among them.

3 Past and Present

· ·

In July 1986, New York celebrated the Statue of Liberty's centennial. The state introduced a new license plate with the statue pictured. A massive four-day event over the first weekend of July, "Liberty weekend," centered on the unveiling of the renovated statue. It was meant to be an open and exuberant celebration of the country's immigrant heritage.[1] Amid the fireworks, tall ships, and splendor, the mayor awarded medals to eighty-six immigrants representing America's diversity. Supreme Court Chief Justice Warren Burger administered the oath of citizenship to several hundred people in a naturalization ceremony on Ellis Island. *New York Times* columnist Anthony Lewis argued that "the languages and the faces have changed, but the miracle of American immigrants goes on." Describing an encounter with an Ethiopian taxi driver, he is left asking, "Is there something about the United States that liberates the spirit, that leads immigrants to strive?"[2]

The Liberty weekend festivities amplified the stories told by immigrants and their descendants and even included the voices of recent immigrants. But the celebration also exposed the ugliness of immigration restriction and its harms. Lewis decried the country's willingness to celebrate its immigrant heritage while simultaneously jailing and deporting asylum seekers. "We are honoring a symbol this weekend while our Government forgets its substance," he lamented.[3]

The Reagan administration was in the process of enacting tax and budget cuts that would harm the poor—a direct rebuke to Emma Lazarus's poem engraved at the statue's base, and a catalyst for increasing inequality in the United States. Further, the *New York Times* reported that around the country some 4,800 immigrants sat in detention, awaiting deportation, as the city prepared its party. "Outside of Liberty Weekend," said Rev. Robert Vitaglione, a priest who represented immigrants in deportation proceedings, "the sentiment in this country is so against the alien. . . . You hear phrases like 'The reservoir's empty.' It's just not reflective of the spirit this country was built on."[4] Immigrants watched TV reports about the celebration of the statue from within the walls of detention centers.

The dissonance depended on the fiction that today's immigrants were different from yesterday's. The long list of nationalities of people being held in detention pointed to the difference between past and present: Cuba, El Salvador, Afghanistan, Zaire, the Dominican Republic, Venezuela. Diverse, nonwhite, and castigated as "illegal." The contradiction between the celebration of the nation's immigrant heritage and the violent treatment of current immigrants was perhaps no contradiction at all.

The Irish belonged to both categories: they were the celebrated immigrants of the past and the disdained undocumented immigrants of the present. Recognizing the apparent contradiction, Patrick Hurley, who was undocumented himself, observed that the public "didn't conceptualize illegal aliens as being like Irish people."[5] As a result, the media became obsessed with "the illegal Irish immigrant" and interviewed him often.

The story of the Irish married the romance of the past with the policy quandaries of the present. "The United States has long been the sanctuary for the Irish in times of oppression and economic difficulty," Hurley wrote in a letter to the editor of *Irish America*. "That right of sanctuary was earned by the contributions of countless Irishmen in the building of this great country. We are no different in nature to the immigrants who came before us. We cherish the same hopes and dreams you once cherished. However, for us, no welcoming sanctuary any longer exists."[6]

It was becoming more dangerous to be undocumented. With new state capacity for rooting out undocumented people, the threat of deportation broadened. A shifting sense of the enforcement landscape was critical to understanding the brewing policy battle and the concerns of the undocumented Irish.

This climate of fear was part of the impetus for the formation of a new organization. Hurley spoke directly to Irish Americans, reminding them of their immigrant pasts: "Irish Americans do not forget us. Do what you can to help change the immigration laws not only for us, but for many more Irish who will surely follow. You owe it to yourselves, as well as us."[7] It was time to make more noise—to use the collective talents of undocumented Irish immigrants and their allies to fight for change, to deepen relationships on Capitol Hill, to persuade the Irish government to act on emigrants' behalf, and to ensure ongoing visas for Irish immigrants.

· · · · · ·

May 20, 1987, was a perfect New York City spring day, the kind where city dwellers seek out patches of grass and sun, lingering outside instead of hurrying into subway stations and skyscrapers. Radio stations were blaring U2's "With or Without You," ubiquitous that summer, the Irish band's first number one hit in the United States. At Shea Stadium, the Mets, still World Series Champions, were playing the Padres. Elsewhere in Queens, some eighty people gathered at the general meeting of the County Cork Association, a long-standing group that had long provided a sense of community and support for Irish immigrants.

There, Hurley spoke up. He and Sean Minihane, a civil engineer and old friend from school, soon came together to form the Irish Immigration Reform Movement—the double-eye-R-M (IIRM). They'd been chatting, talking about the situation, meeting with others. Some wanted to keep a low profile—especially as IRCA was implemented and people began to fear for their jobs. But Hurley and Minihane's instincts were to do the opposite. "Light the explosives, see where the debris comes down," said Hurley.

They gained traction quickly. A reporter with Channel Two News in Boston, for example, called the IIRM "smart, savvy and likeable guys." They were easy to interview—they spoke English, and they were bold and open about publicizing their plight.[8] That boldness came from their upbringing in a modernizing Ireland and confidence in their own talents and capabilities. They believed the Irish government could be pushed to support them in ways that lent them protection. They sensed a broad base of support in Irish America to tap into and deepen. They were also white and thus felt less likely to be identified and deported by the Immigration and Naturalization Service (INS).

In July 1987, the group established a New York office, opening local IIRM chapters over the following months in Boston, Philadelphia, Chicago, San Francisco, Connecticut, and New Jersey, among others.[9] By 1988, the group claimed 10,000 members, with 400 activists actively working toward their goals.[10]

They relished winning media attention, which they used to their advantage when they went to Capitol Hill. They landed on a catchy motto—"legalize the Irish"—and plastered stickers, posters, flyers, and pins everywhere. Sen. Kennedy was photographed with a "legalize the Irish" sticker on.[11] They used occasions like the 1989 St. Patrick's Day parade in New York City to build support and publicity.[12] They raised money by holding dances and engaging Irish and Irish American participants, reportedly raising some $200,000 by the middle of 1988. Irish American publications, including the *Irish Echo* (founded in the 1920s), *Irish America* (founded by Niall O'Dowd in 1985), and the newspaper *Irish Voice* (founded by O'Dowd in 1987 specifically to serve the new Irish immigrants), amplified the work of the IIRM.

Few advocates or policymakers sympathetic to the Irish spoke explicitly about race. But they didn't have to. The popular imagination of immigrants was shaped by what historian Natalia Molina calls racial scripts, constructed socially and historically.[13] The Irish challenged the public's image of the undocumented immigrant, and they used the surprise this caused to gain sympathy for their efforts.

As Congress worked on big-picture legal immigration reform in the late 1980s, the Irish built a case for allowing more "independent" immigrants in the same spirit as the Donnelly visa program. Kennedy proposed legislation to "reopen our doors to potential immigrants who are unable to benefit from the current immigration law," referring to those without close family members to sponsor them. More directly, he added, "It is a question of how we correct an unexpected imbalance stemming from the 1965 act—the inadvertent restriction on immigration from the 'old seed' sources of our heritage."[14]

The hearings featured high-minded talk about justice and fairness. Nearly everyone framed the 1965 act and the immigration it had enabled as an obviously important corrective to past discrimination. Yet in words like "old seed" and "heritage" lurked ideas about the core identity of the American people. Few people would have claimed that there was a singular "American" ethnicity. In popular conceptions like those on display at the 1986 centennial celebration of the Statue of Liberty, Americanness was framed as an identity forged in part through waves of migration and adaptations. Frank Sinatra performed "The House I Live In" at the celebration, a rendition of the song he sang in the 1945 World War II short film, affirming that America was a place for people of "all races and religions."[15]

But advocates and policymakers' thinking about the "classic" immigrant remained shaped by historical processes that had racialized that mythic figure. While some people believed that incentivizing white immigration would help the country maintain its demographic character, or "heritage," the appeal of this discussion was that others could find the images and ideas conceptually inspiring, without being advocates of a whiter America. Still, a century of restrictive policymaking meant that the debate summoned images of turn-of-the-century Europeans rather than their contemporary Mexican counterparts working on farms in the Southwest, Jamaican guest workers in New York, or the Chinese immigrants who'd once outnumbered Italians.

What went largely unsaid was the idea that the difference between the present and the past was unfair. The Irish had *earned* a place in America through their collective hard work in past centuries—as a nationality—and that debt must be repaid. Contemporary discussions about reparations may have also influenced policymakers' thinking; in the summer of 1988, Congress made restitution to Japanese Americans and others held in detention camps during World War II. As the IIRM returned to Capitol Hill again and again, the group hired professional lobbyist Harris Miller.[16] Miller, a former legislative assistant on the House immigration subcommittee, helped the IIRM determine its legislative strategy, critical since Minihane, Benson, Hurley, and the other leaders of the group had no experience lobbying Congress.[17] In addition to drafting talking points, Miller helped the group figure out whom it should target on the Hill and facilitated meetings with congressmen of Irish heritage who might be potential allies and their staffers.[18]

When the IIRM was invited to testify on the Hill, members used some of the same language that their forebears had in the 1960s, when Irish Americans objected to changes in immigration law that disadvantaged them. In testimony, for example, Donald Martin said that "traditional sources of American immigration" had been "virtually shut out" by the 1965 act. Making the system more equitable was a good thing, but the trouble was it had unintentionally created this new imbalance.[19] Congress didn't intend, in passing Hart-Celler, "to repeal the past, or to sever the bonds of culture, tradition and affection which have existed for so long between the people of America and the countries of Europe." Those bonds and traditions deserved to be repaired. Martin reminded Congress members of the "contributions which have been made to American culture by the Irish and other Europeans," including 257 Congressional Medals of Honor bestowed on Irish immigrants over the years. "If those immigrants could speak to you now," he said, "we are certain they would argue for fairness and diversity."[20]

Linking the need for current visas to the deep roots of the Irish in America, the IIRM was engaging in ethnic identity politics. This approach had not worked in the 1960s just after Hart-Celler, but the message hit differently in the 1980s. That's because of a resurgence of white ethnic identity that made these ideas more salient.

· · · · · ·

In 1980's decennial census, census takers asked people about their ancestry in broad terms, requiring no substantiation.[21] While English and German were the most frequently reported ancestry groups, some 40 million Americans reported having Irish ancestry. That was twelve times as many

Americans claiming Irish descent as there were people in Ireland.[22] Advocates believed this figure reflected remarkably strong Irish American heritage.

European immigrants had long been encouraged to melt into the white mainstream. But now many white Americans rediscovered and revived their ethnic roots, particularly in the wake of the civil rights movement.[23] The search for roots connected white Americans to their own family histories and fueled new forms of roots tourism as American families traveled to "old countries" of which they had no living memory. They saw themselves reflected at the Liberty weekend celebrations. The vibrancy of these selected memories of America's immigrant past reflected a shift in the country's syntax of belonging, rooted in what historian Matthew Frye Jacobson deemed the "white ethnic revival."

By the 1980s conservatives drew on the imagery of the mythic European immigrant to bolster arguments about American colorblindness and fairness. If Jews, Italians, and Irish could adjust to life in America, overcome discrimination, and join the ranks of upwardly mobile professionals, why couldn't African Americans and other racialized groups? they reasoned. This story emphasized individuals' capacity to make their own fates, by their own proverbial bootstraps. Such rhetoric distanced white Americans from the legacies of slavery and racial violence, allowing beneficiaries of white privilege to dismiss the idea of enduring structural racism out of hand. Those who could trace their arrivals in America to the nineteenth or twentieth centuries absolved themselves of complicity or responsibility for the racial injustices foundational to American history. Groups that *themselves* had faced hardship and discrimination rebuffed the idea that they could be racists, or beneficiaries of racist systems, now. Instead of recognizing how policies had enabled white ethnic families to accumulate wealth while Black families were shut out of doing so, white ethnics recalled family histories of immigrant hardships overcome, and heartbreak. These memories summoned warm feelings about immigration, especially its role in making America *America*—even as the debate about contemporary immigration was framed around the urgency of restriction.

Lisa Johnston, IIRM's first paid employee, exemplified the trend of reconnecting to one's immigration past. Born in upstate New York, she knew almost nothing about Ireland other than that her paternal great-grandparents had left County Donegal long before her birth, and her father felt a strong sense of his Irish identity. As a kid, she imagined Ireland as a land of leprechauns as depicted on her Lucky Charms breakfast cereal box. But her identity as an Irish American became increasingly important to her as she grew up. She interned in the DC office of Sen. Moynihan (D-NY) and started attending IIRM events. She moved to Brooklyn for law school and began hanging out at Irish bars. What was happening to her friends was unjust, she thought.[24] She could see a clear line linking the past contributions of Irish Americans and the need for future Irish immigration opportunities.

Many congressmen saw themselves in the young Irish immigrants before them. Rep. Thomas Manton (D-NY) recognized that under present law "my parents would probably not qualify to immigrate [sic] from Ireland to the United States."[25] Francis Costello, press secretary to Boston's mayor Raymond Flynn, called the 1965 immigration law a "categorical injustice" to the Irish. How, the *Boston Globe* asked, could this "happen in a country with so many national and state politicians bearing Irish surnames"?[26] An *Irish Voice* story put it succinctly: "It didn't seem right that the Irish, who had done so much to transform America into the great nation it is today, were suffering so badly in the green card stakes, while citizens from other countries were emigrating here in plentiful numbers."[27]

A singer penned unpublished song lyrics for the IIRM. According to a handwritten poem found in the group's archives: "I'm a stranger in a city / Like a hundred thousand more / I'm the one they call illegal alien / As I move from door to door. / Legalize the Irish / Set us free to make our stand / Like our fathers long before us / Help to build God's chosen land."[28] Condensed to a few spare lines was the pain of being undocumented, an argument for justice, and a reference to the contributions of generations of Irish immigrants.

A sense of righteous frustration infused the debate. It masked language about the particular grievances of the Irish in broader language of discrimination, deficit, and moral wrong—without considering how the immigration system created or perpetuated injustices. In the immigration context, the identity politics fostered by the white ethnic revival made it possible for Americans with immigrant roots to celebrate their own heritages while rebuking unauthorized immigration. After all, their ancestors came "the right way" without violating the law, they told themselves. But it wasn't a fair or accurate comparison. The context for European arrivals in the nineteenth and early twentieth centuries was totally different, and, in fact, many Europeans had come *without* permission and later been allowed to adjust their status in ways other groups could not.[29] The stories they told about their families' pasts weren't grounded in history but in their sense of owner-ship of the American story. It was entirely possible for people to proudly celebrate America's heritage as a nation of immigrants while simultaneously casting the immigrants of the day as illegal and unwanted.

Repurposing the language of civil rights, the IIRM argued that the de facto exclusion of Europeans was inherently unjust. Sen. Alfonse D'Amato (R-NY) argued that the law was shutting them out based on their country of origin, just as the national origins quotas once had. "The law shuts them out because they are from countries like Ireland or Italy, whose great days of immigration are long in the past. . . . That is an injustice which I believe we should work to correct."[30] "One of the unintended effects of the changes made in immigration policy in 1965 and 1978 have conspired to increase the problem of discrimination in some areas and not to eliminate it," argued Brian Donnelly in a 1987 plea to extend his visa program. "You cannot solve the problems of discrimination by eliminating it for some and creating it for others."[31]

This rhetorical strategy built on the nostalgic imagery of past large-scale Irish immigration, but it went beyond the frame of ethnic solidarity by us-ing rights language. As the sociologist Eduardo Bonilla-Silva argued, "re-verse discrimination" became a key rhetorical tool for advancing colorblind racism in the post–civil rights era.[32] In this formulation, the Irish and other Europeans should be worthy of visas because they were unwitting victims of reverse discrimination. The strategy reflected the power of rights and antidiscrimination language in political arguments after the civil rights era. Discrimination was broadly understood as antithetical to American ideals. But harnessing "rights talk" and making claims of "reverse discrim-ination" allowed white Americans to resist policies that aimed to address anti-Black racism and to defend systems that benefited them.[33] Framing demands for visas for the Irish in these terms helped build support without saying outright that whitening the immigration stream should be the goal.

· · · · · ·

Together the specific legacy of Irish contributions to the nation and the ar-gument about discrimination in current law gained support. The Donnelly visas (distributed in 1987 and 1988) had been a good start, and in 1988 Con-gress extended the program, making an additional 15,000 visas available per year in 1989 and 1990 for nationals of countries adversely affected by the 1965 immigration law. The extra Donnelly visas were awarded based on the original registration period from January 1987, with entries drawn from those submissions. This was a gift for the IIRM, doing what the group wanted and undoubtedly serving the Irish who had registered in droves for Donnelly visas.

For the Irish, it still wasn't enough. But the activism that had won the Donnelly visas would soon produce something bigger—an immigration lottery.

4 Diversity

....

"The premise is to encourage the kind of diversity we don't get in the present law," Rep. Howard Berman (D-CA), from Los Angeles, told the *Washington Post* in 1989. His own father had immigrated to the United States from Poland in 1920, the paper noted, framing Berman's work on the Hill as part of his own immigration family history. "I can't imagine another country opening up its borders for this kind of opportunity," Berman said. "These are people who want to participate in the American dream."[1]

He was talking about an idea that had emerged from the same debate that produced the Donnelly visa and its extension: a visa lottery. Such a program would invite people without family in the United States to apply to become immigrants ("independent immigrants" was the phrase being knocked around). But where Berman's lottery differed from previous versions was in the list of eligible countries. He looked beyond those nations that had seen their visa numbers plummet after 1965 (those deemed "adversely affected" in the Donnelly visa program) and saw a whole world of people who could not qualify for an immigrant visa through the family system. More than conceiving of the policy as a gift for the Irish, Berman saw his lottery as a program that would contribute to America's diversity.

In 1981, the Select Commission tasked with studying immigration and laying out goals for reform for the 1980s articulated "cultural diversity" as a key goal for American immigration policy. In a supplement to the final report, the staff report stated, "Permitting, and indeed encouraging, the migration of new groups of immigrants broadens the diversity and characteristics of new immigrants and the richness of their contributions to U.S. culture and society."[2]

The commission also cheered cultural diversity as a component of the American creed, *E pluribus unum*, celebrating diversity in the sense of welcoming cultural difference. Commission member Lawrence Fuchs wrote in the report that *E pluribus unum* should be "more than a motto."[3] It made sense that this idea—out of many, one—should surface in a document charting U.S. immigration. The story of migration to the United States, Fuchs wrote, "is one of success in making one powerful, united nation out of many people." While recognizing long trends of nativism and xenophobia in American life, the commission believed that diversity was in the national interest of the United States and that the country could be a land of opportunity for all.

Such thinking elided important histories, including of Indigenous dispossession and the forced migration and enslavement of Africans that indelibly shaped American life. Rather than bringing an inclusive world into being, deploying the myth of the immigrant nation could paper over persistent inequality and obscure the need for transformative change while cutting off imaginative possibilities.

And yet, as dangerous as the "nation of immigrants" idea could be for these reasons, it also appeared as an antidote to a strident ethnonationalism then crystallizing at the fringes. The late 1970s had fostered the rise of a widespread white power movement that would grow in influence into the mid-1990s, with serious consequences for immigration policy. The U.S.-Mexico border was becoming a site for white power activism, with Klan members menacing people they perceived as migrants. Some white Americans resented the resettlement of Southeast Asian refugees and targeted them violently. And in 1980, the arrivals of Cubans in the Mariel boat lift and of Haitian asylum seekers, also arriving by boat, charged the air in South Florida and became politically useful for anti-immigration activists and tough-on-crime politicians. (Nothing about immigration, the commission noted, "seems to have upset the American people more than the Cuban push-out of 1980.")[4] The politics of immigration had the potential to be explosive. Could the story of the "nation of immigrants" help defuse them?

The commission, policymakers, and advocates believed that America should continue to welcome immigrants—for economic reasons, to keep families together, to provide haven for refugees, to increase the country's cultural resources. But they also had less pragmatic and more fundamental reasons. The United States remained "the world's number one magnet," the commission members wrote, not because of the dynamism of its economy but because of American values, including "freedom, equality under the law, opportunity and respect for diversity."[5] Without continued immigration, the promise of the American dream would erode. The story of what made us exceptional would have ended. *That* was a critical reason for the United States to admit independent immigrants, including those from countries with no established "immigration base" in the United States.

They should be welcomed to ensure that America would continue to broaden its boundaries of belonging.

· · · · · ·

Berman urged Congress to create a limited program that would reinforce the importance of diversity in immigration. In contrast to the policymakers working most closely with the IIRM who largely hailed from the Northeast and were either Irish Americans themselves or had districts that were substantially Irish American, Berman represented a district in Southern California that included parts of Los Angeles and the San Fernando Valley. Between 1980 and 1990, the Latino population of LA's metro area grew from 3 million to over 5 million people, and the Asian population more than doubled from just under 700,000 to over 1.5 million people. Many new residents were immigrants or the children of immigrants.[6]

Berman was troubled by visa programs that seemed to cater to Europeans and to elites exclusively. "I will strenuously oppose any backsliding to the days when the United States had a notion of which countries were the source of the most desirable immigrants," he wrote.[7] Among the others who shared his concerns were Charles Schumer, then a congressman from Brooklyn, and Howard Hom, legal counsel to the Chinese Welfare Council. Hom was skeptical about how the Donnelly visa program had identified certain countries as "adversely affected." He suggested that advocates might support a different, random lottery that limited applications to one per person—but only if it would be accessible to citizens of countries around the world. "There are some countries in the world that had traditionally lower immigration figures," Hom said, pointing out how any formula that favored countries with once-high immigration excluded the countries that had *always* been heavily restricted. Any formula that compared post-1965 immigration with midcentury numbers would leave out much of the world, especially countries in Africa and Asia.[8]

To critics, this was deeply flawed and a not particularly subtle way to whiten the immigration stream at a moment of rising panic about demographic change. If you took seriously the idea that the United States should cherish and invest in its diversity, or that the United States was served by having its population represent the whole world, the Irish-centric visa programs were at best a joke, and at worst a form of white supremacy.

And Berman found supporters for his idea who took the idea of immigrant diversity seriously. In 1988 hearings, witnesses expressed their support. They liked the format of a lottery—it was simple, didn't need to be elitist, and could be as open as the United States wished. Congress, embroiled in debate about other parts of the immigration system that year, finally passed a stand-alone bill to create a visa lottery on Berman's plan, one that would be open to Europeans but also to Africans, Asians, and South Americans.

The Berman lottery, known as OP-1, would make 10,000 visas available per year for two years—1990 and 1991—to be distributed through a lottery to people from 162 "underrepresented countries." Some countries always used all their visas and even had waiting lists for eligible immigrants to await their numbers; they were oversubscribed because many people qualified and came. But other countries didn't use every visa allotted to them, in part because there weren't U.S. citizens to petition for family members from those countries. This legislation considered these countries "underrepresented" in the immigration stream. Making visas available to people from these underrepresented countries, proponents argued, would add diversity to the United States.

· · · · · ·

Americans sometimes imagine that our immigration system has a sign-up list or line to queue up in. But in reality, the system is far more complex—and restrictive. The United States has set out a list of preferences to determine who is eligible to become a lawful permanent resident. Only according to narrow, rigid criteria with limited exceptions is applying even possible: in general, be the family member of an American, be recruited by a specific employer for a specific type of work, or be a refugee fleeing persecution. Most of the world was and remains ineligible to migrate. Even those who are eligible face bureaucratic and practical hurdles, and sometimes long waiting times, especially if they are from countries that send many immigrants annually. Furthermore, potential immigrants are subject to deep scrutiny before being issued a visa. The Berman lottery—tiny as it was in the grand scheme of things, and now all but forgotten—actually resembled how people imagined that immigration could work. Sign up to register your interest in migrating and wait for your name to be called.

The world marveled. The Associated Press (AP) wrote that the U.S. embassy in Cairo "was forced to shut down its entire complex and call the local police recently to deal with a crowd of 2,000 people demanding details." In Dakar, Senegal, a dedicated hotline was established, and the phone "never stopped ringing." The embassy in Bangladesh, reported interest "from university professors to rickshaw drivers." Officials in Casablanca,

Morocco, distributed 5,000 information sheets in three days.[9] "Notice of the visa lottery," the AP reported, "was relayed to citizens of 162 foreign countries by radio, television, newspaper and even messengers riding outrigger canoes." It "produced scenes resembling riots" at U.S. embassies and consulates, "from Senegal to Sicily and Morocco to Malaysia."[10] During the March 1989 lottery, some 3.2 million people submitted applications.[11]

Berman called the overwhelming response a testimony to "where the American dream stands for the people of the world."[12]

When the winners of the lottery were notified, OP-1 was found to have achieved the diversity it promised. In the first batch of 10,000 selectees, 123 countries of the 162 eligible nations were represented.[13] The countries that won the most visas were large, populous countries such as Bangladesh, Pakistan, Poland, Turkey, and Egypt. It was, as designed, a very different list than the top sending countries for the overall immigration system. Countries that weren't eligible for the Berman lottery, such as Mexico, the Philippines, and the Dominican Republic, had long histories of U.S. migration and U.S. imperial entanglement. China and India, also excluded, were the world's most populous countries and likewise had histories of U.S. migration going back a hundred years.[14] The Irish won some visas—362 of them. But they fared far worse in this lottery than in Donnelly's program, and although they were happy to embrace the concept of "diversity" to frame calls for more visas, Irish leaders were disappointed.[15] Without a shortened, specially tailored list of eligible countries to favor "adversely affected," countries like Ireland, they feared that they would be drowned out.

Berman's diversity lottery tapped into demand for migration opportunities, especially in countries otherwise not able to use the visa numbers theoretically allocated to them. The lottery was exciting and the prize "priceless." It appeared to have delivered on its promise of prioritizing immigrant diversity. Yet there was something subversive about the idea.

· · · · · ·

The post-1965 immigration system leaned heavily on family ties. This was by design, but some observers began to criticize the system's focus on the family and the outcomes of this system. For example, when the historian John Higham testified in 1986 before the House immigration subcommittee, he pointed out, "Just as the national origins quota system in the early twentieth century suppressed variety in the interest of favored ethnic groups, so the current law does that in the interest of family chains."[16]

Nativists seized on this concept, decrying "chain migration." Drawn from academic analysis, the phrase was coined to illuminate how individuals who migrate tend to create new patterns of migration and links between places, bringing family members and friends along with them, from one place to another. There's nothing nefarious about this—keeping families together is a widely shared priority, and having friends and family members who have already arrived in a destination makes migration safer and perhaps smoother for those who follow. But restrictionists were disturbed that more nonwhite people were migrating and bringing family members with them through the legal admissions system. If this continued, would new immigrants and their descendants unseat white Americans' racial dominance? Worries about demographic change animated the policy debate. While restrictionists tended to focus on the issue of unauthorized immigration in their public messaging, they were also deeply concerned about the legal immigration of people of color since 1965.

Some proponents of diversity visas—whether the Berman lottery or a more permanent, ongoing program—aimed to disrupt these chains of family migration. They wanted to ensure that people outside of Mexico, China, and the other top sending countries had a chance to migrate. Because some 85 percent of legal immigrants now came from Asia and Latin America, most of them through family unification, other regions of the world could be seen as not only underrepresented but excluded.[17] Berman himself said his program was designed to balance inequities in the immigration system that now appeared to favor people from Asia and Latin America—chiefly due to the system's reliance on family migration.[18]

Policymakers treaded carefully when discussing admissions and restrictions, of course. The legacies of nativism, racism, and exclusion in immigration history remained top of mind. When people on the Hill criticized the 1965 act that now governed the immigration system, they didn't celebrate the 1920s restrictions it had replaced, or complain about recent immigrants of color. But they were critical about what they deemed its unintended consequences. In trying to prioritize equality, its crafters were righteous. The problem was that they were wrong in their assumptions.

The law had indeed emphasized equality before the law and non-discrimination—key values in the 1960s, highly prized by congressional liberals. The debate was animated in part by the idea that the United States constituted a "nation of immigrants." As a senator, John F. Kennedy invoked the phrase in a 1958 essay, which he then published as a book in 1963.

The idea was that successive waves of immigration had made America the country it was. It focused almost entirely on different groups of Europeans who had left behind home countries, come to America, and enriched their adopted one. They faced adversity—but overcame it, affirming the American ideal of universal opportunity.

Later, the Select Commission on immigration built on the idea in its recommendations for the policymakers of the 1980s. "Even the Indians were immigrants," the authors wrote. Embracing the notion of a nation of immigrants, they swept aside settler colonialism, white supremacy, and the legacy of slavery, among other basic historical truths.[19] In framing migration as the key to American mobility, the story cast the challenges faced by European immigrants as somehow equivalent to forced migration through enslavement, wars of conquest, or the violent processes that produced refugees in the twentieth century. It ignored how European immigrants had been permitted to become white and to shake off ethnic signifiers to join in racial whiteness, which in many cases was the key to groups' eventual inclusion.

It was a dream story that glossed over painful truths. Aspiring to equality didn't make it so. As Ellen Wu has shown, depicting American democracy as "a succession of triumphs over exclusions" in which "the circle of those included in the polity as full members of society has continued to widen over time" troublingly generated "new modes of exclusion" and delegitimized Black Americans' demands for structural changes.[20]

Even as they passed legislation that ended formal racial exclusions and imposed a new immigration system that put the peoples of the world on even ground, 1965's policymakers weren't terribly concerned about the new modes of exclusion they were generating. Many members of Congress believed and argued that under a system prioritizing family reunification, recent patterns of immigration, and indeed whiteness itself, would be preserved.[21] As Rep. Emanuel Celler (D-NY) said at the time, "There will not be, comparatively, many Asians or Africans entering this country. . . . Since the people of Africa and Asia have very few relatives here, comparatively few could immigrate from those countries because they have no family ties in the U.S."[22] It was an assurance to his segregationist colleagues. But it would turn out to be poor prophecy.

Geopolitics, global economic transformation, and unexpected consequences of the family-based admissions system made immigration to the United States increasingly nonwhite, and this coincided with changes to the U.S. economy and politics that fostered backlash. As immigrants came increasingly from Asia and Latin America, some white Americans, who had always been in the majority and who had long exclusively enjoyed the benefits of American citizenship, came to believe that immigration threatened their own prosperity and place in the world. A national debate about demographic change became entangled with anxieties about an economic system in transformation and the aftermath of urban uprisings in the 1970s—as well as ongoing questions about equality, rights, and racism in the United States.

These were deep, existential questions. What did the state owe its citizens? What would America's economy look like without a strong industrial base, solid union membership, and constant growth? White Americans could feel that they were losing something, between the federal government's efforts to integrate segregated communities and institutions, shocks that shattered the economic basis of American prosperity since World War II, and efforts to unravel public goods and embrace free markets in every part of American life.

In this context, diversity emerged as a framework for understanding American life and for managing racial difference. Wary of appearing to support immigration proposals that would take the United States back to days of open racial quotas, proponents of visas for the Irish embraced diversity, which in blunt terms could be deployed as the opposite of racism. Testifying for the IIRM, Donald Martin had even called diversity "the primary goal of the 1965 Act."[23] It wasn't. But because the immigration system had contributed to making the country less white by the late 1980s, he and others projected diversity as a goal backward onto legislation that had tried to unseat unfair white privilege. As critical as it was of the legislation that had cut Irish visas, the IIRM, in its materials, framed the 1965 ending of the national origins quotas as necessary "because a quota system did not do justice to the principle of diversity."[24]

· · · · · ·

Diversity is a buzzword today. But it wasn't always. A Google Ngram shows a slope of increased references to diversity beginning in the 1950s and 1960s, then a sharper incline beginning in the 1990s, peaking around 2005, falling a little, and then rising again in 2015.[25] The word was popularized in the spheres of business and higher education and came to mean something like the inclusion of people from various backgrounds in American institutions on an equitable basis. Americans do not share a race or ethnicity; we are diverse. The idea of diversity is that we can build a society where we share values, rights and resources while retaining the differences that make us unique. The term also came to indicate the presence of nonwhite people in spaces once maintained as nearly exclusively white: the immigration stream, corporate boardrooms, university campuses.

That the term began its first upward ascent in the 1950s and 1960s is no accident. This was the era of the Civil Rights Act and the end of formal, legal segregation in public facilities and racial discrimination in hiring. Title VII established the Equal Employment Opportunity Commission to enforce civil rights laws and ensure that individuals wouldn't face discrimination on account of race, sex, or other protected characteristics. As important as these mechanisms were in tackling racism in America, few thought they would be sufficient to equalize the playing field and adequately redress centuries of oppression of African Americans. "Freedom is the right to share, share fully and equally, in American society—to vote, to hold a job, to enter a public place, to go to school," said President Lyndon Johnson, in his commencement address at Howard University in June 1965. "But freedom is not enough."[26]

Johnson recognized and acknowledged that further action was needed to combat discrimination against Black Americans. "This is the next and the more profound stage of the battle for civil rights," he said. "We seek not just freedom but opportunity. We seek not just legal equity but human ability, not just equality as a right and a theory but equality as a fact and equality as a result." And so, he issued an executive order requiring *affirmative* action for government contractors to hire and employ women and members of minority groups. Equal opportunity was essential, but not enough.[27]

What he said made sense. And yet, when it came to implementing affirmative efforts to ensure that Black Americans had the same chances to thrive as white Americans, civil rights advocates and others faced dramatic resistance and backlash. White families resisted selling their homes to Black buyers or allowing Black students to attend schools with their children. Efforts to redraw school district boundaries or combine student populations through busing were met with protests. White job applicants complained that affirmative action policies unfairly shut them out.

Opponents of racial equality efforts seized the language of rights, framing themselves as "taxpayers" or "homeowners" defending themselves against "reverse discrimination" created by policies aiming to address discrimination against African Americans.[28] Later, the IIRM would use similar rights language to assert that white Europeans were being shut out of the immigration system. At a moment of deindustrialization and decline, which hastened through the 1970s, any diminution of white privilege felt like oppression. White liberal commitment to racial justice faltered, and the politics of affirmative action frayed nerves and weakened resolve.

In 1978, the Supreme Court weighed in on the constitutionality of affirmative action policies. When Allan Bakke, who was white, was rejected by the UC Davis medical school, he framed his rejection as an example of reverse discrimination and challenged the university's admissions policy. In a fractured ruling, the court framed diversity as a replacement for efforts to affirmatively address systemic racism in American life. Justice Lewis F. Powell Jr., writing a plurality opinion for the court, found that affirmative action in higher education was constitutional under some circumstances. But it wasn't because the state had a compelling interest in producing more Black graduates or in ensuring opportunities for Black Americans. Powell thought that racial classifications were suspect and wanted to believe that a colorblind society was possible. Still, he thought that the state did have an interest in creating a racially diverse student population, and for that reason, it could take race and other characteristics into account when filling the student body.

Diversity could be seen as a value that would enrich the learning experience for every student—*especially white ones.* "The nation's future depends upon leaders trained through wide exposure to the ideas and mores of students as diverse as this Nation," Powell wrote.[29] In other words, some forms of affirmative action were constitutional and could be justified because admitting nonwhite students would ultimately benefit white students too. The diversity rationale was deemed more compelling than dismantling the racist structures that had produced widely disparate outcomes for white and Black students. In a separate opinion, Justice Thurgood Marshall reminded the court that for Black Americans, "meaningful equality remains a distant dream."[30] He urged, "Bringing the Negro into the mainstream of American life should be a state interest of the highest order." But it wasn't.

Instead of recognizing the ongoing need to make American institutions more equitable and to face deep, hard histories of inequality and oppression in American life, we got diversity. Higher education, corporate hiring, and the entertainment industry embraced the concept, finding ways to craft more diverse classes and workforces—but not necessarily equitable ones.

That's not to say diversity initiatives did nothing—the concept brought nonwhite people into spaces from which they'd previously been excluded. But rather than leveling the playing field for Black students, diversity was framed as a perk for white ones. Failing to heed Marshall's argument that the United States must create meaningful equal opportunities for Black Americans as a form of redress, institutions instead touted diversity as the goal for public policies surrounding race in American life. Diversity was a weak, defanged substitute for addressing white supremacy. And it did little to neutralize the backlash against Black progress.

By the 1980s, diversity was understood as a consensus goal, something that CEOs and university presidents could tout as a show of their commitment to core American values, while not doing much else to transform their institutions or make them more inclusive and equitable for Black Americans. It *sounded* antithetical to white supremacy, although of course in many cases it was not. That duality is one reason so many policymakers used the term as they argued about the purpose of immigration policy.

· · · · · ·

By many measures, the United States was already diverse. There was no need to alter immigration policy, which already admitted mostly nonwhite immigrants, to serve the goal of diversity. Unless what was needed was diversity *among* immigrants—as though each year's admissions were like an admitted class at a university. Lawrence Fuchs, an immigration scholar, had pointed out that this vision of immigrant diversity made little sense because "it is not countries that immigrate, but human beings."[31]

As policymakers pondered injecting more diversity into immigration, following the guidance of the Select Commission, they did reduce the measure of diversity to national origin. It was a quiet revival of the thinking that had animated previous restrictions, seeing each immigrant as an emissary of her country of origin. They did so because of the central role played by the IIRM. Even though the Irish were individuals in need of green cards and legal status, their best bet at gaining the visas they needed was their country of origin, which they characterized as both adversely affected by 1965 *and* underrepresented among contemporary immigrants. From their view, adding more white immigrants would diversify the immigration stream by adding variety. "It is difficult to see this as anything but a veiled tilt away from current immigrant source regions," wrote Doris Meissner, the future INS commissioner, in an op-ed criticizing the legislation that eventually created the permanent visa lottery.[32]

Ironically, proponents of diversity visas touted variety as a good thing while tapping into anxiety about the shifting demographics that resulted from the 1965 act and its emphasis on family unification. Because immigrants came overwhelmingly from a handful of countries in Asia and Latin

America, proponents of diversity argued that more visas were needed to break up such concentration. Framed in this way, high levels of Mexican immigration, for example, *threatened* America's racial and ethnic diversity rather than adding to it. If too many immigrants came from the same country, they might form ethnic enclaves and neighborhoods where they'd have no need to adapt to the United States as it had been. This concern dovetailed with debates about multiculturalism that fretted that allowing different groups to retain cultural touchstones and to promote ethnic and racial pride would "shift the balance from *unum* to *pluribus*," as Arthur Schlesinger Jr. wrote in *Time* magazine.[33] Unity required integration and assimilation. Large numbers of people retaining or reclaiming separate identities—something perhaps fostered by the immigration system's family focus—threatened the ideal that pulled diverse Americans together.

Diversity visa programs thus enjoyed a spectrum of support. Liberals like Berman liked the idea that immigrant dreamers could come from anywhere in the world. Advocates for the Irish wanted to see traditional, white sources of immigration revived. And critics of nonwhite immigration who feared ethnic separatism or the transformation of majority-white American institutions could also support the goal of diversity. It was a perfectly American blend of cynicism and idealism.

5 Immigration Act of 1990

It was now or never. "I do not want to sound like the boy who cried wolf, but this is really it. There will be no other opportunity to consider this measure," John Joseph Moakley warned his fellow members of Congress.[1] Pass the immigration act, the culmination of nearly a decade of hearings, debate, and drafted bills, or let all that work be lost. Late October 1990 was a key moment for the Irish and their advocates and, of course, for many others far from policymakers' radar.

Advocates and lobbyists can only go so far. In the end, elected legislators have the power to enact legislation. In 1990, a bunch of white guys passed an immigration law that they knew would add diversity to the country, in part to serve the Irish immigrants who'd established good relationships with them, elicited their empathy, and made the harms of restriction visible and pressing. Some were thinking specifically of the Irish, in fact. Others liked the idea that a diversity immigration program would disrupt the concentration of immigrants from just a few countries in annual admissions, ensuring an assimilationist model for newcomers.

Moakley, for his part, supported the diversity provisions of the final bill, but his primary motivation was to serve Salvadoran refugees denied asylum by the United States by offering a different form of humanitarian relief. That the issue was so dear to him was a result of local advocacy by Salvadoran migrants. His response reflected something deep in his character and his understanding of U.S. global power and its violence. Easing the conditions under which migrants lived in the United States was, to him, a form of repair.

The eventual adoption of the permanent diversity visa lottery program, which would do little for the Irish, shows how the concept of diversity itself helped push policymakers to act—particularly in the moment between the Cold War and its aftermath. At this moment, the five men who played the most direct roles in crafting the permanent visa lottery—Joe Moakley, Alan K. Simpson, Ted Kennedy, Bruce Morrison, and Chuck Schumer—acted with a sense of optimism, grounded in shared consensus that immigration to the United States served its national interests. How it happened is a reminder of where power lies.

· · · · · ·

Senators Kennedy and Simpson were unlikely bedfellows. Kennedy had a long Senate career by this point, and a long trajectory of working on immigration. He had championed the bill that became the Hart-Celler Act in 1965—something the Irish immigration advocates of the 1980s wouldn't forget or forgive. Although he was from the country's most prominent Irish American family, he realized that the previous laws had privileged the Irish in ways that discriminated against others. As his staffer David Burke said later, "Now, how is this son of Irish immigrants going to handle the cutback on Irish numbers, to cut back the number of Irish individuals in this country, in fact? Remember, we're talking families and reunification and so on." But Kennedy took it on because "it just was not right."[2] It wasn't right that a nation of immigrants should choose immigrants based on racist ideas about which countries were most desirable.

But there was another trade-off involved in the 1965 act. The law did end the use of troubling national origins quotas in distributing immigrant visas. But in exchange for a formal commitment to more equality, policymakers had reinforced a framework of restriction. Those restrictions affected the Irish, who remained resentful more than twenty years later about Kennedy's role in cutting off their access to visas.

Kennedy worked on but voted against the Immigration Reform and Control Act of 1986. His chief concern was that its employer sanctions provisions could be used to discriminate against workers who were Hispanic. Although the law allowed millions of immigrants to gain legal status, these measures were paired with restrictive provisions. Now, with that legislation behind them, Kennedy and his Republican counterpart, Alan Simpson, teamed up to address the legal immigration system.

They worked together unusually closely, holding bipartisan, joint hearings between the House and the Senate. While such close cooperation was uncommon, Simpson thought it made sense because immigration "was an issue that was all national."[3] The two men with big personalities—the "liberal lion" and the six-foot-seven cowboy raconteur—had an unlikely bond and rapport.

The debate revolved around key questions like: How many immigrants should the United States accept each year? Should the United States recruit more highly skilled immigrants and accept fewer family members of citizens? In contrast to previous reform efforts, Kennedy and Simpson were not primarily concerned about how immigration policy shaped the demographics of the country or about undocumented immigration but were instead thinking about how legal immigrant admissions could serve U.S. economic needs at the dawn of the 1990s.

Questions about diversity and helping the Irish were also part of the conversation. The Irish had gotten the Donnelly visa in 1986's legislation, become its largest beneficiary in 1987, and seen it extended in 1988. Berman's worldwide diversity lottery in 1989 had been a success for the United States and a disappointment for the Irish. In 1990, the Irish were even more determined to secure a permanent solution. And they turned to Kennedy, a likely ally, but one who had disappointed them before.

But by this time, Kennedy had accepted the IIRM's framing of the issue. They helped him recognize how restrictions harmed the Irish. Kennedy's sense that his own family faced discrimination for being Irish and Catholic made him sympathetic.[4] Kennedy recalled Sen. Jack Brooks (D-TX) joking in conference, "Does Senator Kennedy have his Irish? Are the Irish in this draft?" Kennedy would cringe and change the subject.[5]

He and Simpson eventually proposed a points system to admit "independent immigrants," with points awarded for age, education, English skills, occupational demand, and training and work experience. Kennedy's staffer Michael Myers admitted, "We figured out a way to have a point system in our Senate bill that would favor the Irish. We'd give points for countries that were shortchanged by the current immigration law. That, we thought, was a neutral way of enabling Irish to get green cards."[6]

With both Kennedy and Simpson's backing, the rest of the Senate was likely to support the plan. Of course, the bill they were assembling went far beyond the issue of diversity. Simpson wanted more employment-related visas to help businesses. Kennedy wanted to whittle down the long delays that immigrants from some countries endured while awaiting reunion with their U.S. citizen relatives. Other provisions dealt with investor visas, a visa waiver pilot program for travelers, and visas for people fleeing certain kinds of humanitarian disasters. Holding such varied and complex issues together required compromise and hard work. But the senators were lucky in that, for the moment, immigration was somewhat less of a hot-button issue than it had been earlier in the decade and would be again in the 1990s. The Senate soon passed their bill, which increased immigration numerically to strengthen the nation economically heading into the new decade.

· · · · · ·

The outlook for passing expansive immigration legislation in the House was also looking good. Longtime chair of the House immigration subcommittee Rep. Romano Mazzoli (D-KY), who had worked with Simpson on IRCA, was ousted from his position in 1989. Bruce Morrison, a four-term representative from Connecticut, was next in line by seniority and replaced him. With a secure majority in the House as well as the Senate, Democratic party leadership on the judiciary committee expected him to run the subcommittee with more open discussion, hearings, and space for different voices.[7]

Because of the House's structure, Congress members from far-flung districts approached immigration policy with different priorities. As members proposed immigration bills on various aspects of the system, Morrison sought to bring them under one umbrella as companion legislation to Simpson and Kennedy's bill. Morrison would prove a useful ally to the Irish. Besides being personally drawn to the issue and convinced of the importance of the plight of the Irish, he was particularly attuned to serving the Irish American constituents in his district as he launched his 1990 campaign for governor. Morrison approached his task with the attitude that "immigration policy is not merely a matter of budget priorities, nor of the supply of labor. It is one of the ways we define ourselves as a nation."[8] His professional ambitions would be best served by delivering a generous bill.

The IIRM succeeded in persuading Morrison to keep a version of the Donnelly visa program in the final bill. The "Morrison visa" program was a temporary, "transitional" program that made 40,000 visas available per year for three years, for nationals of "adversely affected" countries, referencing the 1965 act's curtailment of immigration opportunities for some Europeans.[9] A special provision in the transition program reserved at least 40 percent of these for "the foreign state the natives of which received the greatest number of visas issued under section 314 of the Immigration Reform and Control Act"—the Donnelly visas. Ireland was thus guaranteed at least 40 percent of the 120,000 transition visas over three years. Later, when Congress ultimately passed the Immigration Act, Sen. Daniel P. Moynihan (D-NY) acknowledged the role played by the IIRM in "bringing this legislation to fruition. Probably no organization has been as diligent, or played such a helpful role in moving the Congress forward, as the IIRM and they deserve great thanks and hearty congratulations."[10] The only problem was that Morrison's visas were time-limited.

In addition to making sure that the Irish had their visas with the temporary program, Morrison and others also looked for a way to incorporate a permanent diversity visa program into the legal admissions system. An ongoing version of the open global lottery like the one Berman had created in 1989 was appealing. But the IIRM remained wary. The results had reflected "Ireland's inability to compete in a random, worldwide lottery."[11] While the language of diversity was helping to package and sell the idea of admitting "independent immigrants" to legislators—it was expansive, appealed broadly in the late 1980s, and countered charges that such a program was racist—the downside was that it obscured the needs of the Irish, who would be all but lost in a global lottery.[12]

Indeed, the IIRM's desire for "diversity" stopped at the Irish. In the margin of a draft confidential memo to Charles Schumer, someone at IIRM scribbled, "We ought to say straight out that we do not feel that there should be any requirement to produce a system which is so 'neutral' as to create spaces (i.e. visas) for countries, and whole regions of the world such as Africa, where there is currently no demand and more importantly—no lobbying activity on their behalf."[13]

What the Irish needed was a permanent diversity program that on its face appeared race-neutral but in practice would offer them some advantage.[14] Neutrality in the law, like setting equal per-country numerical caps as the 1965 act had, did not necessarily produce neutral outcomes.

· · · · · ·

The IIRM's mention of Africa behind the scenes inadvertently admitted that relative to some underrepresented countries, "adversely affected" countries like Ireland retained key advantages. Recent Irish immigrants were able to tap into long existing networks and use their high levels of education and English fluency to appeal to journalists. Their whiteness elicited sympathy in the American public. Plus, those who'd gained legal status through the Donnelly visa had a more secure position from which to argue for more visas. The Irish *had* seen their numbers plummet after 1965—but no such plummet was possible for countries that had always been excluded.

Congress had a long history of ignoring Black immigration. It hadn't considered the Black population of the country in setting restrictive quotas in the 1920s. African nations were largely denied meaningful visa numbers because the people of African descent living in the United States weren't counted. Centuries of connections between the African continent and what became the United States were intentionally erased in setting these limits— including both the legacy of slavery and a long, numerically small history of voluntary emigration from Africa.[15] The 1920s architects of immigration policy thus flattened the category of Blackness while introducing nuance to the categories for white immigration. Even when some African countries received tiny, minimal quotas, Black immigration remained low, perhaps because anyone wishing to move to the United States would have had to obtain a visa at a consulate, where there was great discretion to deny people.

In the 1960s, of the 3.2 million lawful permanent residents admitted to the United States, fewer than 24,000 were from the African continent. Even in the 1980s, only 142,000 Africans—the world's second most populous continent, containing some fifty countries—were admitted as lawful permanent residents out of a total of more than 6.2 million immigrants. That was less than the number of illegal Irish immigrants the IIRM estimated had come to the United States in just half the decade.[16] Despite the end of formal racist restrictions, Africans remained far more disadvantaged by the system than the Irish ever were.

And unlike the Irish, who easily received visitors' visas to the United States that they were likely to overstay, Africans were often viewed with suspicion at U.S. consulates and denied the temporary visas they needed to study in, attend conferences in, or visit the United States.

But just because few Africans immigrated to the United States under policies that had historically excluded them did not mean that Africans did not want access to visas or would not apply for visas if given the opportunity. African enthusiasm for emigration just couldn't be assessed accurately in Washington. And while Irish American groups had been able to focus attention on the plight of recent Irish immigrants, African American advocacy groups had many pressing issues, beyond immigration, to consider when pushing policymakers to act.

That's not to say African American interest groups had no interest in nondomestic issues. By some measures, the 1980s had been a high watermark for African Americans' influence on U.S. foreign policy, particularly toward Africa. Following Shirley Chisholm's election in 1968, the number of African American members of Congress increased, and they often worked in concert through the Congressional Black Caucus, created in 1971, to advance key issues. In 1977, Black activists formed TransAfrica (later TransAfrica Forum) to advocate within the United States for the people of the African diaspora. In Congress, as the historian Ben Talton shows, Black policymakers like Rep. Mickey Leland (D-TX) pushed to redefine how the United States related to Africa—working to end white minority rule in southern Africa and appropriating funds for famine relief in the Horn of Africa, for example—because of their roots in Black Power organizing and radical Black internationalism.[17]

While African American members of Congress did not dominate debate about migration-related issues, at times they highlighted anti-Blackness in the immigration system and advocated for more humane migration policies. For example, when the Reagan administration suggested it would not protect Ethiopian immigrants from deportation in the early 1980s when the country suffered famine and crisis, groups mobilized to push the administration. The Emergency Committee for African Refugees and the National Association for the Advancement of Colored People (NAACP), along with Black leaders in Congress such as Rep. Julian C. Dixon (D-CA), pushed the Reagan administration to reinstate what was called "Extended Voluntary Departure" for Ethiopians within the United States to protect them from deportation.[18] After this advocacy, the number of Ethiopians resettled as refugees also increased.[19] Black American leaders were also outspoken in the early 1980s and again in the early 1990s against U.S. policies toward Haitian asylum seekers that they recognized as anti-Black.

At times Black public opinion has registered concerns that immigration may harm Black American progress by increasing labor competition, or lowering wages, in theory. And the veneration of immigrants has long been used to reinforce anti-Blackness, through implicit or explicit comparisons. But the scholar Niambi Michele Carter has described African American attitudes over time about immigration as "ambivalent," calling this ambivalence "conflicted nativism." Crucially, Carter argues that such concerns remained distinct from mainstream anti-immigrant sentiment.[20] That's because, she shows, Black Americans have recognized that the white supremacy that animated immigration restriction and deportation was part of the same force that limits Black social mobility within the United States. The advocacy efforts of Black policymakers on behalf of immigrant groups like Ethiopians and Haitians in the 1980s reflected this sense of solidarity.

It is not that there was no lobbying on behalf of aspiring African emigrants and African immigrants in Washington, DC, but that the Black policymakers who were most engaged in these issues saw them in broader terms than just visa numbers. They sought relief for Black immigrants being detained or excluded unfairly, and they sought to deliver aid and support to Black people abroad.

But there were no Black members of Congress on the immigration sub-committee.[21] Of the 143 pieces of immigration-related legislation introduced during the 101st Congress, some mentioned specific places or immigrant groups: Central Americans, Chinese students, Filipino veterans, Soviet Jews, Lebanese. Just one related to Africa: a Concurrent Resolution offered by Rep. Major R. Owens (D-NY) calling on the president to grant asylum to white South Africans who refused to serve in the armed forces in defense of apartheid.[22] Owens, a librarian and civil rights activist, succeeded Shirley Chisholm in representing his Brooklyn district.[23]

The discussion of diversity visas certainly included mentions of Africa. But no policymaker or advocacy group made Africa the focus of the discussion. Instead, the debate remained focused on familiar keywords: diversity, independent immigrants, and the Irish.

· · · · · ·

Schumer had become an ally to the IIRM and had even attended the March 1989 St Patrick's Day parade under a banner of "legalize the Irish." But he suggested that allocating diversity visas to the *adversely affected* countries rather than *underrepresented* countries would "attract a lot of criticism which may cause it to falter."[24] He thought that privileging countries like Ireland in a permanent, ongoing diversity lottery couldn't be justified. A proposal to reserve up to 60 percent of diversity visas for countries like Ireland "has the 'appearance' of being imbalanced," as even the IIRM admitted.[25] As Kennedy's staffer Michael Myers put it, "You can't just have an Irish provision, because that would never pass Congress."[26] To pass, a permanent lottery would have to frame diversity more broadly.

At just shy of twenty-four years old in 1974, Schumer became the youngest person elected to the New York State Assembly since Theodore Roosevelt. He had yet to sit for the New York Bar exam after graduating from Harvard Law School.[27] When Rep. Elizabeth Holtzman ran for the U.S. Senate in 1980, Schumer ran for her seat representing a swath of white ethnic and immigrant Brooklyn (her district included Crown Heights, Midwood, Brownsville, and Gerritsen Beach) in Congress—and won.[28] Although the district lines were redrawn and renumbered over time, Schumer joined a long line of New York City representatives from this area representing immigrant neighborhoods and playing a critical role in immigration policy. In Congress, Holtzman had chaired the immigration subcommittee and co-authored with Sen. Ted Kennedy the Refugee Act of 1980. She'd gained the seat and become one of the youngest women to go to Congress after her 1972 defeat of one of the oldest members of Congress, Emanuel Celler, in the Democratic primary.[29] Celler was eighty-four at the time, having served for a full half century, from 1923 to 1973. He was in Congress to vote against the Reed-Johnson Act establishing national origins quotas in 1924—his first floor speech was against the bill—and four decades later he cosponsored the 1965 act dismantling them. Schumer had begun work on immigration issues in the 1980s, helping negotiate provisions in IRCA, and then turning to the legal immigration bill that Morrison was helping shepherd.[30] The bill, Schumer said, was based on the premise that "immigrants are good for America."[31]

He was convinced by the argument espoused by the IIRM that certain countries had been "left out" by the legal immigration system. "It's wrong that countries like Ireland, or Poland, or Nigeria can't get almost any immigrants into this country, simply because the people who came from those countries came a long time ago," he said. He wanted the diversity visa lottery to say to nationals of these countries: you aren't going to be excluded anymore.

This was not exactly what the IIRM had in mind. To ensure that the Irish could do as well as possible in a worldwide lottery, Harris Miller, the IIRM's lobbyist, created a formula that would be "country-neutral in design, although, of course, it will not be country-neutral in effect."[32] Looking at recent data, he recommended allocating diversity visas in inverse proportion to the family-based preference admissions. Because the Irish and other Europeans were receiving relatively few family-based visas, they would have a leg up in the diversity program, as a complement to the family-based system.

According to this plan, diversity visa allocations would be pegged to region. Because Asia and Latin America received nearly 87 percent of preference admissions, he showed, countries in these regions should be allocated just 13 percent of diversity admissions.[33] A formula sorted the world into the two highest-sending regions (Asia and "Latin America"—including Mexico, Central America, and the Caribbean) and the four lowest-sending regions (Europe, Africa, North America, and Oceania) based on existing immigration levels.[34] Miller's math suggested allocating the most diversity visas to Europe—nearly 47 percent. Africa would receive around 37 percent, followed by Asia receiving 12 percent, with the other regions receiving less than 2 percent each: Latin America, North America, and Oceania.[35] Within regions, the visas should be distributed by lottery so that countries with high demand could win more visas. By dividing and sorting the world in this way, the formula weighted the applications from regions deemed low-sending and advantaged countries with high demand within those regions—like Ireland and Northern Ireland, which the IIRM wanted counted as a separate country for immigration purposes.

Given the concerns Schumer and other policymakers had raised about passing the legislation with a permanent diversity program intact, the Irish could only push so hard. And although it didn't favor them outright, a regionally weighted formula for diversity visas would at least improve the odds for the Irish in a system they knew would be less than optimal but that could feasibly be included in the legislation. It was better than nothing.

The coming deadline—the end of the Second Session of Congress at the end of 1990—proved especially helpful to the IIRM and policymakers who could use the time pressure to prioritize passing the omnibus legislation. Incumbents were sensitive to the notion that they needed to deliver actual legislation, especially before the 1990 midterm elections. Rep. Newt Gingrich (R-GA) had called the 1989 session "an unfinished Congress," which had been beset by its own scandals. House Speaker Jim Wright (D-TX) was forced out over ethics violations in June 1989. The Savings and Loan crisis, which involved the failure of over a thousand savings and loan associations and cost U.S. taxpayers billions of dollars, had become a major scandal by the late 1980s. When Lincoln Savings and Loan collapsed in 1989, it led to what was known as the Keating Five affair, in which five U.S. senators were implicated in a corruption scheme. Congress had been beleaguered by a budget fight and impasse over deficit reduction, and by the reordering of military spending in the wake of changing geopolitics across the Soviet Union and eastern Europe.[36]

Immigration reform had slipped below the radar screen, affording policymakers leeway in working out the details.[37] A January 1990 *Washington Post* editorial made only a brief mention of the immigration bill that "would basically let more people in," but the paper seemed unconvinced that it would pass.[38] The *Post* noted that both Senate and House proposals would increase the number of immigrant visas. As the United States entered the last decade of the millennium, policymakers were looking to immigration as a way to bring in talented workers, as well as to shore up the tax base and address deficit spending.[39]

Morrison's bill on the House side was even more generous in numbers than Simpson and Kennedy's Senate bill, with something for everybody. The bill contained his temporary transition measure that would provide visas to "adversely affected" countries for three years, with 40 percent reserved for the Irish. These became known as "Morrison visas" after the law's passage.[40] The bill also incorporated a compromise with Schumer on the permanent diversity visa provision, using IIRM's basic math and allocating 55,000 diversity visas in inverse proportion to the allocation of preference visas over the previous five years, beginning in fiscal year 1995.[41]

· · · · · ·

Part of the legislative strategy for getting Morrison's bill passed by the House with the key diversity programs intact was to work closely with the chair of the Rules Committee, Rep. John Joseph (Joe) Moakley (D-MA).[42] Moakley, who represented a fairly Irish American Boston district, had found the IIRM's arguments compelling. In August 1990, the group met with him in Boston to urge him to craft a rule to limit floor debate on the bill, which would help it pass.[43]

Although he wasn't on the immigration subcommittee, Moakley had become an unexpected but deep champion for the immigration act. He recognized that the reasons people had to leave home were painful, that restrictions hurt migrants, and that the least the United States could do would be to ease their entry as immigrants. "We cannot ignore the root causes of why people leave their homes," he told the Boston City Council in a 1988 speech.[44]

Moakley was raised in a blue-collar, Irish American neighborhood, the son of an Irish American father and Italian American mother.[45] He'd enlisted in the navy at age fifteen and served in World War II before coming home and making use of the GI Bill to finish high school and attend college. While serving as a state representative, he got his law degree. He went to Congress in 1973, representing the Ninth District of Massachusetts, which contained South Boston neighborhoods such as Dorchester, Roxbury, and Mattapan.

Moakley was known as a "bread and butter" politician who hustled federal funds for his district, helping revitalize the Boston waterfront, undertake the Harbor cleanup, and fund the "Big Dig," among other projects. He had little interest in or expertise in foreign policy or immigration. He once told House Speaker Tom Foley (D-WA), "Foreign affairs to me was going to East Boston and getting an Italian submarine sandwich."[46]

But to his profound surprise, he had become a passionate advocate for refugees fleeing war in El Salvador after meeting with concerned constituents in 1983. He heard directly from Salvadoran refugees who had fled right-wing death squads—only to face and fear deportation by the U.S. government, maligned as "illegal" rather than offered haven.

These testimonials informed how Moakley spoke up about the harms of U.S. foreign policy in the region. "We send arms and supplies to El Salvador to sustain a war. . . . Our policy has forced hundreds of war-refugees to flee that tiny, war-torn nation in search of safe haven in the United States," he said.[47] Yet, the United States was deporting one hundred Salvadorans each week back to dangerous conditions at home, conditions exacerbated by the Reagan administration's policies.

Years later, Moakley credited his unexpected dedication to Salvadoran refugees to his upbringing in an Irish American neighborhood in South Boston. He recalled his father's gruff, "probably Irish" way of teaching him about fighting injustice.[48] He spent the 1980s introducing legislation to secure legal status for the Salvadoran refugees denied asylum by the Reagan administration, which designated them "economic migrants" because of its support for the Salvadoran government.[49] But he couldn't get a stand-alone bill passed.[50] Even as he built momentum in the House, there was more resistance in the Senate, and certainly the administration was staunchly opposed.[51] When six Jesuit priests and two others were murdered in El Salvador in 1989, Congress launched an investigation and appointed Moakley to lead it. This high-profile and shocking violence undermined the administration's arguments that the human rights situation was improving in El Salvador.

And at last, the legislation that Simpson, Kennedy, Morrison, and Schumer were working on offered a vehicle for Moakley's policy for protecting Salvadorans from deportation. He ultimately put a provision in the bill that would provide temporary legal status and work authorization—though no path to citizenship—for people in the United States unable to return to countries with intolerably dangerous conditions. It was called Temporary Protected Status (TPS), and the Immigration Act of 1990 would designate El Salvadorans as eligible.[52]

· · · · · ·

The full Senate had passed Kennedy and Simpson's bill in July 1989, 81 to 17. Morrison had introduced his bill—which contained two diversity provisions as well as Moakley's TPS for Salvadorans—in March 1990, and the full House passed it in early October, 231 to 192. Reconciling the differences between these bills was not necessarily going to be easy. But the immigration policymakers got lucky.

Because of his determination to see the bill passed, Simpson—the most conservative and the only Republican of the group—eventually conceded on the most pivotal issues. He accepted Morrison's transition program, designed to help the Irish.[53] He accepted something he'd previously objected to—the creation of TPS for Salvadorans and others fleeing conflict.[54] He accepted a compromise that raised the overall cap on immigration. When the conference committee agreed on a numerical limit for immigration, it split the difference between the generous House bill and the stingier Senate bill, setting legal immigration at 700,000 per year for the first three years after the bill's passage, then 675,000 thereafter—well above Simpson's previous upper limit.[55] (Immediate relatives of U.S. citizens are not subject to the numerical cap.)

When it came to the diversity programs, negotiators in the conference committee eliminated a points system that Kennedy and Simpson's bill had proposed—it would be too burdensome to administer.[56] Drawing on hearing testimony, the conferees agreed that a complicated formula that awarded points for various criteria was likely to breed fraud.[57]

Instead, they adopted a permanent diversity visa program that was open to all underrepresented countries, to be distributed based on Schumer's regional proportional formula. The only thing Simpson did not compromise on, in the end, was setting qualifications for the diversity visa program. Entrants were required to have a high school education or its equivalent, or two years' work experience at a job requiring at least two years of training.[58]

Legislators finally reached an agreement on the full bill on October 24 and issued a favorable report on October 26. The Senate approved the report the same day. But when it went back to the House for approval, there was chaos.

The controversy wasn't about the visa lotteries, the raised limits on immigration, or even TPS. One priority for Simpson was an immigration enforcement measure. He had included a pilot program for what he deemed to be a more secure identification program for work authorization, something that he believed would make it more difficult for unauthorized immigrants to work and for employers to hire them. The pilot program caused an uproar because some saw it as a fundamental threat to civil liberties. It nearly derailed the whole bill. If the legislation had to go back to the Senate without the pilot program included, Simpson wouldn't support it, but if it went to the full House for a vote with the program intact, it wouldn't pass.

What saved the bill, in the end, was Moakley's dedication. The bill, he implored on the floor, "helps literally thousands upon thousands of people. It helps the Irish; it helps the Polish; it eliminates discriminatory statutes, and it helps thousands of refugees fleeing war whose lives are literally in the balance."[59] Cleverly, he used a procedural mechanism to strip out the secure identification measure that Simpson had fought for, and as a result the bill was able to pass the House, 264–118.[60] Michael Myers, Kennedy's staffer, recalled later, "Moakley, in a conversation with Kennedy, said, 'If my Central American refugee provision hadn't been in there, I might not have found the time in the middle of the night to have a Rules Committee meeting to pull everybody together.' I believe it. I think that ended up saving the Immigration Act of 1990, having it in there, and gave Moakley the impetus to make it happen."[61]

· · · · · ·

Moakley was credited with "saving the 1990 Act from the dust heap of history."[62] Passed on the final day of the 101st Congress session, the Immigration Act of 1990 was signed into law by President George H. W. Bush on November 29.

The Irish had lucked out in the end. Kennedy's staffer kept a memento from the senator, a copy of the Immigration Act. Kennedy had written, in green ink, a note of thanks. "To Michael, who helped take down the sign on the Statue of Liberty that said, 'No Irish need apply.' Many thanks for this and all the other things you did so well. Best Wishes, Ted Kennedy, 1993." Myers noted, "He circled the diversity immigrant part."[63]

But the law did something more than that. The United States was now committed to prioritizing diversity in immigration. The fact of being from somewhere underrepresented in the United States would be enough to create at least the possibility of coming to America. The columnist Ben J. Wattenberg closed out 1990 publishing a book titled *The First Universal Nation*. The *New York Times* gave the book a mixed review but noted that Wattenberg's ideas had undeniable appeal. As the *Times* put it, "For every culture that sends emigrants to this country, this country creates propagandists for its way of life in return. . . . No other country can come close to claiming the diversity with which the United States interacts with the world."[64]

The diversity visa lottery was key to fueling this narrative. And it would prove more expansive than anyone could have thought.

6 Winds of Change

Just as Liberty Weekend had served as the backdrop for the final negotiations of 1986's Immigration Reform and Control Act, the restoration of Ellis Island in 1990 coincided with the passage of that year's landmark immigration legislation. As the *New York Times* reported, organizers for the event "promised a ceremony almost somber by contrast with the hoopla with which the burnished Statue of Liberty was unveiled." There was much to celebrate at Ellis Island—a new museum, an "American Immigrant Wall of Honor" with plaques engraved with the names of immigrants whose relatives donated one hundred dollars or more, and a naturalization ceremony for forty-six new U.S. citizens. Yet some recalled Ellis Island not only as a gateway of welcome but as a site of detention and exclusion. A woman who took her naturalization oath at the restoration ceremony recalled that her grandfather had sought entry to the United States in the 1940s, only to be detained. He then contracted tuberculosis on the island and returned to Grenada, where he died. In the present day, undocumented immigrants from El Salvador and Nicaragua tended the grounds outside the museum, even as boosters touted the restored Ellis Island as a site of welcome and inclusion.[1]

As the new decade dawned, American ambivalence about immigration was reflected everywhere. The idea of immigration remained romantic and sturdy, foundational to the country. Optimism about how immigration would continue to shape the American future had driven the policy debates about legal immigration throughout the late 1980s. IRCA's legalization programs had served as an acknowledgment that immigrants, regardless of status, were often deeply rooted and full members of the community, and the Immigration Act of 1990 expanded immigration opportunities and espoused the value of diversity.

But even as the immigration legislation of the last part of the decade expanded access and granted legal status to millions of people, changes in the law also created new pressures on immigrants. Released in time for Christmas of 1990, Peter Weir's romantic comedy *Green Card* lightly depicted the challenges immigrants faced. The film pairs an American woman with a French man in a marriage of convenience to get him his green card. Immigration authorities haunt the film's protagonists, standing at the ready to haul Gérard Depardieu off, tearing him away from his dreams of American life and blossoming love, putting him on a plane back to France. The film is sympathetic to its protagonists and their plan, and frames the INS as increasingly active and invasive, dedicated to rooting out and expelling immigrants deemed undesirable. Clearly the antagonist, the INS is foiling the efforts of decent people trying to live and love across a border. But the film also hinted that fraud and illicit schemes to evade the immigration system were common. Given the emerging racial dynamics of immigration in the 1990s (though not in this film, where both lead characters are white), this was a dangerous notion—one that would be used to justify ever-harsher policies against immigrants of color.

A 1990 *Time* magazine cover story warned ominously about the "browning" of America, wondering what the United States would be like when whites were no longer in the majority. In a parenthetical aside the story mentioned that *some* Americans considered the white, European-descended majority to be not only traditional but the only "real" America. But already Nguyens outnumbered Joneses in the San Jose phone book. The article rejected open white supremacy but had trepidations. "While know-nothingism is generally confined to the more dismal corners of the American psyche," the piece allowed, "it seems all too predictable that during the next decades many more mainstream white Americans will begin to speak openly about the nation they feel they are losing."[2] A warning: diversity had its limits.

In public debate the United States continued to celebrate individual immigrants and the principle of immigration while simultaneously adopting an increasingly cautious, restrictionist approach at the policy level. Policymakers began ramping up enforcement and finding ways to expel unwanted migrants. Such efforts had been part of legislative debates since the 1970s, when demographic shifts in immigration were already becoming clear. Although advocates defended immigrant rights through the 1980s, restrictionists framed immigration as a drain on scarce public resources, like education, health care, and welfare, not to mention jobs. Even as the government embraced deregulation and the shrinking of the social safety net, restrictionists deflected blame for resulting austerity and inequality onto immigrants themselves.[3] Heeding the strengthening power of restrictionist voices in the 1990s, the U.S. government began using leftover material from the Gulf War to raise a wall along the border between the United States and Mexico near San Diego.[4] Soon, immigration restriction would surge to new heights, providing uneasy context for the rollout of the diversity lotteries crafted in what would come to seem like the last moments of the 1980s.

· · · · · ·

The first lottery held after the 1990 act was the first iteration of the transitional diversity program created by Bruce Morrison. This was a temporary three-year program that took place in 1991, 1992, and 1993, making 40,000 visas available each year to nationals of thirty-five designated "adversely affected" countries, mostly in Europe.[5] Forty percent of Morrison visas were promised to Irish nationals, who were eligible even if they were residing undocumented in the United States. As with the antecedent visa programs of the 1980s, opinion was split. Some were critical of what human rights lawyer Arthur Helton called "an element of bias" in favor of Europeans in the program.[6] But others praised the transition program. For example, a pair of immigration lawyers argued in an op-ed that it would "restore balance" and ensure visas for the immigrants "whose forebears settled and developed America." Martha Siegel and Laurence Canter lauded the program as one that "should help preserve the true melting pot character of the United States and assure that the cultural influences of our earlier immigrants do not disappear."[7] Soon, Canter and Siegel would become notorious for their engagement with diversity visas.

Participation in the Morrison visa program was enthusiastic. Within a single week in October 1991, hopefuls sent in 19 million applications for the 40,000 available visas. Individuals submitted dozens and even hundreds of applications each, sliding applications into different mailboxes to stagger entries' arrivals.[8] Some traveled to the United States from abroad to improve their chances by mailing applications within the country. Thousands traveled to Merrifield, Virginia, in the suburbs of Washington, DC, to submit applications in person at the post office where they would be processed. Because applications would be selected on a first-come, first-served basis, people aimed to get their applications in just in time. Those that arrived before or after the entry period would be disqualified. Fairfax County, Virginia, police and the U.S. Postal Service anticipated that as many as 75,000 people would descend on the Merrifield post office over the weekend, and they set up barricades and portable toilets to prepare for the crowd.[9]

At the suburban post office, nationals of the thirty-five eligible countries gathered and queued. "For 15 minutes on Saturday evening a frenzied throng of about 5,000 immigrants pushed and shoved to get their applications into the collection hampers lined up outside the Merrifield post office," described one reporter. "Many hundreds in desperation, unable to get near the front of the crowd, flung their applications into the air in the general direction of the hampers."[10] The applications formed "a blizzard of white envelopes" that "filled the sky and many chances of legal entry into the U.S. were lost as envelopes fell to the ground under the feet of the stampeding thousands."[11] Witnesses likened it to European soccer riots. While no serious injuries were cited, one immigrant from Northern Ireland suggested that the scene was scarier than being shot at or bombed.[12] With "several languages being spoken in the lines and elsewhere on the Merrifield grounds, the day took on the cast of an international fair, but with a high-stakes edge."[13]

Part of the reason that the lottery was so popular was that the backdrop of rising immigration enforcement made being undocumented ever more precarious. Immigrants said they wanted to be able to stay after graduating from U.S. universities, to work in their chosen fields, and to remain in communities that had become home, without fear of deportation. Being undocumented made the Irish "an underclass," with no choice but to take, as one applicant said, "the crummiest jobs at the lowest wages." Finding work at all had grown more difficult, and the social isolation and fear associated with being undocumented took a toll.[14]

The legalization programs of IRCA in 1986 had provided more than 2 million people with legal status. But by the early 1990s, the undocumented population had begun to grow again.[15] Opponents of immigration would argue that this outcome showed the folly of legalization programs in general; they suggested that IRCA had incentivized people to come without permission to beg forgiveness. But the actual problem was that neither 1986's onetime legalization program nor the slightly increased numerical immigration limits set after 1990 addressed the underlying cause of undocumented immigration: restriction itself. When people needed to migrate to thrive, to work at U.S. jobs that drew them, to reunite with their family members, or to flee intolerable conditions at home, immigration limits denied them legal access but didn't address their needs. Restriction thus fueled unauthorized immigration and would do so as long as demand for visas outstripped supply. When the chance to apply for the lottery arose, eligible people jumped at it, as they would have seized other opportunities to legally migrate.

The U.S. economy also entered a recession in mid-1990 following the Savings and Loan crisis of 1989, with slow economic growth and job losses in construction, manufacturing, and the defense industry. The recession in 1990 and 1991 may have contributed to an uptick in anti-immigrant sentiment, particularly among policymakers who saw the issue as a way to deflect blame.[16] These factors may have heightened the urgency to win one of the Morrison visas to avoid being targeted by immigration authorities.

The very idea of a green card lottery, hosted by a country that restricted legal immigration and rebuked "illegal" immigrants, seemed to offer a wondrous opportunity—and yet it also inspired suspicion. What was the catch? Rumors circulated about the best ways to "beat the system," including sending multiple applications, using different or specific mailboxes to mail applications, and traveling all the way to Virginia to submit entries in person.[17] Applicants reportedly booked DC-area hotel rooms to ensure they were close by.[18] At Merrifield, rumors circulated that 7 P.M. was a "magic hour" and applicants should aim to deliver applications to the collection hampers after that.[19]

When reporters questioned the die-hard lottery applicants in line in Merrifield, people spoke about the once-in-a-lifetime opportunity at hand. "It makes no difference if it's hot and sunny or if it rains," said a Polish man who traveled to Virginia from Chicago. "We came a long way. It's like a dream. I don't know how long we're going to wait for another dream."[20] An Algerian applicant said simply, "America, I swear to God, it's the best."[21] An Irish applicant added, "It's like the lottery; you buy one scratch card, then two, then three," suggesting that part of the program's appeal was that it was a game, that like other gambling, encouraged addictive behavior. Pat Kenneery and his wife arrived at Merrifield with 700 completed applications. When they saw the crowds they purchased another hundred dollars in postage and filled in more applications to up their chances.[22]

Officials seemed surprised by how widespread and persuasive lottery rumors were and spoke out to clarify the program's rules and procedures. Cornelius Scully, an official at the Consular Affairs Bureau, insisted "there are no guarantees. There is more mythology for the right formula for winning. People have different formulas. What's the right way and wrong way? I don't know."[23] Robert Faruq, Merrifield post office's spokesperson, said, "Many immigrants believe they can beat the odds by mailing their applications at Merrifield. . . . We've really tried to put the message out that it doesn't make sense to come here."[24] A State Department employee assured the public that the lottery would be a "crap shoot."[25]

In entrepreneurial fashion befitting the 1990s, immigration attorneys and others saw the program as a chance to generate profit from global demand. Because the program targeted people without U.S. family to sponsor them as well as people outside the United States, applicants may have lacked networks to help them understand U.S. procedures. Prospective applicants constituted a huge potential client base.[26] Denis Guerin invited Irish lottery applicants to drop off their applications for special delivery to Merrifield, touting his own national origin as a native of Kerry County in Ireland as well as being an American attorney.[27] Guerin followed up with an ad wishing "Best of Luck" to Morrison visa applicants, adding, "I have no doubt that the Irish North and South will receive the Lion's share of the Visa's [sic]."[28] Jeffrey Gabel's ad declared "1991 VISA LOTTERY!!" and promoted his immigration law practice.[29] A Washington-based attorney named John F. Kennedy published an ad in the *Irish Echo* offering to mail twenty visa applications "conforming to rules" for a fee of fifty dollars.[30] In 1991 it cost twenty-nine cents to mail a letter first class. Aside from the negligible cost of photocopying, a client paying this fee would net some forty-four dollars in profit for virtually no legal work on the part of the firm. The *Washington Post* reported "law firms around the country are signing up clients, both corporations and individuals, even though . . . no lawyers are needed."[31]

The prominent Washington attorney Michael A. Maggio told the *Post* that "it's a matter of the odds and there are steps you can take to increase your odds." Maggio charged clients $350 to send in one hundred applications.[32] He reportedly posted 20,000 applications in total.[33] Another firm charged a flat fee of $2,550 plus $500 for dependents to register its corporate clients.[34] A Japanese applicant reportedly paid an attorney $1,000 to enter the lottery, plus an additional $2,500 if selected, for the visa application. "It's expensive, but I think it's worth it," the man told the *Los Angeles Times*.[35]

New York City's Department of Consumer Affairs (DCA) tried to crack down on unscrupulous businesses drumming up visa lottery business, announcing it would take legal action against three lawyers and four other companies in Washington and New York offering Morrison visa services. It cited misleading advertisements that guaranteed success, exaggerated claims, or omitted information in several publications including the *Polish Daily News*, *Polish American World*, *The European*, *France Amerique*, and the *New York Daily News*. New York mayor David Dinkins warned that those seeking a Morrison visa "should beware of ads promising more than can be delivered."[36] Mark Green, New York Consumer Affairs commissioner, said, "Roulette is a game of chance, and poker is a game of skill and chance. The visa lottery is roulette, not poker. Since the Secretary of State and the head of the I.N.S. can't promise success in this lottery, no lawyer or visa service can."[37]

The "hail of mail" in Merrifield showed that there was immense demand, unmet through other channels, for legal migration opportunities to the United States. The images of lottery entrants clamoring at the gates had the effect of upholding dear American myths about exceptional opportunities awaiting immigrants here and about the centrality of immigrants to the country's identity. But they also helped contribute to growing anxieties about demographic change. Indeed, a new age of immigration restriction had already begun.

· · · · · ·

Although policymakers had just recently affirmed the importance of immigration to the American story, they had also invested more in immigration enforcement. Now voices calling for the doors to be shut altogether were growing louder. Rather than seeing immigration as a source of cultural or even economic strength, politicians began—more broadly and openly than at any time since the early twentieth century—to express nativist and anti-immigration sentiment.

The rise in anti-immigrant politics coincided with both increasing numbers and visibility of immigrants.[38] Both the passage of the 1990 act and the legalization program of IRCA increased the number of legal immigrants in the United States. After the passage of the North American Free Trade Agreement (NAFTA) in 1992, unauthorized immigration to the United States also increased.[39] The settlement of a high-profile federal court case gave hundreds of thousands of asylum seekers whose claims had been unfairly rejected a second chance to apply for asylum.[40] But without budgeting for more asylum officers, the backlog of asylum cases increased greatly, to over 200,000 people in early 1992. With a growing backlog of cases, applying for asylum was one way to buy time and reside indefinitely in the United States, and as a result, anti-immigrant activists focused more public attention on the asylum system.[41] Asylum was a form of lifesaving protection for people fleeing persecution, but restrictionists' depictions often suggested it was a loophole for unscrupulous migrants without valid claims. Such suspicions fell heavily on immigrants of color, who didn't fit the image of a sympathetic refugee or traditional immigrant.[42] As immigration scholar George Sánchez wrote, "It is not difficult to understand how immigrants from these developing nations can be seen as both drains on our national economy and symbols of countries who threaten American economic hegemony and the dream of a multicultural future in the post-Cold War era."[43]

There were economic factors that fueled Americans' anxieties and created fertile ground for nativist fearmongering. For example, the Cold War's end contributed to a contraction of the defense industry and downturn in the economy, especially in California, where job losses were felt acutely.[44] There, poverty was rising while housing values were falling. Narratives about scarcity in public goods could be explained as an outcome of excessive immigration overtaxing the system.

There were also racial tensions that contributed to a growing anti-immigrant movement. Despite California's self-conception as a liberal, diverse, and forward-thinking place, racial segregation was an enduring issue. As Daniel Martinez HoSang has shown, Californians long used racialized ballot initiatives to shape the state's political culture.[45] For example, voters had defeated a fair employment initiative in 1946 and overturned school desegregation mandates in the 1970s.

In 1992, the Los Angeles uprisings spotlighted deep racial divisions, after LA police were acquitted after the beating of Rodney King, and after the killing of LaTasha Harlins, a fifteen-year-old African American girl, by a Korean American shop owner. The uprisings made racial tensions in California impossible to ignore. It was a moment that called on communities to reckon deeply with histories of spatial segregation, inequality, violent and anti-Black policing and incarceration, and the legacies of U.S. militarism that so often fueled migrations. Some certainly did so, and the moment created opportunities for meaningful Black and Asian American solidarity building.[46]

But some chose to blame immigrants for the unraveling of the California Dream. The state had been a key destination for post-1965 immigration, particularly for immigrants from Asia and Latin America, which had driven the booming economy of the golden state in the 1960s and 1970s. As a 1983 *Time* magazine story had framed it, Los Angeles was akin to "the New Ellis Island," a symbol that was celebrated so long as the state was buzzing, and cultural pluralism was highly valued.[47] Now hostility directed toward immigrants, particularly immigrants of color, shot up.

Initially, immigration was not a galvanizing issue statewide. After all, the state depended on immigrants' labor, particularly in the powerful agriculture business. Then, a tiny grassroots restrictionist movement in Southern California and its connected national partners, like the Federation for American Immigration Reform (FAIR), roused Californians of various political persuasions, races, and classes to see immigration as the chief cause of the state's woes. They launched an effort to pass a strong anti-immigrant ballot initiative in 1994.[48]

Politicians from the Democratic U.S. senator Dianne Feinstein to Republican governor Pete Wilson jumped on the bandwagon, touting the need to make border enforcement tougher and rein in costs, purportedly incurred because of immigrants' use of public benefits, from hospitals to schools to food stamps. The campaign suggested that the border was out of control, that the presence of immigrants and their children was destabilizing, and that good, taxpaying Californians (language that appeared coded as white) were bearing the costs of immigrant deception and federal indifference to their problems.

The dimensions of this battle were local but shaped by events at the national level that helped provide fuel for anti-immigrant narratives.[49] In 1991, for example, the arrival of Haitian refugees on boats in southern Florida gave the appearance of a disorderly border crisis. When the Bush administration implemented a policy of interdicting the boats and returning people either to Haiti, where their lives were in peril, or to detention at the U.S. military base at Guantanamo Bay, litigation sought to stop it, and the courts intervened. This made it seem like the United States, with all its might, couldn't gain control over its borders.

Politicians like Patrick Buchanan and David Duke amplified anti-immigrant ideas during their runs for public office, making clear that what they objected to most was the immigration of people of color. Buchanan said he feared that the new immigrants would "dilute" the country's European character. He told David Brinkley, "I think God made all people good, but if we had to take a million immigrants in, say, Zulus next year or Englishmen and put them in Virginia, what group would be easier to assimilate and would cause less problems for the people of Virginia?"[50] At the Republican National Convention in 1992, the party called for a barrier along the U.S.-Mexico border, anticipating Donald Trump's wall.[51]

After George H. W. Bush bested Buchanan in the 1992 primary, he and Democratic opponent Bill Clinton barely debated the issue. During the campaign, Clinton criticized the Bush administration's policy of interdicting boats carrying Haitian refugees, but that was it. Clinton felt he had been burned on this issue before. He had learned an ugly lesson about immigration politics in 1980. While he was governor of Arkansas, the state provided housing, at Fort Chaffee, for some 25,000 refugees from Cuba known as "Marielitos" who arrived in southern Florida that summer. During his reelection campaign, Clinton's Republican opponent suggested that Clinton had risked Arkansans' lives, proposing that the Marielitos were dangerous and should have been excluded.[52] Although the United States had previously welcomed refugees fleeing Fidel Castro's Cuba, it was possible to cast this group as different. They included more working-class, Black, and queer people. Moreover, Castro himself had advanced a narrative that the Marielitos were undesirable.[53] Clinton lost that election. Immigration policy was dangerous terrain for an ambitious politician.[54] Toughness on the issue came to be understood as a virtue—even if it ran counter to pro-immigration talk that was part of the American creed, not to mention the country's obligations under U.S. and international law.

Fearing political backlash, Clinton, as president, reversed his position on the Haitians and continued Bush's policies. When attackers bombed the World Trade Center in February 1993, early in Clinton's presidency, the event became an unlikely referendum on the U.S. asylum system, because one of the men who planned the attack had claimed asylum at the airport when he entered the United States.[55] FAIR's Dan Stein went on *60 Minutes* to depict the asylum system, which allows people fleeing persecution to find haven in the United States, as a vector of threat. Later that year, when the *Golden Venture*, a ship carrying Chinese migrants, ran aground in Queens, New York, the case captured national media coverage and helped sustain the narrative that the United States' handle on immigration was out of control. Clinton gave a speech in July 1993 saying that the United States must not "surrender our borders to those who wish to exploit our history of compassion and justice," adding, "We will make it tougher for illegal aliens to get into our country."[56]

In November 1994, California voters overwhelmingly (by 59 percent) approved Proposition 187, which would have prohibited unauthorized immigrants from accessing medical care, public schools, and other public benefits. While many of the law's components were struck down by the courts or otherwise suspended, the specter of anti-immigrant, and particularly anti-Latino fearmongering, had sent a message to the state's nonwhite residents that any sense of their belonging was provisional. The fight over Prop 187 would ironically galvanize a movement of naturalization, voting, and political activism among Latinos that transformed California's electoral politics over the following decades.

It also fueled new restrictionist policymaking at the federal level and created a framework for politicians to blame immigration for the ways in which austerity was curtailing the American Dream for the country's citizens. While Prop 187 never went into effect the way its proponents hoped, in September 1994 Attorney General Janet Reno went to Los Angeles to announce the launch of Operation Gatekeeper, an aggressive border enforcement strategy for San Diego, designed to make migration more dangerous and even deadly for crossing migrants.

The measure seemed designed to showcase the Clinton administration's toughness on the border and unauthorized immigration. While efforts to reify the U.S.-Mexico border were long-standing, this particular effort emerged at this moment of shifting political waters, just as Gov. Wilson sought reelection and in anticipation of the signing of NAFTA.[57] The 1994 federal Crime Bill also contained provisions that funneled funding into border control and deportations.[58]

Restrictionists further capitalized on the moment, building support for a trio of federal laws passed in 1996 that made life for noncitizens much more difficult. The new Republican majority that took over Congress in 1994 helped lead the charge, buoyed by the success of Prop 187 in California. The Illegal Immigration Reform and Immigrant Responsibility Act of 1996, the Antiterrorism and Effective Death Penalty Act of 1996, and the Personal Responsibility and Work Opportunity Reconciliation Act of 1996 embedded anti-immigrant policies in federal law. In addition to provisions that made it more difficult for lawful immigrants to access public benefits, the laws stripped noncitizens of certain rights, expanded immigrant detention, and made people more vulnerable to the threat of deportation. Rather than framing immigration as integral to American life, legislators accepted restrictionist arguments that immigration was a threat, that in the 1990s America could no longer afford to be generous, and that American opportunity was shrinking because of immigrants.[59]

And so, at the very moment that the United States was preparing to launch the first iteration of its permanent diversity visa lottery, the politics of immigration within the United States were rapidly ceasing to be welcoming. Restrictionists were eager to take advantage of the shift. As FAIR's Stein wrote in 1994, "There's no more vivid example of the thoughtless, arbitrary and preferential nature of America's immigration than this ridiculous program," of the lottery.[60]

In 1995 the U.S. Commission on Immigration Reform issued an executive summary of its initial report, which had been mandated by the Immigration Act of 1990. Chaired by former Texas congresswoman and civil rights champion Barbara Jordan, the commission adopted a pragmatic tone that emphasized immigration's costs rather than its benefits. The 1997 version of the commission's report later touted the visa lottery's effect on

African immigration as being "particularly noteworthy," since African countries accounted for 35 percent of diversity visas at the time and less than 1 percent of other visas.[61] But the commission also considered diversity immigration to be "lower priority" and suggested eliminating the program and allocating the visas to another category altogether.[62] It recommended eliminating several categories of family-based admissions, including of the adult offspring of U.S. citizens and permanent residents, and siblings of U.S. citizens. Overall, the Jordan Commission's reports advocated a restrictive approach, despite the liberal credentials of its chair and some of its members. They also emphasized a role for the federal government in immigrants' "Americanization" to counter the potential risk that "cultural diversity" would undermine "civic unity."[63]

A bill put forward by Rep. Lamar Smith (R-TX) in 1996 would have eliminated the diversity lottery, in line with the demands of restrictionists. But the program was saved when Charles Schumer offered a compromise amendment. The restrictionist effort to severely cut legal immigration faltered when a coalition of pro-business and pro-family immigration groups united to oppose it.[64] But more broadly the restrictionists had begun the work of dramatically remaking the immigration system in the 1990s, ushering in a new era of restriction.

· · · · · ·

The experience at Merrifield and the proliferation of visa lottery advertisements prompted the State Department to revise the rules for future lotteries. They limited registrants to just one application per person, with selection done randomly at the end of a set registration period, which was extended to a full month.[65] These changes cut down on visa lottery frenzy and the number of applications. In 1992's lottery, for example, the Bureau of Consular Affairs reported receiving just 817,000 applications, compared with 1991's nineteen million.[66] The *Irish Echo* reported "all quiet on the Morrison front.[67]

With just one chance to win, some applicants were even more motivated to get it right. For example, a travel agency advertised special airfares on board Ireland's Aer Lingus for Morrison visa applicants hoping to go to the United States for the 1992 entry period.[68] A local firm in Poland promoted the 1992 lottery, asking, "What would you say to the Grand Prize? . . . Take advantage!" and offered lottery services for 300,000 zloty.[69]

After relatively calm lottery entry periods in 1992 and 1993, the Morrison program concluded.[70] Irish interest in and demand for the Morrison visas began to wane, as many individuals won the lawful permanent resident status they wanted in the United States, and the Irish economy improved at home.[71] The 1990–91 recession also may have slowed Irish immigration to the United States.[72]

The first permanent diversity visa lottery opened during the month of June in 1994. The State Department and consulates prepared, sending news releases and information sheets to local newspapers and radio stations around the world. The U.S. bureaucracy rolled forward, fleshing out the necessary logistics, and creating a system of region-based post office boxes to receive applications from nearly every country of the world. The politics around migration within the United States were growing angrier and more fraught, just as the lottery cracked open the door to an increasingly connected world.

7 Green Card Lawyers

. . . .

Long before the lottery was introduced, navigating U.S. immigration had become a challenge for those who lacked specialized expertise. Different aspects of the system often required lawyers with distinct skills and experiences. For example, businesses might hire immigration lawyers to help them understand the rules for hiring noncitizen workers. Family members petitioning for relatives abroad to join them might consult a lawyer on how to do so. Immigrants in the United States seeking to naturalize as citizens, those held in detention centers, or people making asylum claims had specific needs, and the lawyers serving them could demystify and steer these processes. As the world prepared for the first permanent diversity visa lottery in June 1994, open to nearly every country, what would applicants need?

To be blunt, nothing.

The lottery was designed to be simple to enter and for the government to operate. The requirements were clear and minimal. A lottery with random selection did not need to be scored and judged, which would keep costs down, and minimize opportunities for fraud. Some city governments put out notices to warn immigrants of misleading lottery-related advertisements, assuring them that paid help was not required.

But as the Irish groups had found in the late 1980s, many applicants did want help. The 1994 lottery would operate on a much larger scale than the Donnelly or Morrison programs and would engage people from countries that had previously been ineligible. That was an untapped market of *millions* of people who would soon have the chance to submit applications to the United States, a powerful empire whose policies and procedures could be opaque and difficult to navigate, if not downright intimidating.

As a result, immigration lawyers ramped up their outreach efforts, advertising in foreign newspapers and even traveling abroad to meet clients.[1] Despite notices from the Department of State and U.S. Information Service laying out the process as simple, free, and requiring no professional legal help, American lawyers and their international counterparts offered up their services for a fee.[2]

And this gave two immigration attorneys named Martha Siegel and Laurence Canter an idea. They recognized in the lottery a remarkable opportunity to use new internet technology to attract paying customers. People *wanted* to be able to migrate legally to the United States. The lottery offered a chance to do so. What was needed, the attorneys thought, were middlemen, facilitators.

Canter and Siegel were married, they lived in Arizona, and they practiced immigration law together in a time of rapidly shifting policy. They made names for themselves publishing a do-it-yourself guide to immigration law in 1989 and updating it over the years. They saw the visa lotteries as a chance to drum up business. For example, they advertised for the Donnelly visa in Canadian newspapers in 1987, charging fifty dollars for a telephone consultation.[3]

And then in 1994, they found themselves at the center of a social media hatestorm when they sent what became known as the world's first commercial spam. They flooded Usenet boards, a predecessor to today's online forums, with their message. The subject? The green card lottery.

The early 1990s served as a turning point in U.S. immigration politics, anticipating the revival of deep forces of nativism in American politics and culture. This came with, and indeed was fostered and fueled by, anxieties about America's transforming place in the world. The end of the Cold War presaged increased global trade. Capital and elites were moving with new ease across borders. Alternatives to United States–style capitalist democracy were muted.

And new technology promised to further facilitate trade, exchange, and ideas. More people began using personal computers. While phones with internet access and apps were decades away, by the mid-1990s, more computers were being networked together.

Suddenly, it seemed, the United States—indeed the world—merged onto the information superhighway. In due time, the internet would transform life all over the planet, changing work patterns, consumption, and communications and reinforcing global hierarchies. It would even transform how people would apply for the visa lottery—thanks, in part, to Canter and Siegel's next moves.

· · · · · ·

The internet neither spurred more migration nor crushed it. That might be surprising given how commentators in the 1990s were thinking about the technology's power to shrink space and connect people across borders. In

January 1994, Vice President Al Gore addressed a room of industry leaders at the first public conference on the subject: "By now, we're becoming familiar with the ability of the new communications technologies to transcend international boundaries and bring our world closer together," he intoned.[4] His audience, the CEOs of Newscorp, Bell Atlantic, and Disney, among others, pondered the future of communications and information technology as Gore set out the Clinton administration's principles for expanding access to the internet.

Gore never claimed to have invented the internet, as the political smear turned urban legend claimed. Instead, since 1969, military and academic groups had been working to connect computers together in networks. The first major network, the predecessor to what we think of as the internet, was known as ARPANET and was funded by the Department of Defense during the Cold War.[5] Networking computers that never intended to talk to each other was difficult and expensive. But slowly through the 1970s, ARPANET expanded, as researchers moved from one campus to another. These "migrants" brought knowledge with them, expanding the usefulness of the network.[6] The network grew from its cluster on the West Coast to the East Coast, and then to Norway and the United Kingdom. In 1979 graduate students in North Carolina developed a civilian version of ARPANET, a network communications system known as Usenet. Usenet allowed users to post short written messages to "newsgroups" and then start threaded discussions on boards dedicated to specific subjects.

Users learned how to behave online as they went. On today's social media platforms, users have impassioned debates about moderation, trolls, abuse, harassment, and "free speech." Long ago, Usenet's users were asking similar questions, albeit on a different sort of platform. Throughout the 1980s, Usenet communities negotiated rules and norms that would protect both individual rights of expression and the public good online.

Usenet's structure was decentralized and the newsgroups were designed to be managed democratically and nonhierarchically. Network connection speeds over telephone lines in those days were glacially slow by today's standards, computer memory space was limited, and users paid not only to send information but to receive it. Participating in online discussions thus required each user to consider others. That's why Usenet had topic-specific newsgroups. Keeping conversations on topic was a way to preserve resources, so that users downloaded only the information they wanted and not a bunch of extraneous garbage over their slow, expensive connections.[7] Consideration was a two-way street.

The United States decommissioned ARPANET in 1990, and the U.S. National Science Foundation formed the new backbone for the internet, NSF-NET, which had been created in 1986. This allowed more college campus networks to be connected to each other. Commercial activity on NSFNET was generally prohibited. At the same time, by the late 1980s, commercial internet service providers were appearing and early for-profit computer networks such as CompuServe and America Online were bringing more personal computers "online" over home telephone lines. The internet was a patchwork of networks, email servers, and discussion groups like Usenet, but its patchwork quality was changing. People such as Tim Berners-Lee and Marc Andreessen developed early web browsers, and in 1993 the release of Mosaic broadened access to the networks by offering a point-and-click gateway to a virtual universe of graphics, photos, and links.

Since 1980, when Usenet began to connect to more networks, each September witnessed a new class of college freshmen arriving on campuses and gaining internet access for the first time. They would come online to a whole new world and simply *flood* the Usenet discussion groups. Their arrival was disruptive. A fresh generation of newbies each year, totally unversed in what the place was all about, like aliens from another planet showing up and spoiling a dinner party. They didn't speak the language, held no currency, were foreigners.[8]

But seasoned natives had learned to expect them each autumn. They recognized that newcomers needed guidance on how to use the internet and participate in the community. Teaching computers to exchange data had required developing protocols. So, too, did teaching humans how to talk to each other online. And "Netiquette," as it was sometimes called, was not only a matter of social control and norms, of creating harmony between users. It was also necessary to manage the flow of information in a context of finite resources—remember that users *paid* to download (read) what was posted. Posting off-topic could be expensive not only for the poster but for the people who received the messages. By Thanksgiving break, newcomers had generally been brought up to speed on how to behave on Usenet.

But then the scale exploded. In autumn 1993, "eternal September" came. And there was no going back. That's when America Online began to provide Usenet access to its subscribers. Instead of a bunch of highly motivated, self-selecting computer nerds logging on from college campuses, newcomers could now log on from personal computers in their homes. By 1994, eleven million American households had some access to the internet.[9]

The flurry of activity related to newcomers' arrivals once limited to September became decoupled from the academic calendar. It would *always* be September from now on, a cacophony of novices chattering at each other, unaware of and unbound by the old protocols for getting along.

The internet was becoming mainstream, and legacy media covered it with a sense of wonder that now feels quaint. As *Time* magazine put it, "The magic of the Net is that it thrusts people together in a strange new world, one in which they get to rub virtual shoulders with characters they might otherwise never meet."[10] The norms and rules of online behavior that had been negotiated over the previous decade and a half groaned under the weight of so many newcomers: "Longtime citizens of cyberspace, who for more than a decade had the networks to themselves, are gloomy about the prospects of millions of new settlers unsteeped in Usenet tradition," *New York Times* reporter Peter Lewis noted.[11] They had to contend with new migrants to cyberspace.

In some ways the dynamic echoed the broader climate of skepticism about migration then sweeping the United States, and writers covering tech deployed migration and settlement as metaphors.

· · · · · ·

It so happened that Canter and Siegel, besides being immigration attorneys, were also longtime computer enthusiasts who had subscribed to CompuServe for years. When they finally connected to the internet in 1993, they quickly saw the technology's potential to reach new audiences. Initially, they hung out in newsgroups on Usenet that focused on visa-related questions. Most questions came from users in the United States, but internet access was slowly becoming available in some European countries, Australia and New Zealand, Hong Kong, Singapore, and South Korea. Approximately two people in a thousand in South Africa had internet access—the only country on the African continent to have any connectivity at all in 1994.[12] Despite contemporaneous suggestions that the new technology was flattening difference across national boundaries, internet access tended to track with other measures of national power and wealth.[13] One effect of the centrality of U.S. university campuses to the emergence of the early internet, however, was that the internet's user base was more international than the data reflect. Visiting foreign students typically possessed only temporary visas. Staying to live and work beyond their terms of study would have required seeking out help navigating the immigration system.[14]

Canter and Siegel were no strangers to hustle. They had previously put their expertise down on paper, publishing in 1989 a 600-page tome titled *U.S. Immigration Made Easy*, a guide for fellow immigration attorneys as well as immigrants themselves that promised "inside tips and 'secrets.'"[15] They updated it with new editions and even issued a supplement focused specifically on the Immigration Act of 1990. But the book did not make Canter and Siegel rich: "It was expensive to promote and had a limited market," they explained.[16] It turned out that "not every living soul in the world wants to move to the United States," nor could those who did necessarily afford to buy a lengthy technical book.[17] If it was so easy, why did they need 600 pages to explain it?

On the visa-related discussion groups on Usenet, however, Canter and Siegel found a simple way to connect directly with noncitizens who *did* want to move to or remain legally in the United States and transform them into paying immigration clients. The enterprising couple rapidly recognized the value of tapping a receptive audience at nearly zero cost. Selling traditional legal services over Usenet was no get-rich-quick scheme, of course: legal work for clients still required hours at high prices or high volume to make a profit.

But that conundrum pointed to one appealing thing about the visa lottery in 1994. It required no legal expertise to enter. Canter and Siegel could hang their shingle online, acquire paying customers, fill out clients' forms, and call it a day. Applicants' success or failure at the lottery had nothing to do with the prowess of their immigration attorneys—it was a kind of lottery, after all—but nerves and anxiety about getting the basics right led people to believe that paying a consultant could tip the scales. Hoping to exploit these feelings, Canter and Siegel argued that "the government does its best to make the Green Card lottery as confusing as possible," and offered to file lottery applications for just ninety-five dollars.[18] (The U.S. government, of course, charged nothing to enter.)

After a few false starts where the couple manually posted their message to select Usenet groups, they changed course. They hired a "computer geek," as they called him, to write a program that would simultaneously post a message to numerous newsgroups all at once. They wrote out a message of just 165 words and gave it the header "Green Card Lottery—Final One?" The message warned that this, the first permanent visa lottery, might be the last. Their claim had no basis in reality—the lottery was only just beginning. But the previous programs like it (Donnelly, Berman, Morrison) *had* been temporary. And the anti-immigrant mood in the United States was crystallizing.

By suggesting that it was now or never, Canter and Siegel applied pressure. They promised to send any takers a free pamphlet with further information. The message also provided factual information: stating that most countries qualified, listing the disqualified countries (those that had sent more than 50,000 immigrants over the previous five years), and, most importantly, providing Canter and Siegel's names, mailing address, email address, telephone and fax numbers. They were soliciting responses, after all, and they did not try to obscure their identities.

At 12:30 A.M. on April 12, 1994, Canter and Siegel launched their message, by the stroke of a key, into cyberspace, where it appeared as an original posting in each of 6,000 Usenet newsgroups—all in under ninety minutes of connection time.[19] They had posted their message not only to groups that might be interested, like *alt.visa.us*, but also to thousands of other unrelated groups like *alt.duke.basketball.sucks.sucks.sucks*.[20] The ad, as the *Washington Post* put it, "flew across continents and oceans."[21]

They had just unleashed the first real example of commercial internet spam. "There was nothing very special about the message that made Canter and Siegel the most hated couple in cyberspace," claimed a *Time* magazine cover story on the "battle for the soul of the internet," published that summer.[22] Perhaps it looked that way to technology reporters marveling at the technical breakthrough that Canter and Siegel had just made. But the content of the first spam message was far from incidental. The green card lottery provided Canter and Siegel the perfect opportunity to sell indiscriminately on the internet. They knew that the attention-grabbing post would reach an audience with a global scope. They knew that amplifying their names would help make them known to immigrants in search of an attorney. They knew that even if a few people took them up on the offer they'd make money. And they sensed that a legal migration opportunity to the United States was highly valuable to people, even as—or especially as— the internet seemed to shrink space across borders. No, not everybody wanted to become a migrant, and the whole world didn't dream of coming to America. But enough people did. And Canter and Siegel's message might reach them.

· · · · · ·

On April 12, people across the United States, Europe, Oceania, and Asia woke up to the world's first widespread commercial spam message. "Spam" was called that, most likely in reference to the *Monty Python* sketch of Vikings singing "spam" every time the cheap meat is mentioned. Early internet users had coined the term to mean irrelevant messages that abused people's attention and overused bandwidth. Canter and Siegel's gambit cemented the definition as related to the annoying repetitive messages we receive online that are trying to sell us something.

At first, users tried to parse the message, to understand why it appeared on certain groups: "Why is this being posted here? I have received 5 or 6 copies of this post, and I do not understand why! Am I missing the point?"[23] What did this message have to do with using a CD-ROM or with basketball— the topics that users subscribed to? Unlike normally cross-posted messages, the green card message showed up in every one of a user's multiple newsgroups, rather than being hidden if it doubled up. This ate up bandwidth and slowed people's internet connections.

It also violated the culture and spirit of the place, where commercial activity was tolerated in only narrow circumstances, and where each user was supposed to be considerate of other users' bandwidth.

As it became clear that Canter and Siegel had willfully and indiscriminately posted their ad *everywhere*, it caused an uproar. As scholar Finn Brunton put it, "Two individuals in Arizona had just enormously overconsumed the pool of common resources."[24]

Users found creative ways to address what they perceived as a massive violation of online norms. They sent large files to the couple's email address to overload their internet service provider (ISP), Internet Direct. They set up automatic telephone dialers to call the firm's telephone number and fill up the answering machine tape. They overloaded the firm's fax line by sending "junk faxes" of black sheets of paper, to use up ink and expensive thermal fax paper. Cyberspace might not have been physical, but angry Usenet users were finding ways to punish virtual misbehavior in actual "meatspace." In the days before widespread, cheap digital storage, physical tapes and paper faxes could be targeted. Users also tried to overload Internet Direct itself by sending around emails and large files. "You, Laurence Canter, make me sick," wrote one user.[25]

Internet Direct quickly shut down Canter and Siegel's account, diverting emails sent to them to a hard drive as it tried to get its systems back up and running. Jeff Wheelhouse, system administrator for Internet Direct, told the *Washington Post* that he arrived at work that morning to find hundreds of angry messages. Internet Direct's computer crashed "more than a dozen times."[26] Canter and Siegel were soundly and passionately denounced by thousands of the world's internet users, "and we are talking global hatred, my friends, true internationalism," as an early chronicle of the incident put it.[27] Lewis of the *New York Times* noted that Canter and Siegel were like internet outlaws: "Their digitized photos are posted on computer bulletin boards around the world, like 'Wanted' posters on the electronic frontier."[28]

David Sewell, a longtime Usenet user, posted a literary takedown of the couple in May 1994:

> . . . thus USENET spake,
> Why hast thou, Canter, broke the bounds prescrib'd
> To thy transgressions, and disturb'd the charge
> Of others, who approve not to transgress
> By thy example, but have power and right
> To question thy bold entrance on this place?
> —*Milton, Paradise Lost 4:877-882, slightly altered*[29]

Had Usenet justice worked—had this response effectively shamed Canter and Siegel into backing down—perhaps the story would just be an odd footnote in both internet and immigration history.

But the couple was unrepentant, "shameless," as Brunton wrote.[30] They claimed that their spam message had brought in enough positive responses and paying customers seeking a green card to more than justify their action. Canter, Siegel, and their spam innovation were profiled across major media outlets, including *Time, Washington Post, New York Times*, and tech-specific publications like *Network World* and *PC/Computing.* "In the beginning there were more negative than positive responses," Siegel told the *Times*. "That is shifting. Now almost every response we're getting is positive." In late April, they received 20,000 positive replies, she said, "and we're still getting 500 to 1,000 a day."[31] Later the couple claimed to have made $100,000 by assisting over a thousand clients with their visa lottery applications.[32]

Canter and Siegel relished the limelight and seemed to take perverse pleasure in upsetting the internet's longtime citizens.

This moment raised critical questions about the fate of the internet, where different users brought different metaphors from "real life" to justify and explain their positions.

Canter and Siegel framed their right to spam the internet in American terms. They possessed, they argued, a fundamental right to freely express themselves, as well as a patriotic duty to be entrepreneurial. They had not violated U.S. law, they pointed out. If anything, the users who'd overloaded their fax lines and shut down Internet Direct had harassed *them*. Their right to free speech and entrepreneurship should trump the collective rights of the Usenet community to negotiate and uphold norms for acceptable social behavior. "What's important," Siegel asserted, "is freedom of speech, freedom to operate your business."[33]

For longtime Usenet users, the issue was about community standards and concerns about the public good of the internet—and the form it might take if it became clogged with off-topic and unwanted commercial activity. Shouldn't its residents have a say in how to manage the internet's public spaces?[34]

Rhetorically, Canter and Siegel seemed to agree: "The Internet is public property. It belongs to everyone equally," they wrote.[35] But some "netizens" were more equal than others: "The Internet is too big and powerful to go without official regulation. The public needs to be protected, and we have no doubt it will be. In a very short time, the dust will settle, and the mainstreaming of the Internet will be complete."[36] They adopted the language of American expansion and settlement. They saw themselves as pioneers and "homesteaders" whose mission was to civilize the vast wilderness of the pristine internet, displacing those who came before them—a community they dismissed as outcasts and nerds who had previously occupied the space.

The internet, as they saw it, should belong to those best able to make productive (read commercial) use of it. Forging a civilization online wasn't about hewing to community norms but about opening markets, spreading commerce, and defending their position as pillars of core U.S. principles like free speech and property rights.

Less than a month after sending the notorious spam message, Canter and Siegel moved to launch a new business called Cybersell, a company dedicated to internet advertising. By the end of the year, they had used their ill-found celebrity to publish a book with HarperCollins: *How to Make a Fortune on the Information Superhighway*, where they recounted their expertise and encouraged all readers to launch their own internet enterprises. "In Cyberspace," they advised, "the homesteading race is on."[37] "Like the Old West with which analogies are often drawn, Cyberspace is going to take some taming before it is a completely fit place for people like you and me to spend time."

In the eyes of internet natives, Canter and Siegel were online provocateurs whose brash imperial attitudes reflected their confidence that, as Usenet user Sewell put it, "in America in the '90s notoriety is its own reward—not that book contracts and fees for *Inside Edition* interviews are anything to shake a forked tail at, either."[38] Howard Rheingold, a board member at one of the oldest internet communities, The WELL, said presciently that the "attack of the spammers is probably just the first of many coming collisions between greed and common courtesy on the net."[39]

While Canter and Siegel represented a new frontier in online trolling, they'd stumbled into spaces where users constructed complex layers of inside jokes that depended on deep communal knowledge to poke fun at targets—a form of humor that could trend toward, or be mistaken for, trolling. Frequent Usenet poster and personality Joel Furr commemorated the incident by printing up T-shirts. He screen printed a graphic showing the planet Earth, with a hand extending out and offering a green card.[40] Under a heading "Coming to a news group near you," the words encircling the world read "Green Card Lawyers Spamming the Globe."[41] The image signaled the global reach of both the "green card lawyers" and the internet platform that had connected them with an audience beyond America's borders. When Canter and Siegel threatened to sue Furr, he took to Usenet to find legal advice and support, which people offered.[42] Furr sold his T-shirts for eleven dollars to recoup his costs; Siegel dismissed his actions as juvenile: "T-shirts are a child's game."[43]

· · · · · ·

This incident marked a turning point; the internet as it had been—an insular community that eschewed commercial interference—was gone. Eternal September continued. New users came online in droves. On New Year's Day 1995, NSFNET dropped its ban on commercial activity on its networks, and the internet ceased to be the property of the U.S. government. In 1996 several universities'.edu websites were among the twenty most popular websites. But by 1997 all twenty of the most popular websites were those of private, commercial companies.[44] As the internet became increasingly commercial, spam proliferated, becoming a global business and quotidian annoyance. U.S. policymakers, academics, and others negotiated new norms for internet selling culminating in the legislation of the CAN-SPAM (Controlling the Assault of Non-Solicited Pornography and Marketing) Act of 2003.[45] Although email filters have been developed to keep our inboxes free of much of the spam that is sent, spam via phone call and text message has proliferated. While not all spam contains scams—Canter and Siegel's message was annoying, intrusive, and misleading but not fraudulent—the method lent itself to deception and scams. The FBI and Federal Trade Commission (FTC) have reported that billions of dollars is lost annually through internet and other spam.[46]

Canter—a pioneer or villain, depending on who you ask—was right about one thing: April 12, 1994, would "go down in history as the date the Internet became truly commercial," as he predicted.[47] But whatever celebrity or stardom they'd achieved, it didn't make for a happy ending. In 1996, he and Martha Siegel divorced. In 1997, Canter was disbarred by the State of Tennessee on ethics charges related to his role spamming the internet. He moved to the Bay Area to pursue internet-related work. Siegel passed away in 2000.[48]

But Canter and Siegel left in their stead two important legacies. They transformed the culture of the internet with their brash and unrepentant commercial spam message. Today we take the commercial nature of internet platforms for granted, even as we continue to debate rules around advertising, free expression, and the public good.

And the language they used to defend their actions remains with us. They argued that the internet had been an untamed wilderness, and they asserted their rights, framed as their birthright as *Americans*, to spread their commercial message and seek out new global markets at the newest (final?) frontier. Their imperious attitude reflected deep-seated ideas about the United States and its empire. Grounding their justifications in their understanding of U.S. law and their rights as Americans because they were physically located within the United States, they diminished and denied the possibility of a transnational internet community. Rather, they saw those spaces as something to exploit for profit, transforming what it meant to be a citizen of cyberspace. "Netizenship," in their view, didn't constitute a close-linked community defining its own norms, but instead meant a right to sell and take up space within a broader, more anonymous, more transnational, and less bounded society.

The message was more than the medium. They spread their green card lottery spam through a new global communications platform in hopes of capturing the business of aspiring lottery entrants and would-be immigrants. In this, they seemed to be fulfilling Al Gore's call to use the internet to transcend national borders and bring communities closer together. Columnist Thomas Friedman anticipated that globalization by way of the internet would bring an era of "cultural homogeneity and universal connectivity."[49]

But what Canter and Siegel saw, and what breathless internet boosters couldn't, was that while capital and information could transcend national borders with greater ease, people themselves were far less mobile. Increasing global restrictions on migration and rising xenophobia in places like Europe and the United States would make legal migration opportunities even more valuable. Belonging to a powerful nation-state like the United States had tremendous—perhaps mounting—value in a globalizing world. The experience and results of the first visa lottery, open for the month of June 1994, showed how right they were.

Part II

. . . .

It was from his uncle that Walisu Alhassan first learned about the American lottery. Every school break, he and his eight siblings would leave Kalpohin, a village on the outskirts of town, and head to Tamale, the largest city in northern Ghana. There they would visit their uncle, whose important job working for the national water company connected him to powerful people and big cities to the south, like Accra and Kumasi. On these visits, Alhassan pored over his uncle's journals and magazines, reading and dreaming about the world beyond his own. Seeing advertisements for American hotels—the Marriott, the Radisson—Alhassan developed a hobby of sending them letters to express his admiration for their splendor, and to ask that they reply to his letters with small tokens. It was a kind of game to see if they would reply. When the hotels sent him unwieldy parcels in return, he'd lug them back from the post office, grinning at the other kids. The branded notepads and pens became his school supplies, and he put every bit of soap and shampoo to good use. Since nobody could match his track record at getting hotel goodies back via correspondence, his age-mates asked him to write to hotels, too, on their behalf.

One day his uncle and a friend sat at the dining room table, chatting quietly about winning the lottery and getting a green card. The adults assumed the children were occupied and paid them no attention. But children's ears have special sensitivity for grownup talk, and Alhassan heard them say that visa winners would get jobs in the United States, a place that was already alive for him from what he'd seen in his uncle's magazines, what he'd learned through his hotel chain correspondence, and what he'd seen depicted in movies.

Alhassan's uncle was planning to fill out the form and apply. Because of his job and connections, he had learned about the lottery early—before messages from the U.S. consulate and state press had made their way from the south to the northern part of the country. He figured that if he did the application properly, he would surely be among those chosen. Later, Alhassan stole a glimpse at his uncle's form, with its photocopied image of the Great Seal of the U.S. Department of State. A bald eagle grasps in one talon a bundle of arrows, symbolizing war, while the other holds an olive branch, symbolizing peace. The motto, not quite legible in the photocopy but baked into the symbol, read *E pluribus unum* (Out of many, one). Filling out this simple form, Alhassan deduced, was the key to getting to America, a word that conjured luxury, opportunity, and adventure. He resolved to apply for himself when he could.[1]

Yet information was hard to come by. It seemed that people with connections knew more than others. Alhassan kept asking around until a friend's brother working at the post office told him and his friends what to do and gave them a copy of the form. They made photocopies of the blank form before distributing copies to their friends and filling them out. "We were like, okay. Let's try. Maybe we will be lucky," he later said.

After applying for the first time in 1997, Alhassan became the resident expert among his friends. He knew when to expect replies at the post office. He kept an ear out for rumors, like the one that said that applicants with wives had more luck and were more likely to win than single men. Academic performance seemed not to matter at all, beyond evidence of completing secondary school, a requirement imposed by the United States.

Later, when Alhassan took a job working with a Christian missionary spreading the gospel in rural communities in the majority-Muslim north, he found that the American woman had never heard of the lottery and didn't know anything about it. What was invisible to her was highly salient in the communities where she lived and worked. Alhassan had given much more thought to the intricacies of American immigration policy than the American woman living and working in his country, whose U.S. passport and visa to Ghana had come straightforwardly.

Each year, Alhassan and his friends methodically filled out the paper form during the entry period, typically in the autumn, just before the Harmattan. Because his handwriting was the best, he filled out many forms for his family members and friends, helping mail them off through the Ghana Post. When the United States converted the entry system to an online form in the early 2000s, he went to one of Tamale's two internet cafés, where they did applications, carefully spelling out his name, and providing photocopies of the necessary information. The man at the internet café charged one cedi for the work. He knew of one photographer in town who could take the required passport-sized photo to submit with the application.

He witnessed the limitations on how far luck could carry a lottery winner. Some people who were fortunate enough to be picked then couldn't raise the money to pay for the visa or couldn't find a sponsor in America to guarantee them. Even collecting the necessary documents—a clinical

MyCom Internet Café and Computer Shop, Tamale, Ghana, 2013. Photograph by author.

report, police report, and passport—or traveling to the capital, Accra, for the consular interview could become immovable obstacles to getting a green card. A lot of people flopped. But some didn't.

In 2008 his brother was selected as a lottery winner. They gathered the requisite documents, arranged for a contact in the United States to serve as his guarantor, and traveled down to Accra to sit for the consular interview. Everything cost money, and the whole family chipped in. After a successful interview, Alhassan's brother received the visa and leaned on his network to gather the funds to pay for the airfare. His whole future unfolded differently than it might have had Alhassan not walked him through the steps of entering the visa lottery, accompanied him to the photo studio and internet café, and let him use his post office box as a return address.

When those who'd won the lottery came back home to Tamale for short visits, they held themselves differently, Alhassan observed, and commanded a certain respect for having gone and come back. They had "seen the bigger part of the world." They told stories about life in Georgia, one of the states where so many Ghanaians seemed to settle. They talked about the process of getting a driver's license, and about how the work in America was hard but the pay was fair. Evidence of America's relative luxury appeared in real estate development around Tamale, as expatriates earning U.S. dollars built villas as investment properties to rent out, paid their family members' school fees, put up poultry farms for their families to run and live off of—all while the lottery winner poured himself into the grind of life in America.

Alhassan had grown up in a simple round mud house. It was home. But he could see that there was something else out there. A different life. Peers with American connections simply had more, while those without often went hungry. "America is life, it's good, it is luxury. America would be the choice of most people when it comes to where you would like to go." What he described was no one-way street. A Ghanaian immigrant in America would benefit his new country: "He is going to work, he will pay tax, he is supporting America with his knowledge," Alhassan said.

While the United States was rolling out its global lottery, Africans like Alhassan were facing new pressures to leave home—whether to move to cities where there were more economic opportunities, to neighboring countries when conditions worsened at home, or farther abroad within or beyond Africa. The lottery that enabled people to go to America the legal way, without hassle, was spectacular. And it was making the United States an increasingly desirable destination, at least in people's imaginations. "America is the only country that has given that opportunity. In the whole world, it is only America that is open," he said. Alhassan's optimism about the United States was buoyed by the lottery but was borne of a longer, more complex story.

· · · · · ·

As a country that had once been part of Britain's colonial empire, Ghana continued to use English as its official language and remained connected to the United Kingdom in many ways. As economic and political conditions pushed people like Alhassan to seek opportunities abroad, the United Kingdom might have made sense as a destination. But it wasn't necessarily easy to get there.

Earlier in the twentieth century, imperial networks brought select ambitious Ghanaians to study at British universities. Their experiences helped seed new communities in metropolitan cities like London, where intellectuals, students, and other travelers from colonized parts of the world began exchanging ideas and building power. Britain became a site of Black internationalist, anticolonial, and antiracist organizing in the years between World War I and World War II.[2] Future African independence leaders like Kwame Nkrumah, Jomo Kenyatta, and Nnamdi Azikiwe mingled here before returning to the continent to lead their countries in dismantling colonialism, buoyed by grass roots organizing.

After World War II, labor shortages in Britain led to policies that encouraged migration from the reaches of its empire, from the Caribbean, South Asia, and to a lesser extent, Africa.[3] Anti-Black racism permeated Black Britons' and migrants' experiences, even though as imperial subjects, including those with British or Commonwealth citizenship, they didn't necessarily face the same kinds of border restrictions that people outside of British jurisdiction might have. That changed as colonies discarded British rule and established independence as nation-states. By the late 1960s, British officials sought to define citizenship along racial lines to keep nonwhite British citizens, subjects, and former subjects out.[4]

Even so, a crucial pattern had been established. Going abroad to access educational opportunities and experiences had become an important practice for people of means in Ghana. The name given to a person who went abroad and returned was a "been-to," meaning a person who had *been to* an overseas country and returned.[5] Return was an essential quality of a been-to: travel abroad was a means of achieving education and experience to benefit one's self, family, and country. Returning home, been-tos gained elevated social status.

A related group of Ghanaians were called "burgers." This term was coined in the 1970s to describe people who traveled to Hamburg, Germany (and later other parts of Europe), worked seasonally, and returned to Ghana with enhanced wealth.[6] For both been-tos and burgers, one writer said in a 1994 opinion piece, "Ghana was where the fun was and generally only the failures tarried long in distant lands."[7] A successful been-to or burger went abroad to gain something to bring home: education, experience, or cash. Remaining abroad permanently, in exile, was not necessarily a desirable choice for people of means.

Later, in the 1980s and 1990s, Britain along with other European countries began adopting more stringent border control measures. Unauthorized immigrants, asylum seekers, and migrants from outside Europe—and particularly Africa—faced increasingly draconian punishment as their very presence was criminalized.[8] The systems of power that created migrants, that impelled people to depart home to go elsewhere to survive, also criminalized their migration.[9] The *Daily Graphic*, a state-run paper published in Accra and the most widely read daily in the country, reported that Ghanaians were being deported and repatriated to Ghana in significant numbers after traveling without documents or authorization. It warned that Ghanaians were developing a reputation abroad as "criminals."[10] African migration to Britain and elsewhere in Europe continued, often in the tracks of empire, but barriers and obstacles were multiplying and people encountered rampant anti-Black racism both at borders and within Europe. "Is it a sin to be born in the Dust?" an African couple wrote in their meditation on migration. "If not, then it seems to be a crime for a person from the Dust to be in the Snow."[11]

"Fortress Europe" aimed to close its gates to most Africans, but empire and migration were inextricably linked. As the intellectual Ambalavaner Sivanandan phrased it, "We are here because you were there." Even as restrictionists in Britain treated the migration of Black people as an onslaught, these migratory patterns were shaped by centuries of racism and violence. As Harsha Walia writes, "Mass migration is the *outcome* of the *actual* crises, conquest, and climate change," rather than migrants being the *cause* of an imagined border crisis.[12]

Most profoundly, the transatlantic slave trade was the largest forced migration in history, ultimately ensnaring more than 11 million African people who were taken, ship by ship, year over year, to the Americas in forced servitude and treated as chattel. In what would become Ghana, the slave castles at Cape Coast and Elmina, today tourist destinations, were among the dozens of slave trading forts dotting the coast, becoming for Africans points of no return. Many of these ships flew under the British flag, to British sugar islands in the Caribbean. Sugar—and the African people who cultivated and produced it under a system of racial chattel slavery—made the modern world. Blackness became a marker of and justification for the perpetuity of this system.

The color line continued to structure societies even after the system of slavery was abolished—first and decisively in Haiti, and belatedly by Britain, France, the United States, Cuba, and Brazil. The end of the transatlantic slave trade and the demise of Africa's own slave trading states (like Asante, in what would become Ghana) created opportunities for conquest and the expansion of European territorial empires on the African continent.[13] Building new industrial economies, Europeans looked to Africa as a source for raw materials and untapped markets for European goods. The Berlin Conference of 1884–85 marked a turning point in Europe's colonization of Africa, and by the outbreak of World War I, some 90 percent of the continent was under some form of European rule, with the exceptions of Ethiopia and Liberia. While proponents of colonialism touted the project's "civilizing mission" on a backward, underdeveloped continent, European rule was marked by violence and exploitation. This violence and the drape of humanitarian rhetoric that aimed to mask it were also forged in anti-Blackness. Ideas and images of "Africa" were reproduced throughout Europe and the United States through displays of Black people as inferior at world's fairs and exhibitions touting white superiority. Power reproduced through culture, and colonialism shaped not only the lives of Africans in Africa under European rule but also the assumptions and practices of white Americans and Europeans in their own societies.[14]

Between the world wars, European empires deepened colonial rule, expanding white settlement, displacing indigenous Africans, recruiting local leaders as brokers for Western exploitation, cultivating cash crops, and building up extractive mining operations. Systems of colonial administration were designed to profit Europeans at the expense of African subjects while dismantling older forms of governance and social organization. At great risk of violence, Africans resisted through rebellions large and small, and workers acted collectively to improve working conditions. During the interwar years, elite Africans traveled overseas, typically for education. In some cases, colonial administrators looking to shore up human resources for colonial governance facilitated these opportunities to study abroad. The existence of a tiny cadre of trained Africans would, they thought, help justify the colonial project as doing the work of "civilizing" that boosters of imperialism touted.[15]

It was in this context that independence-era political leaders gained experience abroad, whether through education or military service in the wars. The 1920s, 1930s, and 1940s also saw vibrant Pan-African meetings and conferences, bringing together Black thinkers from the United States, the Caribbean, Europe, and Africa to think in community and foster connections. Seeing Black people across the globe as connected and shaped by global systems of empire, labor, and anti-Blackness, Pan-Africanists conceived of Black liberation as something that transcended national boundaries and that needed to be won everywhere.

During World War II, Africans, recruited into the global conflict as colonial subjects, made critical contributions to the war effort, within Africa and beyond it. The conditions of wartime fighting and production strained people's lives and made colonial rule even more intolerable. Moreover, war veterans returned home with new perspectives gained from fighting abroad, ostensibly to defend "democracy" from the threat of fascism—when they could see as clear as day that the empires they served denied them anything like democracy. European empires, weakened by war and newly aware of how indebted they were to their colonies, acquiesced to economic and political reforms in the wake of the war. Africans demanded more. More control over their own destinies, more self-determination. And by some measures, they got it; in the next decades, almost all of the continent's colonies gained political independence, with dozens of new nation-states coming into existence in the world.[16]

Leading the charge was Ghana, formerly the Gold Coast, in West Africa, which gained independence from Britain in 1957. First president Kwame Nkrumah summarized his philosophy: "Seek ye first the political kingdom, and all else shall be added unto you." Full political independence was a precondition for the growth and prosperity of the new nation. And he saw Ghana's liberation as linked intrinsically with the rest of the continent. "Divided we are weak," he said in 1961. "United, Africa could become one of the greatest forces for good in the world."[17]

Ghana's independence celebration in 1957 drew political leaders and leaders of the Black freedom struggle from all over the world. Martin Luther King Jr., who attended the ceremonies, described the scene as the British flag was lowered and replaced by Ghana's distinctive red, gold, and green flag with a black star in the center. The black star was a reference to Marcus Garvey's Pan-Africanist "Back to Africa" movement and the shipping line he had launched to facilitate the "return" of members of the diaspora. Half a million people came to attend the changing of the flags on March 6. King said, "Before I knew it, I started weeping. I was crying for joy. And I knew about all of the struggles, and all of the pain, and all of the agony that these people had gone through for this moment."[18] He added, "An old order of colonialism, of segregation, of discrimination is passing away now. And a new order of justice and freedom and good will is being born." Lord Kitchener, the Trinidadian calypso musician, penned a song for the occasion: "This day will never be forgotten. . . . Ghana! Ghana is the name."[19]

Africans winning self-rule—often after armed struggle against resistant empires—constituted a world historic event, a transformation of the political map of the globe. African people had been denied not only self-determination but also recognition of their very humanity. When movements and leaders who struggled for independence against powerful, violent empires won, these victories fostered high hopes and optimism about African futures. Patrice Lumumba at Congo's independence said, "We shall show the world what the black man can do when working in liberty."[20]

. . . . . .

Education was central to Nkrumah's vision for African liberation. He helped implement cost-free primary education, which resulted in the expansion of schools and enrolled students.[21] In the early days of independence, going abroad for education and returning to Ghana as a been-to was seen as a way to serve the new nation. Nkrumah encouraged students to go abroad and return to "replace the white man," as Kofi Owusu-Daaku, dean of students at Kwame Nkrumah University of Science and Technology, later put it, meaning that this cadre of trained Ghanaians would help run the country as colonial officials departed. "If anybody went abroad, it was largely sponsored by the government to go abroad and then to come back and manage the country, e.g. by entering the civil service," Owusu-Daaku added.[22]

But soon after independence, the meanings associated with going abroad began to shift. A few decades later, the urge to leave was widespread, with newspaper articles lamenting the "brain drain" of the highly educated as a signal of Ghanaians' dwindling faith in the country. Bitter critics blamed selfish individuals for choosing to depart. As one editorial in the state-owned publication *The Spectator* put it, "No country can develop when its citizens are not patriotic." "Unconcerned whether Ghana rises or sinks," the editor wrote, these unpatriotic Ghanaians "think only about becoming rich."[23] But the truth was more complicated. People didn't necessarily want to depart for selfish reasons, but conditions at home made opportunities scarce. By the time Walisu Alhassan was growing up in the 1980s and 1990s, many people shared the belief that departing Ghana was one of the only ways to advance.

9 Structural Adjustment

· ·

When he landed at Accra's Kotoka airport in 1998, Bill Clinton was greeted by Ghana's president Jerry John Rawlings, along with a huge crowd of people decked out in cloth with the two men's faces screen printed into the pattern and adorning their dresses, shirts, and wraps.[1] The day was hot and "so humid one almost had to chew to breathe."[2] Thousands turned out to greet the Clintons, who were undertaking the first-ever presidential visit of Ghana.[3] In his speech at Black Star Square, a monument to the nation's independence, Clinton emphasized that the United States hoped to foster a healthy trading relationship with Ghana based on the two countries' shared historic connections—the slave trade (which drafts of his speech described alternately as our "national shame," or the more muted "lasting scar") and rising hope for the continent's fortunes.[4] The kind of economic growth and trade he hoped to build in Africa would be driven by Ghana's embrace of free markets and democracy. Draped in traditional Asante kente cloth, with green, yellow, and black woven together in patterns over a magenta wrap, he ended his speech to the thunderous applause of the crowd of some 250,000 people.[5]

It was the first leg of a six-country, eleven-day visit to Africa, the most extensive trip by a U.S. president to the continent in decades. Rawlings appeared happy to embrace Clinton and his envoy. He said in his own speech that "only by allowing the individual to flourish can our communities also flourish."[6] He seemed poised to accept and promote Clinton's optimism about free market ideology. Clinton touted the African Growth and Opportunity Act, then still pending in the U.S. Senate, to encourage African nations to undertake market reforms and embrace the free market.[7]

The visit came amid an energy crisis in Ghana. Electricity was being carefully rationed. Meanwhile, wealthy elites and governmental offices purchased generators and fuel so that they could continue to run their lights, air conditioners, and fans. A member of Clinton's delegation reportedly asked if a large unsightly generator could be moved during the visit and was rebuffed. In fact, Clinton's massive 800-person delegation tested the country's capacity in numerous ways. With only about 500 top-tier hotel rooms in Accra, it was decided that the delegation wouldn't spend the night and would make it a day trip instead. The mismatch between the scale of the delegation and the capital city's capacity to host them "sums up in miniature the gap between rich and powerful America and a largely poor Africa," Howard French wrote in the *New York Times*.[8]

Electricity access in Ghana was and would remain a serious problem. Rolling blackouts, or load shedding, also known as *dumsor*, the Twi word for "off/on," profoundly shaped how families lived their lives and businesses operated.[9] The country's inability to provide consistent, universal, predictable access to electricity exemplified how the promises and ambitions of the nation's founding remained unmet. Just as Clinton was gesturing toward a friendlier post–Cold War America and a more integrated global economy forged in free trade, and just as the diversity visa lottery was beckoning, the difficulties of life in Ghana felt inescapable.

· · · · · ·

At independence in 1957, Kwame Nkrumah drew on existing colonial-era plans to build a hydroelectric dam on the Volta River to generate power for the country, construct an aluminum smelter, and create the infrastructure to support industrialization and modernization.[10] The United States, eager at the time to win the hearts and minds of decolonizing Africans in the global Cold War, threw its support behind Nkrumah's "baby," what would become the Akosombo dam, and suggested that U.S.-based Kaiser industries provide the private funding for the project. Kaiser and a few other aluminum companies would run the project, and funding would come mostly from the World Bank, as well as loans from the United States and Britain. In 1961, Ghana established the Volta River Authority to resettle communities displaced by the dam project, some 80,000 people whose homes and lands would be flooded to form the new Volta Lake, and to oversee the electricity supply.

The dam held the key to the project of making Ghana into a socialist society with a mixed economy—part of the vision of what it meant to end colonialism. By the time Nkrumah ceremonially turned on the power switch at the dam in 1965, however, he had stamped out dissent and implemented one-party rule in the country, dashing many people's hopes for what popular sovereignty would look like in an independent Ghana. The project itself remained incomplete. Although the nation now possessed its own power grid, it failed to connect to the rural parts of the country, leaving many communities out.

The plans for the Akosombo dam were inherited from a colonial state that had created the blueprint to benefit the metropole rather than

Ghanaians. More broadly, Nkrumah had inherited a state that had never been designed for or aimed to serve the needs of African people. Although he wanted to diversify Ghana's economy, its cocoa exports, timber, and mining remained central to the economy as they had been under colonial rule. Africa was still understood by Europeans and others as a source for raw materials and commodities rather than a place where human beings might shape their own destinies. The challenges of forging new nation-states amid the global Cold War were immense. Through the 1950s and 1960s in Ghana, Nkrumah followed what Frederick Cooper called "developmentalist authoritarianism" attempting to modernize the colonial state he had inherited with infrastructure projects.[11] Ghana's mixed economy with both state-owned enterprises and private capital would, Nkrumah hoped, build the funds needed for infrastructure development and social services like education and health care. But then, unstable cocoa prices threatened these ambitions. And the Akosombo dam wound up ceding Ghanaian economic power to multinational aluminum companies (which possessed the needed technology for the massive project) and international financial institutions (which had the money needed to fund it). The project put Nkrumah at the crossroads of the Cold War. While aiming to remain "non-aligned" to either the Communist East or the capitalist West, Nkrumah saw a strong role for the state in developing the economy, while turning to the West for support. The project—and Nkrumah's presidency—ended in disappointment.

In the early years after independence, school enrollments increased, hospitals doubled, and health workers increased. But incomes for most Ghanaians declined, while food prices rose. This was accompanied by growing corruption among those with political and economic power, as government officials amassed wealth through bribes and kickbacks. Supporters and opponents alike grew disillusioned as Nkrumah leaned into authoritarianism, including by introducing the Preventive Detention Act in 1958 to curtail dissent.[12] As consumer prices surged, the state began to drain reserves to pay for social services, making Ghana more indebted. The Akosombo dam project opened up Ghana to further debt. The export agricultural economy collapsed. And in 1966, a coup organized by Ghanaians (but looked favorably upon by, if not encouraged by, the United States) ousted Nkrumah, who lived the rest of his days in exile.

What followed was an era of squeeze and disaster. Ghana's 1969 elections brought K. A. Busia to power, only to be overthrown in 1972. A military leader, Col. Ignatius Acheampong ruled from 1972 until he was deposed in

1978 and executed the following year. The 1970s seemed to mark a global retreat from postwar liberalism and economic growth and stability.[13] Between 1972 and 1982, the World Bank reported that Ghana's economy deteriorated badly, with investments, savings, and incomes plummeting, inflation soaring, and reserves all but depleted.[14]

Acheampong sought to centralize state power and boost agricultural performance to make Ghana less dependent on imports. But his "Operation Feed Yourself" program was undermined by the oil shocks of 1973 and a drought from 1975 to 1977 that badly affected Ghana's cocoa exports and caused mass hardship, particularly in the north.[15] Drought undermined electricity access as well, because of the country's dependence on hydroelectricity. Further, the Acheampong regime was seen as unusually corrupt and became deeply unpopular. Ghanaians decried the regime's *kalabule* (profiteering) as they saw neighbors—"small boys"—transform themselves through illicit means into "big men."

These problems unraveled the state's capacity for infrastructure and development at a time of deepening privation. Ghana's independence remained a source of pride, but what did it mean if the state could not maintain roads, schools, and hospital buildings?[16] Where was any sense of the public good? At the dawn of the 1980s, dire food shortages drove hundreds of thousands of people to seek work in nearby Nigeria. Between 1979 and 1981, Ghana underwent a rapid series of elections and coups, and in 1981 a military officer, Jerry John Rawlings, took power. He would remain there for some time.

· · · · · ·

Rawlings called his government the Provisional National Defense Council (PNDC). He decried the "insidious Western interests" he believed were contributing to corruption in the country and tried to position himself as a revolutionary and firebrand.[17] The PNDC garnered support from students and workers, farmers and radicals. When it imposed price controls to rein in corruption, however, shortages of consumer goods proliferated. Worry about *kalabule* made the state wary of private accumulation of any kind, and Rawlings pledged a "holy war" against corruption.[18] But this made for a troubling pattern: people hoarded consumer goods, worsening shortages, and creating an atmosphere of fear and suspicion.[19] In 1983, Nigeria deported at least 700,000 Ghanaians who had been living and working in the country (when its oil fortunes supported a booming economy) back to Ghana.[20] The event was known as "Ghana must go," giving the name to the woven, plaid-patterned plastic bags that today are used across Africa and the world by people on the go.[21] With the arrival of hundreds of thousands of expelled people, the population suddenly swelled, deepening Ghana's economic crisis. Power cuts at the end of 1983 worsened the sense of despair.[22]

Despite Rawlings's anti-Western rhetoric, he sought help from outside. In 1982, he began negotiations with donors through the International Monetary Fund (IMF) to bring money into the country. In exchange for loans, Ghana became the first African country to adopt what was known as a structural adjustment program (SAP), a set of plans to restructure the economy to align with IMF priorities.[23] The idea was to encourage "free enterprise," strip away government bloat, reduce social spending, focus the nation's farmers on growing crops for export, and encourage more importation of consumer goods. By adopting the SAP, Ghana aimed to assure donors of the country's creditworthiness, to attract loans and aid. The PNDC crafted what it called its Economic Recovery Program (ERP), following World Bank and IMF guidelines, to be implemented beginning in 1983. The program included an austere annual budget, cuts to fuel and food subsidies, and the precipitous devaluation of the Ghanaian currency, the cedi, to appeal to donors.[24]

As more than a half million Ghanaian migrants returned from Nigeria in 1983 in "Ghana must go," Rawlings seized upon the emergency to attract aid without appearing to cede power to foreign donors. He was able to frame the ERP as complementary to its own efforts to handle the migrant crisis.[25] Although the government recognized that the ERP would impose pain on vulnerable Ghanaians, the regime was insulated from democratic accountability.[26] Soon, Rawlings began speaking more openly about "production and efficiency" as the ERP liberalized the economy. The World Bank praised the PNDC for its performance and pledged further aid, which, along with better agricultural performances, improved Ghana's economic situation as the 1980s progressed.[27]

PNDC officials accepted the language of donor agencies, emphasizing statistics, and the "new science of market economics," as the historian Paul Nugent has shown.[28] They loosened the price controls they had imposed on consumer goods, which they hoped would allow people to buy things again and quiet accusations of *kalabule*. More profoundly, structural adjustment entailed shrinking the apparatus of the state. In 1987 and 1988, Ghana reduced the payroll of the state Cocoa Board from 90,000 employees to fewer than 50,000. Economic liberalism appeared to offer solutions to Ghana's problems of dependency, a bloated state apparatus, and corruption.[29]

In 1987, the PNDC began its second ERP to address the structural components of economic growth. This entailed privatizing state functions and divesting from state enterprises, signaling that, unlike in a previous era, the state itself should no longer be seen as the prime driver of economic progress. Such policies rehabilitated the idea of wealth, making private accumulation appear more legitimate and acceptable. Greater wealth was particularly accessible to a pro-PNDC business class, but even Rawlings worried that living conditions for most ordinary people were poor.[30] As part of these reforms, the government began requiring individuals to pay directly for hospital services and drugs, as well as for school and school housing. Although Ghanaians had faced privation, poverty, and even famine before, this shift represented a devastating imposition, particularly in light of what they had come to expect should be provided by the state and independence-era reforms to make education widely accessible.[31] What was celebrated externally as a successful case for austerity-based reforms—as Ghana paid down debts, brought down inflation, and increased production it became the "darling boy" of the IMF—also imposed deleterious effects on ordinary Ghanaians, as it commodified their "life-chances," as scholar Jasper Abembia Ayelazuno put it.[32]

· · · · · ·

Ghanaians navigated the restructuring of their economy as it became more market oriented. And the ruling regime adopted political reforms.[33] In 1992, the PNDC lifted its ban on political activity, and Ghana prepared for the first elections since 1979. Rawlings won, on the ticket of the National Democratic Congress (NDC) party. Ghana's Fourth Republic had arrived, along with a new constitution, implemented in 1993, and new freedoms—private newspapers were finally allowed to operate.[34]

Rawlings deepened Ghana's relationship with the United States, welcoming Bill Clinton for the Americans' visit in 1998. He himself visited the United States in 1999. When the opposition party, the New Patriotic Party (NPP), won power in the 2000 election, sending John Kufuor to the presidency, his administration focused on further developing the private sector and implemented policies designed to bring about what it called a "Golden Age of Business."[35] In the Fourth Republic, all the major parties—despite claiming to hold opposing ideologies—seemed to agree that a market-oriented economy was best.[36]

Ghana's structural adjustment story has sometimes been understood as a success, praised by the World Bank and IMF at times "as a showcase for free-market reform."[37] Yet many ordinary Ghanaians failed to reap the benefits. Growth didn't necessarily translate to better living conditions for all, and even growth slowed during the 1980s, exacerbating inequality and marginalization.[38] The principal beneficiaries of the ERPs were large landowners and foreign investors involved in the production and export of cash crops.[39] Urbanites, the main consumers of imported consumer goods, suffered when prices rose more quickly than their salaries.[40] Due to the state's withdrawal from direct employment, as it shrank the civil service and sold off state-owned businesses and agencies, urban Ghanaians experienced a steady decline in formal sector employment, and thousands lost jobs.[41] The devaluation of the cedi produced an escalation in consumer prices. Scholars estimate that real wages in 1995 were half what they had been in 1970.[42] Reduced state subsidies on food, fuel, and transportation also disproportionately affected urban Ghanaians. More frequent power cuts in the late 1990s destabilized people's ability to reap the benefits when they did gain greater access to consumer goods.

On top of these pressures was the new expectation that individuals would need to pay out of pocket for school fees and health services.[43] To average Ghanaians, noted one newspaper article, the ERPs have "had nothing but a negative and devastating effect on their lives."[44] Praise for the country by international donors wasn't always translating to a sense at home that the government was serving the people. It was in this context that ideas about luck, development, and citizenship shifted. As Lynne Brydon has argued, "luck" came to occupy a significant space for Ghanaians navigating their economic worlds in the era of adjustment.[45]

10 Luck

· ·

Had President Clinton's entourage wandered a few blocks from Black Star Square during their 1998 visit, they would have come across, in the tangle of streets behind Makola Market, the building housing the National Lottery Authority (NLA). Its slogan, "development through games," reflected the country's strategy of using the lottery to raise revenue for public works.[1] A 1999 *Forbes* country report on Ghana suggested that lotteries served as a "painless" form of taxation that allowed ordinary Ghanaians to contribute to the development of their country. To compete with the private lotteries that kept popping up, the NLA decentralized its own regional lotteries in the early 1990s.[2]

Without a consistent source of state funding for public goods, and amid Ghana's dismantling of state-owned enterprises to comply with structural adjustment, for many people playing the lottery seemed no riskier than other forms of participation in capitalism. And the opportunity to get rich was appealing, of course, especially as elites began displaying new symbols of wealth, filling the streets with private cars.

By the middle of the 1990s, Ghanaians had grown used to the proliferation of lotteries as a mechanism for raising state revenue, as a sales gimmick by private companies, as a subject of hand-wringing by moralists, and as a form of income for the desperate. But the introduction, since the summer of 1994, of the new American visa lottery was still something special.

It came in a context of frustration with life in Ghana, and at a time when new barriers to mobility made going abroad more difficult. "Is Ghana such a bad place?" asked a 1994 opinion piece. "The dream of the youth is to leave the country."[3] Dreams of departing took on an epic dimension as Ghanaians encountered slammed doors, criminalization, and racist border regimes as they tried to go abroad.

The lottery debuted, too, as the United States was making efforts to strengthen trading relationships with African nations and pushing countries like Ghana to embrace free markets with enthusiasm. The choice to run the diversity visa program as a lottery, with luck determining the outcome, was fortuitous, given the popularity of lotteries globally in the context of structural adjustment and neoliberalism. Entering the American lottery was not much different from buying lottery tickets from a booth. It was possible to "play" casually.[4] The lottery format suggested that the outcome was a matter of chance or fate, not judgment cast upon an applicant. The role of luck disrupted forms of gatekeeping that had systemically excluded Africans. Why not take a chance?

Together the popularity of lotteries, the role of luck, and the juxtaposition of the diversity visa's prioritization of African immigration with increased global barriers to migration made the program popular. They also inspired industrious intermediaries to offer services to help manage uncertainties.

· · · · · ·

Ghana was far from alone in seeing a proliferation of lotteries as a legitimate source for public funding. In the colonial United States, legislatures often used lotteries to raise funds for public goods. Lotteries were used to distribute property and even enslaved people after an enslaver's death. Rarely, enslaved people entered and won lotteries to purchase their own freedom.[5] When risk taking became more central to American economic life, lotteries became the focus of critics who charged that they exploited the working classes. By the late nineteenth century, most states and then the federal government banned them altogether.[6] That only changed again in the 1960s and 1970s, as states began authorizing lotteries again. As deregulation, low corporate taxes, and veneration of the free market took hold and politicians hesitated to raise direct taxes on citizens, lest they lose reelection, lotteries became a popular method of raising funds.[7] In American history, gambling occupies a strange place; Americans have sometimes embraced the idea that "you make your own luck," and that rewards reflect merit. On the other hand, risk-taking entrepreneurship depends upon a culture of chance, in which luck or fortune governs events and outcomes.[8] The late twentieth century embrace of lotteries and other legalized gambling tracked with growing economic insecurity.

Ghana has held a national lottery since the year after its 1957 independence. The turn to state lotteries in newly independent African nations was born of the practical need to raise revenues.[9] But lotteries became more important in the era of adjustment. Through the mid-1980s, widely circulating lotto newspapers signaled Ghana's urban citizens' interest in playing games of chance in hopes of bettering their circumstances.[10] Newspapers printed state lottery numbers and ran advertisements for privately run lotteries. Political parties used raffles to fundraise.[11] "Ghanaians like to take their chance and gamble. Because we like to live beyond our means. Anything that will make life more comfortable, quicker and faster, they will do it," Kofi Owusu-Daaku, a professor in Kumasi, said.[12] But living beyond our means is encouraged in an economic system that venerates consumerism without ensuring that workers earn sufficient wages.

Ghanaians commented on their own propensity to try their luck in these games of chance. Under the headline "To Lotto or Not To," one writer complained about a self-proclaimed "lotto professor" holding court at Nkrumah Circle in Accra, claiming to hold the secrets to better lottery results.[13] People were vulnerable to "lotto tricksters"—unlicensed people trying to dupe people out of their money—at worst.[14] Even at best, though, Ghana's "national obsession with lottery," warned one 1996 editorial in the *Daily Graphic*, is "threatening to turn Ghana into a nation of gamblers."[15]

The "lotto craze" was having deleterious effects on Ghanaians, causing marital strife, "drunkenness, misery and depression and what-have-you," while imperiling the souls of observant Christians and Muslims, the two major religions to which much of the country belonged. Lotteries, one writer observed, were voluntary but regressive forms of taxation, impoverishing the many to enrich the few.[16]

On the same newspaper page as a 1995 article decrying lotteries, an inset briefly mentioned the Kume preko demonstration in Accra.[17] One hundred thousand people took to the streets to protest the imposition of a value-added tax, as well as the high cost of food, stagnant wages, and other economic woes that they understood were directly tied to structural adjustment.[18] Although elections had been held in 1992, the country's multiple military coups, periods of authoritarian rule, and documented human rights violations meant that street protests and demonstrations were rare in Ghana. Anger at Rawlings—and specifically the economic reforms that people believed were harming them—fueled the march. "Kume preko" meant, in Twi, "You may as well kill me," comparing the slow injury of an economic system stacked against them to violence. Several people at the demonstration were killed.[19] The name of a second march later in the month in Kumasi, "Sieme preko," meant "then just bury me."[20]

One of the planners for the mobilization, Nana Akufo-Addo, would decades later become Ghana's president on a platform promoting free trade and making Ghana more business friendly. In 2016 he would be the candidate of the NPP, the main center-right opposition party to the more left-leaning NDC, Rawlings's party. But back in 1995, the Kume preko and Sieme preko demonstrations in the streets and the lottery grifters and hustlers

Lottery booth in Accra, Ghana, 2013. Photograph by author.

at Nkrumah Circle exposed how Ghanaians were grappling with the turn toward neoliberalism.

A 1998 cartoon printed in *The Mirror* showed a confused man encircled by lottery booths, unsure how to pick his game or his numbers. An operator suggests trying the "Akosombo special lotto" to raise funds to "buy a generator for the country. 99.7% chance of winning."[21] Entering the lottery was framed as a form of civic participation, but one where the impossible odds exposed a sucker's game.

But the cartoon also skewers the government for failing to provide access to the basic public utility of electricity, relying instead on the unemployed and poor's participation in lotteries to raise revenues. Lotteries, people understood, were being run to substitute for functional government and robust state services and infrastructure. In return for putting cedis into these games of chance, people were made to contend with *dumsor* and load shedding. Another 1998 cartoon suggested that Ghanaians were growing accustomed to such inconsistency and unpredictability. "That shows how well we're adapting to the darkness," says one figure in a discussion about "lights out."[22]

· · · · · ·

Lotteries in Ghana were common, accessible, and understood as a legitimate, if narrow, channel for upward mobility—and the United States green card lottery was no different. Although U.S. legislators had considered more complicated formats when creating the diversity visa program, they settled on random draw. They considered this simpler and cheaper to administer than other options, and less likely to generate fraud even as participation in the program was expanded.[23] Framing the program as a lottery also made perfect sense in economic systems that venerated risk taking and speculation.

The United States considered Africa a priority region, after Europe, for diversity immigrants, because these regions sent the fewest immigrants to the United States through the family-based immigration system. Europe had seen its numbers dwindle after 1965, and historically Africa had sent low numbers of voluntary migrants to the United States. The forced migration of the transatlantic slave trade was never considered in calculations that pegged immigration levels to historical movements of people and their descendants.

A formula was designed to allocate diversity visas to regions in inverse proportion to family preference immigration. Countries that sent fewer than

50,000 immigrants over the previous five years were eligible. While citizens of all eligible countries could enter the visa lottery, people from "low-sending" regions of the world—Europe and Africa—possessed a relative advantage, since people living in countries in these regions were guaranteed most of the diversity visas. Nationals of many countries in the high-sending regions of Asia and South America could enter the lottery, but only a small number would receive visas.[24] Some countries, particularly "low-sending" countries within Europe and Africa, would be more likely to win up to the maximum number of visas available, capped at 7 percent of the total, about 3,850 visas (later reduced to about 3,500) per country per year.[25] The lottery was free to enter. The requirements were modest, though not inconsequential. To receive a diversity visa, an applicant had to have a high school diploma or its equivalent, or two years of work experience at a skilled job. This requirement narrowed eligibility substantially.

The number of diversity visas up for grabs was relatively small—55,000 visas in a system that admitted more than 700,000 permanent residents each year.[26] With over 180 eligible countries, millions would participate.[27] The program initially required only that entrants send a piece of paper with their name, date and place of birth, family members' names, and mailing address to a post office box in Portsmouth, New Hampshire, during the registration period.[28] Aside from the cost of postage, there was no fee to enter. Employees at the National Visa Service Center in Portsmouth helped sort the applications by world region and nation, and then a computer selected winners at random.

The introduction of the visa lottery generated uncertainties, questions, and rumors. But soon more information appeared. Flyers and information sheets began to show up at the post office and at the U.S. consulate. Roy Glover, the United States Information Service (USIS) officer in Accra, provided the technical details for this very special lottery to local media and radio stations.[29] Print versions appeared in newspapers. Although Canter and Siegel had been pilloried for their lack of scruples in advertising for the visa lottery online, more high-minded groups like the American Immigration Lawyers Association (AILA) thought lawyers should rise to the occasion. "Having your application selected is only the start of a bureaucratic process filled with pitfalls," Peter Hirsch, former AILA chair, wrote in a letter to the *New York Times*. "Even Einstein would have trouble explaining" the rules of the lottery, he argued.[30] Immigration attorney Michael Maggio told the *Washington Post* that his firm provided free help for lottery applicants, offering to enter clients in the lottery at no cost, to generate potential paid business down the line if they were selected as winners.[31] AILA also recommended that its members file lottery applications for free as a goodwill gesture: "That way, if the applicant wins, then the attorney gets his business in filling out all the paperwork that accompanies the visa application."[32]

Many American companies sought paying customers by advertising in Ghanaian papers.[33] One U.S. immigration attorney who did so, David L. Amkraut, called himself "one of the largest lottery practitioners in the country" and promised clients a special advantage if they paid him fifty to seventy-five dollars to help them enter.[34] Amkraut was later sanctioned by the U.S. Federal Trade Commission for misleading consumers.[35] Would-be agents set up booths—not unlike the lottery booths peppering bus stops and market stalls—this time, to sell a chance at the American dream. "There are these people who have made themselves businessmen in the lottery," Owusu-Daaku said. "People will try to make a bank out of everything." Anything to do with traveling abroad "is like a fortress that you want to get into. So people think they have to get it right."[36]

· · · · · ·

Entering the lottery was designed to be simple, yet many potential registrants were intimidated by the process. The obstacles put up by wealthy, majority-white countries like Britain and the United States to restrict the immigration, or even visits, of Africans helped fuel a sense of unease.

Restrictions on travel and migration were producing visible evidence of Africa's relative powerlessness in the world—and Africans' inability to get through the gate. "I would be surprised if the overnight queue at the American consulate in Accra has vanished," wrote one columnist in *The Mirror*, the state-run weekly.[37] People lined up early to apply for a visa, leaving stones to mark their places in line. "Recent tales speak volumes of turned down visa applications, and appeals, and re-appeals, etc. in a way that keeps tongues wagging—what at all are these consulate people looking for?" he asked. Even receiving a visa was no guarantee against obstacles. "The world appears to have conspired against the Ghanaman traveller, making ports impassable without harassment, handing stowaways over to sharks, turning suitcases inside out—all this after a gruelling bout for a visa!" On the next pages of the same newspaper issue were advertisements for the visa lottery.

Africans seeking even short-term visitor visas to the United States faced long delays at the visa office, steep nonrefundable fees, and refusals offered without explanation. Even as the United States was rolling out a visa waiver program to allow nationals of mostly European countries to enter without a visa at all, Africans seeking to travel for pleasure in the United States needed to apply for a nonimmigrant visa.[38] Consular officers scrutinized their applications and could, at their discretion, refuse a visa to anybody they suspected might overstay and remain in the United States. Restrictions and screening policies that seemed to place extra scrutiny on applicants from African countries, practices that signaled bureaucrats' distrust of African applicants, made them doubtful about the system's fairness. One could be totally deserving of a visa but denied anyway, while someone else might prevail without merit—the gatekeepers had the power to decide one's fate. An unintended effect was that some applicants worked harder to game an opaque and unaccountable system.

Visa refusals felt like another version of austerity imposed on Africans. A 1997 editorial in the *Ghanaian Times* likened the visa regime of wealthy Western countries to colonial rule and its propensity to "take the money of the poor without remorse." Consular officials treated applicants "as if they deserved scorn just for seeking a visa," and the office did not return application fees even when someone's application was denied. Some consular offices "operate like racial registration centers," the editorial said.[39] As Ghanaian-Romanian musician Wanlov the Kubolor put it in his 2007 song "Green Card," "Stand for days at the American Consulate / They're running late / Push back your interview date / So you won't stay / They ask for a bank state / Meant to bring one / Forgot / Now they close gates / Bills ain't paid / Money spent on visa fees."[40] The song wryly described the way long queues, shifting requirements, and onerous fees were deployed by the United States and other powerful countries to limit and exclude African migration, for reasons people could see that were deeply intertwined with racism and colonialism. The indignities continued even if you made it to the United States. One woman described the experience of finally being able to travel from Cameroon to Europe. She noticed that the plane was not full and, annoyed, she wondered "why embassies had to refuse people visas while planes flew empty."[41]

Greater exposure to American movies, music, pop culture, and products at a time of intensifying migration restriction also shaped people's dreams of going abroad. As anthropologists of migration have put it, this exemplified how "images and ideas of the good life, often taking place elsewhere, are circulated all over the globe, while access to legal international mobility circuits is a scarce resource for most people with non-Western citizenship."[42] Stories about emigration took on outsized meaning in part because of the obstacles placed in people's way.[43] As the scholar Eliane de Latour writes in the context of the Ivory Coast, "Migration is not merely determined by poverty and danger, as one often reads; it also belongs to an epic narrative borne by collective imaginings that turn the North into a place where heroes arise."[44]

In Ghana, people talked about going abroad as seeking "greener pastures."[45] Likening traveling abroad to seeking greener pastures framed contemporary emigration as part of an existing widespread cultural narrative, referencing the Bible phrase in an increasingly evangelical Christian Ghana. The pastoral metaphor also made the desire to emigrate sound natural. The phrase was forward looking and aspirational, and it could serve to mask the underlying violence and inequality propelling people's migrations. Talk of greener pastures, moreover, suggested that the collective project of staying or returning home and engaging in shared civic development that had framed the explicitly temporary migration of been-tos and burgers had disappeared. The context of structural adjustment and perceptions of shrinking opportunities at home served to reinforce a sense of marginality, where there was nothing left to be gained by remaining close to home. Emigration, now understood as an individual choice to propel oneself to betterment and improvement through both luck and hard work, appeared to be a critical survival strategy.

· · · · · ·

Although winning a diversity visa was more a matter of luck than convincing gatekeepers of one's worthiness, aspiring emigrants still sought ways to improve their chances. Enterprising American attorneys were joined by African visa services agents who also hoped to exploit the opportunity.

As the state retreated from the public sphere and state enterprises underwent privatization, urban workers were forced to turn to entrepreneurship and small service-oriented businesses to make money and participate in public life.[46] In 1990, the share of employment in Ghana's informal sector was estimated at 45 percent, but by 1997, a survey found that the proportion had increased to 89 percent.[47] The more people turned to the informal economy to offset the grindingly low incomes global marginalization had brought them, the more urban spaces like Accra became crowded with petty traders and hawkers.

Observing the growing popularity of the idea of going abroad to seek greener pastures, visa services agents moved to capitalize.[48] They set up photography shops to produce the required photographs of applicants

Poster outside Landair Travel and Tours, advertising diversity visa lottery registration, Kumasi, Ghana, 2013. Photograph by author.

at the right size, opened travel agencies to arrange travel plans to the United States, and created other local shops.[49] The lottery thus spurred an industry to serve the needs of applicants not only in the United States but in Ghana and countries like it.

Although the U.S. government did not require a specific visa lottery application form, simply asking applicants to write down the required information on a regular sheet of paper, visa agents devised their own forms, which were then duplicated and circulated far and wide.[50] Agents set up temporary pop-up tents during registration time and draped banners across tables outside nursing schools, training colleges, universities, and churches—"any big place" where people would happen by, one agent said.[51] They printed special banners and canopies with American flags adorning them, proclaiming the lottery open.[52] Placards and posters adorned shops where you could apply.

The same reconfiguration of the economy that had made going abroad more desirable had filled urban spaces with an army of entrepreneurs hawking immigration services. Describing the workers who staffed the mobile centers and improvised offerings, one Ghanaian cyber café operator explained, "They do a lot of things. Some of them would just also engage in other petty business, just to survive. And when this one [the lottery] comes, it is their main catch, their biggest catch."[53]

These transformations stretched beyond any one nation's borders. In Ghana's neighbor to the east, Togo, the visa lottery similarly became a cultural practice. In the words of cultural anthropologist Charles Piot, the visa lottery took on "a life of its own and produced its own excess."[54] Visa entrepreneurialism and the annual lottery together drove a larger shift. In Piot's words, it became "an event that collects stories around it, that feeds a collective fantasy, and that produces reputations and markers of distinction." In this way, the lottery did far more than merely increase the number of visas available on a year-to-year basis—it reshaped culture and ideas across multiple nations.

Yet it is important to bear in mind that the lottery's outsize influence was not an inevitability. Many people would have preferred to stay home, if only the conditions allowed it. To play the lottery was not the same as embracing American global supremacy. Those who played were responding to contingent factors—the political and economic conditions that made leaving home more promising than staying, the historical circumstances that had long placed limits on people's mobility, the circulation of stories that cast migration as a heroic act, and of course, the introduction of a visa lottery that made migrating to the United States a slight, but newly concrete, possibility.

Some visa-lottery-related entrepreneurship was illicit. In Togo, Piot has shown that economic activities surrounding the lottery involved extraordinary invention and duplicity, ranging from identity fabrication to elaborate scams and creative economic practices.[55] In Ghana, too, visa lottery agents reportedly helped clients who had been selected as lottery winners produce false documents, like falsified or stolen bank statements.[56] There are accounts of those offering to arrange last-minute marriages of convenience for individuals with winning entries. A 2001 newspaper article noted that there was a "mad rush" in Ghana to register marriages to strengthen people's chances of winning.[57] In 1998, the *Daily Graphic* reported that "applicants notified that they have been selected to apply for an immigrant visa have been known to either sell their notification letters or give them to relatives."[58] Stories also circulated about clients "marrying" their sisters in order to win, or agents coaching lottery winners to say they worked at specific authorized jobs (like tailoring, which made the list in some years) to pass their consular interviews.[59] People would show up at the U.S. embassy with their sewing machines as proof that they were skilled tailors. Some agents would reportedly register applicants, retain the confirmation numbers, and sell winning entries to those willing to pay—and to fraudulently adopt the identity of the winner.[60]

In 2003 and 2004, in the wake of the 9/11 attacks, American critics of the lottery asserted that the program's susceptibility to fraud carried out by visa agents posed a national security risk for the United States. But any evidence of fraud pointed to a different problem; it was ordinary people in places like Ghana and Togo who were being defrauded or extorted by unscrupulous opportunists. They were more likely to be victims than perpetrators of some plot against the United States.[61] Officials responded to these criticisms by pointing out that the lottery was not a substantial vector for threats. After all, U.S. consular officers already applied extra scrutiny to people from countries like Ghana, rumored for racist reasons to have high rates of fraud, and had been imposing ever more secure measures to screen applicants throughout the 1990s and 2000s.[62] These changes served to provide even more incentives for lottery applicants to seek out paid support to navigate the process—leaving them more vulnerable to fraud. Visa agents then spread stories of their own successes—and their competitors' fraudulent methods—to drum up business and find new clients willing to pay for trustworthy help in a sea of potential scams.

· · · · · ·

The uncertainty that arose from people's experiences at the consular office led people not only to pay for assistance but to attribute their success or failure to *luck* alone. One's fate could be attributed to a higher power: "What is required is attention to detail, luck and lots of luck," said a 1998 opinion piece in the *Daily Graphic* about entering the lottery.[63] Those who won the lottery tended to feel singled out: "If you're lucky, you're selected," explained one diversity visa lottery winner.[64] Not winning the lottery, on the other hand, could be blamed on bad luck or fate. As one repeated registrant said, "I am not somebody who is lucky for such things."[65] Yet, failing to win the lottery was not the same as defeat: "I know one day my time will also come," said another applicant in Kumasi.[66]

The visa lottery's format made intuitive sense in a country with so many lottery booths. In contrast to the queues of hopefuls trying for temporary visitors' visas to the United States who felt they were treated without dignity—their fates in the hands of capricious consular officers whose criteria seemed to change constantly, and who looked at applicants as potential criminals rather than peers—the visa lottery's randomness was a virtue. Better to be sorted by fortune's merry wheel than to be looked askance at by consular officers calculating the odds of a visa overstay. Better still would be to travel without obstacles, the way many Americans do.

When the results of the first lottery in fiscal year 1995 were in, more than 2,000 Ghanaian people had received a U.S. diversity visa. Thousands of Ghanaians had applied, and after the 6.5 million applications were processed, Ghana supplied the eighth-highest number of lottery winners globally and the fourth-highest within Africa. Ghana's substantial population size, estimated to be 17 million in 1995, also gave it an edge, since countries that submitted more applications were allocated more visas.[67]

For all the cultural ferment and entrepreneurial energy devoted to the lottery, 2,000 visas may not seem like many lottery winners. It is a small fraction of the hundreds of thousands of people who receive their green cards every year, and even smaller considered as a percentage of Ghana's population. But because of the lottery, 2,000 individuals' lives were upended by the opportunity to do what so many hoped for: go to America to live their dreams.

11 419 and Scams

· ·

No country received more diversity visas in the first year than Nigeria. Perhaps that was unsurprising, given that Nigeria was by far the most populous country in Africa. If only a minuscule fraction of Nigeria's 107 million people, its estimated population in 1995, played the lottery, the country could still max out its potential share of diversity visas—which it did. The newspapers reported a nationwide "spectacular rush by Nigerians of all walks of life to catch the immigration train."[1] As in Ghana, the announcement of the lottery spurred the emergence of "agencies" that were "making a career from 'helping' prospective immigrants to file the visa applications." Despite U.S. officials issuing warnings against hiring them, these visa services entrepreneurs enticed Nigerians to pay to enter the cost-free lottery.

The lottery was not just for those down on their luck in Nigeria. Newspaper reports said that "doctors, lawyers, engineers, nurses, journalists, oil sector executives, bank executives," and other white-collar workers had opted to try their luck. In some regions "almost every school leaver has either applied for the visa or is currently making efforts to do so." One applicant in Port Harcourt said, "Nigeria is good but America would be better."[2] One's nationality could thus be understood as happenstance, a kind of roulette over which we have little control. Why not trade one for another when the opportunity arises?

In Niger State, west of Abuja and north of Ibadan, the *Sunday Champion* reported in 1996, people showed "almost zero awareness of the lottery," although some believed it to be another "419"—slang for an advance fee fraud scam. Visa agencies' eager participation to make a buck from unwitting, perhaps even ineligible, aspiring emigrants no doubt fueled suspicion about the lottery, a program that could seem too good to be true. Scams seemed to thrive in the conditions of uncertainty that abounded in West Africa in the adjustment era, not to mention in the United States since the 1980s. Yet though Ghana and Togo saw their fair share of lottery-related fraud, American leaders and journalists condemned Nigerians above all others.

No scam was more commonly associated with Nigeria than 419. In 1995, CBS's *60 Minutes* aired a segment on Nigerian fraud, and Gen. Colin Powell told the *New Yorker*, "Nigerians as a group, frankly are marvelous scammers. I mean, it is in their national culture."[3] It was absurd for Powell to associate an entire nation of what was then 100 million people with scam and fraud, suggesting such disorder was primordial and universal. After all, Americans' fondness for housing bubbles, Ponzi schemes, and "deal makers" went unremarked as indicative of cultural failure. When Canter and Siegel spammed the internet, their actions were understood as those of individuals, not a signal of fundamental American rot. Likewise, the Savings and Loan crisis of the late 1980s might have prompted soul searching about U.S. deregulation and political corruption, but antiregulatory efforts, risk taking, and speculation remained firmly entrenched.

However, because Nigerian 419 advance fee fraud became associated with email at the advent of the World Wide Web—and for other, racist reasons associating Africa with loose rules and inequity—the connection remained sticky. Nigerian 419 scammers also played on and took advantage of Westerners' assumptions and stereotypes about what "Africa" is like—a site of war, inequality, poverty, and crisis, as well as rich natural resources—offering the shrewd capitalist "the promise of unfettered accumulation," as scholars of the 419 phenomenon have pointed out.[4] Powell and others failed to see how capitalism and political economy structured the production of scams in the United States, West Africa, and elsewhere toward the end of the twentieth century, and how specific conditions in Nigeria at the time helped spur 419 fraud.

· · · · · ·

The scam known as 419 is named for the relevant number in Nigeria's criminal code.[5] But the scam's premise and format long predate and precede the existence of Nigeria as a country. The target receives a letter, fax, or email from an ostentatiously wealthy "Nigerian Prince." He has a staggering amount of wealth but for whatever reason he needs your help to transfer his money for his use. In exchange for your help *now*—which you can provide by sharing your bank account number and sending a small sum in advance to cover the fees for the transfer—you will be thanked *later* with a generous portion of the fortune, to the tune of millions of dollars. Variations on the scheme may involve a bank manager, a deposed African leader or his widow, or an oil executive. But the game always follows a similar pattern.

The modern form of this scam evolved from an older con known as the Spanish Prisoner. The fraudster would tell their mark that a prominent person has been imprisoned in Spain under a false name, and that they need to raise some funds to bail the person out. Putting up the money in advance will not only help the Spanish prisoner out of an unjust situation, the con man would say, but also allow for the mark to be paid back handsomely later.

Variants of the scam date to the late eighteenth century, but the version that emerged in the 1980s and 1990s, strongly associated with Nigerians, had features rooting it in its historical moment and place. As anthropologist Andrew Apter has shown, 419 was in part the product of Nigeria's oil boom and bust. The scam's notion of illicit fortunes held by Nigerian elites was credible thanks to the uptick in oil revenues in the 1970s. But 419 really took off when Nigeria's president Ibrahim Babangida (whose presidency lasted from 1985 to 1993) deregulated the banking and foreign exchange markets, causing the value of the naira to plummet, in 1990.[6]

Nigerian independence followed a trajectory similar to Ghana's—both became independent from Britain, and both had first presidents who had studied abroad and circulated in Pan-Africanist circles. But oil set Nigeria on a different trajectory. Following the curve of the Gulf of Guinea, Nigeria reaches east and north from the Atlantic, encompassing tremendous geographic diversity and the largest population in Africa. The country gained independence from Britain in 1960, and when it proclaimed itself the Federal Republic of Nigeria in 1963, Nnamdi Azikiwe became the first president.

Nigeria's challenge at independence was to remain united, considering its size and diversity. The country's population was enormous—more than 35 million people at the time and growing. Its regions had been administered separately by the British, and strong regional, ethnic, and religious divisions remained potent after independence. Most states have arbitrary borders, and all nations are invented, but the legacy of colonial governance exacerbated difference here. Political parties formed with regional and ethnic strongholds. The constitution recognized these fissures, and the country's federal structure was designed to allow the different regions to hang together in balance. But the discovery of oil off the coast of the Niger delta region in 1958 was a blessing that became a curse.

In 1967, Nigeria's oil-producing region, Eastern Nigeria, seceded as the Republic of Biafra. By 1968, the production of crude oil had jumped to 415,000 barrels per day, all from Biafra.[7] During the civil war that followed secession, the federal government, under the leadership of Major Gen. Yakubu Gowon, fought the Biafrans and imposed a brutal blockade from July 1967 to January 1970 that exacted an enormous human and financial toll. It has been estimated that between 1 and 3 million people died.[8] It was one of the first televised famines, creating a lasting impression of African humanitarian crisis. Following the defeat of Biafra and the end of the war, Nigeria reunited but trust remained elusive.[9] Oil revenues allowed the federal government to function, contributed to a bloated military and civil service, and enriched the people at the top at the expense of the many. When oil prices remained high, the state could invest in national development, increasing spending on infrastructure and education. But this made these projects vulnerable to fluctuations in prices and the whims of leaders.[10]

Whereas the oil shocks in the 1970s caused skyrocketing prices for imported goods and food for Ghanaians, Nigeria benefited from high prices because it produced and exported oil. Key beneficiaries of this largesse were members of the Nigerian military already leading the country. On paper, Nigeria became the wealthiest country in Africa, and the government dedicated some of these revenues toward a National Development Plan that ran from 1970 to 1976. The era saw increased government spending on infrastructure, an expanded university system, and oil-revenue-funded universal primary education.[11] Gowon enlarged the size of the public service, raised civil service salaries, built schools, and massively augmented military spending.[12] And this spending spree was accompanied, as historian Paul Nugent put it, by a "veritable explosion of corruption."[13]

As Nigeria made oil production central to its economy, agricultural output sharply declined. Rural people were drawn to cities, and the country didn't invest in food production, even for export. Ordinary Nigerians, the majority of whom remained agricultural workers, suffered, especially as the country became dependent on imports to feed the small but growing urban population. The military government grew less accountable to average citizens as it depended on oil revenues rather than taxation to fund itself. The state also used oil revenues to shore up support among patrons. A small class of leaders and entrepreneurs became very wealthy even as most Nigerians suffered.

The Gowon regime became synonymous with corruption and abuse of power, and he lost the respect of both civilian and military leaders. Falling short of his timeline for returning the country to civilian rule, Gowon pushed back the deadline for transition to 1976. In 1975 a group of military officers removed him from power. Gen. Murtala Mohammed became the head of state, with plans to return Nigeria to democratic rule. When he was assassinated in an attempted coup, his second in command, Lt. Olusegun Obasanjo, took power. Obasanjo purged both the military and the civil service to reduce corruption, but he was not particularly successful. He did succeed, though, in transferring power to a new democratically elected civilian administration in 1979.

When the oil boom cooled in the late 1970s and then again in 1981, people across the country suffered the effects of high inflation, widespread unemployment, and petroleum shortages.[14] Rather than curbing corruption or redirecting the economy, the federal government increased borrowing and drained its foreign reserves.[15] In 1983, the country expelled thousands of workers from Ghana, blaming immigrants for Nigeria's economic woes in an event known as "Ghana must go." The state sank deeper in debt as oil prices fluctuated, the economy contracted, and ordinary Nigerians faced devastating austerity measures—all while elites flew on private jets and lived in evident opulence. The military ousted the civilian leadership yet again in 1983 and installed Major Gen. Muhammadu Buhari as the head of state. The military remained in power for another fifteen years.[16]

Like Rawlings in Ghana, Buhari oversaw several austerity measures designed to improve Nigeria's international standing among investors and lenders. He curbed government spending, reduced the civil service, rationed commodities, and expanded the role of police and public surveillance to root out corruption and silence criticism of the regime. In 1985, Major Gen. Ibrahim Babangida (also known as IBB) took power by coup. Babangida paid lip service to civil liberties and encouraged debate in the press, while instituting a flexible transition process that extended his time as head of state. He also launched a homegrown structural adjustment program (SAP) that would enable the country to restructure its foreign debts without appearing to cede agency to the IMF. Nigeria pursued structural adjustment without accepting an IMF loan and pushed back repayment of existing loans to 1991 and later.[17]

For the average Nigerian, the consequences of structural adjustment took the form of increasing unemployment and declining wages. The Nigerian currency, the naira, rapidly lost value, reducing people's purchasing power. Hardships were exacerbated by the removal of government subsidies for necessities, including fuel, and reductions in social services and utilities, especially power, and health and education.[18] These changes promoted a loss of faith in the state. As Apter put it, the forms of government inherited from the colonial state were "gradually emptied" by IBB, "deployed not as means of rational administration and taxation to impose order and control, but as technologies of obstruction and interference."[19] Anti-SAP protests were often met with violence. Babangida dragged his heels as he initiated a transition to democracy between 1986 and 1993, amassing a great personal fortune in the meantime.[20]

· · · · · ·

It took until June 12, 1993, for elections to finally take place—a date of infamy in Nigerian history. Babangida's administration controlled the election tightly; only two candidates were to run. Though observers considered the election free and fair, certainly the most free and fair in Nigeria's postcolonial history, its outcome was anything but. Chief M. K. O. Abiola won 58 percent of the vote, but courts intervened to stop the final release of results, and on June 23 Babangida annulled the election results altogether.

A fierce outcry sparked protests, riots, and demonstrations.[21] Wole Soyinka, one of Nigeria's most prominent public intellectuals, suggested that Nigeria might be "a nation on the verge of extinction."[22] By annulling the results, Soyinka suggested, the military "violently robbed the Nigerian people of their nationhood! A profound trust was betrayed, and only a community of fools will entrust its most sacred possession—nationhood—yet again to a class that has proven so fickle, so treacherous and dishonorable."[23] "IBB=419," a sign at the street protests in Lagos and Ibadan, indicated that Nigerians felt conned by the president who'd held out hope for democratic participation on his unwitting "marks," only to renege at the last moment.[24]

In the unrest, Gen. Sani Abacha declared himself head of state in late 1993.[25] Rather than returning the country to democracy, Abacha violently cracked down on his opposition and consolidated power. When the regime executed Ogoni activist Ken Saro-Wiwa, international protests broke out, resulting in Nigeria's suspension from the Commonwealth of Nations for three years.[26] The United States continued to buy oil from Nigeria, but it also reduced official aid. When he visited Africa in 1998, Clinton pointedly avoided visiting Nigeria.[27] Global isolation caused further economic suffering. The naira's value plummeted, and domestic fuel prices soared. Abacha began planning for tightly controlled elections in 1998 that would keep him as head of state, but then he died suddenly of an apparent heart attack.[28] In 1999, Olusegun Obasanjo was sworn in as civilian president. Although his economic reforms over the next eight years improved Nigeria's standing in the world, any gains continued to be distributed unevenly.

That the 419 scam thrived in these conditions is no surprise. Unsolicited emails from Nigerian oil executives or princes promising a big payoff are hardly more absurd than the kinds of wheeling and dealing that enriched the few at the expense of the many in Nigeria in the 1980s and 1990s. Indeed, some Nigerians called the 419 scams a "cheap knockoff" of the examples set by Nigeria's national leaders.[29] The mysteries of capitalist accumulation (how some people get rich while others don't) can be bewildering, and the 419 scams provide a narrative answer.

People get rich by having the luck to receive opportunities *and* having the courage and savvy to seize them. "I go chop your dollar," a song by Nkem Owoh from a 2005 Nollywood film, suggests "419 is just a game / You are the loser, I am the winner."[30]

· · · · · ·

As quality of life and governance collapsed in Nigeria in the 1980s and 1990s, people with the means to do so, particularly professionals, sought to go abroad to seek greener pastures. But they faced obstacles. Consular officers looked upon their visa applications with suspicion and scrutiny. Being associated with global fraud provided an extra layer of humiliation. It was especially painful to be excluded based on nationality when so many Nigerians felt betrayed by a country that ignored their needs, aspirations, and demands for accountable leaders.

At the same time, the visa lottery undoubtedly unleashed new and creative forms of fraud and scams, with visa services agents making unfulfillable promises, pledges to game the system, and recognizable ploys to profit from Nigerians' desire to depart the country. At their least exploitative, visa agents charged for their services—up to 1500 naira for the application at a time when the postage to send the letter cost only forty naira.[31] Reports suggested discount rates for students: "For students, the rate is N350 at Progress Opportunities Limited, Akoka. At Dateline USA, with a branch at Shop 4, University of Lagos Shopping Complex, it is N750 for singles and N950 for a family application. At Afrolinks, it is N1,200."[32] A 2000 article reported "tantalizing advertisements with some listing the names of some winners in the recent edition are finding their ways into newspaper pages while handbills and leaflets adorn the walls of Lagos Streets."[33] A chain of Nigerian banks partnered with a visa agency to lend credibility to the lottery and expand access to clients throughout the country.[34] A 1997 ad adorned with the image of the Statue of Liberty, an American flag, and the Great Seal, featuring attorney Uche Mgabraho in conjunction with a

Houston, Texas–based law firm, proclaimed the lottery the "gateway to the United States of America" and promised a 25 percent lottery success rate for an audience in Lagos, Nigeria.[35] It was an absurd promise, given the number of people likely to enter the lottery and the statutory limit on per-country visas. Another firm, Libertylink, promised to hand-deliver applications from Nigeria to the United States in its 1997 ads.[36]

Yet even as abundant fraud swirled around the lottery, the program was rapidly embraced by the Nigerian public. As the *Sunday Champion* magazine described it in 1996, it was quickly accepted "as a credible process, as almost everyone can point to some distant relative or close friend who is currently in the U.S. courtesy of the visa lottery."[37] The desire to go to the United States, sometimes called "God's own country," had reached a "fever pitch." "Civil servants, students, doctors, journalists, lawyers, accountants, other professionals, traders, even street urchins, teachers, etc have literally fallen over each other in their hundreds of thousands to send their applications" within the deadline, the story claimed.[38] "You can say that one is going in search of greener pasture. Yes!" one young man told the *Sunday Champion*.[39] The editor in chief of *The Week* wrote, the "US Visa Lottery has come to enjoy something close to religious followership in our abundantly blessed country. So irresistible is its lure that even directors-general in the government service are said to be secret worshippers on its altar."[40] Eventually more than 60,000 people in Nigeria would win the lottery and receive immigrant visas to the United States, helping make Nigeria the largest source of African U.S. immigration. In 2015, due to this success, it became the first African nation to "graduate" from the visa lottery by sending so many immigrants that it was no longer considered "underrepresented."[41] The lottery's popularity among Nigerians signaled growing dismay and dwindling faith in Nigeria itself.

12 Post Office Rumors

The lottery in Nigeria generated tremendous activity. A cover story in the *Sunday Champion* magazine ran under the headline "Nigerians Rush for America." The media reported on the strain this placed on Nigeria's postal service, "stretched" by the challenge of processing hundreds of thousands of applications that overwhelmed local facilities.[1] NIPOST officials in Akure, a modest-sized city in southwest Nigeria, reported more than a hundred lottery applicants daily—"an unprecedented influx"—clamoring for information.[2] Benin City, in Edo State in the South, reported "an unprecedented boom in stamp sales as thousands of citizens rush to purchase postage stamps needed to mail their entries for the much publicised immigrant visa lottery."[3] Such news items indicated that the public was eager to seize the opportunity to emigrate. But they also reflected anxieties that Nigerian institutions weren't up to the task of facilitating lottery participation. Soon rumors spread that NIPOST officials were *destroying* lottery applications to thwart Nigerians' attempts to depart and to erase material evidence of Nigerians' dissatisfaction at home. It seemed not only that the post office was struggling to perform its basic functions but that the state was actively sabotaging lottery applicants.

Such rumors were not unique to Nigeria. Rumors circulated elsewhere in Africa about the role played by the post office in the U.S. lottery. Stories that the postal service was failing to process or deliver applications, exploiting customers to raise funds, or conspiring with government officials to destroy applications exposed deeper critiques and anxieties. "Rumours have a way of spreading faster than truth in these parts. Sleek, like hot flames, they disseminate their warmth and quietly but surely roast up everything in their wake," the Cameroonian author and U.S. professor Makuchi writes in her story "American Lottery."[4]

Stories and rumors about the post office and the visa lottery spoke to Nigerians' and other Africans' frustrations with states that no longer seemed concerned with or capable of serving ordinary people. Instead, states themselves and elites at the top were growing rich at the expense of citizens whose daily lives could be punishing. In some cases, the swirling rumors prompted states to shore up capacity and improve mail service, at least temporarily, to avoid embarrassment. Spokespeople for the postal services were pushed to speak out against rumors they claimed were unfounded. In other cases, the rumors reflected and spurred creative efforts to circumvent state services, by facilitating lottery entries through private mail companies or through tapping into individuals' own transnational networks.

Such rumors were so widespread at the time that they also left a paper trail in newspaper articles, cartoons, visa agents' advertisements, and letters to the editor. Whether the rumors of postal sabotage can be supported with archival evidence is an open question. But it is telling that Nigerians, Sierra Leoneans, and others believed them, acted on them, and saw postal services' mishandling of visa lottery applications as evidence of deeper state failures. As the historian Luise White argued, the power of a rumor "lies in the contradictions it brings together and explains."[5] Reliance on rumor also signaled distrust in official sources of information; a 1983 survey in Ghana, for instance, "found that citizens were more inclined on principle to believe rumour than official news."[6] During the 1990s, the relationship between the Nigerian state and citizens reached a nadir. Any faith in the social contract or the notion that the state would or could provide basic services—something that had seemed perhaps within reach during the oil boom—had collapsed. Babangida had hollowed the structures of governance while imposing structural adjustment. The crisis of the failed June 12 election had given way to yet another military authoritarian ruler.

That such rumors flourished during the visa lottery also reflected how the United States exported and reinforced antistatism. Even as the lottery reaffirmed the importance of national citizenship in a global age, positioning U.S. citizenship as the ultimate prize, uncertainty about whether states could even facilitate people's applications fueled larger doubts about state capacity under neoliberalism. Even the United States postal service was implicated in the rumors—it was said to be destroying mail sent from Nigeria, including its visa lottery entries. This prompted people to put trust in private agents, even predatory ones, conditioning them to be consumers, not citizens. Yet the salience of state citizenship could be felt whenever telltale-green Nigerian passports brought looks of suspicion and scrutiny at airport counters, consulates, and banks.[7]

· · · · · ·

The post office is one of the most persistent symbols of national government in most people's lives. In the United States, founder Ben Franklin famously oversaw mail delivery before and after the revolution, recognizing the centrality of the institution to the emerging state. In the twentieth century, Franklin Roosevelt's New Deal built post offices, establishing in even remote villages a physical symbol of the federal government itself. At the time, a special section of the U.S. Treasury Department recruited unemployed artists to adorn the buildings with murals depicting national ideals, linking the state and nation in these physical spaces.[8] These murals can still be found in U.S. post offices today, and mail carriers making the rounds may be the most prominent emissaries of the federal government's reach in Americans' daily lives. Because of this, calls for privatization and delays in mail service during the 2020 U.S. presidential elections were understood to be a threat to the operation of democracy itself— perhaps an intentional one.[9]

During colonial rule in Africa, European administrators established communications infrastructures to secure their political power in the colonies. Colonial-era infrastructures often built on existing precolonial systems of communications established by local rulers and entailed the cooperation of chiefs and local intermediaries. For example, the British used flag post mail relay runners like human telephone lines to share information and administer the colony of British Southern Cameroon.[10] Mail runners were paid wages for their labor, meaning that they could buy consumer goods, which elevated their social status. Runners' access to modernity was predicated on their physical mobility, as they moved mail from one flag post to another. And their footpaths laid the groundwork for future roads, telegraphs, and placement of post offices, as the scholars Walter Gam Nkwi and Mirjam de Bruijn have shown.

After independence, African states inherited and built on colonial communications infrastructure. Leaders used public symbols of nationhood to consolidate their new states. They replaced images of the British monarchy and commodity goods with more aspirational images.[11] President Kwame Nkrumah issued postage stamps in 1957 to commemorate Ghana's independence, and in 1966 to mark the completion of the Akosambo dam and the Volta River Project, his major push to industrialize the country.[12] He understood that postage stamps could serve as "tiny transmitters of the dominant ideologies of the state destined for the imagined community of the nation," as the scholar Igor Cusack put it.[13] When Biafra seceded from Nigeria between 1967 and 1970, authorities there swiftly issued banknotes and postage stamps.[14] Despite the existence since 1874 of a uniform framework for coordinating between postal systems and facilitating international mail, the postal service remains a project of a national scale.[15]

The British had established a postal service in Lagos beginning in 1852 to serve the needs of the empire. At independence in 1960, Nigeria's federal government inherited the colonial mail infrastructure, which included some 176 post offices. But Nigeria's postal service was plagued by a reputation for inefficiency; a mail system built to strengthen British colonial power was ill suited to the task of serving Nigerians' needs. In 1966, the postal service department was made "quasi-commercial" to encourage more efficiency and responsiveness to the public—anticipating similar moves elsewhere.[16] Then, the era of structural adjustment brought new challenges, austere budgets, and further privatization schemes. Private courier services began operating in Africa in the mid-1980s, breaking up state monopolies on mail services and providing an alternative for those who could afford to pay. Competition and state divestment may have worsened the reliability of state postal services while diverting revenue to private companies, exacerbating the problems with mail delivery and tanking the reputation of national postal services and other public enterprises. By 2000, DHL enjoyed a 53 percent market share on the continent.[17]

The U.S. visa lottery's operation depended on the reliability of national postal services, which Nigerians and others had come to regard warily. The lottery itself, of course, was designed to be straightforward. Applicants simply had to write down their name, date and place of birth, and mailing address, and enclose a passport-size photograph in a standard envelope with their name and country written on the upper left-hand corner of the envelope.[18] But the mailing of applications from one country to another aroused anxieties about bureaucratic obstacles and state capacity. Applications received too early or after the last day of the lottery entry period would be disqualified. Timing was a problem.

But the larger issue was that applications had to be mailed through national postal carriers to get to the official post office box in New Hampshire, which was operated by the United States Postal Service. You couldn't simply send something by FedEx and have it delivered.[19]

That left African visa lottery applicants with two main choices. They could send entries to relatives or contacts already in the United States and have them place the forms in America's blue mailboxes.[20] By stipulating that it would only accept applications through the official mail, the United States inadvertently favored applicants with friends or family already in the United States—ironic given the program's aim at making visas available to people without such ties.

The alternative was for visa applicants to try their luck through their national postal services. But these were loudly rumored to be inefficient and unreliable, part of the larger breakdown of state services and the promise of the social contract.

As a result, visa agents preyed upon clients' skepticism about the reliability of their national postal services to drum up private business. Companies promised to hand deliver applications from Nigeria to the United States.[21] A February 1996 ad warned against depending on NIPOST: "Many forms did not get to the appropriate destination due to postal delays" in the previous lottery, it said. One private firm guaranteed that Nigerian visa lottery applications would be received by the United States on time—for a fee of 500 naira.[22] The postage itself should have cost only forty naira, so the promise of more reliable service came at a premium.[23] The company's general manager also told the *Sunday Champion* that his aim was to help Nigerians who had been disqualified in the past due to postal delays.[24] Some agents promised fast delivery to the United States by using private courier services, without mentioning that mail sent by courier would be rejected at its destination.[25] Others specified that they would send applications via private courier to a contact point in the United States, after which point the applications would be delivered to New Hampshire through the official U.S. mail.[26]

While the visa agents may have fanned worries to drum up business, anxieties about the postal service predated their efforts.[27] One woman complained, "You can never trust NIPOST with its laxity."[28] In an era of reduced public services, NIPOST served as a rare, lone outpost connecting citizens to the federal government—and not one that inspired confidence. But it wasn't just that the post office was a site of perceived incompetence, corruption, and failure to serve the public.

Rumors also spread that NIPOST was mishandling visa applications because of direct interference by the federal government. Although the government denied it, some believed that it actually ordered the postal service to *intentionally* destroy Nigerians' visa applications. The goal? To block people from departing and to suppress such visible evidence of the scale of Nigerians seeking to leave a country that was failing to provide them opportunities.[29]

Responding to the proliferation of private agents claiming that only they could be trusted to deliver lottery applications, postal officials fought back with a whisper campaign of their own. They claimed that several visa services firms had collected applicants' money but then dumped their applications, unstamped, at local post offices.[30]

In time, the state took action. As early as March 1996, the *Daily Champion* reported that a Lagos-based visa agency had been shuttered by the state task force on telecommunications and postal offenses, with its directors arrested.[31] The firm, the task force reported, had been operating a courier service without a license and had deceived customers with false promises to deliver the mail to the United States. Then, as part of an apparent public relations campaign, NIPOST announced a new strategy for processing 1997's lottery applications, creating dedicated lottery mailbags in all post offices, to be sent via airmail daily to the United States.[32] Contrary to rumors, NIPOST claimed it was sending out ninety-two bags of visa lottery applications daily.[33] NIPOST spokespeople promised to streamline the process, to alleviate the frustration of spending hours queueing up to mail lottery applications. NIPOST reported that it handled 2.5 million letters during the 1996 registration period.[34]

Yet even reports about the volume of visa lottery mail served to feed rumors that NIPOST was capitalizing on the program to make money through the sale of postage stamps. A cartoon in the *Daily Champion* included a figure, labeled NIPOST, that carried a sack labeled "US Visa Lottery Bonanza" and headed toward the bank.[35] The image evoked corruption and fraud and suggested that the national postal service was enriching itself at the expense of the people and the nation's development.

Nigerians were all too aware that their country had become synonymous with corruption, from the Gowon regime in the 1970s, through the Buhari and Babangida years of the 1980s, and culminating in the 1990s under Gen. Sani Abacha. Abacha, his family, and his government ministers embezzled more than US$3 billion in the five years of his reign.[36] Charges of corruption and inefficiency plagued the public sector. The acronym for the Nigerian electricity company, NEPA, stood for Nigerian Electric Power Authority, but people deemed it "Never Expect Power Always."[37] That the post office now seemed to be profiting from Nigerians' desire to escape the country appeared to be yet another example of the unfair, uneven distribution of resources, and it evoked the constant specter of people gaming every possible system to get rich. It did not seem to matter that rumors that NIPOST was exploiting and benefiting from the lottery were at odds with anxiety that the post office was incapable of handling the volume of mail. The coexistence of these rumors reflected growing certainty that fraud and deception compromised every public good.

Nigerian rumors about the malfeasance of postal workers even extended to the United States. In 1998 and 1999, the United States Postal Service reportedly destroyed 2 million letters from Nigeria entering the United States at JFK airport. These were supposedly 419s, advance fee fraud letters, sent to America to find unwitting marks in the days before 419 became more thoroughly email based. But U.S. efforts to crack down on 419 fraud letters may have also destroyed Nigerians' legitimate visa lottery applications.[38] The United States was thus simultaneously inviting Nigerians to enter the visa lottery and luring talented Nigerians to its shores while callously lumping all Nigerians together as potential scammers and destroying their mail. Such rumors helped exacerbate deep anxieties among lottery applicants, driving them to seek paid assistance to improve their odds, to overcome obstacles at home and abroad.

· · · · · ·

Nigerians were not the only ones who worried that their government ordered the national post office to destroy visa lottery applications. In Ghana, several unsuccessful lottery applicants accused the postal service of destroying their applications on government orders. A Ghana Post spokesperson claimed that the "government does not interfere with our work in whatever form," adding that it had sent 126 mailbags of over 200,000 applications to the United States.[39] Arguing that the visa lottery presented a rare opportunity to make money, a Ghana Post official wrote to the *Ghanaian Chronicle*, explaining "we can, therefore, not afford to kill the golden chick that lays the golden eggs for us."[40] Speculation persisted, however, about the collaboration between Ghana's government and the Ghanaian postal service to destroy visa lottery application forms.[41] When the results of that year's lottery (DV-99) were announced, Ghana had 5,500 winners selected, of whom about 1,800 successfully received green cards, the lowest number since the program's inception.[42] Whether the Ghanaian postal service actually delivered all entries on time or failed to, the persistence of rumors about the government's ill intentions signaled Ghanaians' feelings that the postal service was corrupt and that the state was failing them.

In Cameroon, a short story by the anglophone writer Juliana Makuchi Nfah-Abbenyi highlighted anxiety about the power of the postal service to shape the lottery's operation. In "American Lottery," Makuchi describes a character playing the lottery in the 1990s. At first, protagonist Paul does not quite believe the stories about the program. His brother calls it "some bogus thing about an American immigration lottery that would grant permanent residence to thousands of aliens!"[43] But Paul knows "this was one lottery he had to win."[44] Determined that his application be delivered properly, Paul goes to hand it personally to a friend working at the post office. "There had been too many rumours about instructions handed down to postal workers by the Head of State himself, to withhold all DV-applications. 'Let them leave for America only after the dateline for the receipt of applications,' the order had allegedly stressed."[45] Here the state was not only failing to provide but also putting up obstacles to migration, something people conceived of as the surest path to a more prosperous life. Paul gives his application to a different postal worker, one who unbeknownst to him harbors a grudge against his friend. To exact revenge, she fails to file the application on time. Thus, it is not governmental interference but institutional, and interpersonal, failures that cause his opportunity to disappear.

Such frustrations seemed mild compared with what happened at the post office in Freetown, Sierra Leone, a country embroiled in a brutal civil war from 1991 to 2002. In February 1997, a group of Sierra Leoneans protested outside the post office after bags of visa lottery applications—around 5,000 applications in total—were found dumped in the river and destroyed. While the post office denied destroying the forms, police reported finding them floating near a wharf in the Sierra Leone River. Salpost, the national postal service, had been accused of tampering with the mail in the past. But tensions ran especially high during the war.[46] "I think the Post Office destroyed the forms as the government does not want us to leave Sierra Leone despite the massive hardship and unemployment," one applicant charged.[47] "I had nurtured hope of winning a chance to stay in the United States. Now that hope has been dashed," said another.[48] Armed police were sent to guard the post office after the gathering crowd reportedly threatened to burn it down; some were reportedly throwing stones at the building. Nigeria's *Daily Champion* reported that fifteen people were hospitalized after the police opened fire and shot tear gas at the crowd. Sierra Leone's president Tejan Kabbah reportedly spoke on the radio, appealing to the "rioters" to stop. One protester said he had entered the visa lottery because his family had been displaced by the war in Sierra Leone.[49] The Associated Press reported that up to seventeen people were treated for injuries they sustained at the protest, some with gunshot wounds. Although the police denied that anybody had been injured, the hospital reported that one man had died by gunshot.[50]

In May 1997, after the president of Sierra Leone was forced into exile in neighboring Guinea, the United States evacuated hundreds of Americans and closed the embassy.[51] In the chaos, there was confusion about the visa lottery. The lottery had gone forward worldwide as usual between February 3 and March 5, 1997. In September, the United States announced that it had selected around 100,000 winners globally who were now eligible to apply for the visa itself. The winners selected included 5,364 Sierra Leoneans.[52] With the U.S. embassy in Freetown closed (even the consular section remained closed through 2005), where would visa lottery winners go to apply for their visas?[53]

Eventually the United States established procedures for processing diversity visas under conditions like this, advising Sierra Leonean lottery winners to apply for their visas in Dakar, Senegal, in 1999.[54] But in 1997 no such plans were widely publicized.

Some 700 Sierra Leoneans decided to apply for their diversity visas in Accra, in Ghana. They traveled overland and by air, and almost immediately they encountered a problem. Without appointments, hundreds formed a queue outside the U.S. consular office that persisted for several weeks. "Everyday, we try to put in our documents for consideration but security personnel at the embassy just refuse to let us in. They tell us that they have been instructed not to allow us in," one of the men told the newspapers. Another claimed that the group came to Accra at the invitation of the United States. "We came here because of a letter signed by Ms Barbara Johnson, the Consul in Accra, but it seems she does not want to see us," said twenty-seven-year-old Iddriss Sawaneh.[55] Several news reports echoed this claim.[56] The U.S. embassy in Accra acknowledged that some of the Sierra Leoneans were bona fide visa lottery winners, and it said it had processed thirty-two successful applications.[57] Soon the U.S. embassy announced that all diversity visas for that fiscal year had been awarded—leaving those waiting in line too late to benefit.[58] Later, of the Sierra Leoneans who remained in Ghana after the end of the visa registration period, some 196 were relocated to a refugee camp in the western region of Ghana.[59] Eventually, 500 Sierra Leoneans received diversity visas in the DV-1998 lottery.

· · · · · ·

If the Sierra Leoneans had come at the invitation of the United States, Ghanaian state officials claimed never to have been informed. The *Ghanaian Times* reported on the unexpected entry of Sierra Leoneans through several prominent stories over weeks. "Many Sierra Leonean refugees have flocked here without the Ghana Government being informed," reported one story.[60] Once in Ghana, people who might be categorized as refugees, or perhaps sojourners en route to the United States, needed housing and food, something neither the United States nor Ghana felt obligated to provide.[61] An editorial suggested that the United States had merely feigned surprise at the influx of Sierra Leoneans, arguing that processing Sierra Leone's diversity visa applications in Accra had been the United States' plan. The editorial further complained that the lottery fostered a "brain drain" from Ghana and was done in secrecy.[62]

While the situation was extremely difficult for the Sierra Leoneans who had fled their homes seeking an audience at the U.S. embassy, the coverage in the Ghanaian press mostly focused on what this incident meant for Ghanaians. As Samuel Fury Childs Daly wrote about the "Ghana must go" border expulsion, "migration and attempts to control it were part of what *made* African nation states in the twentieth century, giving a social and political reality to states created by administrative dicta."[63] When Sierra Leoneans showed up in Accra, some Ghanaians interpreted it as a sign that their state was unable to manage its borders, something that was particularly infuriating at a moment when Ghanaians felt themselves restricted by those very borders.

The episode also seemed to reveal Ghana's lack of power in its relationship with the United States. The arrangement to process Sierra Leoneans' diversity visa applications appeared to have been made without any meaningful input from the Ghanaian government. The *Ghanaian Times* coverage highlighted the way Ghana's sovereignty had been compromised, with its capacity to manage migrants limited and undermined.

Through complaints about the postal service, people expressed their distrust of government capacity—to deliver the mail, to support people's ability to participate in the lottery, and to manage borders and diplomatic relationships on equal terms. Each of these incidents and attendant rumors reflected Africans' frustrations with governments that were incapable of providing basic services and states that wouldn't attend to citizens' core needs. People not only distrusted their local post offices. They also saw the postal services' failures as systemic.

Humiliation at the post office and in the conceptual visa queue—in an age celebrated as one of mobility and jet-setting—made people feel powerless. Migrating had come to feel like the only path to a decent life, and obstacles to it came not only from racist gatekeepers abroad but also from people's home countries, unable or unwilling to facilitate their participation in the lottery.

13 Falling Bush

· ·

At the end of the twentieth century, emigration from Africa became more urgent due to economic pressures, as well as neoliberal reforms that diminished states' capacity to provide public services. In the early days of postcolonial independence, going abroad temporarily was often talked about as a way of gaining education and experiences to better serve the nation. But because of structural adjustment and dwindling faith in the state to provide, migration—or at least, the idea of migration—came to seem like a lifeline. Policies of austerity and privatization drew African states into global relationships that encouraged market solutions to social problems, with the pain of adjustment being felt by ordinary people. While complaints about "brain drain" suggested that departing was unpatriotic, states were only reinforcing the idea that individuals had to look out for themselves.

That is the broad story of the context for the introduction of the visa lottery, with its proliferation of economic activity, entrepreneurship, and luck. But it is also perhaps oversimplified. Most people didn't and don't leave home, and those who did migrated within their own country or within the region. And not everybody could qualify for the U.S. visa lottery, let alone want to take on the risks involved with emigrating across the world to the United States if they did happen to win. As I tried to understand how this history unfolded, I became interested by the example offered by Cameroon, a country that is touted as "Africa in miniature," due to its geographic and demographic diversity. Before the lottery's introduction, the population of Cameroonian immigrants in the United States was tiny. For the first years of the visa lottery, Cameroonians won only a few hundred diversity visas each year. Yet, after 2008 Cameroonians were routinely issued over a thousand diversity visas annually. Over the lottery's lifetime, the country joined the top ten diversity-visa-receiving countries in Africa. Why did the lottery gain in popularity as it did?

Part of the answer, I found, lies in Cameroon's colonial and postcolonial history, and the legacy of official bilingualism. Even as new pressures—the economic circumstances of the 1990s, coincident political fractures—made the idea of departing the country in search of better opportunities abroad more urgent, the way people imagined departure varied significantly. In particular, the linguistic fault line that divided the country revealed different evolving attitudes about departing Cameroon and traveling abroad.

· · · · · ·

Cameroon neighbors Nigeria to the east and stretches from the coast at the curve of the Gulf of Guinea to the Sahel in the north and Central Africa to the east. Before World War I, it was occupied as a German colony. Then, after the war, the territory was divided into two League of Nations mandates, with a western strip ruled by Britain and an eastern section under French rule. As elsewhere in Africa, formal European rule came to an end heading into the 1960s. But unlike countries that ousted only one European power, Cameroon ousted two. Following an armed struggle that left tens of thousands of civilians dead, French Cameroun gained formal independence from France in 1960 as the Cameroun Republic.[1] Former prime minister Ahmadou Ahidjo, a French speaker (francophone) from the north, became the country's first elected president. Part of British-ruled Cameroons opted to join the Cameroun Republic rather than neighboring English-speaking Nigeria. In October 1961, together the country became the Federal Republic of Cameroon with a new constitution.[2]

Many newly independent African countries retained the languages of former colonial powers in some formal capacity, while dozens, or hundreds, of African languages were spoken as well. Cameroon was unusual in retaining more than one European language. At independence the country embraced a formal policy of bilingualism, retaining both French and English as official languages. Officials emphasized the importance of unity within the country and suggested that the country serve as a "bridge between French-speaking and English-speaking Africa."[3]

In practice, though, francophone leaders far outnumbered anglophones, and few people spoke both languages fluently.[4] About a quarter of the population was anglophone. Most national government functions took place in French. The country's two biggest cities, Yaoundé (the capital) and Douala (the financial capital), were both in firmly francophone regions. As anglophones would continually point out, Cameroon's independence was shaped by the strong ties retained by the country's leadership with the French government, including its cooperation with the French to militarily suppress the nationalist movement.[5] Emblematic of the continuing relationship, Cameroon adopted as its currency the Central African CFA franc. "CFA" had stood for "Colonies françaises d'Afrique" when the currency was first introduced in 1945. Although it later signified "Communauté française d'Afrique," and postindependence took on another new name, "Communauté Financière Africaine," its value was always pegged to the French franc, and then after 1999, the euro.[6]

The divisions between anglophone and francophone Cameroonians were not necessarily about ancient or ethnic rivalries but about ongoing, active debates about how to share power and resources and ensure that the nation's political and economic structures served its diverse groups of people. Since independence, Cameroonians wrestled with the difficult question of how territories, previously administered separately, could operate together. This question came to the fore in 1972, when a new constitution replaced the country's initially loose federal structure with a unitary state. With a stronger central government, the country adopted the new name United Republic of Cameroon.[7] It would now contain seven provinces, two of them anglophone: Northwest, with Bamenda as its capital, and Southwest, with Buea as its capital. The other five were majority French-speaking. In 1983, some francophone provinces were split up, resulting in a total of ten provinces, just two anglophone. Given the state's close economic and political ties with France, anglophones had reason to worry that their needs wouldn't be addressed by a state dominated by francophones.

Much like his counterparts elsewhere, Ahidjo, Cameroon's first president, restricted civil liberties and eliminated all political parties but his own to cement power.[8] Dissent wasn't tolerated, and the state engaged in press censorship as the French sent military and financial aid to support Ahidjo's rule. With the French military, in 1964 he defeated a nationalist movement that had initially targeted the French colonial administration but continued to fight the ruling regime after power was formally transferred to Cameroonians. Later, when he voluntarily stepped down from the presidency in 1982, Ahidjo retained chairmanship of the sole political party, the Cameroon National Union (CNU), until going into exile in 1983. His constitutional successor was Paul Biya, a francophone from the south who had been serving as prime minister since 1975. Biya renamed the country the Republic of Cameroon and called for presidential elections in 1984 and again in 1988. He was reelected. But the absence of a coup was not a sign of healthy democracy; only one political party was permitted to exist—Biya's. The CNU became known as the Cameroon People's Democratic Movement (CPDM) in 1985.

Though Biya continued the repressive tactics of his predecessor, Cameroon enjoyed something like political stability and economic growth, at least relative to neighboring countries. Ahidjo, and then Biya, pursued a policy of planned liberalism, with the state funding projects on health, education, infrastructure, and various public-owned enterprises. Until the mid-1980s, oil revenues supported many of Biya's state programs, which he touted as a New Deal for Cameroon.[9]

But good fortune declined in the 1980s. The price of oil dropped, and the value of Cameroon's currency, the CFA franc, fell against the U.S. dollar. With less income, the state bureaucracy appeared bloated, and Cameroon began appearing at the top of lists ranking corruption in the world.

Like other African states, Cameroon complied with the World Bank and IMF's recommendations to avert economic collapse and restructure the nation's debts. Beginning in 1987, it adopted structural adjustment programs designed to spur investment and increase efficiency. The World Bank recommended that Cameroon reduce its civil service, restructure its banks, and privatize its many state-owned enterprises. By the late 1980s, Cameroon trimmed its national budget, terminated subsidies for university students, and ended many amenities that had come to be expected by civil servants.

In the early 1990s, Biya continued these measures, cutting public sector salaries and jobs; and in 1994, the CFA was devalued by 50 percent. The stated objective was to improve the performance of African cash crop exports, but one effect was to make consumer goods less affordable for Cameroonians.[10] As one commentator wrote of these policies, "The bulk of Cameroonians have seen their income and standards of living plummeting year after year."[11]

Cameroon's economic difficulties revealed and exacerbated internal political tensions. In 1990, fueled both by economic problems at home and by the international wave of pro-democracy movements that emerged with the collapse of the Soviet Union, Cameroonians pushed to create opposition parties to Biya's CPDM, the single party of the single party state. While some of these efforts were suppressed violently, soon Biya conceded under pressure from international donors that opposition parties could be legalized. But Biya ignored calls for a national conference to revise the constitution, and he imposed a state of emergency that put seven out of ten provinces under temporary military administration.[12]

In response, in 1991, the National Coordination of Opposition Parties and Associations organized the Opération Villes Mortes, or the "Dead Cities" campaign. It was a movement of civil disobedience, including a general strike, boycotts, and refusals to pay taxes.[13] Villes Mortes combined economic activism and political aims. While several political parties signed an agreement with the government, ending the strike and paving the way for the 1992 elections, the government's access to external financial support from France and the IMF allowed it to avoid deeper concessions.[14]

Several parties were permitted to participate in the 1992 elections, but the elections themselves were marred by irregularities. Protests, particularly in the anglophone regions where calls for democratization were strongest, were forcibly suppressed.[15] Opposition parties didn't unite against Biya and the CPDM, often boycotting elections, and Biya and his party remained in power.

Throughout the decade, anglophones would variously call for secession, greater regional autonomy, better representation in national politics, and more power for anglophone citizens.[16] Because Biya was himself a francophone whose strong ties to France helped entrench his power, and because the government appeared to favor French-speaking Cameroonians, anglophones acutely felt the threat of oppression and their lack of access to political and economic power.[17]

While language policy had always been problematic under the rubric of bilingualism, it was not until the political liberalization of the early 1990s that these issues became a prominent and ongoing national crisis.[18] The marginalization of anglophones came to dominate politics and was characterized, tellingly, as the "anglophone problem." Among the grievances of anglophones was that the Southwest region had failed to benefit adequately from its oil reserves. A 1998 front-page story in the independent French-language paper *Le Messager* protested that the state was selling the country to France, referring to the dozen state enterprises undergoing privatization, most likely to be sold to francophone or French interests.[19] But Biya hung onto power, handily winning elections in 1997, 2004, and 2011 after suspending his own term limit.[20]

· · · · · ·

Emigration was frequently an important option for anglophones, from the earliest days of the federation between anglophone and francophone Cameroon. Some anglophones who went abroad were known as "been tos," meaning that the person had "been to" the United States, the United Kingdom, or elsewhere. As in other parts of West Africa, the term was associated with people who went abroad to study and then returned home.[21] When they returned, educated elites often had their choice of job in government, working in the civil services, or working for a state-owned enterprise like Cameroon Airlines.[22] Economic prospects for professionals were generally fine until the mid-1980s, so returning home was appealing. But soon, economic pressures combined with political tensions to shift the decision-making calculus around migration. By the early 1990s, the urgency of departing Cameroon intensified, especially for anglophones who faced on-going repression and marginalization. A new phenomenon of permanent emigration took hold.

It became so widely discussed that anglophones embraced a new expression to describe going abroad to the West. The expressions "bushfalling," "to fall bush," and "bushfaller" drew on a Pidgin expression. "Bush," a word for "wilderness" or "farm," meant the place you go to hunt or harvest food, beyond your home village. The verb "fall" meant to "jump onto" or "rush into" something. To "fall bush" once meant rushing to the farm to do the necessary work of sowing seeds, harvesting, and providing labor at key times, or heading to the wilderness to hunt. "One never returns from the bush with empty hands," the anthropologist Michaela Pelican explained.[23] People began using the expression to mean traveling abroad—to the "white-man kontri," or the West—to work and reap material rewards for it.[24] The phrase also evoked adventure seeking, spirit, and grit. The scholar Maybritt Jill Alpes wrote, "A person who has traveled to bush has to hustle, which means that he or she will accept any kind of work to be able to make money."[25] One Cameroonian man who hoped to emigrate explained to me, "Falling bush—it means that you are going to the white man's world."[26] Bushfallers was also the name chosen for an English-language magazine targeting readers who hoped to travel abroad.[27] The verb "rapidly shoved its way into our sonorous lingua franca in the 1990s, when the phenomenon of Cameroonians emigrating to the West attained new proportions," a Cameroon Post magazine article explained.[28]

For anglophones, bushfalling reflected a kind of aspiration and hope. It indicated that going abroad is the "big dream," as Alpes described it. She also described how bushfalling became a means of fulfilling social obligations rather than fleeing them; bushfallers were expected to send back money or bring back experiences to serve their families and communities. Godlove Song, a technician at an internet café in Bamenda in the Northwest region, explained, "We are struggling. And that's why you see many anglophones, they just love leaving, just moving. The anglophones are a minority, and a lot of them are working hard."[29] The anthropologist and writer Francis Nyamnjoh described bushfalling as "a metaphor for the aggressive search for salvation through migration," though not one without ambiguity.[30]

The language used by francophones to describe emigration revealed even more ambiguity. Francophones had generally assessed their place in

Cameroon differently. The French language had remained central to the state's operation, and the government enjoyed strong diplomatic and economic ties to France. With higher expectations about their place in Cameroon, for francophones, Pelican explained, "migration is seen in a more critical light."[31] Instead of "bushfalling," for example, the 1990s French terminology for international migration borrowed from militaristic language: terms like *aller au front* and *aller se battre*, meaning "going to the front" and "going into battle," were used to describe going abroad.[32] These words associated emigration with struggle, even hardship, and with preparing oneself for something difficult.

France had been a clear destination for elites seeking to study abroad or emigrate, given the tight relationship between Biya and the French government, the continued presence of French interests in Cameroon, and the linguistic legacy of French colonialism. Yet, France worked to close its borders to francophone Africans beginning in the 1970s and then acutely in the 1990s. A 1994 article in the French-language newspaper *Le Messager* complained that trying to get a visa to France, even for elites, was humiliating, raised human rights questions, and was akin to the "*chemin de croix*," the Way of the Cross, a Christian devotion.[33] This sense of humiliation was compounded by the sense that Biya would not or could not intervene on behalf of Cameroon's citizens who were being criminalized abroad, while personally enjoying the support of the French government and his own lavish stays in European destinations.[34]

Safe, straightforward migration options were limited, and shrinking, for almost everyone in Cameroon. But for anglophones, it was perhaps possible to imagine the United States as less of a fortress than France.[35] It is possible that Americans were perceived as less aggressively exploitative than the French and less racist than the British.[36] Of course, getting a visa to the United States was still an ordeal, and Cameroonians were admitted to the United States as students, visitors, or immigrants in only small numbers. In 1989, only 187 people from Cameroon received permanent resident visas.[37] But the continuous presence of U.S. Peace Corps volunteers in anglophone regions since 1962 may have reinforced a sense of connection with the United States.[38] While the national government retained strong ties to France after independence, in the early 1960s, John Ngu Foncha, prime minister of anglophone West Cameroon, sought to promote the English language in the region. Because of the sense that the British had given up its links to the region after independence, Foncha invited the United States to promote English education in Cameroon. The United States sent Peace Corps volunteers to teach, primarily in anglophone Cameroon, which offered good opportunities to spread "American culture and influence."[39] Such interpersonal ties may have helped position the United States as a more attractive destination for bushfallers. Unlike francophones striving to battle their way to Europe, anglophones could aspire to fall bush in America.

· · · · · ·

The introduction of the visa lottery at this very moment may have also sweetened Cameroonians' impressions of the United States. The pressures imposed by structural adjustment, the government's failure to heed calls for democratization and anglophone rights, and the restriction of access to Europe all framed bushfallers' aspirations.

Soon Cameroonians began to have friends, relatives, or acquaintances who played the lottery successfully or who were otherwise already in the United States. "Due to the way people do suggest others to the lottery program makes it popular," a visa agent working in Bamenda, an anglophone city in Cameroon, told me.[40] One man from the Southwest region recalled playing as a child when his parents entered the whole family in the lottery. Information about the lottery traveled slowly and secretly; few people in Cameroon knew much about the lottery before the twenty-first century. But this family's relative who already lived in the United States encouraged them to play.[41] Another man in Bamenda recalled playing as early as 1998. "Sometimes we had people, I don't even know where—by that time we were not so versed with internet—and I don't even know where guys were getting forms. I remember having the first form from a neighbor, in Bamenda, who brought it," he said. "So when you bring a single form, we would do duplication, photocopy, then now we started filling the forms, according to the instructions, in capital letters and black ink. We did and then you have a passport-sized photograph which you clip, and you post. That is how it used to work at first," he explained.[42] Such family and community networks facilitated visa lottery participation, which was initially concentrated in anglophone communities. Private firms and tricksters amplified the efforts of these small networks by spreading word and offering services.

The numbers remained small—546 diversity visa recipients in 1997, 348 in 2000—but they took on outsize importance.[43] Most encounters with white visitors to Cameroon and perceptions of the West were understood as a "gateway to a brighter future in the West itself," as the scholars Francis B. Nyamnjoh and Ben Page described. Framed by the sense of limits and rot in Cameroon, migration came to be seen as critical for accessing opportunity, for hard work to translate into fulfilling one's dreams. The visa lottery put luck at the heart of its operation. Success of any kind, in bushfalling or otherwise, came to be understood as dependent on luck and proximity to the West. Nyamnjoh and Page wrote, "Every visit to the night-clubs, bars, cafes, or beaches frequented by whites, seems like playing the American citizenship lottery—a new game of chance that has come to an-chor illusory hope in the 1990s among the disenchanted, unemployed or underpaid youth of urban Cameroon."[44]

On the second floor of a building in Yaoundé, Cameroon's capital, up a metal spiral staircase, people queued up to apply for the green card lottery. Once they reached a man with a laptop at the top, they gave him their details, which he entered into the computer. Applicants then received a printout with their confirmation number on it. Outside hung a banner decorated with an American flag. In English it proclaimed "American DV Lottery," and in French, "play and win here with the professionals."

The man in charge, Bengha Innocent, had grown up in the anglophone Northwest region but had come to Yaoundé in 2004 to attend university.

The visa lottery was part of the background as he was growing up, but as a high school student, he learned more: "I just heard that there's this contest, which is like a game, that when you play, if you win, you will probably have a visa to go to America, and you live in America like an American."

Although he made his living teaching information management and communications, showing people how to use computers, each autumn he set up shop to assist people in entering the lottery. "So many people are interested in leaving the country. They believe that out there is better than here," he said. "Most of them come here and tell me they've gone to the embassy time and again . . . so they believe this is the only way for them to go." He added that his clients trusted him to improve their chances to win the lottery. "There are people who come, they look at me, and they tell me I am a magician. Because when they want to play, I say, oh you are going to win. And it just happens!"[1]

Innocent's shop—like dozens of places throughout Yaoundé—facilitated Cameroonians' entries in the visa lottery each year, and was made all the more necessary after 2003, when the United States ceased accepting entries through the U.S. Postal Service altogether and shifted to an online format. Entrants would receive an electronic confirmation notice upon submitting their applications to a website. As with the paper-based lottery, applicants were limited to just one application per person, and any entries that failed to comply with the program requirements were rejected. The United States adopted the electronic version of the lottery to lower its own processing

Gates Solution Center, Yaoundé, Cameroon, 2015. Photograph by author.

costs and to use digital tools to screen out ineligible and fraudulent entries.[2]

Removing the postal service from the process allowed applicants more direct access to the program—they didn't have to contend with slow, possibly inefficient national postal systems—but it also limited play to those lucky enough to have access to the internet, which was still rare in West Africa in the early 2000s. As the economist Teferi Mergo observed, the "online-only application requirement seems to be more restrictive than either the education or the work experience requirement" in narrowing the field of eligible applicants.[3]

Although few Africans in 2003 enjoyed internet access at home (internet-connected mobile phones were still years off), a rapidly growing number of people were gaining access through burgeoning cyber cafés. These shops became gathering places, spots to play video games and explore, and places to email pen pals and create social media profiles. Simultaneously, people gained access to seemingly infinite information about life in the United States and the opportunity to connect, while also feeling acutely the limits imposed by borders and national citizenship. Wasn't this the key insight gleaned by early internet spammers Canter and Siegel, and something that internet utopianists had missed? The flow of images, words, ideas, and data around the world would make access to mobility across borders more, not less, valuable—particularly as nations erected walls and other obstacles to migration. The commercial internet and American visa lottery had been born together, and in the twenty-first century they continued to grow up together as cyber cafés became the key physical sites of the visa lottery's operation.

· · · · · ·

Internet cafés made the visa lottery a major part of their business during the one- to two-month registration period each year.[4] Even after personal internet access became more available through the rise of mobile phones in the 2010s, the visa lottery remained a robust source of income for cyber cafés in Africa's cities, owing to lingering questions about accessing the correct website and uploading properly formatted photos.[5] By providing lottery expertise based on previous experience, web savvy, a careful reading of the U.S. Department of State website, a steady hand, and a digital camera, proprietors and workers at these small shops seized the chance to profit and survive.

Cybercafe Telephonie Internationale, Yaoundé, Cameroon, 2015. Photograph by author.

Although the internet originated as a state-driven project funded by the United States Department of Defense beginning in 1969, by the mid-1990s, the technology had come to entail a vastly more complex network of networks stretching around the globe. The invention of the World Wide Web and the advent of spam in 1994 made the internet the far more commercial platform we've become familiar with. The United States Agency for International Development (USAID) launched the Leland Initiative in 1995 to make the internet more widely accessible in Africa; at the time only seven countries on the continent had any internet access at all.[6] It was named after the late Mickey Leland, the African American congressman from Texas who had been killed tragically in a plane crash while on a mission to Ethiopia in 1989. His life ended in pursuit of a radical form of Black internationalism. He saw the fates of Africans and people of African descent in the diaspora as being connected, entwined. The internet initiative might have furthered Leland's vision of strengthening ties between Africans on the continent and Black people the world over; one of its stated aims was to make "African-produced information available to the world"—the rare U.S. acknowledgment that Africans possessed deep knowledge of great value.[7] But it was undertaken after Leland's death and stripped of its lingering radical aims or solidarities, instead aiming squarely at business development and promoting free enterprise.

In keeping with other U.S. projects to spread marketization and especially to push the global South to embrace free-market solutions, USAID recommended privatization and liberalization of African countries' often nationalized telecommunications sectors. In the coming years, the FCC promoted "pro-competitive regulatory policies" in developing countries, especially in Africa.[8] While the Leland Initiative report suggested the use of "telecottages" (community-based facilities for internet training and access) to disseminate information, the initiative's emphasis on the private sector undermined this idea, instead producing a landscape of privately run internet cafés. Between the time of the Leland Initiative's launch in the mid-1990s and the rollout of the electronic visa lottery in autumn 2003, the internet had evolved to a massive network of networks maintained by private for-profit companies where commercial activity was the norm.

Ghana is considered the first country in West Africa to have full internet connectivity.[9] But that connectivity was at first quite limited: in the spring of 1995, it consisted of just ten lines connecting to Cambridge, in the United Kingdom, costing more than $7,000 per month. By 1996 a private internet host company had 140 subscribers in Accra, each of them paying $1,300 per year for the privilege.[10] Only large companies, or perhaps expats and the very wealthy, could afford such astronomical internet access rates.[11] But as more internet service providers appeared in Ghana, the number of subscribers grew and costs declined. Kumasi, Ghana's second-largest city, gained internet access in 1996. Accra's biggest internet café for the first decade of the twenty-first century, BusyInternet, launched in November 2001.[12] By 2003, over 1,000 internet cafés were operating in Accra, and it was estimated that 300,000 people used the internet at least once a month that year. Cyber cafés ranged from sleek professional operations like BusyInternet to scrappy start-ups, with one or two older computers that were slow to boot up.[13] By the mid-2000s, most sizable cities in Ghana, beyond Accra and Kumasi, gained some internet access through a handful of cafés.

The spread of internet access, of course, dovetailed with many Africans' increasing desires to seek greener pastures abroad. As one chronicle of the internet's history in Ghana put it, the growth and spread of internet access in Ghana "was also fueled by Ghanaians' curiosity for the outside world. Many are looking for a way out of the country. Ghanaians are willing to spend a significant part of their income to access the West via the Internet."[14] Mark Davies, a tech entrepreneur and immigrant from Wales who helped launch BusyInternet in Accra, reportedly estimated that 80 percent of his internet customers were looking for a way out of the country.[15] The internet flooded African countries with images and information about rich countries like the United States, fueling people's imaginations about life abroad.

At the same time, the exposure made the dearth of opportunities at home impossible to ignore. It thus helped stoke desire to emigrate at a time when new border and visa restrictions were being erected to block the movement of people of color.[16] "Now we have the internet, we can find out many things we don't know, about anywhere," one cyber café worker in Cameroon told me.[17] This was the dream, wasn't it? It offered a portal to the world's accumulated knowledge. But the juxtaposition of access to a world of possibilities through the internet with the near impossibility of achieving one's dreams at home *or* safely migrating abroad was painful. Such virtual access helped inflate the salience in Africa, of seeking greener pastures, falling bush, and seeing going *somewhere else* as necessary to build a future.[18] The anthropologist Maybritt Jill Alpes argued that "the phenomenon of bushfalling is a symptom of the tensions

Photo Dave in Yaoundé, Cameroon, advertises its past success rate, 2015. Photograph by author.

that have arisen from people's aspirations for mobility at times of heightened migration control."[19]

· · · · · ·

If an internet café could boast one or two people selected as winners one year, the next year it would see twice as many customers trying to tap into that good luck and expertise. As computers and internet connection speeds improved, cyber cafés could promise better service to paying customers.[20] People could stroll into cafés and either register on their own by paying for connection time or register with paid assistance if that was on offer at the shop. Not everyone who was eligible for the lottery possessed computer skills. Many applicants had never learned to use computers at school or at their jobs. Search engines could be hit or miss. As one café worker in Accra told me, "Even to get to the site is not easy for some people. They can't even log in with their credentials. Normally they come—It is a service that we render here. We collect money for that service."[21] A bewildering array of commercial entities popped up when you searched online for visa lottery information. Navigating to the correct page took considerable savvy, with so many possible scams circulating. A good guide or agent could help one navigate and avoid being duped, aspiring migrants believed.[22]

The number of people who registered each year for the lottery at Oceanview Internet in Cape Coast, Ghana, for example, was, as one employee put it, "uncountable. Every day they come."[23] At UNIC, the main café in central Kumasi, Ghana, Bernard Gyasi helped more than a hundred people apply during each year's registration period.[24] Staff at both the British Council and the Kumasi Travel Agency directed potential applicants to Gyasi. In the northern city of Tamale, Ghana, My Com Café became so busy during the registration period that customers would come and wait four or five hours. "People did not even want to step out for prayers and lose their place," an employee told me, referring to Muslims' daily prayers. Hassan Saeed helped so many people apply for the visa lottery one year that his boss rewarded him with a cash bonus that he used to buy a bicycle.[25] Mobility had tremendous value.

In the late 1990s, the internet came to Cameroon, but at high prices, and initially in only very limited areas.[26] A former U.S. Peace Corps volunteer, Paul Mickelson, had retired in the anglophone regional capital of Bamenda, a verdant town ringed by hills and a key site for anglophone political organizing. Having fallen in love with the country, Mickelson opened a computer school in 1997 to help young people learn to use computers and navigate the internet.[27] Paul's Computer Institute was among the first cyber cafés in the country. The sociologist Bettina Anja Frei estimated that by 2003 there were more than twenty cyber cafés in Bamenda, and by 2008, between sixty and seventy.[28] According to a report by the Global Information Society Watch, in 2005 Cameroon gained access to broadband internet services through the Chad-Cameroonian pipeline, and the group estimated that perhaps 1.4 percent of Cameroon's population had access to the internet in 2006—tiny, but likely disproportionately young and eager to learn.[29] A 2013 report suggested that nearly 5 percent of Cameroonians had gained access to the internet—over a million people.[30]

As access to the internet spread, cyber cafés proliferated. Café managers recognized that the annual lottery was an excellent way to draw in business, since few people had access to the internet at home or the computer literacy to apply themselves, and because so many Cameroonians sought to fall bush. When cyber cafés became the site of the lottery's operation, it benefited both proprietors of businesses with internet access and a new customer base: people who previously lacked access to personal networks or other information about the lottery. This is how the lottery became more accessible to francophones.[31]

· · · · · ·

While the lottery was previously more popular among anglophones, the lottery's shift from mail-in entries to online entries helped democratize information about it, broadening participation. Francophone Cameroonians became more likely to play. The same was true elsewhere in French-speaking Africa, in countries like Togo, which saw its visa lottery numbers rise as the lottery went online.[32] Subsequently, Cameroonian immigration to the United States became more numerically significant and more linguistically diverse, as the program came to draw significantly from both francophone and anglophone regions. (In addition to French, English, and Pidgin, Cameroonians speak over 250 languages.) Anglophone visa agents benefited from earlier experiences with the lottery, their familiarity with the old paper version, and their linguistic ability to navigate the online entry system.

One internet café operator in Yaoundé explained, "We help them take pictures and complete the online registration form. And they pay us 1,000 CFA to enter."[33] Businesses crossed the language divide, as cyber café operators seized the program as an entrepreneurial opportunity and promoted it in both French and English languages. As one blogger described Yaoundé during the lottery, "Banners and billboards are prominently displayed, directing passers-by to a nearby Internet café where they would, or could, by

Loterie Americaine visa services in French and English in Yaoundé, Cameroon, 2015. Photograph by author.

a stroke of luck, automatically become American citizens without 'spending much.'"[34] One woman working at a cyber café with her husband told me, "Anglophones comme francophones—les gens s'intéressent"[35] (People were interested). The entrepreneurial activity around the green card lottery "instil[ls] in one the fantasy of one day becoming Uncle Sam's countryman," a Cameroonian blogger argued.[36] As the scholar Joseph Takougang argued, the lottery "has singularly accounted for the tremendous increase in the number of French-speaking Cameroonians in the United States."[37]

Because of their political and economic marginalization and English-language skills, anglophones had long been more likely than francophones to go to the United States.[38] Some received asylum, after showing that they faced political persecution at home, for example, whereas others played the lottery.[39] But it was only in the mid-2000s that francophones too played the lottery in significant numbers, like their anglophone neighbors.[40]

This shift was rooted in changes in border policy in France and elsewhere in Europe. Some francophones who had historically been able to go abroad to France to study or work found that channel now more restricted. Given France's colonial legacy and the ongoing close relationship between Cameroon's president Paul Biya and the French government, francophones might have expected a warm reception in France. Yet, many emigrants found themselves criminalized and without legal status in the former metropole, particularly after 1993 when France's interior minister Charles Pasqua endorsed the idea of "zero immigration" and enacted legislation that toughened requirements, limited visas, and expanded border enforcement.[41] Francophones used language like "going into battle" to describe traveling to Europe, where they encountered a fortress.

But entering a lottery that framed immigration as a positive thing was quite different from going to war. Soon, French speakers began to discuss the visa lottery and immigration to the United States in more positive terms. Although the United States was simultaneously hardening its own immigration restrictions—militarizing the U.S.-Mexico border and increasing immigrant detention and deportation—those shifts were not as apparent in Cameroon, so long as the visa lottery continued to run each year.

A French-language website catering to francophone Africans wrote about the program in 2001 as the lottery of the American dream, which made it possible to live and work "in the country of Uncle Sam totally legally."[42] That the lottery offered an explicitly legal path to the United States dampened the sense that traveling abroad was akin to going to battle. One francophone, Serges Ngueffang, explained in 2005 why the visa lottery was so

Shop advertises photography and lottery entry, at the top of a hill, Yaoundé, Cameroon, 2015. Photograph by author.

appealing: "One has a better chance with it. The Europeans already closed their doors. With this card, we are not illegal."[43] Instead of applying military metaphors to migration, the *Cameroon Tribune*, a state-owned newspaper, used the verb *se bousculer*, meaning "to rush" or "to scramble," language often used in the anglophone context to signal going abroad or entering the visa lottery.[44]

The opportunity to go legally to the United States rather than clandestinely to Europe, however small the odds of winning, helped position the United States as a more attractive destination.[45] An anglophone Cameroonian affirmed this comparison: "People have told me, from all indications, from all information, they told me going to America is like, they are free there. When they go up to Europe, they chase them there, there is a lot of police chasing them away; because in America, if you get your legs in America, it is a free zone."[46]

Each year, as Cameroonians continued to be selected as winners, receive diversity visas, and get their green cards in rising numbers, the lottery became more widely understood as a serious option.[47] The number of winners selected and diversity visas issued in a given year remained limited. By statute, no country may receive more than 7 percent of the total number of diversity visas, an upper limit of about 3,500. Cameroon would not top a thousand winners until 2008. But the process created a feedback loop through which Cameroonians assessed the lottery as a viable option, making it increasingly popular.

Several cyber cafés were founded by or employed anglophone Cameroonians to provide services to francophones. Allomonwing Joseph Ngochi came from the anglophone Northwest region to the capital Yaoundé to pursue his studies at the Université de Yaoundé II. Having learned about the lottery as a young man in Bamenda around 2000, he took a job at Cyber City, where his job, he told me, was "making the world a global village." While he helped diverse clients enter the visa lottery, he said, "Most often it's the English-speaking people who do it. The francophones, once they have an idea about it, they also give it a try."[48]

Menkan Kari, another agent, said, "The irony about it is that the French, too, are interested. America is an English country, but the French, everybody wants to go. The French, too, they are playing even more. It is somehow funny—people who don't even understand English, too, they play."[49] Many of the capital city's internet cafés where the visa lottery is most famously advertised are located in anglophone neighborhoods, like Obili in southern Yaoundé, even though the city itself is situated in a francophone region.[50]

The new electronic system after 2003 made the visa lottery easier to access. Kinga Albert Wirayen, the manager of a cyber café in Bamenda, reflected on the old system, which required a paper application: "That was cumbersome. And most of us did not even have P.O. box addresses before. So we had to use a popular address and the mailing system in Cameroon is not very good. So, even if it's good, when the results come, somebody might hold it back for no good reason."[51] Given the questionable record of postal services, rumors about African government interruption of lottery mail, and the fact that many entrants did not have a mailing address, the paper-based lottery disadvantaged people. While applying now required a person to somehow find a computer with internet access, it also helped applicants ensure their applications were truly received.

A 2006 blog post profiled the internet cafés in Yaoundé that were making good money by arranging the photographs and applications for visa lottery clients.[52] Louis Clovis Ketcha, the manager of a cyber café in Yaoundé, told the *Tribune* that he helped paying customers avoid scams.[53] Some café operators provided legitimate services for reasonable fees, while others cheated their customers, provided false information, and perpetuated fraud. The U.S. government made efforts to intervene against unscrupulous visa services providers, publishing a warning against fraud in French-language newspapers targeting French-speaking lottery applicants, a newly important audience. "Please note," the U.S. embassy in Yaoundé stated in a French-language message in 2012, "that there is no fee for participating in the Diversity Visa program."[54]

Concerned about fraud around the diversity visa, the U.S. consular section in Yaoundé warned in a confidential cable about "rampant corruption and fraud" associated with its immigration screening.[55] Yet, despite the existence of fraud and opportunism, and despite the long odds of winning, the lottery remained one of the few avenues for legal immigration of Cameroonians to the United States. A cable from the U.S. embassy in Yaoundé recounted that the visa lottery "remains an alluring opportunity that embodies much of what draws Cameroonians to immigrate to the U.S." Even after the embassy hosted a long interview on visa-related fraud and heated discussion with a young, foreign-educated Cameroonian journalist in 2007 about how difficult it was to get a tourist visa to visit the United States, the woman told the embassy "that perhaps this year she too would play the DV lottery."[56] Even with stories circulating about its challenges, faith remained strong that bushfalling was the key to a better life.

· · · · · ·

Internet access broadened Cameroonians' access to the United States. One article described the craze as follows: "A unique kind of fever has gripped inhabitants of Yaoundé. The passion and enthusiasm with which Yaoundé city dwellers have welcomed the ongoing registration session cannot be compared to any other."[57] Now, as this author wrote, "everybody wants to live and work in the United States."[58] A 2010 blog post described in French the signs everywhere proclaiming the lottery: "The excitement is palpable."[59]

A spokesperson for U.S. public affairs at the embassy in Cameroon, Bouba Monglo, told a French-language news outlet that the shift to an online

Banner at Photo Prestige Photo Tsinga, featuring the Obama family, Yaoundé, Cameroon, 2015. Photograph by author.

system had resulted in more French-speaking applicants for the lottery program. "Before two years ago [2003], it was more the people in the English-speaking part of the country who applied. In addition, it was more difficult to manage because it had to be done by mail. The advent of the Internet has facilitated the discovery of this medium by francophone Cameroonians."[60] As one visa entrepreneur told me, for a long time, "they thought this thing was all about for those who can speak English. But now, you know, it's like, it's everybody's thing."[61]

The number of Cameroonians who settled permanently in the United States reflected this enthusiasm. In 1989 only 187 Cameroonians received permanent residency visas to the United States, and in 1990, perhaps 3,000 Cameroon-born people resided in the United States.[62] By 2014, the number was over 33,000, an eleven-fold increase in just over twenty years.[63] Half of that number, some 16,000 people, had come through the lottery by receiving diversity visas.[64] By 2020 the number of diversity visas issued to Cameroonians topped 24,000.

It made sense that conditions in Cameroon under Biya's rule and pressures of structural adjustment spurred narratives framing emigration as a necessity. Globalization and the internet delivered images of prosperity and opportunity in the West, and the visa lottery helped make the United States a prime destination. But what people imagined was often at odds with what they encountered when they arrived. And those contradictions could be difficult to square.

15 Soft Power

. . . .

"You thought everybody in America had a car and a gun, your uncles and aunts thought so too," the narrator begins. "After you won the American visa lottery, your uncles and aunts and cousins told you, in a month you will have a big car. Soon, a big house. But don't buy a gun like those Americans."[1]

Expectations of what the United States had to offer the lucky few who won the visa lottery were necessarily abstract. Chimamanda Ngozi Adichie's 2009 story "The Thing around Your Neck" probes the distance between expectations and reality for a visa lottery winner named Akunna. When she is preparing to travel, she imagines gleaming symbols of American wealth and power, soon to be accessible to her. But what she encounters after departing her home city of Lagos, Nigeria, fails to match expectations. "You wanted to write that rich Americans were thin and poor Americans were fat and that many did not have a house and a car; you were still not sure about the guns, though, because they might have them inside their pockets."[2] Back in Nigeria, Akunna's family remains the keeper of that idealized, shining image of American prosperity, which undergirds their expectations for Akunna herself. But she does not write home to explain, does not dispel her family's ideas about life in the United States, does not unravel the image Nigerians back home hold, of American streets paved with gold, of "God's own country."

As it became an annual festival that large numbers of people participated in while facilitating the emigration of the selected few, the visa lottery shaped how people imagined the United States. It made concrete the possibility of actually going to the United States, in contrast to the obstacles encountered by many Africans at consulates, borders, and airports. As a result, the lottery produced and reinforced people's ideas of an exceptional "American dream." The phrase itself and the idea of America as a dreamland built on imagery borrowed from U.S. culture and from the stories America tells about itself. Movies and music, advertisements, and stories beamed in from abroad linked imagined life in the United States with prosperity signaled by purchases made suddenly accessible—like cars and big houses.

Hopefuls imagined a country where things *worked*. Where water flowed from the faucet when you expected it to, and the lights stayed on all the time. Where a person's hard work could produce material gains and stability, where conmen and grifters didn't suck up all the rewards. A place where ordinary people, and not just select elites, could access a piece of the pie and support their children's mobility.

Cyber café workers dreamed of dazzling technology widely available in the United States but limited at home. Chuo Julius, a technician in Cameroon, said his reason for playing the lottery was to seek education, and that his preferred destination was the United States because of its "superior level of information technology."[3]

Students forced to discontinue their studies prematurely under economic duress or because of exorbitant school fees dreamed of accessing education and the stability and upward mobility that it would bring in the United States. "I know in the U.S. you can be working and going to school at the same time. So if I'm able to get there, I can work, pay for my own expenses, and achieve my ambition. . . . If you go there, you can get the best education you'll ever want in this world."[4]

People who had never been able to travel anywhere wanted a U.S. passport, to travel the world without obstruction or the humiliation of applying for visas. To see what was out there was an aspiration for people who felt stuck and without prospects at home.

Visa lottery entrepreneurs promoted these images and ideas in their advertisements and signs. Importantly, emigrants themselves, like the protagonist of Adichie's story, sometimes didn't correct their contacts at home. Even when emigrants shared the truth about the challenges they encountered abroad, their examples failed to unseat confidence in the American dream or certainty that going abroad was the key to a better life. Even friends and family members might not take it seriously if a visa lottery winner claimed to be flailing.

Such dreams mattered, not least because they reflected and reproduced existing inequalities between the United States and African countries. They were more than propaganda or naiveté on the part of aspiring emigrants; they gave voice to something important that felt missing, something, many despaired to think, that could not be gained at home. These images also emerged and circulated in an atmosphere of dwindling formal U.S. diplomacy and focus in the 1990s—and then outlasted it.

As the Cold War ended, the United States stood as the world's lone superpower. In terms of formal diplomacy, the United States directed away

Poster showing happy American family advertising lottery services, Yaoundé, Cameroon, 2015. Photograph by author.

the limited attention it had previously paid to Africa and channeled it toward Europe and the Middle East. Simultaneously, funding for cultural diplomacy and exchanges with Africa dried up, while U.S. corporations and media were expected to grow to fill in any gaps, given their global dominance.

For all the chatter about globalization and mobility that filled speeches and newspaper columns, border restrictions remained as salient as ever for most of the world's people. The idea that the United States offered the lottery out of a sense of generosity, and that it remained a welcoming destination for immigrants, gained adherents. The association of the United States with the promise of dreams fulfilled was strengthened—and it continued to echo even as U.S. policies hardened and the role of the United States in the world became more militant.

* * * * * *

While African countries aside from South Africa had rarely been central to U.S. foreign policy making, during the Cold War the continent became a significant site of U.S. attention, including through bloody military interventions.[5] The United States exerted power widely, including in military operations in Congo and Egypt in the 1960s, Zaire and Angola in the 1970s, and Ethiopia and Somalia in the 1980s, in support of stated Cold War aims like containing the spread of communism and securing access to resources.[6]

As part of its assertion of power, the United States also engaged in cultural diplomacy to win Africans' "hearts and minds"—a mission that was, of course, continually undermined by its reputation for meddling in Africans' affairs through its surveillance, harmful involvement, and support for coups removing popularly elected leaders, as in Congo.[7] Its neocolonial stance was part and parcel of white supremacy, and the sense that Black sovereignty should be, at best, conditional. Yet American racism persisted as a practical thorn in the side of U.S. officials who hoped to win African support in the Cold War, and so efforts were launched to counter it.

The U.S. Information Agency (later USIS) published magazines and broadcasted Voice of America radio shows stressing shared values between Americans and Africans. Successive administrations undertook modernization and economic development programs in Africa in the 1950s and 1960s.[8] The State Department organized American jazz musicians on tours to promote American culture and art, emphasizing the U.S. commitment to racial justice and the deep connections between people in Africa and

Africans in the diaspora. These efforts sought to balance news reports and lived experiences showing the severe limits of that commitment within the United States. This was a priority because of the collapse of European territorial empires in Africa and the emergence of newly independent nations that would gain control over their resources, politics, and destinies.

More important, perhaps, than official propaganda was the way that people used these encounters to form unscripted individual connections and exchanges. Although the United States planned cultural exchange trips, it couldn't control what individual artists shared with locals, what American artists themselves experienced and learned, or how their audiences responded.[9] Louis Armstrong's visit to Ghana in 1956, and later the *Soul to Soul* concert in Accra in 1971, left a lasting impression on Ghanaian music, deepening connections between the United States and Ghana.[10] But musicians spoke their minds, criticizing the United States, and telling truths about the country's violence and inequities. As African students and elites visited the United States and enrolled in universities with the goal of returning home to build up their new nations, they themselves experienced Jim Crow segregation and violence. Such exchanges both undermined U.S. orthodoxy and fostered relationships and solidarities across borders.

At home, African Americans built on civil rights successes to gain institutional power, establishing the Congressional Black Caucus in 1971. The CBC became a potent voice in Congress in the 1980s, and Black legislators used their voices to address enduring racial inequality at home *and* to redirect U.S. foreign policy abroad, particularly in Africa. Most prominently, they decried the U.S. alliance with apartheid South Africa and eventually marshaled support for the Anti-Apartheid Act of 1986, which imposed sanctions on the regime. Even after President Reagan vetoed it, Congress was able to override him to enact the law. Despite the administration's Cold War priorities, African American policymakers pushed the United States to send more than $800 million in aid to support Ethiopians, then under Marxist rule and mired in famine.[11]

But the political tradition of radical lawmakers aligning with global South movements came to an end along with the Cold War. African affairs, historian Ben Talton writes, "grew murky and difficult to pin down in the early 1990s."[12] Formal independence hadn't brought prosperity for most Africans, and African-led states could be exploitative and repressive like their predecessors. Structural reforms undertaken to comply with international donors' demands undermined workers' rights, the provision of public services, and hope for meaningful self-determination. While it was clear to Black policymakers that they and the United States should oppose imperialism and racial apartheid, in the 1990s it was more difficult to know how to support the liberation of diverse African peoples.

Dynamics at the end of the Cold War also shifted U.S. attention away from Africa and away from cultural exchanges to foster positive foreign relations. As superpower and hegemon, the United States no longer worried that communist ideology or alliance with the dissolving Soviet Union would block its access to African resources. The United States had played a key role in destabilizing many African countries during the Cold War, often building relationships with African leaders to serve its own interests. As the Cold War ended, the United States pulled support from allies it no longer needed, leading to the eruption of numerous conflicts.[13] Weapons left over from the Cold War flooded conflict areas, increasing the violence in events like the Liberian Civil War, for example.

U.S. attentiveness to Africa hadn't necessarily benefited Africans during the Cold War, but the erasure of Africa in U.S. foreign policy and aid also had consequences that could be destabilizing. The George H. W. Bush administration proposed allocating $617 million for the whole continent in 1991, a tiny fraction of what it proposed spending elsewhere.[14]

An early post–Cold War crisis set a blueprint for American policy. Amid increasing instability, the United States, which had sent aid to Somalia in the 1980s, closed its embassy in Mogadishu in 1991. Then in August 1992, the George H. W. Bush administration sent U.S. forces to Somalia to support UN relief operations. During the war in Somalia, starvation became widespread. Bush wanted to signal U.S. engagement, attention to the humanitarian crisis, and an interest in working closely with the United Nations. The United States expanded its military presence, and the UN mission expanded beyond the delivery of aid. When eighteen U.S. troops were killed at the Battle of Mogadishu in October 1993, the American public recoiled, and the Bill Clinton administration called for the troops to withdraw by March 1994.[15] This event established a pattern for U.S. involvement on the continent for the rest of the decade. As other humanitarian crises unfolded throughout the 1990s, the United States preferred to avoid direct military intervention.[16] Talk of human rights and democratization remained important, at the rhetorical level, but the administration's focus was on regions of the world other than Africa. Events of the 1990s also helped cement stereotypes of post–Cold War Africa as a site of crisis, with the histories of U.S.

involvement and alliances that had played a key role in Cold War destabilization all but erased from the narrative. Americans could perceive African countries as basket cases or blank slates in need of U.S. assistance, but not as places with deeper histories of entanglements and encounters with the United States and the wider world.

The Clinton administration's priority for Africa was to push states to liberalize trade policies and reduce subsidies as part of its embrace of economic globalization. This push culminated in the passage of the African Growth and Opportunity Act (AGOA), which Clinton signed into law on May 18, 2000, to spur market-led economic growth in Africa and to foster more trade with the United States.

In general, the United States devoted fewer resources to its public diplomacy after the Cold War. Reacting to the needs of the "new world order," the State Department underwent reorganization, including budget and staff cuts.[17] Between 1993 and 1996, while the United States opened twenty embassies in newly created states in Eastern Europe, it shut down thirty-two diplomatic and consulate posts elsewhere and reduced the Department of State staff by 2,500 people.[18] The United States Information Agency saw its budget disappear: its 1998 budget was one-third less than its 1993 budget, before the agency's ultimate dissolution in 1999.[19] As a result, the U.S. diplomatic presence diminished in Africa over the course of the decade.

Although Congress's decision to cut funding to U.S. public diplomacy stemmed from its shifting priorities, it also signaled a belief that globalization and the information age could do some of the work of spreading U.S. culture. For years, the public diplomacy arm of the State Department had built libraries, fostered educational exchanges, broadcast radio shows, and printed and distributed magazines. It had been devoted to "winning the support of foreign publics to further U.S. political, economic and security interests," in the words of a 1995 report by the U.S. Advisory Commission on Public Diplomacy.[20] As *New York Times* columnist Thomas Friedman noted, such programming had been a way of "offering more in the way of American culture than McDonald's and Mickey Mouse."[21]

The decision to defund the State Department and its public diplomacy efforts meant that America's cultural products, like *The Oprah Winfrey Show*, had to pick up the slack in the work of representing the United States abroad.[22] The influential political scientist and Clinton administration member Joseph Nye Jr. famously popularized the term "soft power." He advised that the United States should deploy its culture abroad to win the support of other countries to boost U.S. power. "American popular culture embodied in products and communications has widespread appeal," he argued.[23] The visa lottery supplied an unexpected solution.

· · · · · ·

They were not who Nye had in mind, but it was local visa agents who stepped into the spaces previously occupied by formal public diplomacy efforts, especially in their promotion of the lottery as "the surest way to reach the United States of America."[24] To little avail, U.S. embassies released statements to African newspapers stating that "no outside service can therefore improve an applicant's chances of being selected." The visa agents were louder, more omnipresent, and there to talk with and listen to visa applicants.[25] It was African agents—not the U.S. embassy—that promised people the chance to "feel the greatness of exposure to the hospitality of the American people."[26] Official U.S. communications were not nearly as engaging.

Beyond amplifying ideas of American life that were otherwise being peddled through media, cultural products, and internet access, the lottery produced another set of narratives about the United States and the American dream in Africa. By appearing at a time when emigration was both highly important to people and a diminishing possibility, the lottery tapped into the epic of emigration, served it, and made the United States appear benevolent and open. The lottery also appeared to celebrate cultural difference, and it offered visas broadly, not just to the candidates with the most polished qualifications. As a result, the United States appeared uniquely dedicated to diversity, equality, and democracy. As one visa entrepreneur in Cameroon put it, "Lucky game, like I said, it's not in all about you being so superior, being so powerful, there's nothing about it that can explain."[27] The luck factor made the lottery itself—but also the United States—seem more egalitarian than gatekeeping border regimes Africans were likely to encounter otherwise.

Unlike European colonial powers that had punished former African colonies, criminalized African migrants, and failed to integrate Black citizens and residents, the United States could plausibly be seen as a "no man's land," to borrow a phrase from Cameroon's visa entrepreneurs. The meaning of the phrase echoed the idea that the United States was a "nation of immigrants," not one defined by an ethnic or racial national identity. Instead, the country aspired to define itself by its racial and ethnic diversity. It was a place where Black immigrants could thrive—perhaps. The possibility of migrating legally to Europe or the United States was clearly highly limited.

But stories about the diversity visa, about the individuals who'd gone to the United States through a legal channel reserved specifically for people from the African continent, reinforced the idea that the United States was *more* open than other destinations.

· · · · · ·

When Africans dreamed of immigrating to the United States through the visa lottery, they often pictured material success. Not merely a highly developed and wealthy country, the United States was also prolific at broadcasting idealized images of its own abundance abroad. One visa entrepreneur in Cameroon affirmed that these images attracted visa lottery applicants. "They look at TV and see, it's just too nice for them."[28] Another said, "The movies show us the best life is in the U.S., flashy things they show us in the movies. Majority of the movies. Whenever there is a movie and you see Hollywood, like swimming pools, you see Miami—you want to be there, experience the life."[29]

Many phrases reflected these impressions: "America is just a giant out there with lots of money, money on the floor."[30]

It was a place where "everything is gold."[31]

"Milk and honey flow freely on the streets."[32]

The language describing American largesse was over the top, sometimes delivered with a knowing look indicating that the dream of the United States bore little resemblance to its realities. These images seemed outrageously idealized and absurdly optimistic, but they reflected real critiques of the limits people faced at home.

In a Cameroonian writer's short story about the visa lottery, the whole family, accustomed to watching old episodes of *Dallas*, pictures the lottery winner's life in the United States: "The very bed on which he will lie will be made of dollars, they chanted. Soon, we will receive pictures showing him standing tall, regal, all-African, smiling with his hand on the hood of his huge American car, fondly caressing it."[33]

Repeated mentions of cars and houses reflected the particularly high value of ownership, agency, and mobility for Africans near the end of the twentieth century.[34] These were important in many contexts, of course; cars had been central to American life, infrastructure, and social structures since the midcentury, and home ownership was a primary vehicle for middle-class status and accumulation. But autonomy and mobility were also meaningful in the context of colonial and postcolonial African countries.

The era of structural adjustment brought many imported cars to Ghana, constituting a symbol of illusory prosperity. As historian Jennifer Hart has written, these appeared at first glance to offer "freedom of movement and prosperity for all," but that was, in truth, highly contradictory.[35] The appearance of these physical symbols of luxury masked declining security in most people's lives.

The vast majority of Ghana's urban population relied on tro-tros, privately owned minibuses, and share taxis to get around. The vehicles were often in poor shape, and to optimize revenues, rides entailed being squeezed in tightly. Ride costs rose with fuel costs, which were subject to market fluctuation. On the other hand, being able to afford a private vehicle, particularly an expensive SUV, meant a smoother ride, comfortable seats, space, blasting air-conditioning, and protection from exhaust fumes, heat, sweat, and dust. To be a "myself" driver was to escape the immobility created by infrastructure problems, poor safety, and dilapidated vehicles. But more cars on the road translated to stifling traffic and more frequent, often fatal, traffic accidents, especially for those traveling in tro-tros, buses, and share taxis. Private cars helped individuals gain mobility, but their presence limited the mobility of the many.

Cars, then, were a symbol linking prosperity and movement. Migrating to America was much the same.

Certainly, life in the United States wasn't perfect. But people expected that with hard work, dedication, and ambition, they could find success in America and make decent money—so long as you were "not lazy."[36] It was widely expected. Of the Cameroonian protagonist in the visa lottery story, the family teases, "He will soon be rolling in dollars, their tongues wagged."[37]

Visa agents exploited that expectation, linking winning the lottery with access to American abundance.[38] Their banners and posters featured pictures of the American flag, the welcoming Statue of Liberty, and later, the Obama family.[39] Green card lottery advertisements promised applicants they could "live and work in the USA" without explaining that no particular jobs, let alone housing or other basics, awaited green card recipients.[40] Some messages even promised jobs that did not exist: "The selected persons will receive an offer of employment from employers that will lead to United States permanent residency with all legal, processing expenses paid and one year salary," read one advertisement.[41] Alas, no such support was actually on offer.

These lofty (false) promises reinforced the notion that making it in America would be easily within grasp for a person who was hardworking. A man in Cameroon said, "America is one of the most powerful countries, and there are so many opportunities there, compared to other countries in Europe.

And I think that it is a free land, it's a land of opportunity, and when you are there, if you are somebody who is eager to learn, eager to work, you will make it. You will make it most successful, so I think that is why people are always wanting to travel there."[42] At home, hard work was underpaid and punishing. It was tantalizing to believe that elsewhere things would be different.

The United States would be different in other respects as well. One Ghanaian said of the United States, "They go by the law. No matter who you are, if you have offended, you have to face the law." In Ghana, by contrast, "it doesn't work like that. If you have offended, depending on who you are, depending on what you have, you can be free." He felt that elites and people with connections did not face the same consequences for misdeeds as ordinary people. In Ghana, it seemed that the same rules did not apply to powerful "big men," while ordinary people suffered the consequences of corruption and *kalabule* or profiteering.[43] He assured me, "But the States is not like that. No matter who you are, if you have offended, they always sentence you."[44] It was an interesting interpretation of the United States' sky-high rates of incarceration, which are not applied particularly evenly. Yet the idea that there were measures of accountability in the United States was perhaps less about justice than about idealized perceptions, reinforced through U.S. and international rhetoric, of the importance of the "rule of law" and the existence of safeguards against blatant corruption. The visa agent linked the notion of the rule of law to the market economy. "I believe there are rules and regulations there, which is governing the nation. And it is not easy to violate them," he said. "So I believe that is why the economy is so strong and vital like that."[45]

Another thing the United States offered was mobility—not just to North America but to the world. Because the visa lottery made a green card available (and eventually, U.S. citizenship), it offered African lottery players a chance for something they struggled to access *as* Africans. U.S. passport holders can easily get visas to travel and are often exempt from any visa requirements. As Bengha Innocent, the Cameroonian agent, told me, "Americans can easily get into any other country without any problems. So if I happen to be an American, I will use that means as an American to just go all over, just be moving around."[46] "Tasting the atmosphere of other countries is one of my reasons for entering," Prince Balogun Daisi told a reporter in Nigeria.[47] Through the visa lottery, Africans could imagine becoming jet-setters, something out of reach for most people possessing African passports, for historical, racist reasons.

Africa's marginalization has perhaps made aspiring to global citizenship all the more powerful, a method of rejecting negative stereotypes about Africa and Africans. While many people speak in terms of the places they'd like to visit and see, global travel talk in this context reveals other motivations. For example, as Anima Adjepong writes, the term "Afropolitan," used to describe African immigrant belonging in the world, "provides a foundation upon which some Africans can affirm their belonging to a world in which they strive to exist on equal footing with the global middle class."[48] A francophone Cameroonian put it poetically: "After the United States, I can go to the moon."[49]

A 1997 article in a Nigerian newspaper suggested that by inviting the world to apply for the visa lottery, the United States was showing world leadership. "By further diversifying the cultural components of its large state, the U.S. may well be getting ready to be a miniature world, a model of Marshal McLuhan's Global Village concept."[50] By making itself a model global village, the piece argued, the United States was creating "international persons" who could move fluidly between cultures and countries. Bengha Innocent suggested that the creators of the visa lottery wanted the United States to become "a country with everybody. A country that has, in short, a portion of all the other countries."[51] The aim in diversifying the immigration stream to the United States would benefit the country, not only because immigrants bring drive, labor, and culture.

What if the Cold War–era battle to win African hearts and minds had new salience after the attacks of September 11, 2001? "If you want to talk about terrorism," the Ghanaian agent continued, "maybe a terrorist country would say, no we don't have to attack the U.S. when my people are there. I don't have to do this because the U.S. is like me."[52] By inviting immigrants from around the world, the United States strengthened its political and diplomatic ties—and its economic ones—to all countries. "Cameroonians are there, in numbers, you know," said a longtime visa entrepreneur of the United States. "As a result of that, there is a bilateral relationship that is strong because of that."[53]

· · · · · ·

While many speculated that the visa lottery served U.S. interests, others interpreted it as a measure designed to develop African countries—or at least this was an interpretation that applicants were eager to share with an American visitor.[54] Speculating about the lottery's purpose, Henry Nti Antwi said, "I think they [the United States] wanted to help other nations. When they see their economic background being so weak. They actually wanted to help."[55] Another Ghanaian said that the lottery exists to help "we the Africans."[56] After all, the program created an avenue for African migration that didn't previously exist, and almost everybody I spoke with had known or heard stories about somebody who'd won.

The idea that the United States ran the lottery to help African countries complemented the idea that the lottery was designed to help individuals achieve their dreams. Instead of seeing development as a communitarian project, the lottery and the migration it facilitated framed progress as a matter of individual successes. "To me, it's to help the world . . . to actually realize their dreams. . . . But with the coming of the DV lottery it can help them to actually see how they can make their dreams to come true."[57] Another person said, "Winning the lottery is actually like somebody going to heaven."[58]

By interpreting the program this way, the lottery helped make America dearer to people's hearts, and uniquely so: "America is the only country that has given that opportunity. In the whole world it is only America that is open," Walisu Alhassan told me in Ghana.[59] In a collection of memoirs of Cameroonian Bushfallers, visa lottery winner Victor Mbah writes about winning in 2003. "Not many people get to win a lottery in their lives! . . . This was the opportunity the family had been waiting for. My going abroad could open many doors for other family members to travel overseas as well. And it was not just overseas, it was America!"[60]

This framing of the lottery helped promote uncritical visions of life in the United States. A visa was positioned as a prize of immense value. This fed applicants' ideas about what was appealing about the United States. While people well understood that nothing could be as rosy as they imagined, they still felt sure that something could be found elsewhere that was missing at home. For many, they had the sense that, in a powerful, wealthy country like the United States, they could channel hard work into success. By contrast, they felt this was impossible at home.

· · · · · ·

This imagined vision of the United States reflected critiques of and frustrations with life at home in Africa. People were missing strong institutions, state services, access to education, and opportunities for upward mobility. A francophone man told me, "It's inevitable for the world to have the United States as a dream country, right? It is a way to have a dream each day of something better, something better for tomorrow, most everything, and the

United States, it's a mirror for us—so we say, good, go there for another life, changed one way or another."[61] Couched in language about the United States as a dreamland was a modest, yet still aspirational vision of a country where not everything was broken. It was not that the roads were literally paved with gold, but that they were paved at all.

A hazy impression of the United States, cultivated through myth and Hollywood magic, repeated by those dreaming of the mobility the United States promised through its language about the value of immigration, boosted U.S. power, particularly in a period of formal foreign policy disengagement. In 2015, at an event marking the twenty-fifth anniversary of the Immigration Act of 1990, Bruce Morrison, one of the law's key architects, mused that the visa lottery sprang from the idea that "everyone in the world should believe that you can come to America."[62] That year, 7 percent of Ghana's population, 1.73 million people, applied for the lottery, more than any other country in the world.[63] Although not everyone could come to the United States—far from it—the lottery fueled the idea that *anybody* could. By doing so, the American dream in Africa came vividly alive.

The visa lottery was meant to send a signal to the world that the United States would remain open to the immigration of independent strivers. It did, and the United States benefited—not only by attracting new Americans who would bring their talents and hard work, but also by enhancing its global reputation.

16 Return

The value of winning the visa lottery wasn't just in getting to go to the United States—for many, it was about coming back. Access to the abundance in the United States, through the purchase of a car and house, was one thing, but winning the lottery also meant coming home from America with new status. "When you have been, it implies something, you know. Just getting there, it's something. So a lot of persons, they wish to be going," one lottery agent said.[1] Another added, "If you go to the States and come back home, you get some respect from your friends."[2]

Lottery winners and other emigrants were expected by their families and communities to send money back, to repay debts undertaken to pay for plane tickets and visa fees, and to boost the family's standard of living going forward. The sacrifices of family separation and impossible distances, people hoped, would pay off. On visits home, emigrants were expected to bring suitcases of consumer goods, items impossible to find or prohibitively expensive in local markets. And money sent home on a regular basis was a key element of people's expectations of how migration's benefits should be distributed. The influx of needed funds from abroad could be lifesaving in economically dire situations, or wealth-sustaining in better times. Remittances helped families pay for medical and education expenses, build homes, and set up small enterprises. Talk of going abroad or applying to the visa lottery was inextricable from discussions about *return*, especially the sending of money home.

By the end of the twentieth century, African states recognized that the out-migration of people with needed skills was increasing. Such flows signaled Africa's continuing marginalization in the global economy, in the context of economic policies promulgating free trade and privatization. Consequently, states strategized about how they might harness the power of the diaspora, whether by encouraging citizens to return to stem the "brain drain" or by enabling them to invest at home even if they remained abroad. Efforts to bring people home permanently, by offering better salaries and working conditions, were difficult to implement or sustain. Shoring up public services required revenues states didn't have and went against the tide of economic reforms that states embarked upon with structural adjustment.

The pull of opportunities abroad, and the efforts of Western countries to lure talented workers, was hard for such states to overcome.

Instead, states sought to convert brain drain into brain gain: inviting nationals now living abroad to share expertise and skills back home, while sending money home to circulate in the economy.[3] Experience and salaries earned abroad could be brought back to share with others, to invest in new businesses, to foster new trading relationships, and more. Remittances could boost consumption and let that stand in for broader projects of development without placing demands on the state. Given the appeal of market solutions, encouraging individuals to send remittances was a strategy in line with the times. And the visa lottery served the goals of globalized neoliberalism beautifully.

· · · · · ·

People have always moved—to escape privation or conflict, in search of labor opportunities, to perform seasonal work. But the imposition of strong international boundaries and the global adoption of the modern nation-state as the premiere unit of political organization have made international migration into a political problem, with the category of "outsider" taking on great importance. People continue to move because people have always moved. But today they do so with new labels: labor migrant, seasonal worker, illegal immigrant, asylum seeker, climate refugee.

Migrants with highly valued and sought-after skills have had more freedom to move than their lower-wage counterparts. This is part of a long pattern: wealthy countries have used resources to attract valued workers, even as poor countries have transformed their economies in ways that push out talented people. Going abroad, or having to go abroad, to make a living wasn't inevitable. For example, until the early 1980s, Nigerian professionals stayed home and earned internationally competitive salaries. That changed only after the collapse of oil prices, along with neoliberal reforms that froze wages.[4] Some countries have been pushed to deprioritize industries like medicine, higher education, and science that might have retained professionals, while wealthy nations like the United States have adopted service- and knowledge-based economies.

An estimated 127,000 professionals left the African continent between 1960 and 1989. In 1990, it was estimated that Africa had lost 6 percent of its highly skilled professionals to industrialized countries.[5] The numbers soon increased even further, with some 20,000 African professionals departing the continent annually after 1990.[6] This may understate the scale of the phenomenon by ignoring the movement of professionals within Africa itself. The measure of brain drain may be even larger than reflected in such estimates. In 2002, the Ghana Health Service estimated that 1,200 Ghanaian physicians were working in the United States. Five hundred more worked in the United Kingdom, South Africa, and Canada. More Ghanaian doctors worked abroad than in Ghana itself.[7] The loss of doctors and other medical professionals posed serious problems for the country's health.

Doctors, nurses, lawyers, scientists, university lecturers, and others had many reasons to seek opportunities abroad. Education and national health care systems, so important to independence-era African states, were two areas hit hard by structural adjustment. Yet even in a global system that marginalized people with Black skin and African passports, wealthy countries offered visas, access, and high salaries to individuals with needed skills. With disinvestment gutting those sectors at home, what choice did people have other than to claim those opportunities?

African countries were left to assess the cost of these emigrations to their own societies.[8] Africa, in effect, was providing a subsidy to countries like the United States, educating young people only to have them depart with their talents and skills, in which the receiving country had invested, essentially, nothing. President Rawlings of Ghana called brain drain a "leech" undermining the government's efforts to develop the country.[9] An editorial on brain drain in *The Spectator* decried health professionals who "consider their pockets more important than the national interest." No country, it argued "can develop when its citizens are not patriotic."[10]

Another opinion piece argued that the country's economic woes could not be solved so long as "a multitude of our people, the most precious resource, continue to desert our shores to seek greener pastures abroad."[11] It felt to some like a modern version of slavery—"voluntary slavery"—that Africans' hard work helped benefit the wealthiest nations rather than their own.[12] A 1994 letter to the editor of Nigeria's *Daily Champion* called the lottery itself a form of "neoslavery," a "neo-colonialist mechanism to secure cheap labour and exploit the underdeveloped for the benefit of the U.S." It accused the United States of being "a collapsing civilization" that "waves fake carrots to entice" Nigerians away.[13] In 1996, Ghana's ambassador to the United States, H. E. Ekwow Spio-Garbrah, referred to the visa lottery at a congressional hearing on U.S. trade with Africa. "U.S. green card lotteries aimed at recruiting qualified Africans for the U.S. economy, for instance," he argued, "must be monitored as part of a new international trade in human services. This U.S. immigration policy and practice has the effect of further taxing Africa's economy without the payment of commensurate intellectual property rights to African governments."[14]

Ironically, although the visa lottery facilitated the migration of Ghanaians and other Africans to the United States, it did not strive, to the degree other migration policies did, to select immigrants on the basis of specific professional qualifications like tertiary educations or specific medical skills. Instead, it selected winners with a degree of randomness, although it did set a baseline qualification of a high school diploma or its equivalent, or skilled work experience.

This may have made it more popular given concerns about brain drain. "If it was all about the brain drain," a Cameroonian visa agent said, "then they would somehow, some way they would try to know more about the person playing, instead of some random game."[15] This didn't reflect U.S. generosity or the sudden uncoupling of its notion of "the best and brightest" from class markers and earning potential. Instead, a legislative compromise had stripped more specific minimum qualifications out of the diversity visa program to ensure it continued to admit Irish citizens without advanced degrees. As a result, the lottery may have been slightly less classist than it might otherwise be—and more appealing to applicants.

While concerns about brain drain came up in discussions about trade with Africa, raising the issue wasn't likely to change U.S. immigration policy. The Immigration Act of 1990, after all, aimed to bring in workers whose skills would serve the U.S. economy in a globalizing age. One might expect that those concerned about global inequality would frame policy demands in terms of the brain drain's effects on Africa. But the loudest voices warning against brain drain came from restrictionists eager to stop the flow of *any* foreigners into the United States. John Tanton, who would go on to create the most prominent anti-immigration organizations of the last four decades, drafted a statement for the group Zero Population Growth back in 1973. He argued that the emigration of skilled people from less developed countries would "retard development" there—especially because he believed that retaining doctors and other professionals would help poor countries reduce overall fertility. For population control advocates like Tanton, this was key. Allowing the immigration of talented young people, he wrote, represented a "form of 'reverse' foreign aid."[16] Tanton thought reframing migration as harmful to sending countries would help in his efforts to severely curtail immigration to the United States, but most people who cared about the development of poor countries didn't agree with his prescriptions.[17]

While advocates on different sides of the issue agreed that inequality between countries was a factor in migration, addressing inequality across borders was a substantial challenge. Tanton's organization FAIR didn't tend to focus on the brain drain, since doing so threatened to remind Americans that *they* benefited from the arrival of foreign-born professionals. Instead, they focused on framing migrants as a drain on the United States and argued that it had a responsibility to "screen out the illiterate, the unskilled, the unmotivated and the unassimilable."[18]

If brain drain was a subject for ongoing concern and anxiety, by the late twentieth century it was also a trend that showed no signs of stopping. Some scholars began to theorize that such migrations could ultimately benefit *both* the destination country, where professionals could make best use of their skills, *and* the sending country, which could make up for the loss of human capital by harnessing the power of remittances. Those Africans actively engaged in transatlantic networks and migration might represent, as one scholar wrote, "a bridgehead on which a new global strategy of 'development and migration' can be based."[19]

Some states, including Ghana and Nigeria, began adopting new strategies for coping with and capitalizing on emigration, and hit upon dual citizenship as a solution.

· · · · · ·

Immigration and citizenship are closely related. People born in the United States, regardless of their parents' citizenship, are born U.S. citizens.[20] Immigrants may naturalize as citizens, if they are eligible: typically, if they are lawful permanent residents who have resided in the United States for five years in good standing. Until then, they lack the full rights of citizens. Naturalized citizenship typically grants a person protection from deportation, the right to petition for certain relatives to immigrate, eligibility for jobs available only to citizens, the right to serve on a jury, access to a U.S. passport and its protections, and the ability to vote in local, state, and federal elections.

For immigrants without a green card—those who possess temporary visas, possess other legal statuses, or lack any status—there may be no pathway to citizenship at all. Increasingly since the 1980s, millions live in this liminal place for years, decades, or their whole lives. Many families have mixed statuses: some citizens, some unauthorized, with no access to relief. Citizens and noncitizens alike pay taxes, are subject to criminal and civil laws, and serve in the military. But noncitizens do so without access to formal political power or protection from deportation.

Who can access U.S. citizenship has shifted over time. In the United States, whiteness has long been foundational to citizenship; the country's first naturalization law in 1790 specified that only free white people could naturalize. It was only after African Americans fought for their freedom and citizenship in the Civil War that the Fourteenth Amendment enshrined birthright citizenship. In the twentieth century, others have built on this critical transformation of American citizenship to further broaden access and claim rights. In their struggle for liberation, African Americans expanded the meaning and rights associated with citizenship for other groups as well.

Globally, national citizenship became increasingly important. After twentieth-century European overseas empires began to crumble, independence leaders and social movements imagined forms of political organization that could be alternatives to nation-states, such as Pan-Africanism, or regional confederations that would organize territories, identities, and rights.[21] Instead, former colonies became nation-states.

The continued salience of state citizenship appears almost paradoxical in the context of rapid globalization in our time, an era of swift mobility of goods, capital, and culture, and of people (migrants, refugees, asylum seekers, expats, cosmopolitans) on the move across borders. Although globalization seemed to promise new opportunities for organizing human societies—perhaps in new international, transnational, or even postnational modes—nation-states, and the borders constituting them, persisted. "Far from the nation-state melting away," the political scientist Jeffrey Herbst wrote, "national boundaries, broadly defined, are, in a number of ways, more relevant than ever before."[22]

The restriction and exclusion of immigrants is one method of defining who belongs. "Nationality may be an abstraction, but it does not feel very abstract at a border crossing," as the scholar Samuel Fury Childs Daly wrote about the "Ghana must go" deportations from Nigeria.[23] Recent decades have witnessed the erection of massive walls to fortify borders all over the world.[24] Walls and fences separating "us" and "them" may serve to reinforce national identities but they also reflect anxiety about eroding state power.

Postcolonial African states faced critical state-building challenges even before neoliberalism. Most African independence leaders saw the state as "a key agent of forging a collective vision as well as of building the schools, roads, hospitals, and other facilities needed for a decent life and possibilities of progress in the twentieth century."[25] But they inherited colonial states that had been constructed narrowly to secure metropolitan interests. Initially, national governments pursued developmental programs that expanded state reach, grew public sector employment, and established access to state services, like health care and education, for citizens.[26] Before the 1970s, in most African countries, the historian Frederick Cooper notes that "educational access shot upward, including at secondary and tertiary levels, literacy became more widespread, infant mortality declined, and life expectancy rose. The standard measures of economic growth fluctuated from place to place and time to time, but until the mid-1970s they were on the whole mildly positive."[27] People got something through their citizenship; the state provided. When widespread recession in the 1970s brought economic catastrophe, demands by international donors to balance budgets and cut services resulted in hardship and privation. These market-oriented policies undermined the promises of independence-era state citizenship.[28]

Emigration and the brain drain were responses to these circumstances. In a 1997 article on mass enthusiasm for the visa lottery in Nigeria, a university lecturer reported that more than two-thirds of lecturers at the University of Ibadan had applied for the visa lottery, "noting that teachers had been completely marginalised in Nigeria."[29] A student reported applying for the 1997 visa lottery because of the "unpredictable academic calendar" in Nigeria. "The incessant strikes and inconsistency in education has not been helpful," he said.[30] That teachers and students felt especially disenfranchised speaks to the breakdown of the postcolonial promise of the state, which had made education a core project. The same went for the exodus of health-care professionals, as austerity diminished the prospect of robust national health services that could serve the community.

Frustration with African institutions was a signal of people's disillusionment with their governments, but not necessarily a rejection of national identity. "States may entirely collapse without disappearing as nations from the social imaginary," as Crawford Young writes.[31] Echoing Michael Billig's idea of "banal nationalism"—the idea that national identity is manifest in ordinary interactions and that nationhood is daily reproduced amid globalization—the anthropologist Bea Vidacs has argued, for example, that discursive practices related to sports created and reinforced a distinct Cameroonian nation.[32] Nations might be relatively new—some were "constituent units that had only been encouraged to think of themselves as sharing a national space on the eve of independence."[33] But "sentiments of national solidarity can be grown from diverse seedlings," as Thomas Hylland Eriksen wrote.[34]

External actors such as the IMF and World Bank also treated the nation as the primary unit of political belonging, and an international passport regime based on nation-states further made national borders meaningful to the people living within them.[35] National infrastructure created its own logic that created a physical reality.[36] "All the mobility globalization seems to stand for cannot be interpreted as a 'withering away' of the nation-state," as anthropologist Peter Geschiere wrote.[37]

Questions about belonging became critically important after the Cold War's end. Across Africa, these years witnessed conflicts and episodes of communal violence sparked by fights about belonging within nation-states. The most striking example was the Rwandan civil war and genocide of 1994, but others, like the civil war in Côte d'Ivoire or the crisis in the Democratic Republic of the Congo, centered on questions about who truly belonged to the nation and who should be excluded. African governments were also thinking about belonging in terms of inclusion and outreach to emigrants who'd departed home.[38]

· · · · · ·

In the twentieth century, citizenship, once reserved only for the privileged, grew more expansive. But dual citizenship was rare, since it was understood that a person couldn't be loyal to two different states. Near the end of the twentieth century, something changed. "Where dual nationality was once highly disfavored, if not outlawed, it has become widely accepted," wrote legal scholar Peter J. Spiro.[39]

For example, prior to 2000, any Ghanaian who naturalized as a citizen elsewhere immediately renounced their legal Ghanaian citizenship. This wasn't unusual. Before 1998, Mexican immigrants who naturalized as U.S. citizens automatically lost Mexican citizenship. The United States did not permit U.S. citizens to hold plural citizenship through most of its history either. A 1967 Supreme Court decision began an incremental process through which the United States came to recognize that its citizens could hold a second citizenship without compromising U.S. loyalty.[40]

Immigration has rarely meant cutting all ties with one's country of origin, and even in the nineteenth century, people's paths were more meandering and circular than we sometimes think. Some Europeans settled in the United States and brought their families over, forging permanent lives. Others lived and worked for a while in the United States, and returned home permanently. But migration in the late twentieth and twenty-first centuries enabled new methods of continued connectivity as those in the expanding diaspora could call or email home, travel by airplane at declining costs, send money via electronic transfer, or later keep WhatsApp chats humming in the background of daily life.

As more people lived transnational lives, they began to advocate for changes to citizenship law. Through the mid and late 1990s, a growing population of Ghanaians abroad pressured Ghana to adopt dual citizenship, through a constitutional amendment.[41] It worked. The Ghanaian Citizenship Act of 2000, which took effect in 2002, created the process by which Ghanaians could acquire a second nationality or reclaim renounced Ghanaian nationality.[42]

Instead of fruitlessly trying to stem emigration—or investing in a very long-term project to build opportunities at home that could compel people to stay and reduce transborder inequality—states embraced dual citizenship in response to the brain drain. They wanted to keep emigrants involved in their home countries, through political participation, investment, and remittances. As the political scientist David Leblang has shown, dual citizenship "decreases the transaction costs associated with entering a host country's labor market and makes it easier for migrants to return home."[43] Ghanaians abroad favored the adoption of dual citizenship to participate in Ghanaian politics, to visit more smoothly without a visa, and to invest more easily in their home villages and families.

Ghana was one of many states that decided that dual citizenship served the national interest. As Spiro writes, "Previously, emigrants from these states were considered to have turned on their homelands as part of the brain drain phenomenon. More recently, allowing emigrants to retain their original citizenship after naturalizing in a state of immigration has been adopted as a strategy for cementing the home state tie, with ancillary economic benefits."[44] Leblang calculated that expatriates were more likely to remit and to return to countries that recognize dual citizenship, which multiplied the value of remittances received.[45]

By adopting laws that recognized dual citizenship, African states sought not only to accrue the benefits from transnational remittances and investment but to manage the continuing salience of nation-state membership. By the mid-2000s, more than half the countries of the world, including Ghana and Nigeria, recognized dual citizenship.[46]

The musical artist Wanlov the Kubolor put out a song called "Green Card" in 2007.[47] "We fought to get off the slave yard / Now we fight to get us a green card," he raps in the refrain, taking aim at Ghanaians' widespread impulse to go to the United States.[48] The CD cover features the image of a

Black man entering reluctantly into a marriage with a blonde, blue-eyed American, with the tacit, perhaps paid, approval of a pastor. The specter of the highly prized U.S. passport floats above the couple. The image pokes fun at everybody involved: the white woman smothering her husband with kisses, the priest facilitating the marriage for profit, and the African man desperate for a green card—and, perhaps, a country that has accepted out-migration as a method for its own survival.[49]

. . . . . .

At Christmas, when Africans living abroad traveled home, "one could see them in very good cars, parading the streets of Buea, near the university, with music in their cars turned to the highest volume. We students called these cars 'moving night clubs.' It was so beautiful to stand by the roadside and witness them pass by," recalled one Cameroonian, reflecting on the elevated social status of bushfallers coming home.[50] It wasn't hard to observe the effects of the visa lottery and emigration on winners, their families, and their communities more broadly.

Migrants themselves returned changed by their experiences: "The country is gaining from it, because when you go out of Cameroon, you come home different," the director of a photography shop told me. "You are exposed, you are—you know how to speak, you know how to write, you are educated, so when you come home, you have to change the society in which you live."[51] Although bushfalling was understood as an individual pursuit, the benefits could be seen as serving the broader community rather than draining it.

While these effects were manifold, ranging from personal weight gain to the development of high-end gated communities in suburban Accra, the primary benefit of emigration was the growing role played by remittances. Even before remittances became such an important part of the economies of African countries—Nigeria became the largest recipient of foreign remittances, showing an inflow of $21 billion in 2014—observers linked the opportunity of the visa lottery to the improvement of Africa.[52] As one article put it, "Those who have managed to leave the shores of the country have changed their families fortune for good. By remitting hard currencies, those left behind could boast of living better than those with no one 'outside.' The result? Everyone has set a goal to emigrate, so as to self-actualise and enjoy the good thing offered by the Americans."[53]

Remittances helped support family at home as structural adjustment reduced formal sector employment, devalued currencies, and unraveled the social contract. Instead of the state offering free public education to all citizens, families had to pay school fees as their salaries shrank. But when a family member went abroad, it provided a lifeline. "There are some family members who go and never send anything back to their families, which is of course, not really good," a Cameroonian explained to me. "But the majority send back something and support their families back home."[54] Another man affirmed that an emigrant abroad would "not allow your brother and sister here to languish in poverty."[55] Such observations implicitly suggested that success in America was accessible, and that only moral failure—rather than low wages, discrimination, or high costs of living in the United States—could explain a failure or inability to send such funds.

Because so many people used remittances to pay school fees, studies show that remittance-receiving households "have greater access to secondary and tertiary education, health services, information and communication technology, and banking" than neighboring households that do not receive remittances.[56] Between 1990 and 2010, remittances to Africa quadrupled to $40 billion annually.[57] As Walisu Alhassan, who grew up in a small village in northern Ghana, put it, if a person like him, with many siblings, was to win the lottery to go to the United States, "the family is going to change a lot. . . . It is going to help a lot in the family."[58]

Scholars who study developing countries show that these remittances are more stable than other flows of capital, including foreign aid and direct investment. Not only that, they tend to be countercyclical, meaning they can provide a lifeline in case of emergency.[59] In a case study on Ethiopian diversity visa winners, the economist Teferi Mergo has shown that families with a visa lottery winner experienced greater well-being than their neighbors.[60] They ate better, spent more on energy, owned better consumer goods, and had better access to clean water. Mergo has suggested that the visa lottery may be America's best aid program.[61]

In contrast to other forms of aid fostered by USAID or the World Bank or discourses pegging development to resource extraction, migrant-led development, some have suggested, gives individuals the agency to make their own choices about how to live and improve their lives.[62] Remittance-based development depends on many of the ideas that have animated neoliberal reforms and structural adjustment: individualism, the primacy of markets, and the potential for private enterprise to elevate people out of poverty. Structural adjustment policies, including currency devaluation and facilitating imports, have directly facilitated remittances.[63]

Though some trumpet migration-driven development as a way of giving people a greater sense of agency over their own lives, where structural adjustment and migration restriction had denied it to them, it is important to recognize this strategy's limits.[64] Although the visa lottery has been shown to improve the welfare of families, Mergo's research has also shown that families' business ownership and savings remained unaffected—remittances allowed families to increase consumption but not to build their own enterprises.

And migration-driven wealth has had other unanticipated consequences. Some expatriates have sought to reproduce American living in Africa, through the purchase of large family homes, electricity generators, and large gas-guzzling cars. One man told me about so-called funeral houses—houses that emigrants build back in Ghana but that they cannot really move into, lest they abandon the U.S. incomes they rely on to survive. Instead, the houses, built to stand as grand symbols of the person's success, serve as funeral houses for the person to come back to only after death.[65] The gains earned by successful emigration could be illusory. But such conspicuous consumption reflected a person's raised status, which served to reinforce narratives about the success that could be created only in the West.

Encouraging emigrant Ghanaians to stay connected to Ghana by retaining citizenship, visiting easily, sending remittances, and planning futures back home created notable pockets of wealth. Since the 1990s, metropolitan Accra has witnessed the rapid development of American-style gated communities. A study found that a significant portion of houses in upscale gated communities in Accra were purchased by Ghanaian expatriates living outside the country.[66] Another study showed that demand by Ghanaian expatriates was driving the market for single-family houses in Kumasi. After some time abroad, Ghana expected its emigrants to come home and build their own houses.[67] One Ghanaian opened a business specifically to help expat Ghanaians buy homes in Ghana, sometimes sight unseen. "For a lot of people it's a status symbol of getting out of the position you were in," Austin Batse, a client of the company, said. "You can be someone coming from a village but you return in a totally different class because of the power of what you've been able to earn" abroad.[68] Buying a home in Ghana mattered, argued Kwasi Amoafo, the vice president of the company Ghana Homes. Then, he said, "everyone who matters to you can see you've made it in America."[69]

What benefited the individual, though, could drive economic growth in ways that exacerbated inequality, by raising housing costs, clogging traffic, and fueling the development of inaccessible shopping malls and other luxury services.

· · · · · ·

The visible success of some Ghanaians back home further reinforced mythologies about the United States. The notion that hard work was fairly rewarded in the United States was seemingly illustrated by data showing the impact of remittances on a country's economy. If people weren't being paid generously, how could they afford to send home regular payments? One internet café worker in Ghana explained, "When you are working here, one thing is that there is so much cheating between the employer and the employee. People are not paid for what they should be paid for." In the United States, by contrast, "you work, you always get your pay. So people are able to save there, send the money back for investment."[70] "Nobody has ever left here using the lottery or other means in going to the U.S. and coming back without achieving what he or she wanted to do," is a common refrain.[71]

Few people reported back about adversity in the United States. Messages about loneliness, poor wages, racism, and other difficulties abroad were easy to dismiss as individual problems rather than structural ones. They might reflect a particular emigrant's personal weakness, laziness, or bad luck rather than systemic economic or social hardship in the United States for newcomers and other working people.

Some did express skepticism. One man told me that visa lottery immigrants from Cameroon "don't get the white-collar jobs. They go and [they are] sweeping the streets. So, I don't think it's a positive thing for people like me because I am educated, I have gone to school. I cannot see going to America and sweeping the streets."[72] In a short story about a Cameroonian green card lottery winner, a character rejects the idea of the American dream: "That's exactly what America does. It exports the 'good' side of itself and you spend years of your life dreaming of becoming a carefree Marlboro cowboy, you dream of going to America and becoming the best friend of the Carringtons, to whom you'll proudly show exotic Africa. . . . Then you'll go there and they tell you you're just a black man, you're just a *person-of-color*."[73] A Nigerian newspaper in 1997 quoted a man anonymously saying that emigrating hurt not only the country but the emigrant himself: "A lot of the winners of the visa lottery become worse off in the U.S. than they were before they left the country."[74]

Others contextualized emigrants' difficulties by framing them as temporary or the result of laziness. The good life, after all, was in reach but required hard work.[75] A photographer and entrepreneur whose sons had won the lottery and settled in the United States said, "They tell me things—for three years, things were very difficult, but now it's better. It's okay. You have to adapt, wherever you are."[76] Perhaps the people who suffered—those who accepted low-wage jobs or who failed to send money home—simply hadn't worked hard enough. The narrative of the American dream prevailed when those who failed to achieve it could be blamed in their individual circumstances for not measuring up.

Reports of difficulties were easy to dismiss as exceptional or misguided, given how motivated people were to believe that something better was possible out there, and how states embraced diaspora economics that exacerbated inequality at home. Yet the challenges faced by African immigrants in the United States were profound, not only because of rising xenophobia and anti-immigrant sentiment but because anti-Black racism orders American life profoundly. Even hard work and faith in American ideals could not protect Black African immigrants from violence, policing, and segregation.

Part III

17 Amadou Diallo

. . . .

Amadou Diallo lived in an apartment in the Bronx with three roommates. Each of them had settled recently in New York, finding comfort and connections in the Soundview neighborhood, where many West African immigrants resided. Diallo was born to Guinean parents in the neighboring country of Liberia in 1975, and his childhood was marked by mobility. Owing to his parents' exporting business, he grew up with opportunities to travel and see the world, spending his childhood in Togo, Singapore, and Thailand, as well as in Guinea, as his family moved around. He came to New York in 1996 on a temporary visa. In Manhattan, Diallo spent his days working as a petty trader on 14th Street while saving money for school.[1] "Amadou was the kind of boy who had ambition to go to school and to be somebody," his father, Saikou Diallo, said later.[2] Like millions of others, he believed that the United States would allow him to pursue his dreams.

But Diallo's life was ended when New York City cops fired forty-one bullets at him on February 4, 1999. Nineteen bullets hit him. He was just twenty-three years old. After they killed him, the police claimed to be in his neighborhood looking for somebody suspected of committing several rapes. They said that Diallo resembled the suspect and that he had pulled out a gun. He had not. He was not the man the police said they were searching for.

For many New Yorkers and Black Americans, it was the latest atrocity in a long history of police racially profiling and brutalizing young Black men because they were Black. Diallo's murder came just a few years after New York police famously tortured and sexually abused Abner Louima, another Black immigrant New Yorker, from Haiti, in 1997. And the 1990s' most famous case of police brutality, the videotaped beating of Rodney King, for which the Los Angeles Police Department (LAPD) officers' acquittal fueled days of uprisings in Los Angeles in 1992, had continued to resonate. While each of these events became flashpoints for outrage and activism, they built on decades of organizing and sustained efforts by Black Americans to challenge violent, racist policing.[3] Such calls for transformation periodically provoked state action—LBJ's presidential commission in the 1960s, Supreme Court decisions like *Miranda*, the 1970s Knapp Commission in New York, the use of consent decrees after the 1990s—but racist brutality and killings continued.

Just as the shooting of Michael Brown in Ferguson, Missouri, in 2014 and the murder of George Floyd in Minneapolis, Minnesota, in 2020 would later give rise to mass movements confronting American racism, in 1999 Diallo's case became a rallying cry against police brutality.

Diallo's killing sent the message that being Black was all it took to get a person killed by the police in America.[4] His innocence, clear record, being unarmed, coming from a well-off family, and possession of a convert's love for the United States: none of it had protected Diallo. None of it could have. "I think it was destiny," his mother, Kadiadou Diallo, said about her son's decision to come to the United States. "God sent him here for a mission, and now he has completed that mission."[5]

The case echoed around the world. As the historian Violet Showers Johnson wrote, in every wave of voluntary Black migration "the immigrants have realized the limits of their preparedness, especially to deal with racism."[6] It is said that many people across Africa think America offers a version of "Heaven on Earth"—*until they arrive*. While the visa lottery indeed opened a new channel for African immigration, the prize claimed by its Black winners could be quite different from what they expected. Diallo's fate laid bare a truth that many Black immigrants would learn firsthand: that anti-Black racism defines the American experience.

· · · · · ·

Xenophobia and white supremacy are omnipresent in the United States. But anti-Blackness in particular has shaped the experiences of Black immigrants, in disturbing, sometimes surprising ways. Diallo's mother, after all, emphasized that before he was killed, "Amadou felt good about America."[7] But neither his status as an immigrant nor his class status had protected him from the consequences, in America, of being Black in an encounter with armed police.

Those statuses did shape the media's coverage of his death, however. Even as activists and others made the point that it was all too common and typical of police encounters with Black men, the media framed what happened to Diallo as exceptionally unjust. Part of that was rooted in his identity as an immigrant. That he was Black but *not* African American helped make him a victim worthy of support, while it made the police's extreme use of force worthy of condemnation. Diallo's "Africanness," as the anthropologist Jemima Pierre pointed out, "came to be used to underscore the heinousness of the crime. More specifically, could his immigrant status have allowed him to be implicitly understood as 'innocent' in contrast to the African American often assumed to be guilty of criminality?"[8]

The work done to differentiate Diallo from Black American men killed by the police reflected how, at the beginning of the twenty-first century, African immigrants were sometimes being cast as a new "model minority." It was similar to the construction of the myth designating some Asian Americans as a model racial minority, a process by which, as Ellen Wu has described, groups are "conscripted into the manufacture of a certain narrative of national racial progress premised on the distinction between 'good' and 'bad' minorities."[9] Such narratives served American power and myths about racial progress and inclusion while reinforcing existing hierarchies. The idea was that "African immigrants" constituted an immigrant ethnic group worthy of respect for cultural reasons—for example, the high levels of education that they tended to bring with them, English language skills, or high participation in the labor force. Lifting African immigrants up as embodying such qualities, though, suggested a decisive contrast from native-born Black Americans, who in such discourses were framed as dysfunctional and excluded from the bounty offered universally by the United States.[10] Christina M. Greer argued that, in the case of Black immigrants, such a process did not necessarily convey a "model" status but an "elevated minority status" that placed them above native-born African Americans in America's racial hierarchy but below others.[11]

Toni Morrison wrote in 1993 that immigrant groups' integration "always means buying into the notion of American blacks as the real aliens. Whatever the ethnicity or nationality of the immigrant, his nemesis is understood to be African American."[12] America's racist hierarchies made room for people of color—so long as African Americans remained at the bottom. Working to move up in the racial hierarchy often entailed asserting a particular ethnic group identity, or an "ethnic project," as the sociologist Vilna Bashi Treitler described this process.[13] For African immigrants, "Claiming cultural identity also attempted to move African identity up the U.S. racial hierarchy through distancing from African Americans," Anima Adjepong wrote.[14] Elevated minority status, however, helped reinforce the hierarchy itself, which remained thoroughly intact.

After Diallo's death, some African immigrants spoke out about the discrimination and harassment they faced. They could see how Diallo's identity as an African immigrant hadn't protected him. Mamoudou Jawara, a thirty-year-old Guinean businessman, told the *New York Times* that police officers near his home in Staten Island stopped him frequently, telling him tauntingly to "go back to Africa."[15] Such harassment blended anti-Black racism and xenophobia. Although Diallo's status as an African immigrant made him a sympathetic victim in the mainstream press, African immigrants often encountered insults and attacks grounded in stereotypes about Africa, which was often imagined as a single country, marked by crisis and corruption, or better known as home to exotic animals than people. While mainstream newspapers and magazines could tout the successes earned by African immigrants who were highly educated professionals or essential workers, to illustrate their elevated minority status, such coverage further collapsed differences between immigrant groups and downplayed how much Americans' flattened, stereotypical understandings of the continent shaped immigrants' encounters.

As the experiences of the undocumented Irish in the 1980s showed, any noncitizen could be subjected to surveillance, precarity, and discrimination because of their immigration status, especially as the state ramped up immigration enforcement at the end of the twentieth century. If white immigrants like the Irish worried about being swept up in immigration raids or abuse by their employers, the circumstances faced by immigrants of color were far more unrelenting, as entanglements with the criminal legal system tended to bear out.

And while policymakers had succeeded, in some ways, at liberalizing immigration policy in 1986 and 1990, they had also invited increasingly punitive enforcement mechanisms to accompany those measures. Immigration enforcement at the end of the twentieth century and into the twenty-first depended not only on screening people based on their nationality, immigration status, or work authorization but targeting people perceived to be alien, whether due to race, language, occupation, geography, or contact with the criminal legal system.

This added to the sense that African immigrants, regardless of status, experienced incorporation into American communities as conditional. Hopeful visa lottery applicants didn't and couldn't know this until arriving in the United States. Advertisements for playing the lottery positioned the prize clearly; signs in Cameroon, for example, proclaimed, "Devenez citoyen Américain" and "Jouez et Gagnez la nationalité Américaine." Of course, they didn't clarify that formal status and actual belonging were distinct things, and the United States benefited from the popular idea that it was inclusive. One man in Buea, Cameroon, suggested to me that America's reputation as a multiracial democracy made it a more appealing destination than Europe, where immigrants more visibly stood out. Contrasting it with Europe, in America, he believed, "the police don't disturb you, and so on. You don't have to pay this or that, and so on. So in that way America is good. Because America is like, you have different races: black, white. So you don't know who is American, who is this and so on. So that is why people prefer to go to America."[16] A notion of the United States as a vibrant, multicultural society may have animated people's aspirations before migrating. Arriving in the United States, people found conditions less welcoming than advertised.

· · · · · ·

Diallo was not a visa lottery winner. But his arrival in New York in 1996 put him in the company of an increasing number of Black immigrants from Africa, many of them arriving because they did win the lottery. Though Africans had been immigrating to the United States in small numbers for a long time—for example, Cape Verdean laborers who had been coming since the nineteenth century, and West African exchange students in the middle of the twentieth—it was only at the tail end of the twentieth century that their numbers became substantial (if still small compared with other groups).[17] Still, the word "immigrant" in the American debate rarely summoned images of people from Africa. Even as the demographics of immigration shifted rapidly after the 1960s, stories of Black immigration, and especially African immigration, tended to remain marginal to national discussions and debates.

In 1960, nearly all of the top immigrant-sending countries to the United States were European. Mexicans accounted for under 6 percent of the immigrant population at the time.[18] By 1990—even before the permanent diversity visa lottery was implemented—the top sending countries were already far more geographically diverse and less white and European, with the Philippines, Vietnam, China, Cuba, and Korea all in the top ten, and more than 20 percent of immigrants hailing from Mexico.

Even today, no African country has been among the top sending countries to the United States in any year, although more than 2 million immigrants from Africa now reside here.[19] While this number reflects a huge increase from forty years ago, when just 130,000 people from sub-Saharan Africa resided in the United States, the group still represents just 4.5 percent of the overall population of foreign-born people.[20] Historically, Black immigration has long been kept low. Most Black immigrants come from the Americas, but the rate of African immigration has been rising rapidly too.

About 10 percent of the Black population of the United States is now foreign-born, representing a substantial shift over a short period of time.[21]

African immigration to the United States began to increase for many reasons. The end of formal exclusion in the 1960s was one. The facilitation of student and cultural exchanges during the early Cold War amid decolonization, undertaken to serve U.S. diplomatic goals, was another. Globalization and the availability of more affordable and reliable air travel, yet another. Changes in refugee resettlement mattered too; in 1980, the United States revised its refugee policy and began resettling over 1,000 people from Africa each year, including those fleeing famine, political conflict, or persecution. Ethiopians in the 1980s and people from Somalia, Sudan, and Liberia in the 1990s were resettled in the thousands, establishing small communities in the United States.[22] Others fleeing persecution claimed asylum. Some temporary visitors and students opted to stay when conditions at home worsened. Relative to other immigrant groups in the 1980s and 1990s, African immigrants were less likely to be undocumented—perhaps because of the visa requirements, expense, and travel logistics that restricted their entry to the United States in the first place. African immigrants also came as permanent residents to join immediate family members and relatives in the United States, if they had U.S. citizen family members who qualified to sponsor them, although historically this pathway remained narrow.

And then there was the diversity visa lottery. Fifty thousand immigrant visas each year in a system that assigned nearly a million visas annually is something like a drop in the bucket. But once the lottery began, the percentage of admitted immigrants from Africa doubled, from 2.6 percent (1985–94) to 5.9 and 5.8 percent in 1995 and 1996. The number of African immigrants admitted jumped from 26,712 in 1994 to 52,889 in 1996.[23] Of the latter, 20,806 had diversity visas.[24] As a region, Africa came just behind Europe for most diversity visas issued. The African countries that won more than a thousand diversity visas in 1996 included Egypt (2,219), Ethiopia (3,548), Ghana (3,933), and Nigeria (4,359). But even if smaller countries won fewer visas, they surely mattered for the hundreds of people whose lives were suddenly transformed—for example, Cameroon (329), Kenya (552), Liberia (335), and Sierra Leone (914).[25]

Between 1995 and 2020, thirteen African countries had at least 1,000 diversity visas issued in a single year: Algeria, Cameroon, Democratic Republic of Congo, Egypt, Ethiopia, Ghana, Kenya, Liberia, Morocco, Nigeria, Sierra Leone, Sudan, and Togo.[26] In all, half a million Africans were issued diversity visas over the same twenty-five year period. Africans continued to depend disproportionately on the diversity visa program to gain access to the United States as immigrants. In 2019 over a million people became lawful permanent residents (LPRs) of the United States, about 4 percent of them through diversity visas. But nearly 17 percent of Africa's LPRs had won the diversity visa lottery. Around a fifth of African immigrants in the twenty-first century came through the diversity visa program.[27]

Such figures may even understate the lottery's impact on African immigration. In 2019, of 110,000 African green card recipients, 48,500 were the immediate relatives of U.S. citizens and an additional 11,859 came through the family preference system.[28] That demonstrated a sizable shift since the 1990s. In 1996, only about 16,000 Africans came as immediate relatives, with an additional 5,000 through family preference. These increases are, in part, an outcome of high admissions through the visa lottery. That's because a diversity visa immigrant can bring their immediate family with them or petition for them later. Permanent residents may petition for certain family members to join them through the family preference system, including their spouses and unmarried children. After five years of residency, a permanent resident can typically naturalize as a U.S. citizen. U.S. citizens have further opportunities to sponsor relatives to join them, since our system prioritizes the needs of citizens over immigrants themselves. Citizens' immediate family members (spouse, unmarried child under twenty-one years old, or parent, if the U.S. citizen is over twenty-one) can apply to come, and they are not subject to numerical limits. Likewise, citizens can petition for their adult children and their own siblings through the family preference system.

Nativists have come to decry this system as "chain migration," hinting that it encourages too many people to come to the United States. It's a concern that has arisen at the same time as the demographics of immigration shifted after the 1960s. What was once understood as extending the status quo—white Europeans bringing their white European family members to America's shores—became a vector of the threat of demographic change, as fewer Europeans and more Asians, Latin Americans, and Africans immigrated. Yet family unification remains not only a foundation of the legal immigration system but a pattern that is incentivized and encouraged—not least because Americans rely on family networks in the absence of a robust social safety net. And for very practical as well as emotional and economic reasons, we recognize that families belong together. The visa lottery, just as its legislators intended, created the conditions for "new seed" immigration, planting the possibility of new, ongoing "chains" linking the United States to the rest of the world.

The visa lottery also ensured that African immigration to the United States came from nearly every African country. Populous, largely English-speaking countries like Egypt, Ethiopia, Nigeria, South Africa, and Ghana would have sent immigrants even if the visa lottery never existed. But Togo? Cameroon? Perhaps doctors, professors, and family members of U.S. citizens would have been able to migrate. But someone who never finished college? An IT professional? A student ready to launch her career? The visa lottery thus enriched a small but growing population of African immigrants to the United States, offering formal status and a window of welcome in the name of expanding the country's diversity. But as the lottery did what it promised to do, the resulting diversity it delivered raised questions about race and racism in America.

······

In the 1980s, the proliferation of Ethiopian restaurants in Washington, D.C., resulting from the arrival of refugees fleeing crisis at home, became a celebrated part of the city's food scene. The newcomers were resettled and largely seen as sympathetic people fleeing an inhumane situation, including famine and a Marxist regime. Black and white Washingtonians alike ate at the Ethiopian restaurants that refugees opened, and the *Post*'s star critic reviewed the restaurants favorably. Still, the restaurants were careful to maintain their appeal to white diners, including white suburbanites.[29] Fashioning an image of Ethiopians as ideal immigrants (just like the Italians or Greeks of the past, as one observer noted), bringing their own culture and hard work to their new home, helped to distinguish them from the city's native-born Black population.[30] Buying into this distinction, the area's white liberal residents and yuppies eagerly descended on Adams Morgan, a melting-pot neighborhood in a highly segregated, majority Black city. Here they could demonstrate their cosmopolitan savvy and embrace of diversity through adventurous eating, without necessarily engaging or encountering their Black American neighbors.

The mainstream press approached what it perceived as the novel issue of African immigration gingerly. The *Los Angeles Times*, for example, detailed culture clashes between Black immigrants and African Americans in the city of Angels, exacerbated by misconceptions, surprises, and stereotypes.[31]

The *Washington Post*, on the other hand, found much to celebrate in the restaurant scene and beyond, touting the role played by African immigrant entrepreneurs at sprucing up the Georgia Avenue corridor, and crediting their being "hard working" and "family-oriented" for their rapid rise up the professional ranks.[32] Ethiopians, a real estate developer said, "want to accumulate capital" and do so through their hard work.[33] These traits were described as culturally situated, and that framing could obscure some of the advantages that immigrant groups sometimes enjoyed. Community-based savings groups (*isusus*, *ekub*, or *tontine*), for example, used the collective efforts of working immigrants knitted together in close relationships to fuel new projects and to raise the profile of African immigrant success stories.[34] The visa lottery, one article said, promised to bring yet more "African strivers" with the "potential to work wonders for urban economies."[35]

Yet, such successes were held up against a Black neighborhood in decay. Another *Post* article had likened Georgia Avenue to a declining "city seam that's fraying," ridden with crime. Now African immigrants were engaging in a project of revitalization, serving African American customers, launching businesses, and creating bustling commercial activity where previously there was blight. But "blight" wasn't a natural state. Instead, the term and imagery masked policy failures and deeper questions about access to resources.

And so the press could celebrate a neighborhood's fresh diversity, with Black newcomers bringing new energy, new products, and new dreams to a place that was understood to be desperate for all of these. The context for this feel-good story, however, was long-term disinvestment, encroaching gentrification, and continual displacement of the city's long-term Black residents. Between 2000 and 2013, D.C. would experience the greatest intensity of gentrification of any city in the United States.

A hundred years earlier, D.C. had the largest African American population of any U.S. city and was a key political and cultural center for Black Americans.[36] Even as Black Washingtonians built institutions and lives, they did so amid recurring processes of worsening segregation, discrimination, and displacement. When the city's population surged during World War II it remained highly segregated. While the city's white residents could expect to build wealth through homeownership in desirable neighborhoods, discriminatory housing practices and policies denied similar economic growth to Black families. By the 1950s, though, Black Washingtonians were organizing to demand change. As the capital city representing the nation during the global Cold War, Washington was particularly influenced by shifts in federal policy dismantling official segregation, along with local organizing efforts. By 1957, D.C. became the first big city in America with a Black majority.[37]

Deep inequality persisted, however, and Black frustrations erupted after the assassination of Martin Luther King Jr. on April 4, 1968. The uprisings, subdued by federal troops, resulted in property and businesses destroyed, people left homeless, and many arrests. D.C. was nearly 70 percent Black, and the worst damage occurred in highly segregated Black neighborhoods. Black-led community organizations filled basic needs in the following days and weeks. Building on these grassroots efforts, Black D.C. soon experienced political gains and entered an era of cultural flourishing. D.C. finally gained a measure of "home rule" in 1973, something segregationists had long objected to because of the power this granted to the city's Black residents. Funk band Parliament released 1975's "Chocolate City," granting the city a lasting moniker. Congress even passed a constitutional amendment granting D.C. congressional representation in 1978, though it wasn't ratified by the requisite number of states to become law.

But this moment of relative thriving occurred against the backdrop of a city in trouble, as the population shrank, middle-class families fled, businesses closed, and low-income residents were pushed out—and increasingly criminalized. Crime statistics, persistent problems with drugs and addiction, and images of boarded-up businesses along commercial corridors perpetuated stereotypes about Black dysfunction. Yet in truth, these were the visible traces of decades of policy choices that displaced, disenfranchised, and diminished the city's Black residents.

Such context was missing from sunny pieces celebrating the successes of Black immigrants, who often came to their neighborhoods with advantages, community resources, and opportunities that their African American customers lacked. Immigration-driven revitalization—and rapid gentrification—continued to transform D.C. neighborhoods after the 1980s and 1990s. Despite the new energy brought by Black immigrants, who continued to settle in and around the capital, the Black population of the District actually declined. By 2011, Black residents no longer constituted the majority of the Chocolate City's population.

· · · · · ·

"Hard working," "family oriented," and "law abiding" are elements of a kind of campaign for inclusion that ethnic groups themselves benefit from emphasizing, that advocates reinforce in public-facing communications and in policy debates, and that academics contribute to, wittingly or not. These characteristics have been selected for such campaigns because they tap into—and aim to play up contrasts to—long-running stereotypes that suggest that African Americans were none of these things. Immigrant groups often benefited from differentiation from native-born Black Americans, who have been made to remain at the bottom of America's racial hierarchies even as the country has become more diverse.[38]

Negative and dehumanizing stereotypes about African Americans have roots going back to the institution of slavery, when Blackness became the justification for enslavement, when resistance to enslavement and violence could be framed as "laziness" or "criminality," and when violent family separation became a vicious tool of racial dominance. These tropes were further reinforced after Reconstruction and throughout Jim Crow, and reproduced again even as the civil rights movement remade U.S. institutions, to help explain and justify persistent inequality, discrimination, and disorder.

As Jemima Pierre argued, social scientists' representations of Black immigrants have reinforced such tropes, with scholars accepting and reproducing a flattened, hollow story about native-born African Americans in their work exploring the experiences of Black immigrants.[39] Scholars' ideas about such differences then have been repeated in media coverage, aided by members of ethnic groups eager to position themselves and by advocates making arguments about immigrant inclusion.

Much of the news coverage about rising African immigration in the twenty-first century emphasized positive group traits. On average, African immigrants were younger than the overall U.S. population, more likely to be in the working age range, and less likely to be drawing on social security. Such data helped reinforce the notion that they were contributing more to the country than they took. They were also routinely described as better educated than the broader public. Research showed that nearly 42 percent of African-born immigrants possessed at least a bachelor's degree, compared with 32 percent of the U.S. population overall.[40] Labor force participation rates, likewise, hovered above those of the U.S. population. Compared with other immigrant groups, African immigrants were less likely to be undocumented and more likely to speak English.[41] Given the public's hostility to undocumented immigration and assumptions about language acquisition, such data cast African immigrants as better than other groups, with qualities like education, English, legal status, and high wage employment taking on a moral valence.

In these ways, celebrations of the virtues of African immigrants could do the ugly work of highlighting implied differences between foreign and native-born Black Americans, and between African immigrants and other immigrant groups. Lifting up Black immigrant successes could thus reinforce anti-Blackness rather than challenge it. When law professor Amy Chua and her husband Jed Rubenfeld published their 2014 book *The Triple Package*, they argued that Nigerian Americans (along with seven other groups, including Cubans, Jews, East Asians, and Indians) succeeded in the United States because of a combination of cultural traits that sustained them.[42]

While this version of the notion of "model minorities" eschewed the genetic and racist explanations deployed by Chua's eugenicist forebears, such ethnocentrism was nevertheless as corrosive as race science.[43] It downplayed the advantages that some immigrant groups arrived with (sometimes called "self-selection," many of the people who can afford to migrate to the United States have above-average education levels or wealth) or whether legal structures and policy interventions have given them a boost. It elided the extent to which the United States allows minoritized groups to succeed only within the bounds of a highly racially stratified society. And it suggested that cultural deficits or personal failure, not history or racism, explain disparate outcomes. Because if *some* Black people *do* succeed, then the American dream can be said to work after all. Playing up the successes of Black immigrants, however selective, came in handy for propping up the nation's fraught mythologies and its color-blind racism. Chua gave these ideas a kind of academic gloss, but the logics are omnipresent in how Americans talk and think about race, progress, and persistent inequality and violence.

In other words, the model minority story—even when the model minority in question was Black—reinforced a narrative of Black inferiority that placed the blame for purported Black dysfunction on African Americans themselves. Whether that's for failing to instill the "right" cultural values in their children or for failing to appreciate the bounty available to all who work hard in America, a false notion of ingratitude is pernicious.

Immigrant rights advocacy playing up immigrants' virtues tapped into these narratives. Claims that immigrants commit fewer crimes than American citizens, for example, hinted that this disparity is a result of the moral superiority of immigrants. To be sure, such statistics have been deployed as part of an urgent effort to humanize a population that has often been framed as "illegal" and to counter propaganda that has cast them as dangerous and criminal. Yet this narrative ignores the structural racism of the criminal justice system, the overpolicing of Black communities, and the racial history of the politics of law and order in the United States.

Some Black immigrants and other immigrants of color arrived in the United States having absorbed messages of anti-Black racism or possessing negative stereotypes about Black Americans. African countries themselves are not free from colorism, from the legacies of colonialism, history, and the global color line. Once in the United States, embarking on an ethnic project to avoid being slotted into the lowest ranks of the American racial hierarchy, or situating oneself as a "model Black" person in contrast to perceptions about native-born Black Americans, is perhaps a strategy for survival. But it is one that ultimately undermines projects of solidarity and shared struggle. A potent tragedy of this dynamic is that even as nonwhite immigrants position themselves in proximity to whiteness to succeed, they are able to do so only because they have benefited directly from the sustained work of African Americans to broaden access to citizenship, rights, and opportunities in America.

· · · · · ·

The end of legal restrictions on African immigration, and even the availability of visas through programs like the diversity visa, is only part of the story of what African immigrants navigate when claiming their share of the American dream. As one immigrant wrote, to dispel the myths that circulate abroad about the ease of life in the United States, "The general notion back home is that once you've had your visa, it is the end of hard times, the end of misery, and the beginning of a completely new and happy life for the individual in particular, and his family in general. On the contrary, I must remind you that it is not the end of the journey."[44] This was true not only because of economic inequality and exploitation in the United States but also because of the racism that Black immigrants encounter: "As a person from the Dust, your skin betrays you in the Snow. You are recognized from far off. You may be intelligent or not, you may have the passport of the Snow, or be married to a woman or man from Snow; it does not make you a man or woman of Snow!"[45] To belong, one needs access to formal status, to be welcomed by the U.S. immigration bureaucracy, by employers, by schools, by banks, and by state driver's license agencies. But it is not enough.

Racism shaped the final moments of Amadou Diallo's life. He was killed because he was a Black man in the Bronx. But the media coverage that emphasized his innocence, his particular un-deservingness of this violent end, tended to lift up his status not as a young Black man but an immigrant, someone who believed in the promise of the American dream and who didn't question it prior to his death. But Black immigrants like Diallo, despite contending for the status of "model minority," faced anti-Black racism in the workforce, in their communities, and in run-ins with the police and the criminal legal system.

They also became entangled in an ever-expanding system of immigrant criminalization and immigration enforcement. This trend accelerated through the 1990s and into the twenty-first century. The end of the Cold War produced instability and insecurity. In the early 1990s in the United States, nativism surged on the far right, with far-reaching consequences. After the 1993 World Trade Center bombing, anti-immigration forces gathered strength, passing Prop 187 in California and eventually several federal laws that profoundly shaped and curtailed immigrant rights. In 1996, this impulse manifested in the Illegal Immigration Reform and Immigrant Responsibility Act (IIRIRA), as well as anti-immigrant measures in that year's welfare reform and antiterrorism laws. These laws blurred the boundaries between immigration violations and crime. This approach was already in place before the attacks of 9/11—in their aftermath, it was supercharged.

18 Homeland

. . . .

Both xenophobia and anti-Black racism have long histories in the United States, but at the end of the twentieth century, policymakers simultaneously ramped up policing and immigration enforcement measures, often in combination.[1] The surveillance and criminalization of Black immigrants and an atmosphere of repression reached new heights in the country's responses to the attacks of September 11, 2001. In that climate, the United States launched a boundaryless war abroad in the name of keeping Americans safe, while ramping up its capacity to root out and punish sources of threat at home.

While post-9/11 measures particularly targeted immigrants from Middle Eastern, North African, and South Asian countries, systems of surveillance and detention entangled a broad array of people. The atmosphere was stultifying for Americans who wore the hijab or prayed at mosques.[2] Hate crimes soared against Muslims and others, like Sikhs, perceived to be Muslim. Islamophobia also fueled anti-Blackness. As Spencer Ackerman notes, at the time of the 9/11 attacks, Islam was "a religion that was primarily familiar to most white Americans as a frightening accelerator of Black resistance, thanks to demonized figures like Malcolm X."[3] After the attacks, policymakers, politicians, opportunists, and the media conflated categories of race, immigration, and criminality in the public imagination.

And so, in the new millennium, even as the diversity visa lottery continued to animate dreams of life in America beyond its borders, the vision of American life it seemed to promise withered. Deregulation, free market ideology, and the shrinking of the social safety net had undermined security for many Americans. Now, existing structures of white supremacy and anti-Blackness expanded through amped-up policing, a metastasizing security state, and the global war on terror—undermining the promise of welcome at the heart of the lottery and normalizing anti-immigrant suspicion and exclusion. "They hate our freedoms," President George W. Bush explained just days after the attacks. Soon, the U.S. government was doing its own work to limit people's freedoms in the name of security. The United States stopped treating "immigration as a process for becoming American but as a vehicle for terrorism," as Ackerman wrote.[4] Indeed, the threat of terrorism didn't need to be there at all to treat noncitizens like enemies within.

······

After the passage of draconian anti-immigration legislation in 1996, the apparatus of U.S. immigration enforcement expanded. Funding for the Border Patrol and Immigration and Naturalization Service (INS) increased, the border underwent further militarization, and cooperation between local law enforcement and immigration authorities deepened. It became easier for the system to quickly turn back and remove people without documentation at borders and ports of entry, and to deport and remove people within the country even if they were longtime residents. The use of detention skyrocketed after 1996, with new requirements that the government detain people under certain circumstances. And there was more: people who had previously been "removed" from the country became ineligible for legal status for long periods of time, even if they had a path available to attain it, leaving many families torn apart by borders.

Along with an immigration policy-specific bill (the Illegal Immigration Reform and Immigrant Responsibility Act, or IIRIRA) and a welfare reform bill with key provisions targeting immigrants, Congress passed the 1996 Anti-terrorism and Effective Death Penalty Act (AEDPA), which contained immigration provisions. The precipitating event was the 1995 Oklahoma City federal building bombing, an act of terroristic violence that killed at least 168 people, including children at the building's daycare center. Initially, some commentators suggested that the violence had been the work of Muslim terrorists, perhaps seeing it as a follow-up to the 1993 World Trade Center bombing. But it wasn't. The attack was undertaken by two antigovernment, white supremacist U.S. citizens, part of a pattern of organized white nationalist violence that was nevertheless portrayed as the acts of lone wolf terrorists, the kind likely to evade law enforcement's ability to prevent violence.[5]

Instead of addressing an alarming pattern of white supremacist terroristic violence, though, AEDPA signaled its toughness by eviscerating the right of habeas corpus for people convicted of crimes and in detention, limiting the ability of federal courts to grant habeas relief. It made it easier for law enforcement to convict people with ties to foreign groups. It also targeted noncitizens, requiring mandatory detention of people convicted of certain crimes, a category that Congress expanded dramatically. As a result, the number of noncitizens subject to indefinite detention increased.[6]

"When terrorism was white, the prospect of criminalizing a large swath of Americans was unthinkable," Ackerman writes.[7] But criminalizing an enormous swath of immigrants as an antiterrorism measure was acceptable. Portraying terrorism as nonwhite in an era when immigration was mostly nonwhite—as it had been since the 1980s—put all immigrants in the crosshairs, casting the whole category, comprising millions of people, as potentially suspect.

Even immigrants with legal status—as a person with a diversity visa would be—were made more vulnerable by the 1996 laws. Access to public benefits became more onerous and confusing, especially if one lived in a mixed-status household. People with legal status were made more vulnerable to deportation, without much due process. Permanent residents convicted of certain types of crimes, including minor, nonviolent ones, became ineligible for most forms of discretionary relief from deportation. Instead of treating immigrants as future Americans, the implementation of these changes deepened the sense that belonging was highly provisional—and could easily be taken away.

The attacks of September 11, 2001, and the U.S. government response to them dramatically deepened the state's framing of immigration as a source of potential threat. Immigration touches on many parts of American life: labor, family, economics, culture, and law, to name a few. It was a choice, then, for the government to view the immigration issue increasingly through the lens of law enforcement, conflating immigration violations with the nebulous, but politically powerful, idea of "crime." After 2001, immigration would be viewed first and foremost as a matter of "national security." In fact, a huge proportion of "national security" or "counterterrorism" funds would be dedicated to toughening immigration control, even when no identifiable national security or counterterrorism goal was involved. Forces that had always seen the immigration of nonwhite people as "threatening" the "American" (read white, native-born, Christian, and patriarchal) way of life seized the opportunity to conflate immigrants, potentially *all* immigrants, with a threat to security. A shaken American public accepted the dramatic expansion of the security state, state violence, and an anti-immigrant apparatus wildly out of proportion and disconnected from the threat of terroristic violence.

The consequences of that acquiescence fell heavily on noncitizens, Muslim Americans, and communities of color. Overlapping policies targeted people, threatening and obliterating civil liberties and legal rights. As Tram Nguyen writes, the lens of legal rights and wrongs alone doesn't "strike at the heart of what it means to live, as whole communities of people, at the crossroads of backlash against undocumented immigrants, fear and hostility toward suspected terrorists, and a culture of policing and prison that has increasingly turned toward punitive policies and incarceration as the answer to every problem."[8] Rising hate crimes and harassment, and discrimination in housing, at banks, and in employment due to new pressures and surveillance afflicted noncitizens. As the state expanded its own power, communities' power to survive and thrive shrank.

· · · · · ·

A landscape of expanded law enforcement and an atmosphere of suspicion shaped neighborhoods in the days and years after the 9/11 attacks. Initially, the Department of Justice "rounded up" more than 1,200 Muslim, Arab, and South Asian men, who were detained and held indefinitely. It made no effort to distinguish between people with possible ties to terrorism and those taken into custody by chance. None were ever charged with terrorism-related crimes, but hundreds were deported.[9] A 2013 film, *The Citizen*, dramatized this event, following the story of a Lebanese immigrant who proudly wins the diversity visa lottery, arriving by plane to New York City on—of all days—September 10, 2001, just before the attacks. Rounded up without cause (but for his religion and nationality), the man is held incommunicado in detention for six months and refused a lawyer, before the film's plot moves him into another set of misadventures.[10]

In October 2001, Congress passed the Patriot Act, expanding law enforcement surveillance and broadening the definition of terrorism.[11] It enabled forms of indefinite detention while expanding the government's authority to monitor people in the United States, including both citizens and noncitizens. It also tripled the number of border patrol personnel. In November 2001, the United States created the Transportation Security Administration (TSA) to federalize airport security, forever transforming the experience of flying commercially.[12] In December 2001, INS added 314,000 people with deportation orders to a shared law enforcement database. The Social Security Administration also sent 750,000 letters to employers identifying employees whose Social Security numbers didn't match their identities. It was an effort to expose people working under Social Security numbers not assigned to them, a practice associated with being undocumented, not with committing acts of terroristic violence. In the name of cracking down, however, the policy threatened the livelihoods of three quarters of a million people—workers paying into social security accounts they wouldn't be able to benefit from—and their families.[13]

In January 2002, the first detainees arrived at the U.S. military base on Guantanamo Bay, to be held indefinitely. Bush administration legal advisers had suggested it, as a space outside of U.S. legal jurisdiction. An outpost of U.S. empire and remnant of the expansion of U.S. imperial ambitions at the start of the twentieth century, Guantanamo Bay was considered "foreign, in the domestic sense." Its liminal status, and the American public's indifference to U.S. territorial empire, was handy for U.S. actions that clearly violated its laws and policies.

Prior to its use to hold those deemed "enemy combatants" by the Bush administration, Guantanamo had been the site of a refugee camp between 1991 and 1994, established by Bush's father, where Haitian migrants were brought after being intercepted by the United States Coast Guard. More than 35,000 people were detained, where the ambiguous space became grounds to deny Haitians important legal rights and access. Another camp was used to detain refugees who tested positive for HIV. Many of those seeking refuge in the United States were returned to danger in Haiti. President Bill Clinton then used Guantanamo to house refugees in 1994, including Haitians and Cubans. While the use of Guantanamo to detain captured people during the war on terror was distinct from its use as a refugee camp, the latter echoed and built on the former, making similar use of its lawlessness. As Amy Kaplan wrote, the "routes of American empire today follow well-worn tracks."[14]

The attacks of September 11 generated significant anxiety about the nation's borders. "Our borders today are porous and highly vulnerable to penetration by foreign terrorists," stated a December 2001 border security white paper that Bush administration officials used to push to consolidate immigration functions then spread across multiple agencies and departments.[15] By June 2002, Bush was proposing a dramatic reorganization of the government. More than merely the "Office of Homeland Security" he had created in the White House, the idea was to create a cabinet-level department that would absorb some twenty-two federal agencies, with an urgent mission: "securing the American homeland and protecting the American people."[16] The plan didn't touch the FBI, the CIA, or other intelligence agencies whose failure to prepare for or prevent the attacks of 9/11 was then under scrutiny by Congress. Instead, it combined functions that seemed related to domestic defense or that might be needed in the aftermath of an attack: the Coast Guard, the Secret Service, and the Federal Emergency Management Agency, among others.[17]

Most dramatic was the reorganization of the immigration system. The INS, once operated through the Department of Labor and most recently under the Department of Justice, and the U.S. Customs Service, originally under the Treasury Department, were both restructured and brought into the new Department of Homeland Security (DHS), with their functions divided between three new offices. U.S. Citizenship and Immigration Services (USCIS) would absorb "immigration services"—processing work visas, issuing documents, and adjudicating naturalization applications. Two new agencies would take on border security and law enforcement functions at the edges of the country and its interior, respectively: Customs and Border Protection (CBP) and Immigration and Customs Enforcement (ICE).

As Bush and Congress were creating the DHS blueprint, they promulgated other immigration-related security programs. For example, in September 2002, the Bush administration started the National Security Entry-Exit Registration System (NSEERS), which required the registration of noncitizen men over the age of sixteen in the United States with specific types of legal visas from a list of twenty-five designated countries. Men had to submit themselves for fingerprinting, surveillance, interrogations, and a heavy air of suspicion. The program was discriminatory: all of the designated countries except North Korea were majority-Muslim countries.[18] A total of 290,526 people registered; 13,799 were deported, and 2,870 were detained. The program resulted in no terror-related convictions and was eventually suspended (although not dismantled) in 2011.[19]

In rapid time, the United States had dramatically reorganized its approach to managing immigration. Few people believed that ordinary immigrants posed a security threat to the country. Nevertheless, all noncitizens—as well as citizens cast as foreign on account of race, religion, ethnicity, country of origin, or association with immigrants—would bear the weight of the public's fear and the state's violence. Restrictionists had moved far closer to achieving their longtime goals of ending nonwhite immigration altogether, by framing such efforts as a newly urgent security measure.

· · · · · ·

In July 2002, an Egyptian immigrant named Hesham Mohamed Ali Hadayet[20] went to Los Angeles International Airport armed with a gun and opened fire, killing two people before being killed by a security guard. The

FBI and Department of Justice soon deemed it an act of international terrorism, though authorities were puzzled by the fact that Hadayet had lived in the United States for a decade. A newly renamed House congressional subcommittee on immigration, border security, and claims held a hearing to investigate Hadayet's history of contacts with the immigration system.[21] The thinking behind this investigation was that someone's immigration status, and their onetime path into the United States, was *the* most important information to assess, so that immigration policies could be further tightened to prevent such acts of violence in the future.

The logic was twisted. Given the man's long tenure in the United States, and his roots and family here, it was hard to believe he'd unsettled an entire life in Egypt and immigrated to the United States as part of a years-long plot simply to murder two people. What kind of vetting of U.S. residents could possibly screen for the possibility that they might *ever* commit an act of violence? The vast majority of shootings were done by citizens, and the United States was uninterested in restricting citizen access to firearms or addressing the long- and short-term causes of violence initiated by citizens. But when it came to noncitizens, the issue was identified as an immigration problem, and in the days after 9/11, something to be acted upon.

The INS testified that Hadayet had arrived on a visitor's visa in 1992 and later that year applied for asylum. Although his claim was denied, his case didn't raise any flags when run through various databases. He had no criminal background. He also claimed that his government persecuted him and accused him, falsely, of being involved in a terrorist group, a claim that was difficult to assess. Confirming or checking in with the government in question could imperil an asylum seeker's life or that of their family members. While his case was being adjudicated, he received work authorization, which was mistakenly extended even after being denied asylum.

Then in January 1997 he filed to adjust his status because his wife had been selected as a diversity visa winner in Egypt. She was one of 2,087 Egyptians who received diversity visas in 1996, out of a population of more than 60 million people.[22] The odds of winning had been miniscule. But his wife's good luck would allow him to stay in the country where he'd resided for five years already. When his name was run through the FBI system once more, again nothing appeared, and his application was approved. He became a lawful permanent resident and built a life in California.

The INS acknowledged that certain parts of this story might have raised flags—the extension of his work visa after the denial of his asylum claim, for example—but testified that many of the irregularities or systemic issues that allowed for such a mistake had *already* been addressed through changes to its procedures, after the passage of the 1996 laws and other reforms.

The two non-INS witnesses at the hearing were Daniel Pipes, who ran a conservative, anti-Islam think tank, and Steven Camarota, of the Center for Immigration Studies (CIS), an anti-immigration organization created by John Tanton. Camarota testified that the diversity visa lottery *should* be of special concern to security-minded policymakers because it attracted people with few ties to the United States. That had been its specific purpose—to allow "classic immigrants" like those European forebears of so many members of Congress, without existing family ties to the country, to come, plant roots, and enact their American dreams. But in the view of CIS, and with new resonance in the security-first atmosphere of the early 2000s, that became its vulnerability.

Camarota averred with confidence—but no evidence—that "certainly individuals with few ties to the United States are more willing and more likely to engage in attacks on our country."[23] Given the prevalence of violence in the United States between people with deep, intimate ties, it didn't make much sense. It echoed the "stranger danger" moral panic of the 1980s, which diverted people's attention away from everyday violence while generating outsize fears about a form of random, catastrophic violence that was vanishingly rare. Just as "stranger danger" was deployed to support expansions of policing and mass incarceration, Camarota favored framing diversity visa immigrants as a threat to build up immigration enforcement, restriction, and exclusion.

But as Paul Virtue, a former lawyer for INS, would testify, the lottery didn't pose any "inherent security problems." The lottery itself merely made visas available. But selectees still had to undergo extensive background checks before getting anywhere near receiving a visa.[24] Virtue also mentioned that the State Department had beefed up antifraud provisions for the lottery, including using facial recognition technology to detect duplicate entries.[25] The Department of State later built on this pilot and expanded the use of facial recognition technology to other visa applicant pools. It also prepared to move the diversity visa program to an entirely online system, which it also touted as an antifraud initiative.[26]

The notion that immigration laws were too lax—and that this purported laxness posed a physical threat to Americans—was exactly the message the anti-immigration movement had been hoping to convey. The optimism, abundance, even openness that had characterized the debate around the

Immigration Act of 1990 felt like ancient history, as the country endeavored to armor itself and its borders even further.

While Muslims and immigrants from Middle Eastern countries had been key targets of suspicion right after 9/11 through policies like NSEERS and an atmosphere that enabled acts of Islamophobic violence, immigration hardliners didn't necessarily endorse immigration security plans that singled out people from specific countries or those belonging to certain religions. Instead, what they sought was a dragnet approach to all foreign-born people, any of whom could become a suspect or potential terrorist at any time. While President George W. Bush had, in the aftermath of the attacks, disavowed the notion of collective guilt for all Muslims, the logic of collective guilt was applied through policy anyway—not only in how Muslim and Muslim-American communities continued to be targeted, but in how the entire system of immigration and *every immigrant* were treated as a kind of loophole for imagined threats.

· · · · · ·

Being undocumented had been portrayed as illicit for so long that restrictionists did not have to work hard to extend the association to include criminality, lawbreaking, and even terrorism and violence. The U.S. treatment of Haitian migrants illustrated this logic pointedly. In the 1970s and 1980s, the government roundly denied Haitians' asylum claims, deeming them "economic migrants" rather than people fleeing persecution by a government the United States counted as a Cold War ally. The United States then detained Haitian asylum seekers in one of the country's most notorious immigration detention centers, Krome, in Miami, and in the 1990s at Guantanamo.[27] In the post-9/11 era, mistreating Haitians became additionally justified by the government's unfounded claim that Haiti was harboring Pakistani and Palestinian terrorists. For example, Attorney General John Ashcroft chose to keep an eighteen-year-old Haitian boy, David Joseph, in detention. He didn't argue that Joseph himself posed a security threat but said that allowing him to be free while waiting for his asylum claim to be adjudicated "would tend to encourage further surges of mass migration from Haiti by sea, with attendant strains on national security and homeland security resources."[28]

It was the same logic used in the 1990s to justify expanding border militarization. "Prevention by deterrence" was a policy of "deterring" migration by making the journey more perilous, punishing, and deadly. Humane treatment was understood by proponents of this approach to be a magnet that drew people—too many people, and not the right kind. In practice, such policies immiserated migrants, raised the body count at the border, and did little to "deter" people who were fleeing for their lives, often from conditions that the United States had exacerbated in their home countries. Now, Joseph would remain caged to send a message that the United States would not welcome Haitian asylum seekers. The post-9/11 atmosphere added an extra layer of justification: he must be detained, lest American national security be compromised. If more Haitians tried to come, it would strain *security* resources that needed to be reserved for other imagined threats. But the United States didn't hesitate to expend its resources on keeping a large, ever-increasing number of people in cages, denied adequate care, due process, and freedom simply because they were noncitizens.[29]

That this was framed as protecting the "homeland" signaled how thoroughly the notion was adopted by the Bush administration. At the time of DHS's creation, some criticized the term as seeming kind of un-American. Even Donald Rumsfeld, secretary of defense, thought it sounded "strange."[30] Conservative columnist Peggy Noonan, among others, complained that it sounded German, that it suggested the existence of an American ethnicity. This ran counter to the creedal version of American identity, enshrined since Michel Guillaume Jean de Crèvecœur proclaimed the American a new kind of man, freed from the old blood ties and traditions of stagnant Europe.[31] Moreover, why not just use "civil defense," "domestic security," or even just "national security" to describe a shift in priorities, reflecting new conceptions of threat and technologies that shrank the distance between the United States and other continents?[32]

One of the origins of the term, and its use in the U.S. context, came from a 1997 defense panel report suggesting that security in the near future would entail "a much larger role for homeland defense than today."[33] The report emphasized rising "transnational threats" like nuclear, chemical, and biological weapons with delivery systems that could reach the United States, targeted by either "rogue" states or nonstate actors. While the report mentioned "immigration control" once in 108 pages and noted that the existence of "illegal immigrants" and "drug smugglers" hinted at border insecurity, it didn't frame immigrants as the *source* of threats to the homeland, however.

But the word itself helped ensure that immigration became the focus of homeland security measures. Its "appeals to common bloodlines, ancient ancestry, and notions of racial and ethnic homogeneity," as the scholar Amy

Kaplan wrote, signaled a departure from traditional images of American nationhood as "boundless and mobile."[34] She asked, "Where is there room for immigrants in the space of the homeland as a site of native origins, ethnic homogeneity, and rootedness in common place and past? How could immigrants possibly find inclusion in the homeland?"[35] The word continually demarcated the difference between foreign and domestic, even within the country's borders. Generating such a sense of insecurity was useful for agencies and politicians seeking to expand state power and bring its violence upon vulnerable people.

Manifesting the border as a site of national insecurity helped fuel budget increases for Border Patrol and funding for border fencing and military equipment at the border. To be sure, policies of building up border enforcement predated 9/11—in the 1990s the George H. W. Bush and Clinton administrations had both signaled border "toughness" and claimed that they could prevent migration by deterring it. Migrant deaths, and the number of people captured, detained, and expelled, skyrocketed. The budget for border enforcement tripled from 1995 to 2001; in 2002 it reached US$2.5 billion.[36]

The border had been a site of violence since the U.S.-Mexico War's end redrew it in the middle of the nineteenth century. Now, at the dawn of the twenty-first, organized vigilantes generated considerable attention, framing the issue of migration as one, primarily, of security. Various individuals and groups drew attention to the border in Arizona. Rancher Roger Barnett, activist and retiree Glenn Spencer, who formed a group called American Border Control, and Chris Simcox, who formed Civil Homeland Defense, all encouraged citizens to patrol the borderlands, which they portrayed as a kind of war zone and site of invasion by Mexican immigrants. These groups didn't necessarily believe that Middle Eastern extremists, a focus of the war on terror, were infiltrating a flimsy border—though that notion certainly circulated and gave their project salience in the political atmosphere of the time. Rather, they saw *immigrants*, including people seeking refuge, those coming to labor in the fields, or those coming to reunite with U.S.-based family, as an invasion force, not for terroristic violence but as bringers of dangerous demographic change. Spencer fretted about the conquest of "Aztlán," a white supremacist conspiracy theory about Mexican "reconquest" of the Southwest. Others complained that pregnant people who crossed the border were doing so to deliver their (dehumanizingly framed) "anchor babies." The image combined stereotypes about Latina fertility and the notion that immigrants were draining public services through their use of schools and hospitals, which both explained the shrinking of the social safety net and justified immigration restriction. Now, such women were framed as threatening to transform the country from a majority-white one into something else.

Such ideas had long circulated among white supremacists but gained new traction as the U.S. government embraced the notion of "homeland." In 2005, Jim Gilchrist brought his Minuteman Project to the border for a spectacle event to push the Bush administration to ramp up immigration enforcement. The Bush administration didn't seem to appreciate the specter of armed white supremacists openly gathering at the border, but the display helped push the president's hand, and he announced that more border patrol agents would be deployed along the Arizona border. The Senate approved funding for even more.[37]

If the U.S.-Mexico border was a focus of anxious violent obsession, the U.S. war against terror could not be constrained by borders. While the focus of U.S. military aggression was its wars in Afghanistan and Iraq, war defined against "terror" was boundaryless. The CIA used a series of "black sites," including as far afield as Thailand, to torture and interrogate men suspected of terrorism—at least 119 people over six years; a far greater number were sent to be tortured by partners.[38] The United States imported methods and torture—which it labeled "enhanced interrogation" to provide an air of legal authority—from Guantanamo back to Iraq, where it held detainees at a prison at Abu Ghraib. In the summer of 2004, images and accounts of this treatment were exposed publicly. The whole world could see, without question or doubt, the violence and debasement that U.S. counterterrorism entailed.

· · · · · ·

Soon U.S. foreign policy became more focused on Africa again—its fight was global, after all, and threats could be anywhere. Attention to the threat of terrorism replaced what had once been attention to the threat of communism. Instability and poverty in Africa, policymakers reasoned, could foster a breeding ground for extremism, extremism that must be contained to protect U.S. interests. But efforts to bolster stability and reduce poverty were superseded by concerns about security.

In 2002, the United States opened its first military base on the continent since the Cold War, in Djibouti on the Horn of Africa. Within a few years, more than 4,000 U.S. troops were stationed on the base at Camp Lemonnier. The United States began pouring funding into counterterrorism activities throughout East Africa. It gained access to bases in Kenya, Ethiopia, and the Seychelles.[39] It directed attention to the Sahel region, creating the Trans-Sahara Counterterrorism Partnership (TSCTP) in 2005. The United States funded counterextremism efforts in Muslim-majority countries, and the U.S. military provided training and equipment to its counterparts, now expected to bulk up their own border control and terrorism prevention activities. Soon large swaths of northern and western Africa were involved in these exercises.

The Pew Global Attitudes survey showed large declines in favorable opinions of the United States, even among allies, especially because of the unpopularity of the Iraq War. But in Nigeria in 2003 and 2006, polling showed more than 60 percent of people held a positive opinion of the United States. A 2006 poll showed that only a quarter of Nigerians believed that the U.S. presence in Iraq represented a great danger to world peace. Perhaps this was because polls showed that only 22 percent of people in Nigeria had heard about the abuses at Abu Ghraib and Guantanamo Bay. And a huge gap was emerging between Nigerian Muslims and Christians, with nine out of ten Christians having a favorable view of the United States; the same was true for only 32 percent of Nigerian Muslims. Same with views of the American people—Nigerian Christians held them in "extraordinarily high regard," while only 23 percent of Nigerian Muslims had a favorable opinion.[40]

By the end of the Bush presidency, the United States established an Africa Command within the Department of Defense, AFRICOM, in 2008, with responsibility for U.S. military operations across Africa, although headquartered in Germany. While proponents of AFRICOM argued that it would show that Africa was a high U.S. priority, critics pointed out that it tended to view all issues through the lens of post-9/11 counterterrorism—not necessarily a fit for the problems facing residents of fifty-four diverse African nations.[41]

When George W. Bush visited Ghana on a five-nation tour of Africa in February 2008, he downplayed suggestions that the United States would add to the military presence there, calling a rumor that the United States was planning to build a big military base "bull."[42] Instead, Bush tried to emphasize how his administration was sending aid to address tropical diseases, and to deflect criticism that his administration's AIDS initiative required spending on programing promoting abstinence.

But Bush's protest that the United States wasn't building bases was disingenuous. While the United States government stated that it had just the one base on the continent in Djibouti, it was also setting up and gaining access to a vast array of small base sites and "lily pads" (small, secret military installations)—at least thirty-four by one count in 2018.[43] In Cameroon, the United States occupied or regularly used up to five different bases to support the fight against Boko Haram, for example. The United States continued to gain access to sites for drones, surveillance aircraft, and other forces in an array of countries, including Ghana, plus sites for fuel bunkers for aircraft and naval vessels in another half-dozen countries, including Nigeria.

And the formation of AFRICOM did pave the way for the military to take over humanitarian and development programs, weakening these efforts, and even harming U.S. strategic interests. "Washington's failure to understand the complex situation on the ground and its pursuit of short-term counterterrorism objectives over long-time human development goals embroiled American personnel in local conflicts that intensified anti-American feelings," the historian Elizabeth Schmidt argued.[44]

Choosing war obscured alternative approaches to global safety, cooperation, and counterterrorism. For example, the 2005 Pew Global Attitudes Project showed that Morocco had the most favorable view of the United States of any predominantly Muslim country. One explanation was that the U.S. mission in Rabat had noted in a cable that Moroccans' "positive views of U.S. lifestyle and economic opportunity are also reflected in the record number of Moroccans who have won the annual diversity visa lottery." In a focus group conducted by the U.S. embassy, one participant said, "Everyone dreams of winning the [visa] lottery to go to the U.S."[45]

Even as the visa lottery continued to make the United States an appealing destination, the country seemed determined to shut itself off from the world. More open migration had the potential to connect communities across borders and foster new American dreams, but America's focus on security was rapidly shrinking those possibilities. Even a less bellicose president with roots in Africa would default to harmful forms of militarized globalization and immigration exclusion.

19 Obama's Return

On July 11, 2009, President Obama made international headlines when he, with wife Michelle, their children, and Michelle's mother, visited Cape Coast Castle. He wasn't the first U.S. president to visit Ghana—Bush had visited the previous year, Clinton in the 1990s—but he was the first to make this particular stop part of his diplomatic journey. It was framed as a poignant, painful moment, the return of a son of Africa to the continent, to a site of violence and tragedy, a place that stood in for the global slave trade that linked Africa, Africans, and the Americas.

The Obamas' visit was highly anticipated. Ghana's government posted photos on giant billboards around Accra, and the excitement exceeded even that of previous American presidential visits. It was a world-historic moment, a Black man elevated to the most powerful position in the world coming back to the continent of his roots and confronting the global color line that sought to make his rise impossible. Vendors sold Obama T-shirts and Obama cloth, printed specially for the occasion. The press described the phenomenon of "Obama-mania."[1]

Obama's historic campaign placed "hope" front and center, and that hope extended across the world. George W. Bush had become deeply unpopular, with the Iraq War languishing, the publicized use of torture bringing global shame, and his economic policies contributing to the Great Recession by the end of 2007. Obama's promises of change and unity energized voters and signaled a round rejection of the path that Bush had charted.

But Obama's cries for unity and for a new direction were undermined by a simmering backlash against the progress his election represented, fueled by a politics of white grievance—which was further amplified by the language and policies of the war on terror. The movement that arose to stymie Obama was fueled by politics privileging the "homeland" that sought to define American identity as white and to exclude those deemed outsiders.

Rather than dismantle those same policies, however, Obama embraced them. He showed remarkable continuity in the realms of foreign policy and immigration—the issue areas most closely related to the diversity visa lottery and its operation. Under Obama, the United States ramped up its militarization in Africa and increased official hostility against immigrants. Even

Billboard in Accra, pictured in 2011, marking President Obama's visit to Ghana. Photograph by author.

as the figure of Obama inspired great enthusiasm for the visa lottery, his exercise of U.S. power destabilized people's lives in Africa, and immigrants' lives in the United States.

But hope soared that the Obamas' poignant visit to Cape Coast Castle would augur change. Standing on the soil that had once been home to so many African Americans' ancestors, Obama said, "The winds always blow in the direction of human progress."[2]

· · · · · ·

Cape Coast is a small seaside city west of Accra. It takes a bit over four hours by car to get here from the capital. Ocean breezes bring relief from the heat and humidity. Small hills afford vistas as you walk through the town. Five hundred years ago it was a small fishing village, but over the next few centuries it became a major trading center and site for the transatlantic slave trade. From Europe, first the Portuguese came, and they were followed by Swedes, Danes, Dutch, and English. It was the Swedish who built a permanent fort, Cape Coast Castle, in the mid-seventeenth century before it passed into the hands of the British in 1665.

As a guide would have explained to the Obamas and other visitors of the historic site, for 143 years Cape Coast served as Britain's slave-trading headquarters, with hundreds of thousands of souls captured, moved through its stone walls, enslaved, and shipped in squalid conditions to the New World. Many Americans who visit are familiar with the history, but here they touch it, at just one site of the world-splitting horror that remade the modern world and seeded a forced global diaspora of African people. This place is part of the story of a new people, African Americans, born on the water beyond the sea's edge.

The Cape Coast Castle tour brings people into the slave dungeons beneath its statelier rooms, which include a chapel for devout enslavers. One visitor described the underground segment of the tour as follows: "The stench of musty bodies, fear and death hung in the air. There was no noise except the thunderous crash of the waves against the outer walls and the roaring sound of the water."[3] You go deeper, still, into the men's dungeon and the women's dungeon. The feeling of being trapped, the darkness, is palpable. A door to the sea—deemed the "door of no return"—when opened provides a moment of relief from the dark swelter of these airless cages, where frightened people spent their last moments on familiar earth. But the air disappears again: this was a gate to hell. For 143 years, people were forced to march out, through the shallows, to ships where they were crammed in so tightly that many perished on the ocean, shackled to each other but separated from their families, communities, and life as they had known it. The tour forces its visitors to time travel, to imagine viscerally what it was like then.

Obama and his family were visibly moved by the tour. His comments on the visit, respectful and somber, reflected both his temperamental investment in a postracial reading of history, especially American history, and his sense of himself as outside of the African American experience of slavery. He admitted that the Cape Coast experience must be a different one for Michelle Obama, who, in a campaign speech the year before, he'd said was "a Black American who carries within her the blood of slaves and slaveowners."[4] That wasn't his legacy. His father, Barack Obama Sr., was born in Kenya when it was still under British rule. He was part of a generation of independence-era students selected to study abroad in the United States, where he met Obama's mother, who was white and American.[5] His father died in 1982, and when a young Obama first visited Kenya in 1987, his homecoming was warmed by visits with family he'd never known. The experience moved him profoundly, giving him a sense of the past to which his own story was indelibly linked, and of connection to place.[6]

He told Anderson Cooper, in a taped segment for CNN, that his own voyage of "return" was different from that of most African Americans, for this very reason. Africa was a place where he had direct family ties, living links to his ancestors. When African Americans visited Ghana, many also felt a sense of homecoming—of return to a place that lingered in them. But, Obama remarked, other people's encounters in Africa only served to reinforce how *American* they were.

But many people yearned to feel a connection to roots. This was especially true for the descendants of enslaved people whose own family trees had been destroyed.[7] Destroyed at sites within Africa, as ancestors were stolen away from kin and place to be made into global commodities, and destroyed in the Americas, where forced family separations were a feature of ongoing enslavement. African Americans were never supposed to survive a global system built on their oppression, let alone to resist and to thrive, let alone to seek to build and repair the ruptures of centuries past. Return tourism and the rise of practices of genealogy and DNA testing were for some people bridges to a plundered past. As the writer Jacqueline Woodson would write of her family's visit to Ghana a decade later, "There is nowhere in this country where the eye can land and the body not feel, at once, both a deep pain and an immense joy."[8]

The tour of the Cape Coast Castle wasn't the only stop on the Obamas' whirlwind visit—he also met with the president and delivered a speech to parliament—but it was its centerpiece. It made intuitive sense that the visit's planners should select this site, weighted with meaning. But the choice also cast Ghana as a place stuck in time, relevant primarily for its place in the transatlantic slave trade and then forever frozen in that moment— without its own colonial and liberation histories or identity or place in the world *now*. Narratives about Africa in the United States and elsewhere tended to frame it as unchanging and timeless. In fact, Obama's visit was the outcome of a particular, quite recent, history that established the castle as a tourist attraction and heritage site.

The Ghanaian government had invested in such sites of slavery tourism, with a particular goal of attracting African American visitors to the country. It was only in the 1980s and 1990s, aided substantially by funding from the United States government and U.S. nongovernmental organizations, that Cape Coast and other slavery sites were developed and given fresh facades and new historical materials to contextualize them for visitors.[9] The importance of these sites for foreign visitors was often prioritized over Ghanaians' own interpretations and ideas about their history.

Ghana joined other West African states in the pursuit of projects of "heritage" tourism. These aimed to "recall the country's racialized heritage in the service of economic development," as Jemima Pierre demonstrated.[10] Encouraging tourism was not only an opportunity to foster a shared sense of Black identity between the continent and Africans in the diaspora, but a survival method in the age of structural adjustment. Cape Coast Castle stood not only as a historic site illuminating Africa's place in the transatlantic slave trade of centuries ago, but as a present-day expression of its marginalization.

These measures coincided with efforts to harness the power of the diaspora through the adoption of dual citizenship at the dawn of the twenty-first century. In an earlier era, gatherings and events like Ghana's independence celebrated the shared concerns and aspirations of Black peoples everywhere, situating Pan-Africanism as a form of liberation. But now such commemorations and events drawing the African diaspora back to the continent appeared less political and more oriented toward countries' immediate economic needs, aiming chiefly to bring tourists and their dollars to the continent. Tourism was an indirect outcome of the liberalization of Ghana's economy, and as Pierre noted, the state's actions here reflected, "at least in part, the country's marginalized position within the global political economy."[11]

Kwabena Akurang-Parry, a Ghanaian poet and professor of history at Shippensburg University, wrote that Obama's visit illustrated "the tyranny of neocolonialism" and its grip on Ghanaians.[12] This tension suggested something revealing about the terrain upon which Obama approached Africa, not with a sense of radical solidarity as many African American leaders had before the 1990s, but on the turf of economic liberalism.

· · · · · ·

Obamamania had washed across the African continent like a wave in 2008 and 2009. The former Nigerian president said, "Obama's election has finally broken the greatest barrier of prejudice in human history." Kenya's president said that Obama's victory was "our own."[13] Chop bars and hotels were named after Obama; taxi drivers hung little American flags with Obama's face on them. His name and likeness were depicted in the painted signs outside of barbershops. Vlisco, the Netherlands-based textile company, sold a wax print for the African market known as "Le sac de Michelle Obama," featuring overlapping purses piled against a simple background. To wear the print "is both to honor and to aspire to be ravishingly beautiful and powerful like Michelle Obama," as an Ivoirian friend explained to the anthropologist Nina Sylvanus.[14]

When Obama told the Ghanaian parliament on his July 2009 visit that the twenty-first century would "be shaped by what happens not just in Rome or Moscow or Washington, but by what happens in Accra, as well," it suggested that he recognized the centrality of Africa to an interconnected world and that he would reject narratives that relegated the continent to the margins.[15] The United States would go on to receive more favorable ratings from Africans than from the peoples of any other world region during his presidency.[16] Many of the signs and images would remain plastered in place through the duration of Obama's two terms, long after the words of his speeches stopped resonating.[17]

Africans hoping for a significant shift from the foreign policy of either the Clinton or the George W. Bush administration may have been disappointed. Despite suggesting that Africa's fate was central to that of the world, Obama did not prioritize Africa as a site of U.S. engagement. He also reiterated his predecessors' free market ideas, emphasizing "trade, not aid." He spoke of strengthening democracy but didn't pay close attention to grassroots pro-democracy movements on the continent.[18] Further, Obama cut democracy and governance funding, leaving the military to take on a greater role.[19]

Obama didn't just continue the status quo; he deepened it, devoting more resources to counterterrorism and quietly expanding the U.S. footprint in its conflicts. The Bush administration's war on terror had been accomplished only with significant complicity by liberals. Then, as the American public cooled on the war in Iraq and other elements of post-9/11 counterterrorism, Obama was able to position himself as a candidate of change, someone who sought to break sharply with the past. His campaign harnessed "an unapologetic antiwar boldness," even if some of his comments suggested a modest approach.[20] Once in office, though, he didn't disentangle the United States from the war on terror. Instead, he made drone strikes its centerpiece. Drone strikes continued the war quietly and expanded the geographic scope of U.S. targets. Framed as "precise" and "lawful" in contrast to the Bush administration's sloppiness and embrace of torture, these strikes often killed civilians and children. The U.S. public paid little attention.

He had also said early on that "we need to look forward as opposed to looking backwards."[21] It was an accidental echo of a Kwame Nkrumah quote: "We face neither East nor West; We face forward." Both were pleas to build a future free from the constraints of the past or even the present.

But the headwinds of history proved powerful. Nkrumah could not forge a future untangled from the global Cold War. And Obama's desire to avoid investigating or imposing accountability for the Bush administration's crimes of torture, "enhanced interrogation," and lawlessness made him complicit in smoothing over atrocities and continuing them.

The war would continue with an expanded footprint. Bush had said that the U.S. military must be able "to strike at a moment's notice in any dark corner of the world."[22] It was an expansive, imperial vision. And it guided U.S. entanglements in Africa. U.S. military dominance was never solely about counterterrorism, but was grounded in ideas about white racial dominance, geopolitical competition with China, and protecting access to resources, especially oil in the Gulf of Guinea and across West Africa.

· · · · · ·

What the United States military was doing in Africa and when was often shrouded in secrecy and well outside the view of the U.S. public.[23] But occasional reporting revealed a broad range and scale of activities that came as a surprise to Americans. In 2014, for example, Obama announced that the United States had sent eighty troops to Chad in Central Africa. They were being deployed to search for the Nigerian girls in Chibok kidnapped by Boko Haram. The *Washington Post* reported that, at the time, the United States *also* had a military presence in Burkina Faso, Central African Republic, Democratic Republic of Congo, Djibouti, Ethiopia, Kenya, Mali, Niger, Nigeria, Somalia, South Sudan, and Uganda. The *Post* warned that there was a "blurred line" between military and CIA operations in Africa.[24]

Military deployments focused on various threats. In Congo and Central African Republic, troops were deployed to search for Joseph Kony and the Lord's Resistance Army. Four thousand troops were stationed at Camp Lemonnier in Djibouti. The United States established a drone base in Niamey in Niger in 2013 and stationed one hundred troops there. The base in Ouagadougou, in Burkina Faso, a country north of Ghana, Togo, Benin, and Côte d'Ivoire, and south of Mali and Niger, had since 2007 acted as a hub for a U.S. spying network to search for al-Qaeda in the Islamic Maghreb (AQIM).

Burkina Faso was understood by the United States to be a stable, peaceful country. The former French colony achieved independence in 1960. Blaise Compaoré served as the head of state from 1987, when his predecessor Thomas Sankara was assassinated, until his resignation in 2014. Although he was elected and reelected president, the elections themselves were questionable. The politically motivated killing of a journalist in 1998 betrayed the regime's authoritarian violence and discontent among the public. Popular protests in 2011 revealed widespread dissatisfaction with the country's inequality, impunity, and corruption.[25] Compaoré retained power and legitimacy, however, in part because of the role he assumed as a mediator in regional conflicts, which garnered him international support.

The United States provided funding for Burkinabé troops, weapons, and equipment and sent U.S. advisers, making the Ougadougou base a center for its broader approach to the region. At the time, AQIM was seen as active primarily in northern Mali. But acts of militant violence began ticking up within Burkina Faso, from 3 attacks in 2015 to 516 from 2019 to 2020. A humanitarian crisis began unfolding even before the coronavirus pandemic struck and worsened it.

According to the journalist Nick Turse, a cause of this violence was the U.S.-led intervention in Libya that overthrew Gadhafi in 2011.[26] In its aftermath came a military coup in Mali, undertaken by soldiers who had been trained by the United States. Conflict in Mali then spilled across borders. U.S. and French counterterrorism efforts pushed al-Qaeda groups closer to Burkina Faso's border, worsening the problem. The growth of militant groups associated with al-Qaeda or the Islamic State was particularly dangerous for people in northern Burkina Faso, near the border with Mal, especially members of the minority ethnic group the Fulani.

But the Fulani were threatened in other ways as well. They were caught in the crosshairs between such groups and the Burkinabé security forces that were being trained, armed, and funded by the United States. These forces also targeted Fulani civilians, whom they would accuse of supporting terrorism without evidence. Some local activists said these attacks amounted to "ethnic cleansing."[27] Such abuses may have then fueled the recruitment of young people into militant groups.

A powerful pro-democracy movement in Burkina Faso emerged amid the rising violence. Demonstrators protested Compaoré's effort to amend the constitution to extend his time in office. Their popular movement became the first since the Arab Spring to topple an autocrat in Africa south of the Sahara. Compaoré, a key ally of France and the United States, stepped down. (In 2022, a military tribunal convicted him, in exile, in the killing of Thomas Sankara, his friend and predecessor.)

But the United States continued to pour funding into an effort that coincided with increasing instability and violence.[28] In January 2016, a stunning and devastating attack by al-Qaeda militants left thirty people dead. The deteriorating security situation helped feed the idea that the

United States should put more resources into counterterrorism.[29] U.S. militarization of the government's response to overlapping crises (militant groups' attacks, soldiers' attacks) thus escalated violence that, by 2020, had killed an estimated 1,735 civilians and displaced more than a million people.[30]

The United States continued to secure its own interests at the expense of people who had to live with the instability exacerbated by U.S. actions.[31] U.S.-trained troops, for example, overthrew democratically elected governments in Mali, Mauritania, Niger, and Chad. Elsewhere, the U.S. presence strengthened repressive regimes.[32]

· · · · · ·

Another example came in Cameroon—"Africa in miniature" and long a stable presence in Central Africa. The United States fostered a close relationship with Cameroon to fight Boko Haram, establishing a military presence at the Salak military base in the far north by 2013.[33] In 2015, Obama sent another 90 U.S. military personnel, later joined by 200 more, in addition to maintaining a drone base in Garoua, also in the far north.[34] Civilian residents of the north found themselves in the crosshairs of violence between Boko Haram militants and zealous security forces. Amnesty International issued an alarming report in 2017 about Cameroon's use of torture in its fight against Boko Haram, which it said was widespread and practiced with impunity.[35] Individuals accused of supporting Boko Haram, with little or no evidence, were arrested by local police, army soldiers, or members of the Rapid Intervention Battalion (Bataillon d'Intervention Rapide, BIR) and subjected to torture, held incommunicado, and detained. At least thirty-two victims interviewed by Amnesty had witnessed the deaths of others following torture. The country's minister of defense denied that detainees had been tortured, "insisting it was merely 'enhanced interrogation,' ('exploitation approffondie')," borrowing the phrase from the Bush-era war on terror.[36]

It should come as no surprise that Cameroonian officials imported this language along with the U.S. approach to counterterrorism, personnel, training, equipment, and aid. U.S. personnel were regularly present at the Salak military base, the headquarters for the soldiers carrying out a campaign of torture against locals swept up in the fight against Boko Haram and site of at least eighty documented cases of torture.[37] Cameroonian government officials did not meet with Amnesty to discuss these findings, suggesting indifference to news of widespread human rights abuses. The reports did little to disrupt the relationship between Cameroon and the United States and their shared effort in the war on terror.

In Yaoundé in October 2015, banners and signs, flyers, and postcards proclaimed the visa lottery open, in both French and English. Cafés touted the numbers of people who'd played there in years past and won. An image of Barack Obama holding a green card appeared on one poster. A banner showed Obama with an amendment to his famous catchphrase: "Yes You Can Win." Another banner featured a portrait of the Obama family. His image remained potent, even as the U.S. military lent support to security forces terrorizing Cameroonians in the north of the country.

And Paul Biya's regime would soon have a new target for its military forces. During the 1990s, Cameroon's "anglophone problem" had flared as the country undertook steps to democratization. Various anglophone groups had demanded everything from better representation to more regional autonomy to full secession from the bilingual country where francophones dominated. Those protests were suppressed and Biya hung on to power, imposing repressive measures. Meanwhile, the Southwest and Northwest anglophone regions remained politically and economically marginalized. Anglophones embraced opportunities to emigrate, or "fall bush," including by participating in the diversity visa lottery and envisioning new lives in the United States. Others fled and sought asylum abroad. These dynamics allowed the diaspora to continue to play an activist role in Cameroon itself, with emigrants able to make use of the internet and social media to connect groups within and outside of Cameroon.

In the 2010s, the anglophone problem transformed into crisis. Lawyers, teachers, and others began making more prominent demands and denouncing anglophone marginalization, focusing attention, for example, on the lack of translated government materials in English. These efforts led to calls for strikes in 2016. The movement was joined by students, politicians, religious leaders, and others, who protested. After 2017, Cameroonians in the diaspora joined in. Although the demands of the movement were fluid, with some advocating for federalism in Cameroon, some for decentralization, and others for secession, their prominence reflected deep problems within the country—as Biya himself neared age ninety, and his rule neared forty years—that went beyond anglophone questions.[38]

The regime met demonstrations in Buea and Bamenda in the autumn of 2016 with tear gas and bullets, killing six. Dozens were arrested, and the government cut internet services to the anglophone regions. When students at Buea went on strike that winter, the police beat, arrested, and extorted them. The zeal of security forces' responses escalated the conflict. Following those protests, a separatist movement launched in support of an

Banner advertising visa lottery services, Yaoundé, Cameroon, 2015. Photograph by author.

independent state called Ambazonia. This movement too was met with violence, which only intensified after the heavily contested presidential election of 2018. More than 4,000 people were killed, and three quarters of a million were displaced. The United Nations estimated that 3 million people in the anglophone regions were affected by the humanitarian crisis.[39] Amnesty International reported that both sides of the conflict had committed human rights abuses. It appeared in 2020 that security forces had committed mass rapes.[40]

During the Obama administration, U.S. forces had played a role in training the very BIR forces in Cameroon that were now directing violence against civilians in marginalized corners of the country. The United States and its security goals added fuel to a fire not necessarily of its making, helping undermine good governance rather than enhance it.[41] Those attuned to the history of migration will recognize a deeper pattern: the United States had played a destabilizing role that made emigration a matter of survival. The United States, meanwhile, frequently denied Cameroonian asylum claims and deported Cameroonian immigrants, with more than 190 people deported from 2019 to 2020. Human Rights Watch reported than more than eighty deportees were subjected to human rights abuses upon their return to Cameroon.[42] It was only belatedly in 2022, after repeated calls to grant Cameroonians in the United States legal status and protection from being deported to a country in turmoil, that the United States eventually designated Cameroon for Temporary Protected Status.[43] It was estimated that up to 38,790 Cameroonians would benefit from a TPS designation.[44] The annual American diversity visa lottery became that much more potent as people sought to depart a desperate situation and find haven abroad.

During Obama's tenure, the number of Islamist militant organizations in Africa increased from five major groups in 2012 to twenty-one in 2017, according to the military. One estimate put it at fifty groups by 2015.[45] Another report showed that terrorist attacks in Africa spiked from 400 in 2007 to over 2,000 in 2016, before falling again.[46] The U.S. military presence appeared counterproductive when it came to fulfilling its stated goals, and harmful, by fueling anti-U.S. sentiment and helping entrench authoritarian regimes, as in Cameroon.

And although few Americans paid attention to U.S. policy in Africa, U.S. combat injuries and deaths were reported in Mali, South Sudan, Niger, Somalia, Kenya, Tunisia, Nigeria, Cameroon, and Chad between 2013 and 2020.[47] These casualties didn't rival the number of U.S. casualties in wars in Afghanistan and Iraq. But the toll of waging endless, secret wars on many fronts was substantial. Rather than representing a break with the past, Obama had continued it. Obama said in his final State of the Union address in 2016, "The world respects us not just for our arsenal; it respects us for our diversity and our openness."[48] But deploying an actual arsenal undermined the promises of diversity and openness.

· · · · · ·

Obama's harsh prosecution of the war on terror was invisible and irrelevant to conservatives in the United States, who vilified the president as illegitimate and an enemy within, because he was Black. During the 2008 Democratic primary, the "birther" conspiracy theory circulated that he was not a U.S. citizen at all, but a Muslim noncitizen. Nativists blended demands to see Obama's birth certificate with stories about his foreignness, his roots in Muslim Africa (his father was Christian but was born Muslim), and criticisms of his cosmopolitan liberalism to argue that he represented a threat to the United States. Even after a decisive election victory, the conspiracy theory dogged his presidency, animating a politics of white grievance, including within the mainstream of the Republican Party. As Adam Serwer wrote, birtherism was "a statement of values, a way to express allegiance to a particular notion of American identity."[49]

Anti-Muslim groups spent the early years of Obama's presidency pushing "anti-sharia" laws in state legislatures, channeling anger about the first Black president and simmering war-on-terror Islamophobia to harass Muslim Americans. Figures like Frank Gaffney and Pamela Geller waged crusades, seizing issues like the purported building of an Islamic center in lower Manhattan (deemed the Ground Zero mosque) to channel white rage. Obama's continuation of U.S. wars abroad, and his embrace of programs like Countering Violent Extremism (CVE), which targeted Muslim communities at home, did nothing to mitigate attacks from the Right.

Obama was also stymied by right-wing institutional forces, such as the Tea Party movement, which ferociously protested federal government responses to the financial crisis and Obama's health-care bill, with funding from antiregulation, antitax corporate figures like the Koch brothers. Racism and anti-Obama animus were enmeshed in critiques of his policies, which cast his very person as illegitimate.

Such vitriol casting Obama as a radical belied his careful cultivation as a postracial figure. Obama spoke sparingly about race, and he often couched his comments in terms that would be nonthreatening to white voters, that affirmed the possibility of the American dream, of progress itself.[50] His ascendancy to the presidency was thus positioned both as a breakthrough triumph over past oppression and as a signal that progress was real and the worst was behind us. Michelle Obama's 2016 Democratic National Convention (DNC) speech situated the story of the country as one of progress fought for and built by the formerly enslaved and their descendants, whose striving delivered an African American family to the seat of U.S. power and a "house that was built by slaves."[51] The power of the moment was undeniable. But the dream did not endure.

The enormity of the backlash against Obama revealed the fragility of the postracial myth.[52] Soon, his successor came to power by radicalizing and racializing the white electorate in novel ways. He would also build on much of what Obama himself did—continuing drone strikes and evading accountability abroad, while continuing to align immigration enforcement, criminal justice, and counterterrorism at home. These efforts hadn't satisfied the nativist Right, but stoked it. And while the diversity visa lottery would outlive the Obama administration, his compromises on immigration would lead to its endangerment.

· ·

The diversity visa lottery remained largely under the radar as the post-9/11 United States radically redesigned its immigration enforcement system and expanded its militarized role in the world. Without congressional action, the Immigration Act of 1990 remained the basis for legal admissions, and for people entering the lottery around the world each autumn, there was no reason to expect that its basic operation had changed. Yes, in 2003 it had shifted to an electronic-only system with added security features, and yes, those selected as lottery winners would face the scrutiny of new immigration screening measures. But the lottery remained open, cost-free, and popular.

Within the United States the lottery almost never made headline news. It rarely received media coverage or surfaced in debates about immigration, which remained focused on "security" issues like the border, detention, and deportations, undocumented immigration, and tightening the asylum system. The lottery was a niche program in a niche area of policy and law, and few Americans knew or thought much about it.

But those people and groups who sought to severely restrict and end immigration, including legal admissions, hated the lottery. For them, ethnic and racial diversity seemed less like something the United States should be encouraging, and more like potential sources of conflict and balkanization within America. What made the program unique in the immigration system—its whimsy, global reach, foundational understanding that immigration served American interests, its effort to bring in people without existing ties to the country—made it detestable to restrictionists. They saw the program as especially vulnerable because it didn't serve obvious constituencies like U.S. citizens petitioning for their family members or businesses.

The lottery lacked strong defenders, and restrictionists saw it as a clear target for elimination. Questions about the lottery's usefulness surfaced within a broader debate about the purpose, functioning, and efficiency of the entire system. A series of bills and debates framed as "comprehensive immigration reform" during both the Bush and Obama administrations proposed restructuring the whole system, marrying increased enforcement measures with a reformulated admissions policy and provisions to provide legal status for undocumented people. Security and enforcement were framed as particularly urgent in the post-9/11 world.

Although both presidents supported passing comprehensive reform, they both struggled to do so, and the politics of homeland security they each embraced may have added to the obstacles. Reform plans that seemed to reflect broad agreement on the issues faltered under the pressure of hardcore restrictionists, who were gaining institutional power within the government through the expansion of DHS and within the Republican Party.

Inaction in Congress kept the diversity visa alive, for the time. But the consensus in favor of welcoming more immigrants and fostering diversity that had brought the lottery to life just a few decades before had fully splintered. Immigrants instead encountered an increasingly chilled atmosphere. And the politics of immigration restriction and revived nativism soon nurtured an array of cultural forces that would bring Donald Trump to power in 2017.

· · · · · ·

The new immigration-as-national-security paradigm offered critics an opening to frame the lottery as a source of American vulnerability rather than strength. At a 2004 hearing, Rep. Steve King (R-IA) suggested that immigration policy as constituted undermined the goal of "assimilation." King wondered what the country would look like in ten, twenty-five, or fifty years.[1] Later King would more openly embrace the nativist language of the "great replacement theory," the idea that white Americans were being "replaced" by immigrants and their children over time. ("We can't restore our civilization with somebody else's babies," he wrote in 2017.[2]) But he was already drawing attention to questions about how immigration could alter the future demographics of the United States and diminish its whiteness.

Rep. Bob Goodlatte (R-VA) had introduced a bill—the Security and Fairness Enhancement or SAFE for America Act—that would eliminate the diversity lottery, which he claimed "encourages a cottage industry for fraudulent opportunists."[3] While the State Department had previously flagged a problem with duplicate entries, it typically identified and disqualified them—2.4 percent of the almost 10 million envelopes submitted in 2002, and 6.2 percent of the almost 6 million entries submitted electronically in 2003.[4] If applicants tried to game the system, the system identified them. That didn't make those who submitted duplicates dangerous. It mostly signaled that they desired to win the lottery. Multiple entries had once been permitted in the temporary programs that preceded the permanent diversity visa lottery, and nobody seemed to mind when the Irish won a plurality of them by stuffing mailboxes full of applications. But now Goodlatte suggested that such behavior indicated that such people *were* dangerous, especially individuals who came from countries designated as state sponsors of terrorism. Instead of perceiving emigrants from such countries as fans of the United States and its famed freedoms—who might even share Goodlatte's criticisms of their own governments—Goodlatte suggested that they should be considered suspicious, as potential terrorists lying in wait.

By attracting immigrants from "corrupt" countries such as Nigeria, argued Steven Camarota of the restrictionist Center for Immigration Studies (CIS), the lottery should be perceived as a threat. Moreover, he asserted, the program was irresistible to terrorists because it served as a magnet for people without a strong attachment to the United States. "After 9/11 immigration fraud of any kind is a national security nightmare," he opined. He called the green card "the Holy Grail for the terrorists" because it allowed them to get any job they wanted.[5]

What was worse, he argued, the lottery served no purpose. "There's no humanitarian reason for it," he testified. "Unlike employment-based immigration, it does not select people based on their skills nor does it unite families." Even the program's official aim of diversity, he reasoned, wasn't really achieved through the lottery; the list of top immigrant-sending countries each year remained consistent, with or without the visa lottery.[6]

Another critic was Jan Ting, then a law professor at Temple University, and previously assistant commissioner of the INS from 1990 to 1993. He argued that the lottery was "unfair and expressly discriminatory on the basis of ethnicity and implicitly race." The lottery, he said, perpetuated exclusion in the law by leaving out the many Asian countries, Mexico, and other non-European nations that already sent many immigrants to the United States. He also seemed to echo the conservative critique that, like any race-conscious admissions policy, it was discriminatory and counter to the color-blind meritocracy it purported to support.

Ting objected to the program's origins, noting that it was conceived "transparently" as "a device to bring more Caucasians to the United States." He added, "And I think the fact that it now also brings significant numbers of Africans and Bangladeshis to the United States does not mitigate the discriminatory nature of the program which continues to this day."[7] He scoffed at the old language of white countries being "adversely affected" by reforms of 1965. "When discrimination against women, minorities and the handicapped is ended by law, should able-bodied white males receive a legal remedy because they have been adversely affected by having to compete against others who are finally treated equally?"[8] Ting called the hope that the lottery purportedly inspired in people abroad "an illusion" because so few people could win.[9]

King spoke in plainer terms about his objections to the lottery's purpose. "Do we have an obligation to put the perfect multicultural formula into our immigration policy so that we get the balance from the rest of the world?" he sneered, in a rebuke to the logic and open-mindedness that had framed the lottery's legislative birth just fifteen years prior.[10]

A rare voice defending the lottery piped up. Sheila Jackson Lee (D-TX), an African American congresswoman from Houston, thought the lottery fostered dreams, something the United States should take seriously. The lottery benefited both immigrants and the United States, she said, mentioning the young football star Freddy Adu, from Ghana, whose parents had won the lottery, and who, in the absence of such a policy, would not be in the United States or representing it on a soccer field.

Goodlatte's bill failed. Because President Bush and Republican policymakers were hoping to address immigration reform more comprehensively, the visa lottery survived for the time, despite the restrictionist atmosphere. While the failure to pass legislation kept the lottery in place, it also left millions of American residents facing dragnet immigration enforcement without access to a path to citizenship.[11]

Undeterred, Goodlatte continued his antilottery campaign. A 2005 hearing aired the usual complaints from the usual suspects. Goodlatte and witnesses from the ardent restrictionist groups CIS and NumbersUSA suggested it was a source of dangerous fraud and terroristic threat. They complained that it reintroduced nationality-based discrimination into the immigration system.[12]

Defending the program, Bruce Morrison, one of its key legislators in 1990, testified that it had evolved, with the major accomplishment of opening the door to African immigration, something that the United States had blocked for most of its history.[13] "I think that is a very good contribution to our country and to an understanding in our own population that the doors of this country are open to people everywhere in the world as long as they follow the rules and as long as there are numbers available," he said.[14] In his written testimony he wrote, "There is no better antidote to the challenges of globalization than to attract the 'self-selected strivers' from every corner of the globe."[15] Goodlatte remained unmoved. But again, despite Republican majorities in the House and Senate, Congress did not amend or end the program.

· · · · · ·

In 2006 Congress finally came close to passing comprehensive immigration reform. Harking back to legislation passed in 1986 and 1990, the "grand bargain" framework for reform married border security and legalization. Bush wanted legislation to pass. His own state of Texas had a large immigrant population and many businesses that depended on immigrant workers. He and others hoped that if immigrant legalization passed under his tenure, it would help rally Hispanic voters to the Republican Party. He also said that the vast majority of immigrants without legal status, were "decent people who work hard, support their families, practice their faith, and lead responsible lives."[16] They deserved to live outside the shadows, he said, echoing language that had animated reform in the 1980s. He still touted the importance of fortifying the U.S.-Mexico border, in part for vague terrorism reasons, and in part to prevent further migration. He also supported a guest worker program that would supply growers with the labor they required, without accepting more permanent immigrants.

Rhetorically he touted the idea of a nation of immigrants, "bound together by our shared ideals," and he appeared eager to reject the idea that America was a nation defined by whiteness. "Our new immigrants are just what they've always been: people willing to risk everything for the dream of freedom," he said.[17] "And America remains what she has always been: the great hope on the horizon, an open door to the future, a blessed and promised land. We honor the heritage of all who come here, no matter where they come from, because we trust in our country's genius for making us all Americans—one nation under God," he said. The crucible of the migration experience would ensure that newcomers would adapt and become American. When he added that immigrants must assimilate, speak English, and add to rather than divert from America's unity, he appeared to be speaking to his nativist critics. He also accepted that immigration should be limited. The 2006 Senate bill proposed reducing the visa lottery to about 18,000 visas, allocating what remained of the program to people with advanced degrees only. A door would remain ajar, but only to those deemed most worthy.

Bush's immigration speech came amid a massive uprising and protests against anti-immigrant policies. In the spring of 2006, millions took to the streets in an immigrant-led protest of a bill passed by the House in late 2005. Known as the Sensenbrenner bill for the congressman from Wisconsin, it required more fencing (more "prevention through deterrence") along the U.S.-Mexico border, more mandatory detention, and electronic verification of work authorization. It imposed new fines and penalties, made it a crime to "assist" undocumented people, ended the diversity visa lottery thanks to Goodlatte's amendment, and more.[18] It rejected the very notion of the grand bargain, offering nothing in exchange for its draconian measures.

Four hundred protests involved an estimated 6 million people across the country over the course of the spring. The crowds proclaimed boldly that immigrants were people, members of communities, neighbors, and colleagues. They refused to accept the dehumanization and silencing of immigrant voices that had long characterized immigration debates. It would be a watershed for Latino organizing, as protests against Prop 187 in California in 1994 had been a dozen years before. It also galvanized Far Right responses—Fox News and others used the images of protesters waving Mexican flags to cast the population as irrevocably alien; the Minutemen project registered new members. In retaliation, workplace ICE raids terrorized undocumented workers.[19]

Ultimately the Sensenbrenner bill didn't become law—but neither did the comprehensive Senate bill that Bush supported. Conservative Republicans like Rep. Tom Tancredo (R-CO) launched a concerted effort to defeat any legislation that provided legalization, deploying nativist, white supremacist talking points and disseminating them through conservative media like Rush Limbaugh's radio show. He argued that America's multiculturalism was undermining its effectiveness in the "clash of civilizations" against what he deemed "Islamo-fascism."[20] The war on terror and the immigration debate met at the shoals of whiteness. The bills passed by the Senate and House couldn't be reconciled, and nothing passed.[21]

Another Senate bill in 2007 also failed. Like the 2006 bill, it contained border security measures, added thousands of border patrol agents, and created a legalization path for unauthorized immigrants. It also eliminated some admissions categories, including jettisoning the lottery altogether.[22] The public largely supported the provisions in this and other bills that would have provided legal status to the undocumented.[23] But that vague sense of support faltered under the pressures brought by anti-immigration groups like NumbersUSA, which launched a fax campaign to cajole policymakers to vote against the bill.[24]

The collapse of the economy in 2007 and the recession that followed, along with the dire unpopularity of the Iraq War, helped usher out the Bush administration and its legislative priorities. But despite campaign trail promises to address immigration reform, it was not the first priority for President Barack Obama. The policy and political issues remained unaddressed, and restrictionists continued to gather strength.

· · · · · ·

As with his prosecution of the war on terror abroad, Obama continued his predecessors' work in pouring resources into immigration enforcement at home. Despite rhetoric that emphasized diversity as America's strength, his policies continued to treat immigrants as enemies within. Soon critics deemed him "deporter-in-chief." While he spoke about immigration reform as a candidate, in office—even with a Democratic-controlled Senate—he focused his energies instead on the economic recovery from the Great Recession and health care. He also faced a particularly intransigent Congress. No Republicans were willing to work with him, even though members of the GOP had contributed productively to previous immigration reform efforts.

Obama did push for passage of the DREAM Act, a bill initially proposed in April 2001 to allow people who entered the United States as children and who met certain requirements to become permanent residents and citizens after several years.[25] Elements of DREAM had been included in the 2006 and 2007 attempts at immigration reform. The DREAM Act was popular, especially because of its focus on young people. The immigrant-led movement that had been galvanized in 2005 against Sensenbrenner's bill had continued to gain power, and in 2009 and 2010, immigrant youth led a massive push to pass the DREAM Act. Young people, undocumented themselves, put their lives on the line for legislative change. The House passed a 2010 version of the act. But it failed to pass the Senate by the five votes needed to get cloture. Five Democrats voted against it. Restriction enjoyed bipartisan support.

With nothing moving in Congress, Obama acted through the executive branch. He used discretionary power and the architecture of the existing deportation machine to increase deportations to signal that he was serious about enforcement and security.[26] Some argued that doing so would help build support for comprehensive reform legislation and legalization.[27] In the process, millions of people saw their lives disrupted, including the hundreds of thousands of individuals "removed" from the country that had been their home. Deportations destabilized whole families and communities.[28]

Obama's bet did not pay off. Between the growing power of the nativist Right within the Republican Party and the politics of white grievance aroused by the figure of Obama himself, Republicans were not eager to provide him a political win. Furthermore, Obama's own rhetoric did nothing to derail the machinery of immigrant dehumanization and narratives of immigrants as threats. When he said he would deport "felons, not families," in setting his priorities, he reinforced some people's view that all immigrants were criminals. The phrase erased the humanity of people with criminal convictions, signaling that they were disposable. Moreover, it ignored and obscured the policy choices that framed how the public conceived of the very notion of criminality, which was deeply racialized. These priorities not only ensnared an enormous number of people despite sounding tailored, but also disproportionately focused on people of color, who were more likely to have contact with the criminal legal system.[29]

The Democrats lost their House majority in the second half of Obama's first term, which slowed the push for comprehensive reform—despite the president's use of deportations to demonstrate his restrictionist bona fides. As a result, the 112th Congress did little on immigration.

· · · · · ·

Goodlatte continued to push his stand-alone bill to eliminate the visa lottery and held another hearing.[30] Chairman of the subcommittee and restrictionist Elton Gallegly (R-CA), who had argued that the children born to undocumented immigrants should be denied birthright citizenship, attacked the lottery as an illicit means for terrorists to enter the country. Immigration policy, he argued, "should be based on something more than just the luck of the draw."[31] Janice Kephart, testifying for CIS, called the program "a terrorist gamble" and deemed it a national security vulnerability that "has outlived its usefulness in a post-9/11 world"—a convenient argument for an anti-immigrant group that had seen the lottery as useless in the pre-9/11 world as well.[32]

While the mood of the 2011 hearing was decidedly anti-lottery, the program did have compelling defenders. Rep. John Conyers (D-MI), the African American congressman from Detroit, for example, defended the program as "the way more African immigrants get into this country than any other way."[33] He suggested that efforts to eliminate it had more to do with people's feelings about diversity than about security. Ending the lottery "would basically eliminate African immigration to this country," he cautioned.[34]

No one at the policy level had framed the lottery's value in these terms before. In the congressional debates that produced the lottery, its creators had focused overwhelmingly on white, European immigration. Defenders of the lottery over the years had pushed back against unfounded arguments that it had no value. Rep. Zoe Lofgren (D-CA) had pointed out that the average diversity immigrant came with a university degree. She also touted diversity as an American value in a broad sense. Some media coverage credited the lottery with adding to the life-giving diversity of cities like New York, because it had facilitated immigration from places like Bangladesh and Nigeria.[35] But Conyers recognized the lottery specifically as a channel for Black immigration that was now being threatened, likely disingenuously, based on hollow security arguments.

Johnny Young, the well-respected African American diplomat and former ambassador, argued that the visa lottery served American foreign policy goals. Testifying on behalf of the U.S. Conference of Catholic Bishops, Young said that it was important that there be a mechanism for bringing diverse immigrants to the United States who otherwise would have no opportunities to immigrate. "Immigrants, in turn, benefit from U.S. freedom and opportunities while contributing to the economic and cultural fabric of our great Nation," he said.[36] "The diversity immigrant visa program generates goodwill and hope among millions across the globe ravaged by war, poverty, undemocratic regimes, and opacity in government," he said. "Through the diversity immigrant visa program, the United States makes a counterpoint to that reality, a chance at becoming an integral member of an open, democratic society that places a premium on hard work and opportunity."[37]

Showing the world that the United States was a "place of unparalleled openness and opportunity . . . is crucial to the maintenance of U.S. and American leadership," he said. The lottery furthered these objectives. Programs like the lottery "help shape the minds and hearts of those within their borders to regard the United States and the democracy it enjoys as a beacon of hope and opportunity, and therefore a leader, in the world. The Diversity Immigrant Visa Program . . . engenders hope abroad for those that are all too often without it."[38] Young's experience as ambassador to Togo and Sierra Leone, as well as Bahrain and Slovenia, gave him access to an international perspective that was otherwise missing at most immigration hearings that focused singularly on domestic perspectives and politics. Having lived abroad, he saw how people imagined the United States, what border control looked like on the other side, and the unique role the visa lottery played. Youths abroad, he said, "think of the United States in a very positive way, and I think that is a very good thing for our image, and I think that helps us. And as I said, the most important thing is that we offer—this is an opportunity for hope."[39]

His own biography also lent credibility to his faith in the American dream. Young was born in poverty in Savannah, Georgia, under Jim Crow, and his mother died shortly after his birth. The Ku Klux Klan would terrorize the family and their neighbors, burning crosses in the street. He was raised by an aunt and brought to Philadelphia in the mid-1940s, part of the Great Migration of African Americans from the South to northern cities, where people found that racism and discrimination persisted without a southern accent. After a chance trip abroad to Lebanon, he developed higher aspirations for himself, only to be locked out of corporate opportunities because of his race. He was able to join the foreign service only because the federal government had ended formal discrimination. He became one of very few Black foreign service officers, a path that exposed him to the world. He was able to observe what French colonialism had wrought in places like Guinea, for example, and understood that constraints on people's opportunities were the outcomes of global power imbalances.[40]

His analysis of these injustices did not extend to recognizing or raising for this audience the role played by the United States in perpetuating poverty and undemocratic regimes abroad during and after the Cold War. But his faith in human dignity, grounded in his Catholicism, drove him to support the visa lottery. And he recognized quite clearly that the United States itself stood to benefit doubly from newcomers' talents and from the good image the lottery projected.

Rep. Pedro Pierluisi (D-PR), a member of the immigration subcommittee, agreed: "I just believe that messages we send to the rest of the world are very important. And by having this program, we are sending a message that we continue to welcome immigrants from a diversity of backgrounds and nations of origins, and that is an important message."[41] As resident commissioner of Puerto Rico, he was a nonvoting member of the House.

It was striking that the lottery's staunch defenders—Conyers, Young, Pierluisi—had backgrounds that gave them perspectives on America's deep inequalities that were often ignored in halls of power. Goodlatte had suggested that "there is not a person in this room who can't go back a few generations or several generations and find somebody in their family who came to the United States to better their lives for themselves and their family."[42] Lofgren mentioned her own grandfather who did just that. But the

African American men who testified did not root their support for the program in the "nation of immigrants" mythology that didn't reflect their families' or communities' history. That story also excluded the people who came under U.S. power because the United States expanded across *their* borders, like Puerto Ricans. Their support for the diversity visa wasn't biographical; it was grounded in their ideas about what America meant and about the necessity of being a welcoming place for people of color.

Those subtleties were lost on the committee, which construed national security in the narrowest terms. The bill killing the lottery was favorably reported out of committee, but the legislation went no further.

· · · · · ·

Pressured by the immigrant youth-led movement during his reelection campaign, Obama unveiled an executive action in June 2012, Deferred Action for Childhood Arrivals (DACA). This allowed some undocumented people, brought to the United States as children, to apply for a two-year renewable status that allowed them to work legally. It was far less than what people demanded, but it was something.

In Obama's second term, Congress tried once again to mount a comprehensive immigration reform effort. A bipartisan group of senators crafted a bill in the spring of 2013. It followed the models of the 2006 and 2007 bills with yet more resources poured into border security, paired with a lengthy path to legalization for undocumented people and the inclusion of the DREAM Act's provisions. The bill, which passed the Senate, also created a new points-based ("merit") system to eventually replace some of the family-based system, made changes to employment-based immigration, and eliminated the visa lottery altogether.[43]

This time, instead of focusing on the visa lottery's potential security flaws—those arguments had failed to convince Goodlatte's opponents for many years—the proposal to do away with the program argued that those visas should be allocated differently. This idea reflected the zero-sum thinking that long characterized immigration reform. Proposals pitting one visa category against another had worried advocates in 1989 and 1990, but eventually the Immigration Act of 1990 had opted to add visas instead of subtracting or substituting them. Two decades later, stinginess reigned.

The idea was to take the 50,000 diversity visas and create a "merit-based" system to attract immigrants based on key employment skills, as measured by education, employment experience, and occupation. (Other provisions created categories for "lower skilled" and lower paid, but still essential, work.) Points in the merit system could also be awarded based on English-language skills, a family relationship to a U.S. citizen, and "country of origin diversity"—a nod to the purpose of the lottery that would be eliminated.[44]

Some of this echoed the debate in 1989 and 1990 that balanced "diversity" against other national interests like attracting well-educated and "highly skilled" workers. Back then, provisions that would have selected immigrants by allocating points for specific qualities were rejected as being too onerous to manage. But it had turned out that even without selecting specifically for such skills, the lottery *had* brought highly educated and skilled immigrants to the country. Of course, diversity of origin and sought-after skills were not opposites, but overlapping categories.

One of the lessons of the lottery's operation was that immigrants are multifaceted. Selecting people for specific jobs could be unnecessarily limiting and could reduce workers' autonomy. Doing so also reflected a lack of imagination about the American future that noncitizens could help create. The admissions system treated immigration channels as distinct: family-based, employment-based, diversity, humanitarianism. But family members immigrated and joined the economy. Workers brought family members. People selected through the diversity visa lottery did both. American economic life was dynamic.

Goodlatte, now the chair of the House Judiciary Committee, was overseeing several bills that reflected Congress's narrower vision of immigration and its role in the U.S. economy. An expanded agricultural guest worker program would keep Americans fed and would not bind workers to a specific employer, but it would also deny those workers a path to permanent residency. A second bill would allocate visas to noncitizens with doctorates in STEM (science, technology, engineering, or mathematics) fields from U.S. universities.[45] STEM was all the rage, amplified by the dazzling wealth being generated in Silicon Valley. A lack of STEM skills was widely understood to be the major cause of America's problems, a stand-in for the story of America's diminishment on the global stage. Obama himself had lauded STEM education efforts as necessary to affirm "America's role as the world's engine of scientific discovery and technological innovate," casting the challenges of the future as primarily technical.[46] While such language had become the stuff of common sense among media voices and policymakers, it was also a distinct ideology in its own right, one that fueled the growth and power of Silicon Valley, supported a lax regulatory environment, and exacerbated inequality. While people would become more circumspect about idealizing Big Tech in the aftermath of the 2016 election, the pro-STEM ideology had captivated many policy arenas, including immigration.

· · · · · ·

Unlike in previous debates, the provision of the 2013 bill eliminating the visa lottery attracted attention and the lottery's defenders came out of the woodwork. In a 2002 article, the political scientist Anna O. Law had noted, "It is unclear whether there is a constituency supporting the diversity lottery today and who that constituency may be because there has been no serious policy discussion about the lottery since 1990."[47] The people who had rallied to create the lottery in the first place had largely resolved the problems that motivated them. Many of the members of that generation of undocumented Irish immigrants had attained legal status. Others returned to Ireland to enjoy the Celtic Tiger economic boom.

During the 2004, 2005, and especially 2011 hearings, some witnesses defended the lottery against the charges that it was bad for America. Only a few argued affirmatively for it. Indeed, the people who cared most about the lottery were people outside the United States. Winners already in the United States may have thought of it fondly, but its continuation didn't affect them directly. Few U.S. citizens ever thought about the lottery at all.

But finally, the lottery began to generate its own American supporters. Emboldened by the power of immigrant-led movements speaking out for policy changes, new voices appeared. At last there was recognition that Black immigrants were "underrepresented" in the broader immigration debate, which still often pitted the categories of "African Americans" and "immigrants" against each other.[48] There were no Black members of the so-called Gang of 8, the bipartisan group of Congress members who were negotiating immigration reform.[49] Could the Congressional Black Caucus (CBC) have helped preserve the lottery in the bill, had one of its members been at the table?

Among those speaking out to save the lottery was a group of Cameroonian Americans. The African immigrant community in Washington, D.C.'s metropolitan area was proportionately the largest in any U.S. city, and the area had the second-most African immigrants, in terms of numbers, anywhere in the United States.[50] Douala native Sylvie Bello sought to harness the power of this community and created the Cameroon American Council, based in Washington, to advocate on behalf of the broader constituency of African immigrants. As Bello pointed out, "The only visa type that has a high proportion of Africans that come through, is the Diversity Visa."[51] More than just amplifying what was clear in immigration statistics, Bello helped translate a sense of Africans' enthusiasm for the lottery to policymakers in D.C., who had all but ignored them. Yes, Africans may qualify for other visas, like STEM or agricultural, but these weren't "made with us in mind," she said.[52]

She organized small rallies and visits with White House officials and legislators for diversity visa winners to make their case personally. Dominic Tamin, whose father won the lottery, came to New York from Cameroon in 1997. Tamin produced a hip-hop song (sung by Trinidadian artist Mayja Money) called "DV Lottery" to build support. The song calls the United States "where dreams turn into reality / because of the DV lottery" and claims "the only reason we escaped poverty / was because of the green card lottery." The refrain pleads, "To take away hope for our future, it would be robbery / so please reinstate the DV lottery."[53]

Both the NAACP and CBC spoke against the elimination of the lottery because it would reduce the number of immigrant visas available to Africans.[54] Rep. Yvette Clarke (D-NY) issued a statement expressing disappointment and concern that awarding points for diversity within the proposed merit-based system "isn't robust or sustainable enough to adequately protect the future flow of racially and socioeconomically diverse immigrant populations."[55] Rep. Hakeem Jeffries (D-NY) reiterated that it was important that "immigrants from underrepresented parts of the world have an opportunity to pursue the American Dream."[56]

Many African American groups well understood that immigration was a Black issue. For decades, the abusive treatment of Haitian asylum seekers, for example, was recognized as being motivated in part by anti-Black racism. In the 1980s, issues like the resettlement of refugees from African countries animated Black congressional action. Now, the swell of voices speaking in support of the lottery amid a dizzying comprehensive immigration reform negotiation signaled that this generation of leaders understood how something like the diversity visa lottery affected Black communities.

The growing size and political power of Black immigrant communities played a key role. The number of African immigrants has roughly doubled every decade between 1970 and 2010, to over 2 million people by 2020.[57] A rising share of the Black population (one in ten people) was now foreign born. African immigrants drove the recent growth, with some 16 million Black African immigrants in the United States in the 2010s.[58] While some scholarship has characterized the relationship between African Americans and foreign-born Black Americans as one shaped by ambivalence or conflict, it was notable to see Black members of Congress not only speaking out on the immigration issue in service of existing constituents but also arguing that it was important that Black immigrants be able to immigrate into the future.[59]

Their effort to save the lottery succeeded, but not because they persuaded Congress to amend their bills. While the Senate passed its bill with the lottery elimination intact, the bill died in the Republican-controlled House. The 113th Congress was unable to pass comprehensive immigration legislation. The 114th Congress only considered bills focused on enforcement, nothing that would regularize the status of millions of immigrants living in the shadows, and nothing that would slow deportations or immigrant detention. In a 2014 House Report on a bill that would have increased STEM visas, a dissenting view noted that the "elimination of the diversity visa program would undercut the significant foreign policy goal of sustaining the American dream in parts of the world where obtaining a diversity visa represents the only realistic opportunity for immigrating to the United States."[60] It would also "drastically reduce immigration from certain parts of the world and harm our ability to sustain a diverse Nation."[61] A politics that saw immigrants as a threat to the domestic interests of the United States, in terms of both the economy and national security, won the day.[62] And the triumph of anti-immigration rhetoric and politics would have consequences not only for immigrants and their communities but for American democracy itself.

21 "Shithole Countries"

. . . .

"There are always rumors that it will end next year. My wish is that it shouldn't end," a visa entrepreneur in Cameroon told me, alarmed. He was born in the Southwest region but had been living in Bamenda and working at a cyber café on Foncha Street for the previous three years. When he was a kid, his family played the lottery by mail. Now, in 2015, he helped about 300 people enter the lottery online, for 1,000 CFA francs (about US$1.75) each. He hadn't won, but familiar rumors circulated about those who did and traveled to the United States, which he preferred to Europe, where immigration policies were "really strict." When people win, "it just changes the family's situation. . . . You see the changes that result from that, maybe the victory that happens in that family. Because winning the lottery is actually like somebody going to heaven."

"So, Donald Trump should not win the elections," he warned. "Because I know if he wins, he will definitely stop programs like this."[1] Our conversation took place on November 7, 2015, a year and a day before Trump's election victory.

Trump's campaign rhetoric was so inflammatory that his reputation on immigration was well understood around the globe, even before he took office. Although there were long-standing rumors that the lottery would end—stoked by visa agents to encourage maximum participation, fueled by policy reforms that aimed to cut it—this was the first time its fate seemed to hinge on the outcome of a U.S. election.

Trump hadn't mentioned the lottery on the campaign trail, but his presidential announcement speech in the summer of 2015 had centered on immigration and the politics of white grievance. "The U.S. has become a dumping ground for everybody else's problems," he said. It was a bizarre inversion—or perhaps reflection—of recent history in which the United States had generated problems where it went, bringing surveillance, policing, and military force, to say nothing of marketization, to all corners of the world.

But what Trump meant was that the growing racial diversity of the United States reflected too much generosity in accepting the "wretched refuse" of too many teeming shores. His speeches rambled, but he was clear: he believed that America's social problems could be blamed on the presence of immigrants, whom he cast as "rapists" from Mexico.[2] Using his celebrity podium, Trump had amplified the birther conspiracy during the Obama administration, aligning himself with the voices of Far Right media personalities, and building himself a voter base in the Republican Party. From that foundation, he grew his following by insisting that Obama's race marked him as an outsider who had left America vulnerable to decline because of his weak and obsequious stance toward immigrants. Being the deporter in chief had failed to burnish Obama's image as a tough defender of the border, because Trump and his supporters saw the border as a line in a race war—with Obama belonging to the wrong side.

Toughness was long touted as necessary for the state to have credibility on immigration issues, and the state's capacity to block, remove, and surveil noncitizens had increased markedly in the decades since 1990. Official policies that cast immigrants as a threat to the dominance of white Americans didn't assuage white Americans, however. They helped keep the issue alive and potent. Trump seized the opportunity to radicalize his audience further, to make subtext loud and blaring. The diversity visa lottery became a particular target.

· · · · · ·

From his days of stoking the Obama "birther" conspiracy in 2011 to his incendiary rhetoric on the campaign trail, Trump was consistent. "Make America Great Again," his campaign slogan, had clarity and purpose. He would deport immigrants, ban Muslims from the country, and deliver it back into the hands of white America, too long, he suggested, besieged. What had in previous years appeared to be a politics of consensus around the notion of a pluralistic, multiracial democracy was in fact, as Jamelle Bouie put it, détente. "And Trump shattered it."[3]

By some measures, Trump failed to deliver for the white Americans who put him in office. His presidency was marked by incompetence, corruption, scandal, and a careless, politicized response to the global pandemic that, over time, would disproportionately take the lives of his constituencies.[4] Populist promises to revive the wages and dignity of the white working class went unfulfilled.

But Trump succeeded in using the machinery of the immigration system to hurt and scare noncitizens. The cruelty he doled out, and his exercise of power over people's lives, caused a widespread outcry as many Americans paid attention to the immigration system's violence for the first time. Trump's supporters seemed emboldened by these measures.[5]

A week after his inauguration, Trump signed his first attempt at the Muslim ban he had promised to implement. It banned foreign nationals of seven countries (Iran, Iraq, Libya, Somalia, Sudan, Syria, and Yemen) for ninety days, suspended entry of Syrian refugees, and imposed a 120-day pause on all refugee admissions. The ban was issued without notice or guidance on implementation, and the result was chaotic. People who'd boarded flights abroad with valid visas found themselves banned and held up upon landing. Immigration attorneys and volunteers flocked to U.S. airports to help support those denied entry. Within weeks the ban was blocked by the courts. The Trump administration tried again in March, this time blocking new visas from being issued to nationals of a list of six countries (Iraq was taken off the list). It too was tangled up in the courts. Only a third, revised version of the ban issued in the autumn of 2017 (with North Korea and Venezuela added to the list, Chad added temporarily) went into effect on a permanent basis in December 2017. It was upheld by the Supreme Court in June 2018.[6] These bans were life-altering for the thousands of people who were barred suddenly from the United States, and Trump's focus on majority-Muslim countries sent a chilling message to Muslims everywhere.

While nationals of these countries could continue to participate in the annual diversity visa lottery, selectees struggled to get visas issued to them. The permanent version of the travel ban included a waiver process for people who would suffer undue hardship if they were denied a visa, if the issuance of the visa was in the "national interest" of the United States, and if the person didn't pose a security risk. The Trump administration made clear to consular officers that they should find every reason to deny visas, however.[7] The State Department told Congress that ninety-two diversity visa applicants in banned countries had met the criteria for a waiver, and seventy-two visas had been issued between December 2017 and October 2018.[8]

Iran had received 2,106 diversity visas in 2017, but only 318 in 2018. Yemen likewise dropped from 267 to 28, and Syria from 128 to 55. Diversity visa numbers vary from year to year for many reasons, but the effect of the bans on participants from these countries was stark, as intended.

· · · · · ·

On October 31, 2017, a man plowed a rented truck into the pedestrian path along the Hudson River in lower Manhattan, where cyclists, joggers, walkers, and strollers were enjoying the mild weather. Some were just leaving school, while others walked excitedly to Halloween festivities. In what was quickly deemed an act of terroristic violence, the man driving the truck left eight people dead and eleven injured. The attack, the deadliest in New York City since 9/11, took place not far from the memorial site where the twin towers had once stood.

The driver of the truck, Sayfullo Saipov, was an immigrant from Uzbekistan who had arrived seven years earlier in 2010. He was just twenty-two years old when he had won the diversity visa lottery. More than 3,000 people from Uzbekistan won that year. The lottery was popular, and Uzbekistan annually received a good share of the generous allotment of visas for the European region, especially after the shift to the online lottery in the twenty-first century.

Reporting showed that Saipov arrived from Tashkent with dreams of making it in America. In Uzbekistan he had worked in accounting in the hotel industry after attending university. But he struggled to find work in his industry in the United States. He landed a job as a trucker and got his own apartment in Ohio. Then he married a woman, also an immigrant from Uzbekistan, and they had two daughters together. He started a couple of businesses. He showed up to pray at a local mosque but didn't seem particularly devoted. The trucking life had him on the road a lot. Acquaintances later said they'd noticed that he was becoming argumentative and aggressive. The family relocated to New Jersey, near his wife's family, and she became pregnant again, now with a son. He started driving for Uber and wondered if he should move back home.

Unhappy, he began downloading ISIS videos and plotting an act of violence.[9] Moments after the attack, the Department of Justice reported, he yelled out "Allahu Akbar," meaning "God is great."[10] Attorney General Jeff Sessions didn't hesitate to describe the act as one driven by "hate and a twisted ideology," casting it as part of a global war. He suggested that the Trump administration might transfer Saipov to Guantanamo, as though he were an enemy combatant.[11] It was later uncovered that Saipov's communications had been recorded on an FBI wiretap, although this surveillance had not been able to stop the attack from unfolding.[12]

Using vehicles as weapons to kill civilians was a form of terroristic violence with clear appeal in a country like the United States, where cars are omnipresent and kill a lot of people, especially pedestrians.[13] Just two months before Saipov used a truck as a weapon to kill eight people, a white supremacist plowed into a crowd in Charlottesville, Virginia, killing Heather Heyer and wounding dozens of others. In the aftermath of the Charlottesville "Unite the Right" rally, Fox News pulled a video it had been running that showed a reel of car attacks against antiracist protesters and seemed to encourage the tactic.[14] A few years later, in the summer of 2020, at least fifty vehicle-ramming incidents were reported, with right-wing extremists using cars to plow into racial justice protests, signaling an alarming increase.[15]

Had Saipov been native-born, Christian, and white, his murderous act of violence might have drawn attention to the tactic rather than his motive. But Saipov was Muslim and hadn't been born in the United States. That created the possibility for President Trump to trumpet his idea of the true source of deadly threat: the diversity visa lottery itself.

By the morning after the attack, Trump had decided to frame Saipov's act of violence as the outcome of a too-lax legal immigration system that left Americans vulnerable to terrorism. "The terrorist came into our country through what is called the 'Diversity Visa Lottery Program,' a Chuck Schumer beauty. I want merit based," he proclaimed.[16] He used the moment to argue for a transformed system. "We are fighting hard for Merit Based immigration, no more Democrat Lottery Systems. We must get MUCH tougher (and smarter). @foxandfriends."

He was building on the language of the comprehensive immigration reform debates to suggest that the lottery was an irrational, even dangerous, program. He never called it the "green card" lottery, preferring to emphasize that it was built to foster diversity, and that doing so was something that Democrats foolishly prioritized. Trump was still tweeting about it on November 2. "I am calling on Congress to TERMINATE the diversity visa lottery program that presents significant vulnerabilities to our national security," he wrote. A follow-up ten minutes later broadened his targets to include the family-based immigration system. "Congress must end chain migration so that we can have a system that is SECURITY BASED! We need to make AMERICA SAFE! #USA," he wrote.

Defenders of the visa lottery mobilized in response. The UndocuBlack network held a news conference to argue that the program was a beacon of hope. Rep. Yvette Clarke (D-NY) said the program was designed "to ensure that the United States remains a multi-racial, multi-ethnic, and multi-faith nation for the benefit of us all."[17]

The New York Immigration Coalition credited the lottery with helping create a "strong, vibrant, diverse immigrant community in New York." Threatening to eliminate the program would send a "message upholding xenophobia, islamophobia, and racism," said Darakshan Raja, codirector of the D.C. Justice for Muslims Coalition and a diversity visa recipient himself.[18]

It seemed like no accident that the program's legislation had been possible when the likely participants were imagined to be white immigrants. Now that the program had become a clear channel for Black immigration, it was vulnerable to such attacks—even though the perpetrator of the New York attack was not himself Black. The anti-Blackness at the heart of Trump's fury at the program would not go unremarked.

· · · · · ·

For several decades, politicians from both parties had embraced a framework that treated the United States as fundamentally insecure, casting immigration as a source of threat. But most mainstream figures, gauging public opinion and Americans' widely held sense that admitting immigrants was enmeshed in the idea of the American dream, had focused primarily on unauthorized immigration. Recognizing that the public didn't really understand the immigration system well, policymakers of both parties allowed that undocumented immigration was a symbol of disorder. Clinton, Bush, and Obama, to varying extents, didn't paint all immigrants with the same brush. Most immigrants, they suggested, were good people and contributors. But they also used the idea of disorderly immigration to build up the country's enforcement and immigration policing powers, knowing that these efforts would touch ordinary people, simply trying to live their lives, and not just the imagined figure of the "criminal alien." A mainstream consensus formed that immigration was good, but that unauthorized immigration was a problem to be solved. Who was imagined to be good and who was imagined to be bad was not necessarily tied to legal status, but the binary held.

Trump innovated by blurring the line even further between the categories. He was able to do so because his predecessors had been willing to demonize immigrants; when Obama said he wanted to deport "felons, not families," he helped cement a link between criminality and immigration. Now Trump wanted to end pretty much all immigration, from the diversity visa lottery, to the family unification system that had been at the heart of admissions policy for fifty years, to the refugee admissions system, to the asylum system, and more. He framed this all as wanting "merit"—language that had purchase during the debates for comprehensive immigration reform. But his racism and xenophobia clarified what was meant by merit. He wanted immigration to be white.

Trump made this abundantly clear in January 2018 when it leaked that he'd expressed his disdain to a group of senators, who'd come to the Oval

Office to discuss immigration legislation, about immigrants coming from "shithole" countries. He was referring to immigrants from Haiti and El Salvador, and also African nations. "Why are we having all these people from shithole countries come here?" he reportedly asked. Couldn't the United States bring more people from countries such as Norway? He was justifying his decision, subsequently challenged, to end Temporary Protected Status (TPS) for Haitians in the United States, but he was also referring to his desire to see the diversity visa lottery ended. He saw no benefit to admitting immigrants from Africa.[19] Trump had reportedly previously complained about Nigerian immigrants, saying that once they came to the United States, they would never "go back to their huts," blending stereotype, colonialist racism, ignorance, and xenophobia in the shortest of phrases.[20]

It wasn't that he framed immigrants from these "undesirable" places as a security issue, or a matter of insufficient vetting, as recent critics of the lottery had. His language was more an echo of that of the 1920s, when eugenicists argued about who should be admitted and who should be blocked based on their racial and ethnic desirability. Now, he laid bare that anti-Black racism animated his ideas about what America should be.

The comments traveled the world. The African Union was "alarmed." "Given the historical reality of how many Africans arrived in the United States as slaves, this statement flies in the face of all accepted behavior and practice," spokesperson Ebba Kalondo said, adding that it was "particularly surprising as the United States of America remains a global example of how migration gave birth to a nation built on strong values of diversity and opportunity."[21] Kalondo's comments suggested two things. Admitting African immigrants now should be understood as a kind of global repair, connected to the legacies of the transatlantic slave trade, from which white America benefited outrageously. And the lottery served U.S. interests, projecting an image of a nation where diversity and opportunity were strongly linked.

Trump wasn't fazed as he sought to curtail legal immigration to transform the demographics of the nation, as his 1920s forebears had done so effectively. He would ultimately prove remarkably successful at curtailing legal immigration. But, unlike in the 1920s, it was not through Congress.

· · · · · ·

His proposed framework for immigration reform became a sticking point in negotiations. He demanded legislation that would end the visa lottery, restrict family-based immigration, increase border wall funding, and, recognizing the idea's popularity and in a nod to previous compromise efforts, provide a narrow path to citizenship for some DACA-eligible people.

In contrast to previous proposals to eliminate or reallocate visa numbers from the diversity lottery, it now became impossible to ignore that the voices calling for its elimination were motivated by a desire to curtail nonwhite—and particularly Black—immigration. The Congressional Black Caucus called Trump's proposal "un-American" and suggested he was pitting Black and brown immigrants against each other, trading permanent status for DACA recipients, most of whom were Latino, against future immigration opportunities for people from Africa.[22] The CBC amended the "nation of immigrants" frame in calling the lottery's elimination unpatriotic: "America is, by its very nature, a beautiful patchwork of immigrants of all races, nationalities, and religions. Indeed this country and its wealth was built on the backs of African slaves brought here against their will and forced to toil for centuries under despicable bondage and domestic terrorism through slavery, Black Codes, Jim Crow, and every other backlash to the marginal advancement of African Americans in this country."

What was key about the statement was that the CBC recognized the elimination of the lottery as *part of the backlash* to the advancement of African Americans. "Ending the Diversity Immigrant Visa Program will undoubtedly diminish the future flow of African immigrants and further marginalize those who depend on the program for a shot at the American Dream."[23] Restrictionists had accused liberals of passing the 1965 act to transform America's demographics, to weaken the power of whites. That wasn't the case. But their own efforts to curtail certain forms of legal immigration clearly aimed to keep whites in the majority. Trump made the motivations of the restrictionist movement impossible to ignore.

As a result, in February 2018, the Senate voted on but didn't pass four different immigration bills—including a bipartisan bill that gave Trump his wall in exchange for a version of the DREAM Act. Trump torpedoed it because it didn't do enough to curtail legal immigration.[24] That gave the true goal away. Much of the public had conceived of the key "problem" of immigration as related to undocumented immigration, and it had been primed to recognize immigration legislation compromises as matching enforcement with legalization. Policymakers agreed to do just that. But Trump and the restrictionists would rather see *no* compromise than one that didn't address future *legal* immigration, a source of ongoing demographic diversity that threatened those who considered America a white country.

In June, the House considered two bills. Both eliminated the visa lottery, a Trump priority. Debate took place against the backdrop of searing headline news exposing the cruelties of Trump's family separation policy at the border, which had first been reported in the fall of 2017 by journalist Lomi Kriel and had become front-page news everywhere and the subject of widespread protests by mid-2018.[25] Both a hardline version and a "compromise" bill with Republican "moderates" failed to pass.[26] Even with control of Congress, Trump was unable to get legislation passed that would permanently alter the legal admissions system.

· · · · · ·

Trump followed in Obama's footsteps by using executive power to effect policy change in immigration. Restrictionist organizations that knew the policy terrain well had a list for him to tick off before he even entered office. During his term, he issued more than 400 executive actions. His interventions touched every corner of the immigration system. Each year, Trump reduced the ceiling number of refugees to be resettled, and gutted state capacity to process even the reduced number the United States said it would resettle. Border policies made it impossible for many people to apply for asylum, and new guidelines made asylum cases harder to win. The travel bans contributed to a decline in the number of spouses, children, and parents of U.S. citizens being able to reunite in the United States. A new "public charge" rule deterred families from using public benefits and made it easier to deny their immigrant visa applications for having used benefits. USCIS, the services and benefits branch of the immigration bureaucracy, increased its role in enforcement. The list went on.

The constant stream of new immigration restrictions began to become *normal*.[27] The news became a torrent of cruelties, lawsuits, and protests. Trump was often portrayed by critics as sui generis, but in substantial ways he built on the policies of his predecessors, using the tools they had innovated and funded. Where he differed was in raising the issue's profile to rally supporters, and in speaking openly about immigrants with contempt.

An unexpected consequence of focusing so much public attention on immigration was that it became salient not only for his nativist supporters but also for Americans who hadn't paid close attention to the issue. His actions inspired those who recoiled from and reviled him to act and speak out in protest. Voters didn't reward the Republican Party for embracing nativism in the 2018 midterms, and public polling continued to show broad, rising support for immigrants. Trump's actions helped unite disparate groups against him—from those appalled by the overreach of state violence, to business owners and Big Tech firms seeking foreign workers, to religious and ethnic community organizations, to liberals who felt that xenophobia betrayed U.S. values, to prison abolitionists, to immigrant-led advocacy groups.[28] Organizers were able to show the connections between the state oppression of immigrants and other forms of white supremacist violence in the United States.

At the end of January 2020, Trump added more countries to his "travel ban" list, targeting immigration from Nigeria, Eritrea, Sudan, Tanzania, Myanmar, and Kyrgyzstan. The ban also prevented people from Sudan or Tanzania from immigrating to the United States through the diversity visa lottery.[29] The country most affected by the "African ban" was Nigeria, Africa's most populous country and the country with the largest African diaspora population in the United States. Trump had once reportedly said that Nigerians, once in the United States, would decline to "go back to their huts," a nakedly racist comment.[30] Now he had blocked them from coming at all under the guise of "national security." The fact that it didn't apply to nonimmigrant visas (visitors, students, and tourists) but to immigrants signaled that it was primarily an effort to curtail the permanent settlement of nationals from those countries, whose children would be born U.S. citizens. Groups like the NAACP recognized the move as an "attack on the rights, the dignity and the identity of Black communities."[31] It was part of a plan to slow the demographic change that threatened white dominance.

· · · · · ·

Heading into 2020, an election year, it seemed certain that immigration would be central to the presidential campaign. Seeing how the issue had begun to excite likely Democratic voters, candidates began staking out leftward positions. With Trump embroiled in his first impeachment for abuse of power, a different future seemed possible.

And then, quietly at first, news of a novel coronavirus began to make international headlines. In early January the news barely registered in America. But by the end of the month the virus was confirmed to be in the United States. The World Health Organization (WHO) declared a global health emergency on the same date that Trump issued his African travel ban. (Tellingly he was more eager to block the immigration of Africans than to impose travel restrictions from Wuhan.) A few days later, the United States also declared a public health emergency. But the virus got the barest of mentions in Trump's State of the Union address on February 5. WHO declared it a pandemic on March 11, with Director General Tedros Adhanom Ghebreyesus expressing concern about "alarming levels of inaction" by world leaders.[32] Trump declared a national emergency on March 13, and Congress acted at the end of March to provide aid to hospitals, small businesses, and state and local governments, as well as sending payments to Americans to sustain them, with so many paychecks on pause and uncertainty abounding.

Trump's response reflected his broader approach to state action. He touted the use of unproven drugs to treat the virus, which combined conspiratorial thinking, profit seeking on the part of drug and supplement manufacturers, and an individualist rather than collective approach to the idea of public health. Painfully aware of the dire state of the stock market on which he had pinned his reelection hopes, he wanted to rush to reopen "the economy," to send workers and consumers into spaces with no mitigation measures to contain the spread of the respiratory virus—even as the death toll mounted. He tried to pit states against each other to win competitive contracts for needed protective gear, rather than using the power and purse of the federal government to ensure its availability. Eager to stoke xenophobia, Trump called COVID the "Chinese virus," stigmatizing Chinese Americans and other Asian Americans. His rhetoric was linked to a rapid rise in racial profiling and anti-Asian violence, which continued through the pandemic.[33]

Where he didn't hesitate to use state power was at the country's borders. Realizing that the pandemic could serve his goal of curtailing immigration, he issued travel directives that were unlikely to slow the spread of the virus. On February 2, 2020, the United States barred foreign nationals who had been in China in the previous two weeks from entering, although the restriction didn't apply to U.S. citizens and permanent residents who were still flying back from China. The virus remained unconcerned with what passport a person held. New flight restrictions were announced at the end of February (Iran) and mid-March (European nations). The travel bans proved both discriminatory and ineffective.[34]

Trump also blocked noncitizens from entering by using a public health authority called "Title 42," although the Centers for Disease Control and Prevention initially opposed its use. Beginning on March 20, Trump used it to block the entry of people who came to the border to claim asylum, a right under international law. This denied asylum seekers any process and turned them back or put them into detention before being flown back to the countries they fled.[35] Keeping people out did nothing to slow the pandemic within the United States.

A month later, on April 20, 2020, as the official U.S. death toll surpassed 45,000 people, Trump issued Presidential Proclamation 10014, suspending entry of all immigrants outside the United States without a valid visa. Consulates suspended processing of diversity visas. Because diversity visas must be issued by September 30 of each year, the suspension meant that thousands of people selected in the lottery would miss their chance for a visa altogether. Trump virtually ended legal immigration during the pandemic. By the end of Trump's term, 400,000 Americans would be dead. But the border was all but closed. Trump's metaphorical wall was in place.

Instead of safety, the state offered border violence and encouraged individualistic and market solutions to a public health emergency. America's investments in sprawling wars, policing and incarceration, and mechanisms of immigration restriction all undermined the country's ability to protect people's lives when pandemic struck. Jails and prisons accelerated the spread of illness; the detention and deportation of immigrants spread the virus, too.

It soon became clear that the pandemic was disproportionately ravaging certain groups of people, including those deemed "essential workers" who could not easily work from home or cloister in place. They also tended to be people of color, Black Americans, and immigrants: hospital and nursing home staff, grocery clerks, meatpackers, agricultural workers, and bus drivers. People in institutional settings like jails, prisons, immigration detention, and nursing homes were also at high risk of contracting the virus and becoming ill. After the pandemic started, the share of Black immigrants in detention soared. According to RAICES, 44 percent of families in ICE detention in the summer of 2020 were Haitian.[36] The lives of vulnerable people—especially Black people—appeared to be expendable.

And the fact that the pains of the pandemic were not being evenly shared helped give rise to a conservative backlash against mitigation measures and public supports that would allow people at risk to stay home from jobs that exposed them to the virus. When the victims of the pandemic were largely Black, Latino, or elderly, white America accepted a half-hearted response.[37] Faced with a deadly public health crisis that was claiming lives, the Trump administration had clarified and reiterated *whose lives* had value in America, laying bare the country's racial contract.

Anger stirred at Trump's authoritarianism and cruelty, and at the administration's abandonment of the very idea of the public good during the pandemic. And then in the summer of 2020 a spark lit the country up. The police killing of George Floyd, an African American man, in Minneapolis,

Minnesota was captured on video and widely shared. Soon the country—and the world beyond its borders—was undergoing a racial reckoning of a scale not seen since the civil rights movement and Reconstruction before it.

The Black Lives Matter movement became the largest in American history, with millions of people taking to the streets to protest anti-Black racism in large cities, towns, and rural areas alike. More than 40 percent of counties in the United States had a protest.[38] The scale was unprecedented, almost unfathomable.[39] This momentum built on prior major protest events over the previous decade and a half: the immigrant-led protests in 2006, the Occupy movement against economic inequality in 2011, the emergence of Black Lives Matter in 2013 after the acquittal of George Zimmerman in the killing of Trayvon Martin, the 2014 protests in Ferguson, Missouri, and New York, the Women's March of 2017 to protest Trump's presidency, and the January 2017 airport protests of his first Muslim ban. The work of activists, organizers, and social movements supplied attendees of the summer 2020 marches with interpretive language that helped them better understand their country's problems and the intersections between them. Americans could recognize the deep connections between histories of slavery, colonialism, and nativism and their present-day legacies: racist police violence against Black Americans, Trump's fanning of anti-Asian hate, and the deportation of immigrants. On a large scale and collectively, Americans acted in solidarity and recognized that our fates are linked together.

· · · · · ·

When Trump won the 2016 election, he won as a defender of white America. Ta-Nehisi Coates called him "America's first white president."[40] When Trump lost the 2020 election, he denied his loss. What was rightfully his had been illegitimately taken. The point was made most momentously on January 6, 2021, as Congress convened to certify the results of the election. Soon, crowds from a pro-Trump rally where the president had spoken gathered outside the U.S. Capitol. And then the mob forced its way into the building, violently breaking windows and doors. Their threat was potent; Congress was forced to adjourn and evacuate, with members fearing for their lives and safety. Trump encouraged the mob, repeating his claims that the election was invalid. It was only after more than four hours that the Capitol was secured, the crowd cleared, and Congress was able to reconvene to certify the election results securing Joseph Biden's victory.

It was a violent, deadly event. Five people died in the mob, including four Trump supporters and one officer in the Capitol police. Four additional police officers died by suicide in the days and months that followed. Trump's crowd had occupied spaces of power, of deliberation and governance, and made it, for the moment, *their* place. They sat in the chairs of Congress members, rifling through their papers, ransacking offices, taking objects from chambers, recording themselves with fearlessness and glee. They carried zip ties with them, hinting at further violence. They not only sported Trump gear—T-shirts, flags, hats—but also wore the symbols of other Far Right and militia groups, like the Three Percenters, Proud Boys, and Oath Keepers.[41]

They understood that these actions were rooted in longer histories of American white supremacy. A noose and gallows were set up outside the Capitol, providing a chilling visual echo of racial lynchings that terrorized African Americans through Jim Crow and of vigilantism at the "frontier." Confederate flags, symbolizing Black oppression, waved in the Capitol. Participants were overwhelmingly white, many hailing from counties with a shrinking proportion of white residents, where messages about their diminishing relative power resonated most.[42] Emboldened by a leader with a plan to take the country by force when the movement was unable to win by the ballot, the crowd acted with faith that the country was the birthright of white Americans alone.[43]

The mob didn't succeed that day in nullifying the election and installing their leader in power. But Trump had done much to buoy their movement, not only in the days since his electoral loss, but throughout his term in office. Trump had openly framed immigration as a threat to white dominance. Now, he had all but ended legal immigration that made the country more racially diverse. He brought the diversity visa lottery—a small program, but one wildly antithetical to the ethnonationalism he espoused— nearly to a halt. Immigrants remained the nation's "essential workers," but they would be treated not as Americans in waiting but as invisible and expendable—even more so during the pandemic.

He also conveyed a sense that restriction should apply to immigrants not only at the gates but in all parts of American life: voting rights, public goods, public health, safety, the history that can be taught, and freedom itself should all be restricted and reserved exclusively for white Americans. Such restriction impoverished American life and denied the promise of democracy itself.

Coda

The Lottery Age

∙ ∙

Therese Patricia Okoumou scrambled up the base of the Statue of Liberty in an act of protest on the Fourth of July in 2018. Seeking to draw attention to Trump's policy of separating migrant children from their families at the border, she stood alone, holding her ground in the summer heat for three hours until police removed her. She was responding to audio recordings of children screaming in terror, answered by the jeers of border agents, which had recently gone viral. The Statue of Liberty is at the heart of the country's self-conception as a nation of immigrants. The image of Okoumou, herself a Black immigrant from the Republic of Congo in Central Africa, claiming space at its feet represented a courageous demand for liberty.[1]

America had always been cruel. The cries of those children reverberated with the weight of history. In the time of slavery, the soundtrack was anguish, that of people torn from their homes and packed into hard, dark ships. In the United States, domestic slavery auctions echoed with the wails of children and mothers who would never see each other again. An 1859 auction in Georgia became known as the Weeping Time, for the sky that opened up before the sale. Heavens wept along with the people.[2] Trump's systemic separation of children from their families, imposed as a punishment and to deter them from seeking haven, seemed to echo practices like North America's Indian boarding schools, a program of cultural genocide.

This example of immigration cruelty brought deep pain to the surface like moss saturated with rain. It wasn't only these families that were torn apart by the violence of the border. Families were forced apart by the economic constraints that pulled adults to the fields across the border each year to pick food and send money home, in the hopes of providing something better for their children. Deportations of mothers and fathers left children parentless. A voracious criminal legal system and system of mass incarceration swallowed parents, leaving children behind. Even migration stories with the most hopeful of arcs, like those of many diversity visa lottery winners and others who found welcome in a new land, contained pain, separation, and loss. When dreams require uprooting, there are costs.

Arrested, convicted, and sentenced after climbing the Statue of Liberty's base, Okoumou told the court, "I am not a criminal." It was not a defense, but a rejection of the premise of criminalization that underwrote the whole system. Her climb had potently illustrated the intersections between the militarized border restrictions and racist policing. She also drew attention to how border policy and restrictions shaped the experiences of Black immigrants.

Thanks in part to the diversity visa lottery which positioned the United States as a dreamland, African immigration rose in recent decades. But it grew simultaneously with harsh restrictions, nativism, and reactionary forces in America. This left African immigrants to face overlapping, hostile, racist systems, the criminal legal system and the immigration system. "Every arm of our country's incarceration and deportation machine brings down a hefty amount of its weight onto the backs of Black people," as the journalist Jack Herrera noted.[3] Although the majority of those deported have been Latino immigrants subject to these systems, Black migrants face disproportionate rates of arrest, detention, and deportation. While some African immigrants who came to the United States through the diversity visa lottery were hailed as a new "model minority"—with high rates of English-language skills and college degrees—many have rejected this framing. As Nekessa Opoti of the UndocuBlack Network put it, "A spotlight on 'exceptional' black immigrants often erases and makes invisible the lived experience of black immigrants who experience police brutality, state surveillance, poverty, and workplace discrimination, among other things."[4]

Trump's immigration policies had revealed starkly how white supremacy and anti-Blackness shaped restriction. The path forward would require deep solidarity and collective action. Okoumou's protest showcased the argument that, in immigration, Black lives matter.

• • • • • •

By many measures, 2020's election was a referendum on white supremacy. The summer's protests had reflected broadly felt anger at America's inequities, violence, and racism. The pandemic and the Trump administration's response deepened the urgency of confronting American racism and division. When Joseph R. Biden emerged as the Democratic candidate for the moment, however, it wasn't because of a strong record on issues related to race and immigration. Critics warned that he had a poor record on criminal justice reform, and he had served as vice president under Obama, the deporter in chief. Still, in 2020 Biden spoke about the issue as one of morality, and he made clear that Trump's positions were moral failures. While noting that the "nation of immigrants" myth wasn't comprehensive—it left out, he recognized, Indigenous people and enslaved Africans and their descendants—he also affirmed its salience. "Immigration is essential to who we are as a nation, our core values, and our aspirations for our future," his campaign declared.[5]

Early in office, Biden struck down Trump's African and Muslim bans. He halted some wall construction along the U.S.-Mexico border. He raised the cap on refugee admissions, although the number of refugees resettled remained low. Recognizing that symbols mattered, U.S. Citizenship and Immigration Services replaced the word "alien," a dehumanizing term that Trump had relished, with "noncitizen."

But just as previous Democratic presidents had criticized the system while on the campaign trail before embracing the same tools as their predecessors, Biden showed remarkable continuity with the past. He retained Title 42, the purported public health provisions that Trump had put in place early in the pandemic to rapidly turn back immigrants at the border. Biden brought the total number of Title 42 expulsions to over 1.8 million.[6] He continued other Trump asylum policies like "Remain in Mexico," which the administration only ended in the summer of 2022. He continued to deport immigrants. As the first Black History Month of his presidency dawned in 2021, advocates pointed out that Biden was continuing to expel asylum seekers to Haiti, on what they called "death flights." ICE was supposed to prioritize serious cases for deportations. But that turned out to mean deporting Black immigrants.[7] Patrice Lawrence of UndocuBlack said her organization was demanding legal residency for all the Haitians who had been deported. "That is the reparations they are due," she said. Guerline Jozef of the Haitian Bridge Alliance said of the 2020 election that brought Biden to power, "This election was said to be a fight for America's soul, but we continue the same cruel and inhumane practices that we saw under Trump."[8]

What did it say for America's soul that Biden continued his predecessor's work? Using Title 42 as a justification, Biden expelled some 4,600 Haitians in September 2021, including families and children. Although the administration recognized that country conditions were poor in Haiti, especially after a recent earthquake and the assassination of the president, the expulsions continued.[9] The expulsions were seen as so inhumane that Ambassador Daniel Foote, special envoy for Haiti, resigned immediately.[10] In December, the Haitian Bridge Alliance and Innovation Law Lab sued the

Biden administration, alleging that its treatment of Haitian asylum seekers was discriminatory and driven by anti-Blackness.[11] Viral images of border patrol agents on horses menacing Haitian migrants provided visual evidence that echoed centuries of anti-Black racism. The images resembled those of overseers on sugar plantations in the Caribbean, disciplining enslaved workers in the eighteenth and nineteenth centuries. They looked like the Texas Rangers, who worked as slave catchers and who massacred Indigenous and Mexican people in the nineteenth century. In the early twentieth century, photographs circulated of Texas Rangers on horseback, with lassos and ropes tied around people's corpses. As the historian Monica Martinez pointed out, some Rangers had gone on to join the brand-new border patrol in 1924.[12] Nearly a century later, the border patrol's show of force against desperate Black asylum seekers seemed to embody this longer history of anti-Black racism and border violence. By February 2022, Biden had deported or expelled 20,000 Haitians.[13] Another 4,000 were expelled in May, with no end in sight.[14]

Anti-Blackness in immigration didn't begin under Biden, or even Trump, and it has been thoroughly bipartisan. U.S. policies of denying Haitians' asylum claims go back to the 1970s.[15] Reagan, George H. W. Bush, and Clinton each deepened the pattern of discriminating against and dehumanizing Haitians. U.S. policy toward Haitians presaged the expansion of a system of immigration detention that has caged millions of people over the years. Post-9/11 policies further ensnared Black immigrants during the Bush administration. Despite making up less than 5.4 percent of the undocumented population between 2003 and 2015, Black immigrants constituted 10.6 percent of those in removal proceedings.[16] Obama's policies exacerbated the disparity. By focusing on deporting people with a criminal record, he claimed to be showing his compassion for families, not felons. But Black communities are already overpoliced with higher conviction rates. As a result, Black immigrants were more likely to be overrepresented among those targeted for deportation.[17]

Trump spoke disparagingly of Black immigrants, and he even banned immigration from several African countries. But Biden also targeted travelers from the African continent when the omicron variant of COVID was discovered in South Africa in November 2021. He blocked travelers from South Africa, Botswana, Zimbabwe, Namibia, Lesotho, Eswatini, Mozambique, and Malawi, even though the variant was already circulating in Europe and the United States. Without using Trump's crass language, Biden's move suggested that some countries were sources of pandemic threat—even though it was thanks to South Africa's sophisticated science that information about the new variant had been uncovered.

Although Biden ended this policy quickly, as COVID surged again through the United States, the ban made no mistake about Africa's place in the world. Public health experts, African leaders, and historians warned against marginalizing Africa in global efforts to contain the pandemic. Vaccine inequity across borders was not only making people in poor countries more vulnerable; now vaccine hoarding by wealthy countries was creating the conditions for new variants to spread and circulate everywhere—and Africans could be cast as the problem's cause, even though they were its primary victims.[18]

· · · · · ·

The continuity of anti-Blackness in immigration policy across administrations pointed to how extraordinary it was that the diversity visa lottery existed at all. It very nearly didn't—the Immigration Act of 1990 passed only in the final hours of the 101st Congress. Even as it began to operate in the mid-1990s, growing nativism at home nearly derailed it as policymakers adopted new immigration restrictions. Even as those restrictionist efforts expanded in the new millennium, and critics framed the lottery as a security threat, the program persisted, surviving several failed attempts at immigration reform. That the lottery continued over the years managed to signal something precious about the United States and its welcoming ways abroad—even as successive administrations made the country more hostile to immigrants, undermining its promise as a land of dreams.

Only during the Trump and Biden administrations did the visa lottery face extinction. With Trump's travel bans, the lottery became a bit less open. Then the public health emergency of the COVID pandemic supplied Trump with the tools he needed to more substantially halt the program. Although diversity visa selectees—those who'd won the lottery but hadn't been able to receive a visa—sued the Trump administration and received some forms of relief, for many the opportunity disappeared.[19] Around the world, people hoped that the new administration would reverse Trump's harmful policies. Memes circulated juxtaposing Biden's face, American flags, and messages like "We have faith in the new administration to revoke proclamation 10014." One motto was "Diversity is an American Strength." A diversity visa winner from Côte d'Ivoire wrote in the *Washington Post* about what it felt like to be blocked from starting her new life in the United States. She had eventually received her visa after the courts intervened. "I'm grateful to

A man walks by a shop advertising diversity visa lottery services, featuring the Statue of Liberty, Yaoundé, Cameroon, 2015. Photograph by author.

America. It remains a place of promise and hope," she wrote. But she cautioned, Trump's orders continued to make the "nation of immigrants into a colder, crueler, less inclusive place."[20]

The Biden administration didn't act with urgency to undo Trump's harms.[21] Although courts ordered the administration to issue certain visas, winners of the DV-2021 lottery complained that visas were being issued slowly, owing to huge backlogs at U.S. embassies and consulates, which were closed or understaffed during the pandemic, and which were not making diversity visas a priority. More lawsuits followed, including for DV-2022 lottery winners.[22] Even when a court ordered Biden to act to issue diversity visas, the administration defended itself and appealed.[23] Congress worked on a solution that would be more comprehensive. One proposal would have allowed diversity lottery winners who didn't receive a green card between 2017 and 2021, because of either Trump's travel bans or COVID-related delays, to apply for a visa under a provision of the Build Back Better bill. It was calculated that there were 43,326 diversity lottery winners from travel ban countries who didn't receive visas.[24] When Biden's legislative agenda stalled, the possibility disappeared. Although Biden had rolled back some of his predecessor's barriers to diversity immigration, he didn't make more transformative changes. Such complacency signaled how deeply the new era of restriction had rooted. The diversity visa lottery remained part of U.S. law, but the state appeared unable or unwilling to run it robustly and in good faith. That outcome was a success for restrictionists, who saw the lottery as a threat to their vision of a white America. It was an unlucky break for aspiring immigrants who dreamed of coming to America. And it was a blow to those seeking to unroot and unseat anti-Black racism in the United States.

· · · · · ·

The diversity lottery is by many measures a small part of a large, complex immigration policy, but over the course of its existence, it has become powerfully important, especially as a channel for Black emigration from Africa and as a lens to understand anti-Blackness in our immigration system.

Between 1995 and 2020, more than half a million people from Africa received diversity visas, including 72,000 from Ethiopia, 40,000 from Ghana, nearly 62,000 from Nigeria (before the country began sending so many immigrants to the United States that it was no longer eligible for the lottery), 26,000 from the Democratic Republic of Congo, and 24,000 from Cameroon. There is no African country that has not sent at least one person to the United States through the visa lottery. Because people who immigrate with a diversity visa can bring their immediate families, and later petition for other relatives to join them—the process that Trump derided as "chain migration"—over time the visa lottery introduced new, sustained paths of migration from once underrepresented countries. Beyond the hundreds of thousands of visa lottery winners, many more have had the opportunity to migrate through the family preference system as a result of the lottery's existence.

These migrations, the lives people have built in the United States, and the rippling effects on communities have also helped provide support for an alternate articulation of U.S. identity to the one embraced and amplified by Trump's presidency. "America is a land of nobody," an IT technician in Bamenda, Cameroon, told me in 2015. "Meaning that, people come from every part of the world, bringing in their talents."[25] "The USA is the no-man's land," another man in Bamenda told me.[26]

Relative to other programs, the visa lottery recognizes what it can't predict, which is who among aspiring immigrants is most deserving. Like other immigration policies, it excludes—setting an education minimum, rooting out fraud, imposing certain bars. But unlike many programs, it also includes, recognizing that it has no place assessing what will make a person's contribution worthwhile or valuable, confident that we all have something to give. Proposals to replace the lottery with programs that would select only a few immigrants with the highest levels of skills have come into fashion in our era of restriction. These align well with an economic worldview that claims that our systems work, provide opportunity broadly, and reward merit and hard work with success. But such assumptions paper over deep inequalities and foreclose possibilities rather than open them. Many advantages are structural, but chance and luck play more of a role in our outcomes than we would like to admit.

That the United States created space for immigrants of every different nationality has projected a global image of welcome. This stands in contrast to other countries where African immigration has been aggressively criminalized. And the notion has endured despite the corrosive role played by the United States in rising violence, militancy, and instability, as well as its role promulgating free market ideology that has imposed further harms around the world. "The U.S. is known as a no-man's land," another man repeated, owing to "the opportunities, the tolerance—*not quite tolerance, but as compared to other developed nations.*"[27] The existence of the visa lottery lends itself to generous interpretations of American life, even those unearned.

The visa lottery was born within structures of white supremacy, with white immigrants using frameworks and stories that recalled past immigration to promote a future of white immigration, to push mostly white policymakers to bring something new into being. In doing so, they used concepts that did as much to exclude as to include. They called it "diversity," a weak substitute for equality, and in this case partial code for reversing a decline in white immigration. They invoked the "nation of immigrants" myth, a story that explained the success of white immigrants and their children in color-blind terms that aimed to erase the histories of conquest. slavery, and plunder that made us. They sought restitution, something owed them—visas—in return for the past contributions of their group.

Yet the immigration act was negotiated at a time of seeming consensus that the United States was and would remain a pluralistic, multiracial democracy. In this moment of apparent consensus came space for empathy. It was undergirded by faith that immigration was and would be central to the nation's core values and grandest successes. Without particularly intending to do anything more than appear fair, to comply with America's stated but often shallow priorities, policymakers produced a program that became more than the sum of its parts. They embraced the idea at a time when they could imagine the future as abundant.

Recent decades have undermined that optimism. We have witnessed the retreat of the state from many parts of life, and with it the foreclosure of opportunity. To thrive seems more and more to require good luck. The atmosphere of restriction has given rise to an emboldened nativist Right and open white supremacy. These forces would answer the challenges of the future with hard borders, violence, and more restriction.

While it has not always been clear what the lottery has done and means for the United States, retaining it has become more critical over time. The lottery keeps open the possibility of migration in an age when efforts to curtail it are powerful. With new people come new ideas, new dreams, new connections the world over, and with them the possibility for solidarity, for seeing more clearly our interconnected fates.

The lottery has increased the number of Black immigrants in the United States, adding to the richness and diversity of our communities, deepening encounters between peoples and countries, whose collective contributions helped make visible the fact that immigration is a Black issue. Defenders of the lottery in recent years haven't framed the need for the program in terms of restitution alone, haven't relied solely on stories about diversity immigrants' contributions, although there are many. Instead, they have affirmed that the lottery should be retained because it makes the opportunity to migrate available as a form of repair, an acknowledgment of the violence of borders and inequality of our world.

That was the message embedded in Patricia Okoumou's action on July 4. A Black woman, a U.S. citizen, an immigrant, climbing the iconic green copper of Lady Liberty, she asserted a vision of liberty for all and cry for justice.

Acknowledgments

I feel lucky to have been able to write this book. I am especially fortunate to have Andrew Chess Thomas as my spouse. What a gift to have traveled and learned with you all this time. Thank you for the conversations, support, and encouragement. I thank my daughters, Sylvia and Rose, who force me to focus on what matters in the present and to envision the future we need. I am grateful to the teachers and caregivers at Friends Child Care Center, whose labors have enriched my daughters' lives and made my work feasible.

Our family wouldn't exist without the histories of migration that preceded us, and I recognize the sacrifices of our predecessors who moved and fostered hope for a better future. My sister, Dr. Lesley Goodman, is a model teacher, loving aunt, and treasured confidant. My father, Fred Goodman, gifted me an education and instilled a stubborn sense of righteousness that has been tempered only by a conviction, also Fred's gift, that curiosity is to be nurtured and followed. I learned humility from my mother, Linda Land, who passed away in 2015. I hope you would be proud of what I've done since. My in-laws Kenneth and Alicia Mena Thomas have been unfailingly supportive and generous. My grandparents, Ben and Sylvia Goodman, who were there for the beginnings of this project, are no longer with us, but their decency and kindness are with me still. I would like to thank all the caregivers who attended to my family members at the ends of their lives—sacred, essential work.

Had I not traveled to West Africa in 2011, I could not have understood or connected the stories of the diversity visa lottery, and I am indebted to every person who spoke with me, hosted me, or endeavored to help me then and in subsequent trips in 2013, 2015, and 2016. I realize that these visits and our conversations were a tremendous privilege, and my aim has been to honor them. Individuals to whom I owe special thanks include Aunt (Dr.) Patricia Thomas in Cape Coast, Lillian in Kumasi, and Walisu Alhassan and Dr. Bill and the late Dr. Patricia Turner in Tamale. At Kwame Nkrumah University of Science and Technology I am thankful to Dean Kofi Owusu-Daaku and Dr. Wilhelmina Donkoh. The International Research and Training Center (now the Congo Basin Institute) in Yaoundé was indispensable. Thanks to Dr. Kevin Njabo, to my hosts in Bamenda, Foinbi Mildrate Yibe and Akomboh Walters, and to Ruth Nsang and Rilindis Okafor for research assistance during my visit. Thanks also to the team at the American Corner in Buea. I am thinking of you all.

Thank you to the good people at University of North Carolina Press, for your conviction that humanities scholarship matters and deserves readers. I am grateful to my editor Brandon Proia for his honesty, always constructive suggestions, and faith in and enthusiasm for this project. Thanks also to Sonya Bonczek, Iris Levesque, Carol Seigler, Lindsay Starr, and everyone at the press for their hard work. Special thanks to the readers of the manuscript. What a gift to receive the close and careful reviews of scholars I admire greatly for both their insights as historians and determination to write history that engages the world around us. Daniel Immerwahr and Ellen Wu offered critique and encouragement in a spirit of generosity that sustained me through lonely writing days and pushed me to think harder. I am also grateful for the attentive copyediting by Liz Schueler, production editing by Kristen Bettcher, indexing by Amy Murphy, and proofreading by friends and colleagues. Finalizing a book and a new baby at the same time was a challenge, but we made it work.

Editing the *Made by History* blog at the *Washington Post* has been an education. I am thankful to every author I've worked with for sharpening my historical understanding and making me a better writer. I also learn daily from my coeditors— brilliant scholars, excellent writers, and generous human beings: Kathryn Brownell, Brian Rosenwald, Nicole Hemmer, Keisha N. Blain, Julio Capó Jr., Diana D'Amico Pawlewicz, Stacie Taranto, and Felicia Viator. Thanks also to our partners at the *Post* for believing in *Made by History*.

The two years I spent as a visiting assistant professor at La Salle University shaped me as a scholar and teacher. Sincere thanks to my colleagues in the history department, to all the La Salle colleagues whom I talk to online, and above all to my students, whose engagement in my courses pushed my thinking and shaped how I approached sections of this book. Before becoming a professor, I spent two wonderful years as the Mellon/American Council of Learned Societies Public Fellow at American Friends Service Committee. It is always an honor to work in a community guided by love. Working on migration issues as the Trump administration accelerated anti-immigrant cruelty was an urgent reminder of our need for deep historical reckoning. Before graduate school, I first began to think about migration policies at Human Rights First, where I was fortunate to have the chance to work with dedicated and brilliant advocates.

I am thankful for the opportunities I've had to publish research related to the work in this book. Thank you to editors Kathleen Belew and Ramón Gutiérrez for feedback on the essay that became part of *A Field Guide to White Supremacy* (University of California Press, 2021). Thanks to Sam Lebovic for the wonderful experience revising my essay for a special 2019 volume on neoliberalism of the *Journal of Social History*. Thanks to María Cristina García and Maddalena Marinari for including my essay on the diversity visa lottery in *Whose America? Immigration Policy Since 1980* (University of Illinois Press, 2023).

I relished these chances to push my thinking and share in conversation. I am also grateful for discussions about teaching, research, writing, and editing with Bose Abosede, Barbara Allen, Chloe Angyal, Danielle Battisti, Dan Berger, Carl Bon Tempo, Melissa Borja, Christopher Capozzola, Giulia Casentini, Elizabeth Cohen, Amira Rose Davis, Gaby Del Valle, Daniel Denvir, Ruthie Epstein, Adam Goodman, Robert Greene, Jennifer Hart, Hidetaka Hirota, Jane Hong, Reece Jones, Anil Kalhan, S. Deborah Kang, Paul Kramer, Julia Rose Kraut, Anna O. Law, Erika Lee, Heather Lee, Dara Lind, Drew McKevitt, Tanvi Misra, Natalia Molina, Daniel Morales, Hiroshi Motomura, Brendan O'Connor, Arissa Oh, Alison Okuda, Ivón Padilla-Rodríguez,

Abigail Perkiss, Charles Piot, Emily Prifogle, Andrew K. Sandoval-Strausz, Yael Schacher, Kate Scott, Tina Shull, Alexandra Minna Stern, Karen Tani, Evan Taparata, Laura Tillman, Kimberly White, Jonathan Wilson, Lacey Wilson, Audra Wolfe, Philip Wolgin, and Ellen Wu.

I am thankful to the organizers, scholars, journalists, attorneys, abolitionists, advocates, and immigrants sharing knowledge and vision on Twitter.

I first embarked on this project as a graduate student at Temple University, where I was fortunate to be supported by a champion in Richard Immerman, whose trust in my ability and vision was a gift. I learned so much from Beth Bailey, Lila Berman, David Farber, Aziz Rana, Bryant Simon, and Ben Talton, who each saw different strengths in this project and encouraged and pushed me to go further. Grad school colleagues Jess Bird, Manna Duah, Dylan Gottlieb, Melanie Newport, Dan Royles, and John Worsencroft became dear friends, and I am grateful for the ongoing intellectual sustenance, compassion, and encouragement in the years since Gladfelter became a distant memory—including offering feedback on this book. How lucky I have been to learn from Carol Gluck, who allowed me in her graduate seminar as a sophomore at Columbia, and who modeled boundless energy and generosity in the study of history. She encouraged us to look for the commonalities and connections, and to recognize trends and processes unfolding in multiple places.

I am grateful for the research support and expertise I encountered at many libraries and archives. The project came together at Tamiment Library and Robert F. Wagner Labor Archives at New York University; American Heritage Center at University of Wyoming; Thomas J. Dodd Research Center at University of Connecticut; Moakley Archive and Institute at Suffolk University; the Historical Society of Pennsylvania; Bentley Historical Library at University of Michigan; Special Collections at George Washington University; and the Massachusetts Historical Society. Thanks to the invaluable Cooperative Africana Materials Project (CAMP) via the Center for Research Libraries, and to Bea Vidacs for her collection of Cameroonian newspapers. In Ghana, I spent time at Balme Library at the University of Ghana, at Legon, and the University Library at Kwame Nkrumah University of Science and Technology (KNUST) in Kumasi. In Cameroon I enjoyed visiting the National Archives in Yaoundé, and the University Library at the University of Buea.

None of this would have been possible without the financial support I received while I was conducting research. I received funding through Temple's Presidential Fellowship, the Graduate School, College of Liberal Arts, Temple University Global Studies, the Center for the Humanities at Temple, the Department of History, and the Center for the Study of Force and Diplomacy. I was grateful to receive external funding from the American Society for Legal History, Society for Historians of American Foreign Relations, the John Joseph Moakley Archive and Institute, Association of Centers for the Study of Congress, American Heritage Center at the University of Wyoming, History Project of the Harvard Center for History and Economics and Institute for New Economic Thinking, and Humanity in Action's Diplomacy and Diversity Fellowship. My research at the Bentley Historical Library was supported by the Bordin-Gillette Fellowship. My mom was dying when I learned that I'd been selected to receive SHAFR's Marilyn Blatt Young Dissertation Completion

Fellowship. Receiving such support at that time was life-sustaining. Later, I was deeply honored to learn that my work was recognized with Honorable Mention for the Oxford University Press USA Dissertation Prize in International History. Extra thanks to all the friends who hosted me or otherwise traveled with me on the journey.

For more than a decade I have lived with the stories and ideas of the diversity visa lottery. I'm convinced that this history, and the questions it probes about who we are, has much to teach us if we listen. We all have a stake in the task ahead, to build a more humane world, to repair the pain inflicted by borders that cut through us, to welcome with dignity. We can only do so by listening to those on the front lines of these battles, who every day contend with and challenge systems of immigration enforcement and global anti-Black racism, and by confronting our history. Errors and mistakes are all mine.

Notes

Introduction

1. FTC v. David L. Amkraut, "Complaint for Injunction and Other Equitable Relief," 1997, https://www.ftc.gov/sites/default/files/documents/cases/1997/01/amkrautc.htm.

2. FTC v. David L. Amkraut, "Stipulated Final Judgment and Order for Permanent Injunction and Other Equitable Relief," 1997, https://www.ftc.gov/sites/default/files/documents/cases/1997/01/amkrauto.htm.

3. Fleegler, *Ellis Island Nation*.

4. HoSang, *Wider Type of Freedom*; Halter and Johnson, *African & American*.

5. Liz Stark, "White House Policy Adviser Downplays Statue of Liberty's Famous Poem," *CNN.com*, August 3, 2017, https://www.cnn.com/2017/08/02/politics/emma-lazarus-poem-statue-of-liberty/index.html.

6. Pamela S. Nadell, "President Trump's Violent Threats against Migrants Betray American Ideals," *Washington Post*, October 3, 2019, https://www.washingtonpost.com/outlook/2019/10/03/president-trumps-violent-threats-against-migrants-betray-american-ideals/.

7. Stovall, *White Freedom,* 82–92.

8. Gillian Brockwell, "The Statue of Liberty Was Created to Celebrate Freed Slaves, Not Immigrants, Its New Museum Recounts," *Washington Post*, May 23, 2019, https://www.washingtonpost.com/history/2019/05/23/statue-liberty-was-created-celebrate-freed-slaves-not-immigrants/.

9. Berry and Gross, *A Black Women's History of the United States*, 209.

10. Paul A. Kramer, "Who Does She Stand For?," *Slate.com*, March 5, 2018, https://www.paulkrameronline.com/wp-content/uploads/2018/05/kramer-who-does-she-stand-for-1.pdf.

11. Lois Beckett, "Interview: 'A System of Global Apartheid': Author Harsha Walia on Why the Border Crisis Is a Myth," *The Guardian*, April 7, 2021, https://www.theguardian.com/world/2021/apr/07/us-border-immigration-harsha-walia.

Chapter 1

1. For the first visit, he came on a J-1 visa and received a Social Security card while working in finance. He next arrived in October 1985. Sean Benson, interview, November 29, 2005, Ireland House Oral History Collection, AIA 030, Archives of Irish America, Tamiment Library/Robert F. Wagner Labor Archives, New York University.

2. About 360,000 Irish citizens left home between 1981 and 1991. Almeida, *Irish Immigrants in New York City*, 61.

3. Marvine Howe, "Working to Help Irish Immigrants Stay, Legally," *New York Times*, November 27, 1988, http://www.nytimes.com/1988/11/27/nyregion/working-to-help-irish-immigrants-stay-legally.html.

4. Almeida, *Irish Immigrants in New York City*, 62.

5. "Irish-Catholic Immigration to America," Library of Congress Classroom Materials, https://www.loc.gov/classroom-materials/immigration/irish/irish-catholic-immigration-to-america.

6. Schrag, *Fires of Philadelphia*.

7. Hirota, *Expelling the Poor*.

8. "Table 2: Persons Obtaining Legal Permanent Resident Status by Region and Selected Country of Last Residence, Fiscal Years 1820 to 2019," in U.S. Department of Homeland Security, *2019 Yearbook of Immigration Statistics*.

9. Keogh, O'Shea, and Quinlan, *Lost Decade*.

10. Benson, interview.

11. Howe, "Working to Help Irish Immigrants Stay, Legally."

12. "Table 2: Persons Obtaining Legal Permanent Resident Status by Region and Selected Country of Last Residence, Fiscal Years 1820 to 2019."

13. Ignatiev, *How the Irish Became White*; Jacobson, *Whiteness of a Different Color*; Roediger, *Working toward Whiteness*.

14. "Census: Americans More Irish Than Irish," *Philadelphia Daily News*, June 1, 1983.

15. Inga Saffron, "Well-Traveled Irish Now among the Illegals," *Philadelphia Inquirer*, May 2, 1987, http://articles.philly.com/1987-05-02/news/26164733_1_illegal-irish-immigrants-gaelic-football-irish-american.

16. Benson, interview.

17. Peter Anderson, "The Twilight Society," *Boston Globe*, December 14, 1986.

18. Lee, *At America's Gates*; Lee, *America for Americans*.

19. Ngai, "Architecture of Race."

20. Lee, *America for Americans*, 114.

21. "Immigration," U.S. Congress, House, Committee on the Judiciary, *Hearings Before the United States House Committee on the Judiciary*, 51.

22. Ngai, "'Nation of Immigrants.'"

23. Dudziak, *Cold War Civil Rights*.

24. Marinari, *Unwanted*; Wolgin, "Beyond National Origins."

25. Philip Hart (D-MI) was the grandson of Irish immigrants; Emanuel Celler (D-NY) was the grandson of four immigrants from Germany, three of them Jewish.

26. Ngai, *Impossible Subjects*.

27. Benson, interview.

28. Benson, interview.

Chapter 2

1. Patrick Hurley, interview, October 31, 1997, Ireland House Oral History Collection, AIA 030, Archives of Irish America.

2. Walia, *Border & Rule*.

3. Cohen, *Illegal*, 101–106; Battisti, *Whom We Shall Welcome*; Ngai, *Impossible Subjects*.

4. It was only after the settlement of a class action suit by more than 500,000 Guatemalan and Salvadoran asylum applicants that Salvadorans and Guatemalans in the country in 1990 received a substantive hearing of their asylum claims. Blum, "Settlement of *American Baptist Churches v. Thornburgh*."

5. *Chicago Metro News*, January 30, 1982.

6. "Billy Rowe's Note Book Chicago Is a Hell've Town," *Chicago Metro News*, June 12, 1982.

7. The undocumented population reached an estimated million people by 1975, and then tripled by 1980. Bobadilla, "'One People without Borders'"; Warren and Passel, "Count of the Uncountable."

8. Bon Tempo, *Americans at the Gate*.

9. Belew, *Bring the War Home*; William K. Stevens, "Klan Inflames Gulf Fishing Fight between Whites and Vietnamese," *New York Times*, April 25, 1981, https://www.nytimes.com/1981/04/25/us/klan-inflames-gulf-fishing-fight-between-whites-and-vietnamese.html.

10. Bobadilla, "'One People without Borders,'" 104–142.

11. Sandoval-Strausz, *Barrio America*.

12. Reagan, *Public Papers*.

13. Reavis, *Without Documents*.

14. Tracy Gray, "Jackson South of the Border," *National Leader* (Philadelphia, PA), July 1, 1984. He was echoing language used by Rep. Edward Roybal (D-CA) in the late 1970s.

15. "Chisholm Testifies on Immigration Law Reform," *Chicago Metro News*, June 5, 1982.

16. Manuel Guzmán quoted in Bobadilla, "'One People without Borders,'" 177.

17. Only about 600 Irish people qualified for legalization under IRCA. Bill Breen, "Irish and Illegal in America. 'Ireland Has Lost Another Generation,'" *Christian Science Monitor*, March 23, 1989, http://www.csmonitor.com/1989/0323/piris.html. Sandoval-Strausz argues that the program should have been designed to be more expansive. A. K. Sandoval-Strausz, "A Path to Citizenship for 11 Million Immigrants Is a No-Brainer," *Washington Post*, February 24, 2021, https://www.washingtonpost.com/outlook/2021/02/24/path-citizenship-11-million-immigrants-is-no-brainer/.

18. Hurley, interview.

19. American Irish National Immigration Committee, "Irish Need Not Apply," *New York Times*, at http://www.jscjohnpcollinsret.com/uploads/3/4/6/1/34611293/ny_times_ad.pdf.

20. Niall O'Dowd, "Visa Man," *Irish America*, May 1989, IIRM Records, AIA 016, box 162, folder 11, Archives of Irish America.

21. Donnelly, "Foreign Affairs, Drug Interdiction, and Immigration," 271.

22. Donnelly's program was included in the bill introduced by Judiciary Committee chair Peter Rodino (D-NJ). Immigration Control and Legalization Amendments Act of 1986, H.R. 3810, 99th Cong. (1986). H.R. 3810 was adopted by the House and incorporated into the Senate bill, Immigration Reform and Control Act of 1986, S. 1200, 99th Cong. (1986).

23. Quinlin, *Irish Boston*, 155.

24. U.S. Congress, House, Committee on the Judiciary, *Legal Immigration: Hearing Before the Subcommittee on Immigration, Refugees, and International Law*, July 30, 1986.

25. Ethan Bronner, "Kerry Plans Bill on Irish Immigration," *Boston Globe*, September 20, 1985.

26. "The Year of the Illegal Aliens," *Irish America*, December 1988, IIRM Records, AIA 016, box 13, folder 19, Archives of Irish America.

27. Self, *All in the Family*.

28. Select Commission on Immigration and Refugee Policy, *Final Report and Recommendations of the Select Commission on Immigration and Refugee Policy with Supplemental Views by Commissioners*.

29. U.S. Congress, House, Committee on the Judiciary, *Legal Immigration*, July 30, 1986 (statement of Thomas Flatley), 62.

30. U.S. Congress, House, Committee on the Judiciary, *Legal Immigration*, July 30, 1986 (statement of Rev. Joseph A. Cogo, American Committee on Italian Migration), 44.

31. "Nonpreference Immigration Visa Availability under Section 314 of the Immigration Reform and Control Act of 1986: Determination of Areas 'Adversely Affected' by the Enactment of Public Law 89-236," box 369, folder 3, Alan K. Simpson Papers, Collection 10449, American Heritage Center, University of Wyoming.

32. The nations identified as "adversely affected" were Albania, Algeria, Argentina, Austria, Belgium, Bermuda, Canada, Czechoslovakia, Denmark, Estonia, Finland, France, the Federal Republic of Germany, German Democratic Republic, Great Britain and Northern Ireland, Guadeloupe, Hungary, Iceland, Indonesia, Ireland, Italy, Japan, Latvia, Liechtenstein, Lithuania, Luxembourg, Monaco, the Netherlands, New Caledonia, Norway, Poland, San Marino, Sweden, Switzerland, and Tunisia. No. 92, 52 *Fed. Reg.* 17948 (May 13, 1987). IIRM Records, AIA 016, box 12, folder 35, Archives of Irish America.

33. "U.S. Visa Lottery," *Irish America*, February 1987, IIRM Records, AIA 016, box 162, folder 9, Archives of Irish America.

34. "One-Time Visa Offer Swamps U.S. Consulates," *Vancouver Sun*, January 8, 1987.

35. "Non-preference Immigrant Visas for the United States—Procedure for Submitting Applications," *Irish Echo*, January 10, 1987, IIRM Records, AIA 016, box 26, Archives of Irish America.

36. "Over a Million Seek U.S. Visas," *Irish Echo*, January 31, 1987, IIRM Records, AIA 016, box 26, Archives of Irish America.

37. Benson, interview.

38. Michael Farber, "Many Trying U.S. Roulette," *The Gazette (Montreal)*, January 8, 1987.

39. Benson, interview.

40. "Irish Win 3112 Visas in Lottery," *Irish America*, April 1987, IIRM Records, AIA 016, box 162, folder 9, Archives of Irish America; "10,000 Non-preference Visas to Be Issued by U.S.," *Irish Echo*, January 10, 1987, IIRM Records, AIA 016, box 26, Archives of Irish America.

41. O'Dowd, "Visa Man."

42. James O'Shea, "Brian Donnelly to Be Recognized on 25th Year Since Donnelly Visas," *Irish Central.com*, October 26, 2011, http://www.irishcentral.com /news/brian-donnelly-to-be-recognized-on-25th-year-since-donnelly-visas -132606733-237419521.html.

43. This was true to a point. Some observers did object that the program was an obvious response to Irish lobbying and that the "adversely affected" formulation favored predominantly white nations. One lawyer reportedly filed suit in federal court to stop the program, an effort that did not affect it. Don Shannon and Marita Hernandez, "U.S. Launches Controversial Visa Lottery," *Los Angeles Times*, January 22, 1987.

44. Patrick, "The Right to Dream," letter to the editor, *Irish America*, June 1987, IIRM Records, AIA 016, box 26, Archives of Irish America.

Chapter 3

1. Lee Iacocca was chairman of the Statue of Liberty-Ellis Island Foundation and reportedly raised $265 million for the statue's restoration and the $30 million weekend extravaganza. Martin Gottlieb, "Iacocca Says Liberty Fund Surpassed Its Goal by $12 Million," *New York Times*, July 2, 1986, https://www.nytimes.com /1986/07/02/nyregion/iacocca-says-liberty-fund-surpassed-its-goal-by-12-million .html; Joyce Purnick, "Koch Presents Liberty Awards to 86 Immigrants," *New York Times*, July 2, 1986, https://www.nytimes.com/1986/07/02/nyregion/koch-presents -liberty-awards-to-86-immigrants.html.

2. Anthony Lewis, "Abroad at Home; of Thee I Sing," op-ed, *New York Times*, July 3, 1986, https://www.nytimes.com/1986/07/03/opinion/abroad-at-home-of-thee-i-sing .html.

3. Lewis, "Of Thee I Sing."

4. Samuel G. Freeman, "While Liberty Fete Nears, 219 Aliens in City Face Expulsion," *New York Times*, July 1, 1986, https://www.nytimes.com/1986/07/01/nyregion /while-liberty-fete-nears-219-aliens-in-city-face-expulsion.html; Sam Dolnick, "Removal of Priest's Case Exposes Deep Holes in Immigration Courts," *New York Times*, July 7, 2011, https://www.nytimes.com/2011/07/08/nyregion/priests-former-caseload -exposes-holes-in-immigration-courts.html.

5. Patrick Hurley, interview, October 31, 1997, Ireland House Oral History Collection, AIA 030, Archives of Irish America.

6. Patrick, "Undocumented Alien from County Cork Now Resident in Queens," letter to the editor, *Irish America*, June 1987, IIRM Records, AIA 016, box 162, folder 9, Archives of Irish America.

7. Patrick, letter to the editor, *Irish America*, June 1987.

8. "The Year of the Illegal Aliens," *Irish America*, December 1988, IIRM Records, AIA 016, box 13, folder 19, Archives of Irish America.

9. "Story of the IIRM," IIRM Records, AIA 016, box 9, folder 3, Archives of Irish America; "The Year of the Illegal Aliens."

10. "The Year of the Illegal Aliens."

11. "The Year of the Illegal Aliens."

12. Sean Benson, interview, November 29, 2005, Ireland House Oral History Collection, AIA 030, Archives of Irish America, Tamiment Library/Robert F. Wagner Labor Archives, New York University.

13. Molina, *How Race Is Made in America*.

14. U.S. Congress, Senate, Committee on the Judiciary, *Legal Immigration Reforms on S.1611*, October 23 and December 11, 1987, 2.

15. Frank Sinatra, RKO Radio Pictures, Alex Stordahl, and Albert Maltz, "The House I Live In." 1945, Video, https://www.loc.gov/item/mbrs00009167/.

16. Harris Miller started his career as a congressional staffer in the House Judiciary Committee, before starting his own lobbying firm. Jeffrey L. Pasley, "The Aides Virus: The Hill's New Influence-Peddling Epidemic," *New Republic*, October 19, 1987, 22–24; and Chris L. Jenkins, "Miller Defends Lobbying Stances," *Washington Post*, June 9, 2006, http://www.washingtonpost.com/wp-dyn/content/article/2006/06/08/AR2006060801650.html.

17. Richard Day to Harris Miller, March 31, 1982, box 350, folder 8, Alan K. Simpson Papers, Collection 10449.

18. Sean Minihane, interview, October 25, 2007, Ireland House Oral History Collection, AIA 030, Archives of Irish America.

19. U.S. Congress, House, Committee on the Judiciary, *Reform of Legal Immigration*, September 7 and 16, 1988 (statement of Donald Martin on behalf of IIRM), 542.

20. U.S. Congress, House, Committee on the Judiciary, *Reform of Legal Immigration*, September 7 and 16, 1988, 545–552.

21. U.S. Department of Commerce, *Ancestry of the Population by State*.

22. "Census: Americans More Irish Than Irish," *Philadelphia Daily News*, June 1, 1983.

23. Jacobson, *Roots Too*.

24. Lisa Johnston, interview, March 16, 2009, Ireland House Oral History Collection, AIA 030, Archives of Irish America.

25. Thomas Manton to John Whelen, September 20, 1988, IIRM Records, AIA 016, box 9, folder 1, Archives of Irish America.

26. Peter Anderson, "The Twilight Society," *Boston Globe*, December 14, 1986.

27. Debbie McGoldrick, "The Way We Were, the Way We Are," *Irish Voice*, December 9, 1997.

28. Kevin Molloy, "Legalize the Irish" (1989), IIRM Records, AIA 016, box 10, folder 9, Archives of Irish America.

29. Between 1925 and 1965, 200,000 unauthorized European immigrants legalized their status, gaining formal access to both U.S. citizenship and white ethnic American identity. Ngai, "Strange Career of the Illegal Alien."

30. U.S. Congress, Senate, Committee on the Judiciary, *Legal Immigration Reforms*, October 23 and December 11, 1987 (statement of Sen. Alfonse D'Amato), 41.

31. U.S. Congress, Senate, Committee on the Judiciary, *Legal Immigration Reforms*, October 23 and December 11, 1987 (statement of Rep. Brian J. Donnelly), 51.

32. Bonilla-Silva, *Racism without Racists*. See also Fraser and Kick, "Interpretive Repertoires of Whites."

33. Deslippe, "'Do Whites Have Rights?,'" 934.

Chapter 4

1. Karlyn Barker, "Visa Lottery: Drawing for Diversity; 20,000 Applicants Chosen by Computer Win Chance to Enter U.S.," *Washington Post*, May 16, 1989.

2. Select Commission on Immigration and Refugee Policy, *Supplement to the Final Report and Recommendations of the Select Commission*, 358.

3. Select Commission on Immigration and Refugee Policy, *Supplement to the Final Report and Recommendations of the Select Commission*, 123.

4. Select Commission on Immigration and Refugee Policy, *Final Report*, 5.

5. Select Commission on Immigration and Refugee Policy, *Final Report*, 1.

6. "Table 1: Growth of Regional Population by Race-Ethnicity, 1980 to 1990," in Myers, "Demographic Dynamism," 930.

7. U.S. Congress, House, Committee on the Judiciary, *Legal Immigration Legislation: Hearing before the Subcommittee on Immigration, Refugees, and International Law*, June 21, 1988 (statement of Rep. Howard L. Berman), 2.

8. U.S. Congress, House, Committee on the Judiciary, *Reform of Legal Immigration*, September 7 and 16, 1988 (statement of Howard Hom, immigration attorney), 565.

9. Susanne M. Schafer, "Around the World, People Line Up for Chance to Receive a U.S. Visa," *Philadelphia Inquirer*, March 27, 1989.

10. Associated Press, "Pakistani, Iranian and Kuwaiti Are First Winners in Visa Lottery," *Boston Globe*, May 16, 1989.

11. "3 Million Win a Chance to Enter U.S. 'Visa Lottery,'" *Los Angeles Times*, May 10, 1989, http://articles.latimes.com/1989-05-10/news/mn-2797_1_visa-lottery-immigrant-visa-state-department.

12. "Winners of Visas Announced," *New York Times*, May 16, 1989.

13. Espie, "Bachelor from Pakistan Is First Winner in Worldwide Lottery," 18.

14. Thirteen countries were ineligible because they used most of their available visas each year: China (mainland and Taiwan), Colombia, Dominican Republic, El Salvador, Guyana, Haiti, India, Jamaica, Korea, Mexico, Philippines, and the United Kingdom.

15. Townsend, "Undocumented Irish Need Apply"; Margaret Curley, "Ireland Gets Only 362 of 20,000 Berman US Visas," *Irish Times*, June 15, 1989.

16. U.S. Congress, House, Committee on the Judiciary, *Legal Immigration*, July 30, 1986, (statement of John Higham, historian), 3.

17. "Talking Points for Discussion with Senator Simpson," IIRM Records, AIA 016, box 9, folder 2, Archives of Irish America.

18. Marvine Howe, "Immigrants to Get Visas by Lottery," *New York Times*, March 1, 1989, http://www.nytimes.com/1989/03/01/us/immigrants-to-get-visas-by-lottery.html.

19. Select Commission on Immigration and Refugee Policy, *Final Report*, 30.

20. Wu, *Color of Success*, 8.

21. Reimers, "Unintended Reform."

22. Quoted in Reimers, "Unintended Reform," 16.

23. U.S. Congress, House, Committee on the Judiciary, *Immigration Act of 1989*, September 27, 1989 (statement of Donald Martin), 238.

24. Irish Immigration Reform Movement, "The Case for Immigration Reform: A Presentation to The Honorable John Joseph Moakley," August 14, 1990, Moakley Papers, Record Group 3.4, box 5, folder 74, Moakley Archive and Institute.

25. Google Ngram viewer, https://books.google.com/ngrams/graph?content=%22diversity%22&year_start=1900&year_end=2019&corpus=26&smoothing=3#.

26. Johnson, "Commencement Address at Howard University."

27. Johnson, *Undermining Racial Justice*; Katznelson, *When Affirmative Action Was White*.

28. Delmont, "Rethinking 'Busing' in Boston."

29. Regents of the University of California v. Bakke, 438 U.S. 265 (1978), http://www.digitalhistory.uh.edu/disp_textbook.cfm?smtID=3&psid=4095.

30. Caplan, "Thurgood Marshall."

31. U.S. Congress, Senate, Committee on the Judiciary, *Legal Immigration Reforms*, October 23 and December 11, 1987 (statement of Lawrence Fuchs, immigration scholar), 179.

32. Doris Meissner, "Yes to Immigrants, No to Quick Fixes," *Los Angeles Times*, October 26, 1990.

33. Arthur Schlesinger Jr., "The Cult of Ethnicity, Good and Bad," *Time*, July 8, 1991, https://time.com/vault/issue/1991-07-08/page/29/.

Chapter 5

1. Congressional Record Proceedings and Debates of the 101st Congress, 2nd Session, Volume 136 Part 25, October 27, 1990 (GPO, 1990), Statement of Rep. Moakley, 36798–36799, https://heinonline.org/HOL/P?h=hein.congrec/cr1360025&i=795.

2. "Ted Kennedy, LBJ, and Immigration Reform," Miller Center, University of Virginia, June 15, 2016 (including excerpts from the Miller Center's Edward M. Kennedy Oral History Project), https://millercenter.org/issues-policy/us-domestic-policy/ted-kennedy-lbj-and-immigration-reform.

3. The GOP controlled the Senate during the 97th, 98th, and 99th Congresses (1981–1987), and Simpson chaired the immigration subcommittee. Democrats maintained control of the House throughout the 1980s. Alan Simpson, interview, May 10,

2006, Edward M. Kennedy Oral History Project, Miller Center, University of Virginia, http://web1.millercenter.org/poh/transcripts/ohp_2006_0510_simpson .pdf.

4. Michael Myers, interview, August 28, 2006, Edward M. Kennedy Oral History Project, Miller Center, University of Virginia, https://millercenter.org/the-presidency /presidential-oral-histories/michael-myers-oral-history-2006.

5. Edward M. Kennedy, interview, October 8, 2007, Edward M. Kennedy Oral History Project, Miller Center, University of Virginia, http://web1.millercenter.org /poh/transcripts/ohp_2007_1008_kennedy.pdf.

6. Myers, interview.

7. "House Judiciary Committee Ousts Chairman of Immigration Panel," *Los Angeles Times*, February 2, 1989, https://www.latimes.com/archives/la-xpm-1989 -02-02-mn-2742-story.html; "Rep. Mazzoli Loses Helm of Judiciary Subcommittee," *Washington Post*, February 3, 1989, https://www.washingtonpost.com/archive /politics/1989/02/03/rep-mazzoli-loses-helm-of-judiciary-subcommittee/48424d68 -1e72-4799-9125-37f361dfobd8/.

8. "1989 Speech," box 26, folder 608, Bruce A. Morrison Papers, Archives & Special Collections at the Thomas J. Dodd Research Center, University of Connecticut Libraries.

9. Negotiators cut the House bill's allocation of 15,000 additional transition visas for eastern Europeans and Africans.

10. Congressional Record Proceedings and Debates of the 101st Congress, 2nd Session, Volume 136 Part 24, October 26, 1990 (GPO, 1990), Statement of Sen. Moynihan, 35619, https://heinonline.org/HOL/P?h=hein.congrec/cr1360024&i=1137.

11. IIRM, "The Case for Immigration Reform, a Presentation to the Honorable John Joseph Moakley," August 14, 1990, Record Group 3.4, box 5, folder 74, Moakley Archive and Institute.

12. The IIRM was critical of Berman's lottery, and so was Sen. Simpson's office. Staffer Carl Hampe advocated for the repeal of such an open-ended program. In a note, he indicated that Sen. Kennedy would join Simpson in repealing the Berman provisions "if we 'held our nose' on the 'Irish bill for 'disadvantaged countries.'" Carl Hampe to Alan K. Simpson, March 1989, box 405, folder 2, Alan K. Simpson Papers, Collection 10449.

13. Sean Minihane to Congressman Schumer, Draft Memo, November 13, 1989, IIRM Records, AIA 016, box 12, folder 26, Archives of Irish America.

14. Harris Miller to Michael Myers, April 26, 1989, Robin O'Brien Hiteshew, Collection 3059, box 11, folder 12, Historical Society of Pennsylvania, Philadelphia, PA.

15. Johnson, "Black Presence in U.S. Immigration History."

16. "Table 2: Persons Obtaining Legal Permanent Resident Status by Region and Selected Country of Last Residence, Fiscal Years 1820 to 2019," in U.S. Department of Homeland Security, *2019 Yearbook of Immigration Statistics*.

17. Talton, *In This Land of Plenty*.

18. Bernard Weinraub, "State Dept. Reverses Policy on Ethiopian Exiles in U.S.," *New York Times*, July 7, 1982, https://www.nytimes.com/1982/07/07/world /state-dept-reverses-policy-on-ethiopian-exiles-in-us.html; Akalou, "Ethiopians and

Afghans in the United States." Edward G. Brooke, the African American former U.S. senator from Massachusetts, was chairman of the Emergency Committee. See Edward Brooke, "Africa's 6.3 Million Forgotten Refugees," letter to the editor, *New York Times*, December 13, 1981, https://www.nytimes.com/1981/12/13/opinion/1-africa-s-6.3-million-forgotten-refugees-129862.html; Leslie Wybiral, "The Ethiopian Committee on Immigration, Inc.: Social Justice in Action," Hidden Heritage Collections, April 28, 2016, http://hiddenheritagecollections.org/2016/04/the-ethiopian-committee-on-immigration-inc-social-justice-in-action/.

19. Veney, "Effects of Immigration and Refugee Policies."

20. Carter, *American While Black*.

21. In the 101st Congress, the House Subcommittee on International Law, Immigration, and Refugees was chaired by Bruce A. Morrison (D-CT) and included Democrats Barney Frank (MA), Charles E. Schumer (NY), Howard L. Berman (CA), and Romano L. Mazzoli (KY) and Republicans Lamar S. Smith (TX), Bill McCollum (FL), D. French Slaughter Jr. (VA), and Hamilton Fish Jr. (NY). "Congress Profiles," History, Art & Archives, United States House of Representatives, https://history.house.gov/Congressional-Overview/Profiles/101st/.

22. H. Con. Res. 67 Calling Upon the President to Grant Asylum to Those Individuals Who Seek Asylum in the United States Rather Than Serve in the South African Armed Forces in Support of Apartheid, https://www.congress.gov/bill/101st-congress/house-concurrent-resolution/67/text?r=93&s=6.

23. Joseph P. Fried, "Major Owens, 77, Education Advocate in Congress, Dies," *New York Times*, October 22, 2013, https://www.nytimes.com/2013/10/23/nyregion/major-r-owens-congressman-who-championed-education-dies-at-77.html.

24. Schumer agreed in principle with the diversity visa scheme being proposed by the IIRM in late 1989: 100,000 visas, with 60 percent reserved for adversely affected countries, 20 percent for underrepresented countries, and 20 percent for the rest of the world. Sean Minihane to Charles Schumer, "Attention: Courtney Ward," October 24, 1989, IIRM Records, AIA 016, box 7, folder 4, Archives of Irish America.

25. Sean Minihane, IIRM, to Charles Schumer, Draft Memo, "Alternative Proposals for Diversity Visas," November 13, 1989, IIRM Records, AIA 016, box 13, folder 8, Archives of Irish America.

26. Myers, interview.

27. Alfonso A. Narvaez, "Legislature Welcomes 46 Freshmen," *New York Times*, January 26, 1975, https://www.nytimes.com/1975/01/26/archives/legislature-welcomes-46-freshmen.html.

28. Holtzman was elected to represent the 16th District, which is now a Bronx-based district. "NY District 16 - D Primary," Our Campaigns, https://www.ourcampaigns.com/RaceDetail.html?RaceID=140328. Schumer won the 16th in 1980. In 1982, his district was redrawn as the 10th, to include some of Park Slope, Windsor Terrace, and Canarsie. "NY District 10," Our Campaigns, https://www.ourcampaigns.com/RaceDetail.html?RaceID=37496. In 1992 he won reelection in the 9th District, which by then encompassed parts of Queens. "NY District 9," Our Campaigns, https://www.ourcampaigns.com/RaceDetail.html?RaceID=28185.

29. Richard L. Madden, "Despite Issue of Age, Celler Is Confident," *New York Times*, June 18, 1972, https://www.nytimes.com/1972/06/18/archives/despite-issue-of-age-celler-is-confident.html.

30. Charles E. Schumer, "Back to Immigration," *New York Times*, May 21, 1985, https://www.nytimes.com/1985/05/21/opinion/back-to-immigration.html.

31. "Schumer Immigrants 1990," C-SPAN, October 27, 1990, https://www.c-span.org/video/?c4711011/user-clip-schumer-immigrants-1990.

32. James S. Holt and Harris N. Miller, Holt Miller & Associates, to Sean Minihane, IIRM, October 30, 1989, IIRM Records, AIA 016, box 7, folder 4, Archives of Irish America.

33. Sean Minihane, IIRM, to Charles Schumer, "Alternative Proposals for Diversity Visas," November 13, 1989, IIRM Records, AIA 016, box 13, folder 8, Archives of Irish America.

34. By counting Mexico, a high-sending country, as part of a region designated "South America, Mexico, Central America, and the Caribbean," this scheme would diminish the number of diversity visas for South Americans. Harris N. Miller, IIRM, to Amy Friend, Subcommittee on Criminal Justice, U.S. House of Representatives, "Comments on 'Diversity Immigrants' Provisions of Draft of 'Employment-Related Immigration Act of 1990,'" February 26, 1990, IIRM Records, AIA 016, box 13, folder 8, Archives of Irish America. The language adopted in the law specified that region (vi) includes South America, Mexico, Central America, and the Caribbean. Immigration Act of 1990, Pub. L. No. 101-649, 104 Stat. 4978, https://www.justice.gov/sites/default/files/eoir/legacy/2009/03/04/IMMACT1990.pdf.

35. Holt and Miller to Minihane, October 30, 1989, IIRM Records, AIA 016, box 7, folder 4, Archives of Irish America.

36. Robin Toner, "Congress Ends '89 with Long List of Work Undone," *New York Times*, November 24, 1989, http://www.nytimes.com/1989/11/24/us/congress-ends-89-with-long-list-of-work-undone.html. See also Black, *Best Way to Rob a Bank*; Thompson, "Mediated Corruption"; and Stephen Gettinger, "A Speaker's Downfall," *CQ Weekly*, November 11, 1995, 3435–3437, http://library.cqpress.com.libproxy.temple.edu/cqweekly/WR409330.

37. "The Cloud over Congress," editorial, *New York Times*, January 23, 1990, http://www.nytimes.com/1990/01/23/opinion/the-cloud-over-congress.html.

38. "Congress Returns," editorial, *Washington Post*, January 22, 1990.

39. Julian L. Simon, "More Immigration Can Cut the Deficit," *New York Times*, May 10, 1990, https://www.nytimes.com/1990/05/10/opinion/more-immigration-can-cut-the-deficit.html.

40. At an event reflecting on the twenty-fifth anniversary of the Immigration Act of 1990, Morrison admitted that the transition visa program was "nothing but political log-rolling" and lamented "it didn't win me the governorship so what good was it? I still can get a free drink in any Irish bar." Morrison, "Reflecting on the Immigration Act of 1990."

41. "Irish Immigration Reform Movement Lobbying Day," September 18, 1990, IIRM Records, AIA 016, box 13, folder 6, Archives of Irish America.

42. Harris Miller to Sean Minihane, "Strategy on Immigration Reform," August 9, 1990, IIRM Records, AIA 016, box 13, folder 7, Archives of Irish America. Moakley became chairman of the Rules Committee on June 7, 1989. See Resolution naming Moakley Rules Committee Chairman, H.Res.168, 101st Congress, Congressman John Joseph Moakley Papers (MS 100), 1926-2001, Record Group 3.5, box 8, folder 89, Moakley Archive and Institute.

43. "The Case for Immigration Reform: A Presentation to the Honorable John Joseph Moakley, Chairman, Committee on Rules, U.S. House of Representatives by the Irish Immigration Reform Movement, Tuesday, August 14, 1990," Moakley Papers, Record Group 3.4, box 5, folder 74, Moakley Archive and Institute; IIRM to the Honorable John Joseph Moakley, Re: H.R. 4300, the "Family Unity and Employment Opportunity Act of 1990," August 16, 1990, IIRM Records, AIA 016, box 7, folder 7, Archives of Irish America.

44. Congressman Joe Moakley, Statement before the Boston City Council, March 31, 1988, Moakley Papers, Record Group 8.2, box 8, folder 186, Moakley Archive and Institute.

45. Speech for "Irishman of the Year" event honoring Congressman John Joseph Moakley at the John F. Kennedy Library, March 6, 1994, Moakley Papers, Record Group 8.2, box 12, folder 296, Moakley Archive and Institute.

46. Melissa B. Robinson, "Quintessential Irish Democrat marks 25 years in Congress," Associated Press, January 30, 1998. https://advance-lexis-com.libproxy .temple.edu/api/document?collection=news&id=urn:contentItem:3RX4-0250 -007D-K4VW-00000-00&context=1516831.

47. Congressman Joe Moakley, Statement before the Boston City Council, March 31, 1988, Moakley Papers, Record Group 8.2, box 8, folder 186, Moakley Archive and Institute.

48. Speech for "Irishman of the Year" event.

49. Edmund G. Crotty, interview by Francis C. Weymouth Jr., April 21, 2003, John Joseph Moakley Archive and Institute, available at https://dc.suffolk.edu /moh/8/.

50. He introduced H.R. 4447 in the 98th Congress. In the 100th Congress, H.R. 618 passed the House but didn't move in the Senate. In the 101st, he tried again, introducing H.R. 3506 and H.R. 45, the latter of which passed the House.

51. Crotty, interview.

52. Chinese and Central American Temporary Protected Status Act of 1989, H.R. 45, 101st Cong. (1989); "Sizable Boost in Immigration OK'd," in *CQ Almanac 1990*, 46th ed. (Washington, DC: Congressional Quarterly, 1991), 474–485, 478; Daniel Golden, "Massachusetts Muscle: Long Obscured by More Flamboyant Colleagues, Joe Moakley Has Emerged as One of the Most Influential Members of Congress, Wielding Power on Everything from Redistricting to a Controversial Courthouse," *Boston Globe Magazine*, September 29, 1991; Rick Swartz and Wade Henderson to Chairman Joe Moakley and Jim McGovern, confidential memo re "Strategy on Temporary Safehaven for Salvadorans and Other Groups," September 10, 1990, Moakley Papers, Record Group 3.4, box 5, folder 72, Moakley Archive and Institute.

53. Negotiators cut the House bill's allocation of 15,000 additional transition visas for eastern Europeans and Africans.

54. Simpson argued that special protection for Salvadorans was unnecessary because the violence and political killings in El Salvador had declined. Tracy Wilkinson, "Bill to Give Salvadorans Temporary Haven Immigration," *Los Angeles Times*, November 9, 1990, http://articles.latimes.com/1990-11-09/news/mn-4117_1 _safe-haven-program.

55. Alan K. Simpson to Sen. Pete Wilson, October 22, 1990, box 403, folder 11, Alan K. Simpson Papers, Collection 10449.

56. David O. Williams cited in Jacob, "Diversity Visas," 316.

57. In a 1988 memo responding to written questions from the subcommittee, the secretary of state noted that a random lottery would probably be less costly to administer than a qualified, points-based system where applicants would be evaluated and sorted. "The unqualified registration system requires only the clerical function of data entry to create the record of registration. Since there are no requirements for registration, there would be no need to adjudicate the application substantively." He added that an unqualified registration system "would produce a much larger pool of registrants." A qualified, points-based system would be "the most conducive to fraudulent claims that could be imagined." Written Responses to Questions, February 29, 1988, 4-5, box 369, folder 9, Alan K. Simpson Papers, Collection 10449.

58. Dick Day wrote a note on a copied AP story on the diversity visa lottery: "our only contribution to the program." Dick Day to Alan K. Simpson, Re: Diversity Program from 1990 Act, July 15, 1994, box 458, folder 17, Alan K. Simpson Papers, Collection 10449.

59. Congressional Record Proceedings and Debates of the 101st Congress, 2nd Session, Volume 136 Part 25, October 27, 1990 (GPO, 1990), Statement of Rep. Moakley, 36798-36799, https://heinonline.org/HOL/P?h=hein.congrec/cr1360025&i=795.

60. Sean Benson, interview, November 29, 2005, Ireland House Oral History Collection, AIA 030, Archives of Irish America; Cong. Rec. 136 (October 27, 1990). Congressional Record Proceedings and Debates of the 101st Congress, 2nd Session, Volume 136 Part 25, October 27, 1990, (GPO, 1990), Roll No. 530 on HR4300, 36848, https://heinonline.org/HOL/P?h=hein.congrec/cr1360025&i=795.

61. Myers, interview.

62. Myers, interview.

63. Myers, interview.

64. Christopher Lehmann-Haupt, "America, the Evermore Beautiful," *New York Times*, December 31, 1990, https://timesmachine.nytimes.com/timesmachine /1990/12/31/726090.html.

Chapter 6

1. Tim Golden, "Ellis Island Doors Reopening, This Time as Haven to Tourists," *New York Times*, September 10, 1990, https://www.nytimes.com/1990/09/10/nyregion /ellis-island-doors-reopening-this-time-as-haven-to-tourists.html.

2. William A. Henry III, "Beyond the Melting Pot," *Time*, April 9, 1990, https://time.com/vault/issue/1990-04-09/page/33/.

3. Coleman, *Walls Within*.

4. David Ellis, "Do Big Fences Make Better Neighbors?," *Time*, July 8, 1991, https://time.com/vault/issue/1991-07-08/page/13/.

5. It was thirty-five instead of the previous list of thirty-six because of German unification. The eligible countries were Albania, Algeria, Argentina, Austria, Belgium, Bermuda, Czechoslovakia, Denmark, Estonia, Finland, France, Germany, Gibraltar, Great Britain, Guadeloupe, Hungary, Iceland, Indonesia, Ireland, Italy, Japan, Latvia, Liechtenstein, Lithuania, Luxembourg, Monaco, Netherlands, New Caledonia, Northern Ireland, Norway, Poland, San Marino, Sweden, Switzerland, and Tunisia. Ashley Dunn, "U.S. Plans Lottery with Jackpot of Legal Residency," *Los Angeles Times*, September 6, 1991, http://articles.latimes.com/1991-09-06/news/mn-1739_1_visa-lottery/3.

6. Marvine Howe, "Irish-Americans Praise New Immigration Bill," *New York Times*, October 7, 1990, https://www.nytimes.com/1990/10/07/nyregion/irish-americans-praise-new-immigration-bill.html.

7. Martha Siegel and Laurence Canter, "More Immigrants: Is the Immigration Act of 1990 the Right Way to Adjust the Flow?," *Christian Science Monitor*, November 19, 1990.

8. Robert F. Howe and Brook A. Masters, "Green Card Applicants Hold On to Hope," *Washington Post*, October 14, 1991.

9. Jane Seaberry, "Officials in Va. Prepare for Immigrants' Visit: Number at Post Office Grows," *Washington Post*, October 12, 1991.

10. John O'Mahony, "A Hail of Mail in Merrifield," *Irish Echo*, October 16, 1991, IIRM Records, AIA 016, box 36, Archives of Irish America, Tamiment Library, New York University.

11. O'Mahony, "Hail of Mail in Merrifield."

12. Jane Seaberry and Marylou Tousignant, "Crowd Stampedes in Green-Card Lottery: No Serious Injuries Cited at Va. Post Office," *Washington Post*, October 13, 1991.

13. Howe and Masters, "Green Card Applicants Hold On to Hope."

14. Al Kamen, "Immigration 'Sweepstakes': Odds Will Favor the Irish," *Washington Post*, July 28, 1991.

15. Fix and Passel, *Immigration and Immigrants*.

16. Massey, *Immigration and the Great Recession*.

17. Cheong Chow, "New Visa Lottery Will Favor Irish, Boston Official Says," *Boston Globe*, August 8, 1991.

18. Seaberry, "Officials in Va. Prepare for Immigrants Visit."

19. Seaberry and Tousignant, "Crowd Stampedes in Green-Card Lottery."

20. Seaberry and Tousignant, "Crowd Stampedes in Green-Card Lottery."

21. Seaberry and Tousignant, "Crowd Stampedes in Green-Card Lottery."

22. Howe and Masters, "Green Card Applicants Hold On to Hope."

23. Kamen, "Immigration 'Sweepstakes.'"

24. Seaberry, "Officials in Va. Prepare for Immigrants Visit."

25. Chow, "New Visa Lottery Will Favor Irish, Boston Official Says."

26. Pat Hurley, "Morrison Visas: Mail Now!," *Irish Echo*, October 9–15, 1991, IIRM Records, AIA 016, box 36, Archives of Irish America, Tamiment Library, New York University.

27. Advertisement, "Morrison Visas Special Delivery," *Irish Echo*, October 9–15, 1991, IIRM Records, AIA 016, box 36, Archives of Irish America.

28. Advertisement, "Best of Luck, Denis C. Guerin," *Irish Echo*, October 16–22, 1991, IIRM Records, AIA 016, box 36, Archives of Irish America.

29. Advertisement, "The Law Offices of Jeffrey Gabel," *Irish Echo*, October 2–8, 1991, IIRM Records, AIA 016, box 36, Archives of Irish America.

30. Advertisement, "***Visa*** Application, Washington D.C. Attorney John F. Kennedy," *Irish Echo*, October 2–8, 1991, IIRM Records, AIA 016, box 36, Archives of Irish America.

31. Kamen, "Immigration 'Sweepstakes.'"

32. Kamen, "Immigration 'Sweepstakes.'"

33. Jane Seaberry, "Immigrants Line Up in Merrifield to Play 'Green Card' Lotto," *Washington Post*, October 11, 1991.

34. Kamen, "Immigration 'Sweepstakes.'"

35. Dunn, "U.S. Plans Lottery with Jackpot of Legal Residency."

36. Quoted in Pat Hurley, "Firms Cited for False Visa Ads," *Irish Echo*, October 2–8, 1991, IIRM Records, AIA 016, box 36, Archives of Irish America. Dinkins was also quoted stating that "swift action" would be taken "against those who would deceive and mislead." Debbie McGoldrick, "Countdown to Visa Lottery," *Irish Voice*, October 8, 1991.

37. Dennis Hevesi, "Lawyers and Visa Services Charged in False Ads," *New York Times*, September 28, 1991, https://www.nytimes.com/1991/09/28/nyregion /lawyers-and-visa-services-charged-in-false-ads.html.

38. Zolberg, "Immigration Control Policy."

39. Fernández-Kelly and Massey, "Borders for Whom?"; Luckstead, Devadoss, and Rodriguez, "Effects of North American Free Trade Agreement."

40. The *ABC cases* was a class action settlement that provided Salvadorans and Guatemalans in the country in 1990 a substantive hearing of their asylum claims.

41. Schrag, *Well-Founded Fear*, 33.

42. García, "National (in)Security and the Immigration Act of 1996."

43. Sánchez, "Face the Nation," 1025.

44. Vincent J. Schodolski, "The California Dream Deferred," *Chicago Tribune*, July 26, 1993, https://www.chicagotribune.com/news/ct-xpm-1993-07-26 -9307260004-story.html.

45. HoSang, *Racial Propositions*.

46. Nadia Y. Kim, "The Unexpected Alliance Forged after the Rodney King Verdict," *Washington Post*, April 21, 2021, https://www.washingtonpost.com/outlook /2021/04/21/unexpected-alliance-forged-after-rodney-king-verdict/.

47. Kurt Anderson, "Los Angeles: America's Uneasy New Melting Pot," *Time*, June 13, 1983, https://time.com/vault/issue/1983-06-13/page/1/.

48. HoSang, *Racial Propositions*; Jacobson, *New Nativism*.

49. Deborah Sontag, "Calls to Restrict Immigration Come from Many Quarters," *New York Times*, December 13, 1992, https://www.nytimes.com/1992/12/13/weekinreview/the-nation-calls-to-restrict-immigration-come-from-many-quarters.html; Andreas, "Escalation of U.S. Immigration Control."

50. Stephen L. Carter, "Nativism and Its Discontents," *New York Times*, March 8, 1992, https://www.nytimes.com/1992/03/08/opinion/nativism-and-its-discontents.html.

51. Deborah Sontag, "Across the U.S., Immigrants Find the Land of Resentment," *New York Times*, December 11, 1992, https://www.nytimes.com/1992/12/11/nyregion/across-the-us-immigrants-find-the-land-of-resentment.html.

52. Steen Teske, "Cuban Refugee Crisis," *Encyclopedia of Arkansas*, updated March 12, 2015, https://encyclopediaofarkansas.net/entries/cuban-refugee-crisis-4248/.

53. Julio Capó Jr., "The White House Used This Moment as Proof the U.S. Should Cut Immigration. Its Real History Is More Complicated," *Time*, August 4, 2017, https://time.com/4888381/immigration-act-mariel-boatlift-history/.

54. Mark Matthews, "Refugee Riot in 1980 Gives Glimpse of Clinton in Crisis," *Baltimore Sun*, October 19, 1992, https://www.baltimoresun.com/news/bs-xpm-1992-10-19-1992293110-story.html; Justin Wm. Moyer, "The Forgotten Story of How Refugees Almost Ended Bill Clinton's Career," *Washington Post*, November 17, 2015, https://www.washingtonpost.com/news/morning-mix/wp/2015/11/17/the-forgotten-story-of-how-refugees-almost-ended-bill-clintons-career/; David A. Graham, "Rejecting Syrian Refugees," *The Atlantic*, November 16, 2015, https://www.theatlantic.com/politics/archive/2015/11/paris-backlash-governors-reject-syrian-refugees/416151/.

55. García, *The Refugee Challenge in Post-Cold War America*.

56. "U.S. Immigration Policy," C-SPAN, July 27, 1993, https://www.c-span.org/video/?46688-1/us-immigration-policy.

57. Nevins, *Operation Gatekeeper*.

58. Violent Crime Control and Law Enforcement Act of 1994, Pub. L. No. 103-322, https://www.congress.gov/103/statute/STATUTE-108/STATUTE-108-Pg1796.pdf.

59. Coleman, *Walls Within*.

60. 1994 Press Releases, box 1, folder 8, Federation for American Immigration Reform Records, Special Collections MS2195, George Washington University.

61. U.S. Commission on Immigration Reform, *Becoming an American*, 5.

62. U.S. Commission on Immigration Reform, *Becoming an American*, 63. Higher priorities were the same as those advanced during the legislation of the Immigration Act of 1990: the long backlog of family members awaiting visas, including the spouses and minor children of lawful permanent residents.

63. U.S. Commission on Immigration Reform, *Legal Immigration: Setting Priorities*, xxxi.

64. Gimpel and Edwards, *Congressional Politics of Immigration Reform*, 234. Splitting Simpson's bill, and then the Chrysler-Berman-Brownback Amendment, kept the status quo intact.

65. Dylan Foley, "All Quiet on the Morrison Front," *Irish Echo*, September 2–8, 1992, 5, IIRM Records, AIA 016, box 38, Archives of Irish America.

66. Kevin McHugh, "Most Visa Winners in Ireland," *Irish Echo*, December 30, 1992–January 5, 1993, IIRM Records, AIA 016, box 39, Archives of Irish America.

67. Foley, "All Quiet on the Morrison Front."

68. Advertisement, "Tara Travel: Attention Morrison Visa Applicants: Aer Lingus Is Offering $100 off Its PEX," *Irish Echo*, July 22–28, 1992, IIRM Records, AIA 016, box 38, Archives of Irish America.

69. Advertisement, "A co powiedzialbys na Wielka Wygrana, Bureau of tourist services Panorama," 1992, box 28, Polish Subject Collection, Hoover Institution Archives, Stanford, California, trans. Daniel Pratt. Because the zloty was undergoing continuous devaluation, its conversion rate cannot be determined.

70. "Morrison, Round Three," editorial, *Irish Echo*, February 3–9, 1993, IIRM Records, AIA 016, box 39, Archives of Irish America.

71. The State Department notified winners of the 1993 lottery well into 1994 because so many lottery winners had failed to follow up to apply for the visa. Kevin McHugh, "State Department to Notify 5,000 Morrison Winners," *Irish Echo*, June 15–21, 1994, IIRM Records, AIA 016, box 43, Archives of Irish America.

72. Foley, "All Quiet on the Morrison Front."

Chapter 7

1. Anthony M. DeStefano, "Green Card Lottery Warning," *Newsday*, June 1, 1994; Ann O'Hanlon, "Immigrants' American Dream: Winning a Visa," *Washington Post*, July 1, 1994, https://www.washingtonpost.com/archive/local/1994/07/01/immigrants-american-dream-winning-a-visa/3dc9d087-e8a0-4fe1-948c-12cdd63d43a6/.

2. "Going to the United States?—USIS Explains Visa Lottery Programme," *Free Press*, June 24, 1994; Deborah Sontag, "Aspiring Immigrants Misled on Chances in Visa Lottery," *New York Times*, June 20, 1994; U.S. Government Accountability Office, *Fraud Risks Complicate State's Ability to Manage Diversity Visa Program*.

3. Peggy Berkowitz, "Give Us Your Tired, Your Poor, Your Huddled Mailbox Stuffers," *Wall Street Journal*, January 19, 1987.

4. Al Gore, remarks, The Superhighway Summit, Royce Hall, UCLA, Los Angeles, California, January 11, 1994, https://clintonwhitehouse1.archives.gov/White_House/EOP/OVP/other/superhig.html.

5. Tarnoff, *Internet for the People*.

6. Giovanni Navarria, "How the Internet Was Born: From the ARPANET to the Internet," *The Conversation*, November 2, 2016, https://theconversation.com/how-the-internet-was-born-from-the-arpanet-to-the-internet-68072.

7. Brunton, *Spam*.

8. Paul Simon, "You Can Call Me Al," *Graceland*, Warner Brothers, 1986.

9. "World Wide Web Timeline," Pew Research Center, March 11, 2014, http://www.pewinternet.org/2014/03/11/world-wide-web-timeline/.

10. Philip Elmer-Dewitt and David S. Jackson, "Battle for the Soul of the Internet," *Time*, July 25, 1994.

11. Peter H. Lewis, "Business Technology: Anarchy; a Threat on the Electronic Frontier," *New York Times*, May 11, 1994, https://www.nytimes.com/1994/05/11 /business/business-technology-anarchy-a-threat-on-the-electronic-frontier.html.

12. Map shows South Africa had 0.247 percent of its population using the internet in 1994. "Individuals Using the Internet (% of Population)," International Telecommunications Union (ITU) World Telecommunication/ICT Indicators Database, The World Bank, https://data.worldbank.org/indicator/IT.NET.USER.ZS ?end=2020&most_recent_year_desc=false&start=1998&view=map&year=1994.

13. Even the infrastructure of the internet tends to trace the paths of earlier technologies of colonialism. Starosielski, *The Undersea Network*.

14. Some 450,000 international students were studying in the United States in 1994. Davis, *Open Doors*, 22.

15. Canter and Siegel, *U.S. Immigration Made Easy.*

16. Canter and Siegel, *How to Make a Fortune*, 2.

17. Canter and Siegel, *How to Make a Fortune*, 2.

18. Canter and Siegel, *How to Make a Fortune*, 16.

19. Canter and Siegel, *How to Make a Fortune*, 21.

20. Google Groups hosts an archive of Usenet posts including many copies of Canter and Siegel's message. Post by Laurence Canter, "Green Card Lottery— Final One?," Usenet, April 12, 1994, 3:45:39 A.M., https://groups.google.com/d/msg /bit.listserv.cdromlan/UM6EtDwXwiY/5aoEXLf2-ZAJ.

21. John Burgess, "Who'll Make 'the Net' Gain? Global Computer Community Wrestles with Issue of Advertising," *Washington Post*, April 26, 1994, https://www .washingtonpost.com/archive/business/1994/04/26/wholl-make-the-net-gain /aoe558e2-1822-45c9-a549-e1678adc6c9d/.

22. Elmer-Dewitt and Jackson, "Battle for the Soul of the Internet."

23. Scott Yates, reply to "Green Card Lottery—Final One?," Usenet, April 13, 1994, 9:32:08 A.M., https://groups.google.com/d/msg/bit.listserv.cdromlan /UM6EtDwXwiY/7MZWqVcM_30J.

24. Brunton, *Spam*, 55.

25. Burgess, "Who'll Make 'the Net' Gain?"

26. Burgess, "Who'll Make 'the Net' Gain?"

27. K. K. Campbell, "A Net.Conspiracy So Immense . . . ," Yenta, October 1, 1994, https://web.archive.org/web/20210615070247/http://bella.media.mit.edu/people /foner/Yenta/green-card-lawyers.html.

28. Peter H. Lewis, "Business Technology; Sneering at a Virtual Lynch Mob," *New York Times*, May 11, 1994, https://www.nytimes.com/1994/05/11/business /business-technology-sneering-at-a-virtual-lynch-mob.html.

29. David Sewell, "Laurence Canter and the Devil," Usenet, May 26, 1994, https://web.archive.org/web/20210516022639/http://www.people.virginia .edu:80/~drs2n/Netwriting/canter.html, linked from David Sewell, "Netwriting Archive," March 2003, https://web.archive.org/web/20120121034650/http://people .virginia.edu/~drs2n/Netwriting/index.html.

30. Brunton, *Spam,* 57.

31. Lewis, "Sneering at a Virtual Lynch Mob."

32. Canter and Siegel, *How to Make a Fortune,* 32.

33. Rob Pegoraro, "CyberSurfing: Commotion on the Internet," *Washington Post*, February 16, 1995.

34. Elmer-Dewitt and Jackson, "Battle for the Soul of the Internet."

35. Canter and Siegel, *How to Make a Fortune,* 207.

36. David Freedman, "Email with . . . Spammers," *Inc.*, Summer 1995, 44.

37. Canter and Siegel, *How to Make a Fortune,* 216.

38. Sewell, "Laurence Canter and the Devil."

39. Richard Leiby, "Style: Traffic Jam on Internet E-mail Overload Sends Netiquette Out the Window," *Washington Post*, May 31, 1994, https://www.washingtonpost.com/archive/lifestyle/1994/05/31/traffic-jam-on-internet/4a3f9060-be62-4ae2-964c-72e82dc3c0d2/.

40. The T-shirt is cataloged at the Computer History Museum. Catalog Number 102757853, "Object is a long sleeved medium t-shirt. with a five-color silk screen on the front reading, 'Coming to a news group near you . . . Green Card Lawyers Spamming the globe,' Design and art (c).McCall and Furr," 1994, Gift of Glee Willis, https://www.computerhistory.org/collections/catalog/102757853.

41. Joel K. Furr, "Final Notice: Deadline to Order Green Card Lawyers and/or McElwaine T-shirts," Usenet, August 17, 1994, 7:41:24 A.M., https://groups.google.com/g/misc.legal/c/bByeMuDOXPQ/m/d-wGbHdsvYYJ; Joel K. Furr, "Legal Wrangling about T-Shirts," Usenet, August 8, 1994, 9:30:53 A.M., https://groups.google.com/g/misc.legal/c/RSw-xzr-jno/m/kE1EuBdP-tEJ.

42. Rob Pegoraro, "T'd Off over T-Shirts," *Washington Post*, August 18, 1994.

43. Campbell, "Net.Conspiracy So Immense."

44. Philip Bump, "From Lycos to Ask Jeeves to Facebook: Tracking the 20 Most Popular Web Sites Every Year Since 1996," *Washington Post*, December 15, 2014, https://www.washingtonpost.com/news/the-intersect/wp/2014/12/15/from-lycos-to-ask-jeeves-to-facebook-tracking-the-20-most-popular-web-sites-every-year-since-1996/.

45. CAN-SPAM Act of 2003, Pub. L. No. 108-187, 117 Stat. 2699 (2003).

46. Federal Trade Commission, *Fraud Reports*, based on data updated February 22, 2022, https://public.tableau.com/shared/6Y6XQ4HT4?:display_count=n&:origin=viz_share_link; Federal Bureau of Investigation, *Internet Crime Report, 2021*, https://www.ic3.gov/Media/PDF/AnnualReport/2021_IC3Report.pdf.

47. Freedman, "Email with . . . Spammers."

48. Ashley Craddock, "Spamming Lawyer Disbarred," *Wired Magazine*, July 10, 1997, https://web.archive.org/web/20220121151909/https://www.wired.com/1997/07/spamming-lawyer-disbarred/; Board of Professional Responsibility of the Supreme Court of Tennessee, Canter, Laurence A., BPR#006032, https://docs.tbpr.org/006032-19970605-0-a.pdf. In 1987 the couple was reprimanded and suspended temporarily by the Florida Bar. The Florida Bar v. Siegel, 511 So. 2d 995 (1987). See also Ray Everett-Church, "The Spam That Started It All," *Wired Magazine*, April 13, 1999, http://www.wired.com/politics/law/news/1999/04/19098; "The Father of

Modern Spam Speaks," interview with Canter, *Cnet.com*, March 26, 2002, https://www.cnet.com/news/the-father-of-modern-spam-speaks/.

49. Thomas L. Friedman, "The Mouse That Roars: A Global Tale," *New York Times*, July 18, 1998, section A, page 11, https://www.nytimes.com/1998/07/18/opinion/foreign-affairs-the-mouse-that-roars-a-global-tale.html.

Chapter 8

1. Walisu Alhassan, interview by the author, March 12, 2013, Tamale, Ghana.

2. Yosola Olorunshola, "How the West African Students Union Drove the Anti-colonial Agenda in 20th Century London," *Quartz Africa*, March 21, 2021, https://qz.com/africa/1979035/how-west-african-students-in-london-fought-for-african-independence/.

3. Perry, *London Is the Place for Me*; Matera, *Black London*.

4. Patel, *We're Here Because You Were There*.

5. Miescher and Ashbaugh, "Been-To Visions"; Padmore, *Pan-Africanism or Communism?*; Akyeampong, "Africans in the Diaspora."

6. Nieswand, "Burgers' Paradox."

7. "Is Ghana Such a Bad Place?," editorial, *Daily Graphic* (Ghana), November 14, 1994.

8. The 1986 Single European Act mandated the abolition of internal borders and stressed the need to tighten control over external frontiers, and the Schengen and Dublin Conventions of 1990 became the pillars of "Fortress Europe." Loescher, "State Responses"; Zaiotti, *Cultures of Border Control*.

9. Walia, *Border and Rule*, 2.

10. "Unlawful Migrants," editorial, *Daily Graphic*, February 20, 1995.

11. Germaine Mbongue and Joe Mbongue, "From Dust to Snow," in Ngwa and Ngwa, *From Dust to Snow*, 75.

12. Walia, *Border and Rule*, 3.

13. Clarke and Getz, *Abina and the Important Men*; Getz, *Long Nineteenth Century*.

14. Johnson, "Largest Human Zoo in World History."

15. Conklin, *Mission to Civilize*.

16. Nugent, *Africa Since Independence*; Cooper, *Africa Since 1940*; Cooper, *Africa in the World*; Shillington, *History of Africa*.

17. Nkrumah, "I Speak of Freedom."

18. King, "Birth of a New Nation."

19. Lord Kitchener, "Birth of Ghana."

20. Lumumba, "Speech at the Ceremony of the Proclamation of the Congo's Independence."

21. Ahlman, *Kwame Nkrumah*, 117–122.

22. Kofi Owusu-Daaku, interview by the author, January 30, 2013, Kumasi, Ghana.

23. "Comment: Those Unpatriotic Ghanaians," *The Spectator*, November 20, 1999.

Chapter 9

1. Richards, photograph of Bill Clinton and Jerry John Rawlings.

2. James Bennet, "Throngs Greet Call by Clinton for New Africa," *New York Times*, March 24, 1998, https://www.nytimes.com/1998/03/24/world/throngs-greet-call-by-clinton-for-new-africa.html.

3. AP Archive, "Ghana: Thousands Turn Out to Welcome US President Clinton," posted July 21, 2015, YouTube video, 2:52, https://www.youtube.com/watch?v=5RW8IDf3N4s.

4. Clinton, National Security Council, Speechwriting Office, and Widmer, "Africa—Ghana [POTUS Address to the People of Ghana, March 23, 1998]."

5. Clinton Digital Library, "Kente Robe."

6. Bennet, "Throngs Greet Call by Clinton for New Africa."

7. Eric Schmitt, "Bill to Push Africa Trade Is Approved," *New York Times*, March 16, 1998, https://www.nytimes.com/1998/03/16/world/bill-to-push-africa-trade-is-approved.html.

8. Howard W. French, "Accra Journal; African Hospitality No Match for Clinton's Hordes," *New York Times*, March 19, 1998, https://www.nytimes.com/1998/03/19/world/accra-journal-african-hospitality-no-match-for-clinton-s-hordes.html.

9. Aidoo and Briggs, "Underpowered."

10. Miescher, "'Nkrumah's Baby.'"

11. Cooper, *Africa Since 1940*, 89.

12. Gerits, "'When the Bull Elephants Fight.'"

13. Rodgers, *Age of Fracture*.

14. Assan and Kharisma, "Political Economy."

15. Hart, "'NIFA NIFA'"; Kobo, "'We Are Citizens, Too,'" 83–88.

16. Nugent, *Big Men, Small Boys, and Politics in Ghana*.

17. "Military Coup in Ghana Alarms West African Governments," *New York Times*, January 4, 1982, https://www.nytimes.com/1982/01/04/world/military-coup-in-ghana-alarms-west-african-governments.html. The *New York Times* called Rawlings a "charismatic revolutionary." James Brooke, "In Ghana, the Leader at Full Sail," *New York Times*, December 11, 1988, https://www.nytimes.com/1988/12/11/world/in-ghana-the-leader-at-full-sail.html.

18. "Ghana's New Ruler Names a Civilian Cabinet," *New York Times*, January 23, 1982, https://www.nytimes.com/1982/01/23/world/around-the-world-ghana-s-new-ruler-names-a-civilian-cabinet.html.

19. Joseph Appiah-Nkrumah, interview by the author, February 19, 2013, Kumasi, Ghana. Police and military aggressively enforced price controls and rules against "hoarding."

20. Some estimate that up to 1.2 million Ghanaians were deported in 1983, but others use the figure of 700,000. Henckaerts, *Mass Expulsion*, 67–68.

21. Daly, "Ghana Must Go."

22. Miescher and Tsikata, "Hydro-power and the Promise of Modernity and Development in Ghana."

23. Williams, "'Rawlings Revolution.'"

24. Nugent, *Big Men, Small Boys, and Politics in Ghana*, 112.

25. "The Reality of IMF Policies," editorial, *Daily Graphic*, October 11, 1997.

26. Williams, "'Rawlings Revolution,'" 369.

27. Nugent, *Big Men, Small Boys, and Politics in Ghana*, 113–115.

28. Nugent, *Big Men, Small Boys, and Politics in Ghana*, 131.

29. Nugent, *Big Men, Small Boys, and Politics in Ghana*, 130–133.

30. Kelsall, *Business, Politics, and the State in Africa*, 78; James Brooke, "Ghana, Once 'Hopeless,' Gets at Least the Look of Success," *New York Times*, January 3, 1989, https://www.nytimes.com/1989/01/03/world/ghana-once-hopeless-gets-at-least-the -look-of-success.html.

31. Nugent, *Africa Since Independence*, 169.

32. Ayelazuno, *Neoliberal Globalisation*, 165.

33. Perhaps Rawlings was eager to satisfy the donor community, which insisted on good governance and democratic norms. Oquaye, "Ghanaian Elections of 1992."

34. As Oquaye notes, despite the lifting of the ban on private press, campaigns of harassment continued to target them.

35. Kufuor was reelected in 2004. In 2008 NDC regained the presidency with the election of John Atta Mills. In 2012 Mills passed away, and Mills's vice president, John Mahama, took office. In the 2012 elections, Mahama was elected. The 2012 election was subject to an appeal by opposition party NPP on behalf of their presidential candidate, Nana Akufo-Addo. However, in August 2013 the Supreme Court affirmed that Mahama was the legitimate winner of the election. Arthur, "Ghana's 'Golden Age of Business.'"

36. Ayelazuno, *Neoliberal Globalisation*, 166; Ayee, "December 1996 General Elections in Ghana."

37. Kenneth B. Noble, "Ghana Falters after Years of Growth," *New York Times*, June 24, 1991, https://www.nytimes.com/1991/06/24/business/ghana-falters-after -years-of-growth.html.

38. Ferguson, *Global Shadows*, 11.

39. Steger and Roy, *Neoliberalism*, 114.

40. In 1994, Ghana's minimum wage was under one U.S. dollar per day. "Minimum Wage Timeline (1963-2015)," Mywage.org/Ghana, http://www.mywage.org /ghana/home/salary/minimum-wages/minimum-wage-timeline. In 2013, the daily minimum wage was increased 17 percent to 5.24 Ghana cedis, the equivalent of less than three U.S. dollars. "Ghana Increases Daily Minimum Wage by 17% for 2013," *Ghana Business News*, April 30, 2013, http://www.ghanabusinessnews.com /2013/04/30/ghana-increases-daily-minimum-wage-by-17-for-2013/.

41. Obeng-Odoom, "Neoliberalism and the Urban Economy in Ghana," 95.

42. Overa, "When Men Do Women's Work"; Fine and Boateng, "Labour & Employment Under Structural Adjustment."

43. Ayelazuno, *Neoliberal Globalisation*, 175.

44. Victor A. Osei, "ERP: How Are Ghanaians Abroad Contributing Towards It," *Daily Graphic*, November 30, 1994.

45. Brydon, "'With a Little Bit of Luck . . .'"

Chapter 10

1. Ghana National Lottery Authority website, http://www.nla.com.gh/.

2. Department of National Lottery, "A Short History of the Department of National Lotteries," archived electronic version of *Forbes Magazine*, October 6, 1999, https://web.archive.org/web/20120729023405/http://www.winne.com/ghana/cr12int.html.

3. "Is Ghana Such a Bad Place?," editorial, *Daily Graphic*, November 14, 1994.

4. Paulina Johnson, interview by the author, April 11, 2013, Accra, Ghana; Ibrahim, interview by the author, April 11, 2014, Philadelphia, PA.

5. Tankus, "Jackpot."

6. Anders Bright, "Ohio's Vaccine Lottery Scheme Is Working—So Why Does It Bother Us?," *Washington Post*, June 1, 2021, https://www.washingtonpost.com/outlook/2021/06/01/ohios-vaccine-lottery-scheme-is-working-so-why-does-it-bother-us/.

7. Worsop, "Gambling Boom."

8. Lears, *Something for Nothing: Luck in America*, 4.

9. Van Wyk, "Postcolonial Africa and its Lotteries."

10. Nugent, *Big Men, Small Boys, and Politics in Ghana*, 190.

11. Various newspapers and dates, including *Daily Graphic*, *The Mirror*, *The Pioneer*, and *The Spectator*, found at KNUST.

12. Kofi Owusu-Daaku, interview by the author, January 30, 2013, Kumasi, Ghana.

13. Rev. Apostle Kwamena Ahinful, "To Lotto or Not To," *The Mirror*, May 13, 1995.

14. Efam Awo Dovi, "Watch Out for Lotto Tricksters," *Daily Graphic*, June 2, 1994.

15. "Of Raffles and Lotteries," editorial, *Daily Graphic*, August 27, 1996.

16. Ahinful, "To Lotto or Not To."

17. May 11, 1995. "'Kumepreko' Demonstration in Accra," *The Mirror*, May 13, 1995. See also The Statesman, "'Kume Preko' on CNN, BBC," *Modernghana.com*, May 23, 1995, http://www.modernghana.com/news/172/kume-preko-on-cnn-bbc.html; Research Directorate, Immigration and Refugee Board, Canada, "Ghana: Information on the Kokomelemele Mechanics Association and the Alliance for Change," February 1, 1996, https://www.refworld.org/docid/3ae6acdb2c.html; John Pender, "Recent Demonstrations in Ghana Show That There Is No Future for Africans under Structural Adjustment," Robinson Rojas Archive, October 1995, reprinted from *Living Marxism*, no. 83, October 1995, http://www.rrojasdatabank.info/ghanasa1.htm; "Today in History: The 1995 'Kume Preko' Protest That Rocked Ghana," *Ghanaweb.com*, May 11, 2020, https://www.ghanaweb.com/GhanaHomePage/NewsArchive/Today-in-History-The-1995-Kume-Preko-protest-that-rocked-Ghana-948484.

18. Osei, "Political Liberalisation."

19. Alhaji Abdul-Rahman and Harruna Attah, "Kume Preko: Setting the Record Straight," *Modernghana.com*, May 26, 2020, https://www.modernghana.com/news/1004675/kume-preko-setting-the-record-straight.html.

20. Ayelazuno, *Neoliberalism and resistance in Ghana*, 181–182.

21. *The Mirror*, June 27, 1998.

22. *The Mirror*, June 20, 1998.

23. David O. Williams, cited in Jacob, "Diversity Visas," 316. In a 1988 memo responding to written questions from the subcommittee, Secretary of State George Shultz noted that a random lottery would probably be less costly to administer than a qualified, points-based system where applicants would be sorted according to criteria. "The unqualified registration system requires only the clerical function of data entry to create the record of registration. Since there are no requirements for registration, there would be no need to adjudicate the application substantively." He added that an unqualified registration system "would produce a much larger pool of registrants." Yet, a qualified, points-based system would be "the most conducive to fraudulent claims that could be imagined." Written Responses to Questions, February 29, 1988, 4–5, box 369, folder 9, Alan K. Simpson Papers, Collection 10449, American Heritage Center, University of Wyoming.

24. For diversity visa admissions, Mexico and the nations of Central America were grouped as part of the "South America" region, drastically reducing South American countries' chances in the lottery. Wardle, "Strategic Use of Mexico."

25. Initially, the law made 55,000 diversity visas available annually, but in 1997 the Nicaraguan and Central American Relief Act (NACARA) stipulated that up to 5,000 of the annually allocated diversity visas be made available for use under the NACARA program, reducing the available diversity visas to 50,000 beginning with DV-99. The per-country cap was therefore reduced to about 3,500. Only the most populous or enthusiastic countries in low-sending regions neared the cap. These numbers are also inexact because more winners are selected in the lottery than receive visas.

26. In fiscal year (FY) 1995, more than 700,000 people obtained permanent residence status in the United States, and only around 55,000 of them did so via the lottery. "Table 1: Persons Obtaining Legal Permanent Resident Status: Fiscal Years 1820 to 2012," 2012, U.S. Department of Homeland Security, *Yearbook of Immigration Statistics: 2012*.

27. Randolph Ryan, "Millions Enter Lottery for US Citizenship: Eligibility Expanded to Over 180 Countries," *Boston Globe*, June 15, 1994.

28. "Going to the United States?—USIS Explains Visa Lottery Programme," *Free Press*, June 24, 1994.

29. "Going to the United States?"

30. Peter Hirsch, "LTE: Green Card Lottery Would Foil Einstein," *New York Times*, June 15, 1994, https://www.nytimes.com/1994/06/15/opinion/l-green-card-lottery-would-foil-einstein-403970.html.

31. Ann O'Hanlon, "Immigrants' American Dream: Winning a Visa: But Many Need Lotto Luck in State Department's First 'Diversity Lottery,'" *Washington Post*, July 1, 1994.

32. Maria Puente, "Beware Promises of Winning Entries," *USA Today*, April 6, 1994.

33. Various advertisements: "The U.S. Green Card Lottery, '94," *Free Press*, April 29, May 6, 13, 20, 27, June 3, 10, 17, 1994; "Going to America or Canada—the Law Office of Mark Carmel USA Immigration Lawyer Is Ever Ready to Help You,"

Daily Graphic, October 16, 1998. In 1999, the *Ghanaian Chronicle* reported that Vision 2000 Associates had promised clients they would win the lottery if they paid a fee of twenty dollars. Compilation of News "The Dispatch," April 1, 1999, https://web.archive.org/web/20220329155629/https://www.ghanaweb.com /GhanaHomePage/NewsArchive/artikel.php?ID=5725.

34. Deborah Sontag, "Aspiring Immigrants Misled on Chances in Visa Lottery," *New York Times*, June 20, 1994, https://www.nytimes.com/1994/06/20/nyregion /aspiring-immigrants-misled-on-chances-in-visa-lottery.html. I found his advertisements in the following Ghanaian newspapers: "USA to Give 55,000 'Green Cards' (David L. Amkraut)," *The Mirror*, January 20, 27, February 3, 10, 17, 24, March 2, 9, 16, 23, 30, April 13, 1996; "USA to Give 55,000 'Green Cards,'" *The Pioneer*, February 7, 8, 12, 13, 14, 15, 16, 20, 22, 26, 27, 1996.

35. Federal Trade Commission (FTC) v. David L. Amkraut (C.D. Cal. 1997), http://www.ftc.gov/enforcement/cases-proceedings/952-3182/amkraut-david-l-dba -law-offices-david-l-amkraut; Angie Chuang, "Lawyer Misled Consumers, Agency Says," *Los Angeles Times*, January 25, 1997.

36. Owusu-Daaku, interview.

37. Kwoi Yankah, "Woes of a Kwatriot: Come Back Home, Sir," *The Mirror*, December 9, 1995.

38. The Immigration Reform and Control Act of 1986 initiated a Visa Waiver Pilot Program for eight countries. Subsequent legislation modified the program requirements and made it permanent. Kolker, *Visa Waiver Program*.

39. "They Exploit Visa," editorial, *Ghanaian Times*, October 14, 1997.

40. Wanlov the Kubolor, "Green Card," https://wanlov.bandcamp.com/track /green-card.

41. Geraldine Ayiehfor, "Europe: Heaven on Earth?," in Ngwa and Ngwa, *From Dust to Snow*, 11.

42. Kleist and Thorsen, *Hope and Uncertainty in Contemporary African Migration*, vii.

43. Sylvie Bredeloup associates migratory paths with a "mystic journey," drawing on how hope is embedded in Muslim and Christian religions. Bredeloup, "Migratory Adventure as Moral Experience"; Bayart, *Global Subjects*,186.

44. "La migration n'est pas seulement déterminée par la misère et le danger comme on le lit souvent, elle appartient aussi à une geste épique portée par des imaginaires collectifs qui font du Nord un lieu où les héros s'élèvent." De Latour, "Heros du Retour," 172.

45. The phrase "greener pastures" references Psalm 23 in the Old Testament and reflects the increasing dominance of imported and domestic charismatic churches and the role of evangelical Christianity in the social life of Ghana broadly, and particularly its southern cities, coinciding with structural adjustment.

46. And engaging in "Atlantic African" economic practices that have long characterized African economic activity. Guyer, *Marginal Gains*.

47. Overa, "When Men Do Women's Work," 541–543.

48. Brydon, "'With a Little Bit of Luck'"; Ferguson, *Global Shadows*; and Nugent, *Big Men, Small Boys, and Politics in Ghana*.

49. Edward [pseud.], interview by the author, April 4, 2013, Kumasi, Ghana; Cornelius Ayensu Noonoo (Kwesi), interview by the author, May 16, 2013, Cape Coast, Ghana; and Prince Nyarko, interview by the author, May 13, 2013, Kumasi, Ghana.

50. "To the agents, the process involves special technicalities. To this end, forms were printed which the applicants then obtained." Austin Avwode, "Mad Rush to America," *The Week*, March 11, 1996.

51. Noonoo (Kwesi), interview.

52. Noonoo (Kwesi), interview; Mabel Sarpong, interview by the author, May 21, 2013, Accra, Ghana; Anonymous, interview by the author, May 21, 2013, Accra, Ghana; and Nyarko, interview. Dates for the lottery varied each year. For FY 95, the registration period was June 1–30, 1994. Registration dates for successive lotteries were as follows:

FY 96: January 31, 1995–March 1, 1995
FY 97: February 12, 1996–March 12, 1996
FY 98: February 3, 1997–March 5, 1997
FY 99: October 24, 1997–November 24, 1997
FY 00: October 1–31, 1998
FY 01: October 4, 1999–November 3, 1999
FY 02: October 2, 2000–November 1, 2000 (beginning with DV-2002, applications had to be received at the Kentucky Consular Center, which opened in 2000, rather than the National Visa Center; "Registration for the Diversity Immigrant (DV-2002) Visa Program," *Federal Register*, https://www.federalregister.gov/documents/2000/07/31/00-19363/registration-for-the-diversity-immigrant-dv-2002-visa-program)
FY 03: October 1–31, 2001
FY 04: October 7–November 6, 2002
FY 05: November 1, 2003–December 30, 2003 (Beginning of the electronic lottery)
FY 06: November 5, 2004–January 7, 2005
FY 07: October 5, 2005–December 4, 2005
FY 08: October 4, 2006–December 3, 2006
FY 09: October 3, 2007–December 2, 2007
FY 10: October 2, 2008–December 1, 2008
FY 11: October 2, 2009–November 30, 2009
FY 12: October 5, 2010–November 3, 2010
FY 13: October 4, 2011–November 5, 2011
FY 14: October 2, 2012–November 3, 2012
FY 15: October 1, 2013–November 2, 2013
FY 16: October 1, 2014–November 3, 2014
FY 17: October 1, 2015–November 3, 2015
FY 18: October 4, 2016–November 7, 2016
FY 19: October 18, 2017–November 22, 2017 (Original dates were October 3, 2017–November 7, 2017, but due to technical problems entries received before October 10 were discarded and dates were revised)

FY 20: October 3, 2018–November 6, 2018
FY 21: October 2, 2019–November 5, 2019
FY 22: October 7, 2020–November 10, 2020
FY 23: October 6, 2021–November 9, 2021

53. Noonoo (Kwesi), interview.

54. Piot, *Nostalgia for the Future*, 95.

55. Piot, *Nostalgia for the Future*.

56. Laura Lomokie Teye, "Visa Deal—Woman before Court," *The Mirror*, September 2, 1995.

57. William A. Asiedu, "Mad Rush to Register Marriages—for Easy Visa Acquisition," *The Mirror*, May 12, 2001.

58. Jojo Hagan Annobil, "US Green Card Lottery . . . Suspense and Agony," *Daily Graphic*, October 27, 1998.

59. Kofi Owusu-Daaku said one year he saw eight women, who had won the visa lottery, who showed up at their consular interview with sewing machines to demonstrate that they had tailoring skills. Owusu-Daaku, interview. Piot also describes this phenomenon in Togo, with applicants purporting to be tailors (in 2003, when the job was added to the skilled jobs list) and house painters (in 2006). Piot, *Nostalgia for the Future*, 80.

60. Stephen Atta Owusu, "Visa Contractors and U.S. Diversity Visa Lottery Fraudsters Drain Gullible Victims in Ghana," *Modernghana.com*, August 28, 2012, http://www.modernghana.com/news/414171/1/visa-contractors-and-us-diversity-visa-lottery-fra.html.

61. U.S. Congress, House, Committee on the Judiciary, *Diversity Visa Program and Its Susceptibility to Fraud and Abuse*, April 29, 2004; U.S. Government Accountability Office, *Fraud Risks Complicate State's Ability to Manage Diversity Visa Program*.

62. U.S. Government Accountability Office, *Fraud Risks Complicate State's Ability to Manage Diversity Visa Program*.

63. Annobil, "U.S. Green Card Lottery."

64. Rita Ofori-Frimpong, interview by Susan Thomson and Christoph Strobel, November 8, 2007, University of Massachusetts Lowell Center for Lowell History, Oral History Collection, https://archive.org/details/CLHOH-OforiFrimpong; Malam Faisal, interview by the author, May 9, 2014, Philadelphia, PA; Hailu et al., "Lived Experiences of Diversity Visa Lottery Immigrants in the United States."

65. Henry Nti Antwi, interview by the author, April 24, 2013, Kumasi, Ghana.

66. Bernard Gyasi, interview by the author, April 8, 2013, Kumasi, Ghana.

67. Ghana's population grew from an estimated 11 million (1980) to 19 million (2000) to 31 million (2020), according to the World Bank. "Ghana," World Bank, accessed August 10, 2022, https://web.archive.org/web/20190308144306/https://data.worldbank.org/country/Ghana. Ghana won the fourth highest number of visas of any African country in 1995, after Nigeria, Ethiopia, and Egypt (the top three most populated countries in Africa at the time), while Ghana was the twelfth most populous African country.

Chapter 11

1. Biodun Sonowo, Chukwudi Nwabuko, and Chris Okereafor, "Nigerians Rush for America," *Sunday Champion (Nigeria)*, February 25, 1996.

2. Hilary Okwessa to Joseph Anagboso, quoted in Sonowo, Nwabuko, and Okereafor, "Nigerians Rush for America."

3. Henry Louis Gates Jr., "Powell and the Black Elite," *New Yorker*, September 25, 1995, 64–80, 76. See also Howard W. French, "Lagos Journal: Nigerians Lament 'Locusts' That Pick Nation Bare," *New York Times*, October 12, 1995, http://www.nytimes.com/1995/10/12/world/lagos-journal-nigerians-lament-locusts-that-pick-nation-bare.html.

4. Smith, "Nigerian Scam E-mails and the Charms of Capital."

5. Nigerian Law, Criminal Code, Part 6, archived at https://web.archive.org/web/20050308040611/http://www.nigeria-law.org/Criminal%20Code%20Act-Part%20VI%20%20to%20the%20end.htm.

6. Apter, "IBB=419."

7. Nugent, *Africa Since Independence*, 95.

8. Osaghae, *Crippled Giant*, 69.

9. Daly, A History of the Republic of Biafra, 228.

10. Falola and Heaton, *History of Nigeria*.

11. Apter, "IBB=419," 274.

12. Falola and Heaton, *History of Nigeria*, 183.

13. Nugent, *Africa Since Independence*, 219.

14. Nugent, *Africa Since Independence*, 219.

15. Falola and Heaton, *History of Nigeria*, 181–208.

16. In 2015 Buhari was elected president of Nigeria, describing himself as a "converted democrat." "Buhari: From Coup Leader to 'Converted Democrat,'" *Vanguard*, May 27, 2015, http://www.vanguardngr.com/2015/05/buhari-from-coup-leader-to-converted-democrat/.

17. Falola and Heaton, *History of Nigeria*, 217.

18. Falola and Heaton, *History of Nigeria*, 219.

19. Apter, "IBB=419," 289.

20. Nugent, *Africa Since Independence*, 372.

21. Kenneth Noble, "Nigerian Military Rulers Annul Election," *New York Times*, June 24, 1993, https://www.nytimes.com/1993/06/24/world/nigerian-military-rulers-annul-election.html.

22. Soyinka, *Open Sore of a Continent*, 18.

23. Soyinka, *Open Sore of a Continent*, 8–9, quoting a 1994 article in the Nigerian media titled "The Last Despot and the End of Nigerian History?"

24. Apter, "IBB=419," 287.

25. Falola and Heaton, *History of Nigeria*, 224–229.

26. Mikell and Lyman, "Critical U.S. Bilateral Relations in Africa," 81.

27. Campbell, *Dancing on the Brink*; Baker and Stremlau, "U.S.-European Stakes in Africa's Largest State."

28. Nugent, *Africa Since Independence*, 421.

29. French, "Nigerians Lament 'Locusts' That Pick Nation Bare."

30. Nkem Owoh, "I Go Chop Your Dollar." Owoh is a Nollywood star who was featured in several films in the mid-2000s in which the visa lottery was a plot point. This song is referenced in Smith, "Nigerian Scam E-mails and the Charms of Capital," 5–6.

31. Chukwudi Nwabuko, "Going to America," *Sunday Champion (Nigeria)*, March 10, 1996.

32. Austin Avwode, "Mad Rush to America," *The Week*, March 11, 1996.

33. "Nigeria: Business Centres in Visa Lottery Boom," *P.M. News (Lagos)*, October 3, 2000, http://allafrica.com/stories/200010130258.html.

34. Olayinka Oyebode, "Nigeria: Coop Bank Renders Services for US Visa Programme," *Post Express (Lagos)*, November 1, 2000, http://allafrica.com/stories/200011010110.html.

35. Advertisement, "Uche Mgabraho: 1998 American Visa Lottery," *Daily Champion*, February 14, 1997.

36. Advertisement: "Libertylink: Best Bet in the American Visa Lottery," *Daily Champion*, February 6, 1997.

37. Nwabuko, "Going to America."

38. Nwabuko, "Going to America."

39. Cyprian Nwafor and Don Uwak, "Why We Are Desperate," *Sunday Champion (Nigeria)*, March 10, 1996.

40. Isaac Umunna, "From the Editor," *The Week (Nigeria)*, February 10, 1997.

41. Migration Policy Institute, "The Nigerian Diaspora in the United States," June 2015, http://www.migrationpolicy.org/sites/default/files/publications/RAD -Nigeria.pdf.

Chapter 12

1. Biodun Sonowo, Chukwudi Nwabuko, and Chris Okereafor, "Nigerians Rush for America," *Sunday Champion (Nigeria)*, February 25, 1996.

2. Sonowo, Nwabuko, and Okereafor, "Nigerians Rush for America."

3. Sonowo, Nwabuko, and Okereafor, "Nigerians Rush for America."

4. Makuchi Nfah-Abbenyi, *Your Madness, Not Mine*, 93.

5. White, *Speaking with Vampires*, 70.

6. Ellis, "Tuning in to Pavement Radio," 325.

7. Modenine, feat. Sage Hasson, "Green Passport."

8. Park and Markowitz, *Democratic Vistas*; Matthews, "Arts and the People."

9. Richard R. John, "The Founders Never Intended the U.S. Postal Service to Be Managed Like a Business," *Washington Post*, April 27, 2020, https://www.washington post.com/outlook/2020/04/27/founders-never-intended-postal-service-be-managed -like-business/; Richard R. John and Joseph Turow, "Cutting Back the U.S. Postal Service Would Hurt the Lifeblood of Democracy," *Washington Post*, August 18, 2020, https://www.washingtonpost.com/outlook/2020/08/18/cutting-back-us-postal -service-would-hurt-lifebood-democracy/.

10. Nkwi and de Bruijn, "'Human Telephone Lines,'" 218.

11. Adedze, "Nigeria: A Philatelic Essay."

12. Fuller, *"Civitatis Ghaniensis Conditor"*; Fuller, *Building the Ghanaian Nation-State.*

13. Cusack, "Tiny Transmitters of Nationalist and Colonial Ideology."

14. Prestedge, *Postal History of the Rebel State.*

15. Shulman, "Ben Franklin's Ghost"; "Website of Universal Postal Union," https://www.upu.int/en/Universal-Postal-Union/About-UPU/History.

16. For example, in 1970 the U.S. Congress transformed the Post Office Department into a government-owned corporation called the United States Postal Service, and in 1982 Congress stopped direct government subsidies to the USPS. The USPS is subject to competition from private companies.

17. Neta Nwosu, "DHL Courier Company Launches Africa First Campaign," *Post Express*, August 24, 2000, http://allafrica.com/stories/200008240424.html. DHL began operations in Ghana in 1984. "DHL: Corporate—DHL's History," https://web .archive.org/web/20210523035349/http://wap.dhl.com/info/history.html.

18. United States Information Service, "Europe and Africa to Receive Largest Number of Visas," *The Democrat*, February 12, 1996.

19. Beginning in 2000 for the DV-2002 lottery, entries were processed at the Kentucky Consular Center (KCC) in Williamsburg, Kentucky. U.S. Department of State, Office of the Spokesman, "Press Statement: New Consular Center Opens in Williamsburg, Kentucky," October 25, 2000, https://web.archive.org/web/20201229113434 /https://1997-2001.state.gov/briefings/statements/2000/ps001025a.html/.

20. Atabe Nzunse, interview by the author, November 7, 2015, Bamenda, Cameroon. Nzunse's family was an early adopter of the lottery, and he recalled his family playing some fifteen years earlier. "Most of the times, we had pictures taken and then sent to alderman who was in the U.S." through the mail, he told me.

21. Advertisement, "Libertylink: Best Bet in the American Visa Lottery," *Daily Champion,* February 6, 1997.

22. Advertisement, "Vio Investment Limited: US Visa Lottery!," *Daily Champion*, February 16, 1996.

23. Sonowo, Nwabuko, and Okereafor, "Nigerians Rush for America."

24. Chukwudi Nwabuko, "Going to America," *Sunday Champion*, March 10, 1996.

25. Nwabuko, "Going to America."

26. Austin Avwode, "Mad Rush to America," *The Week*, March 11, 1996.

27. "Nigeria: Business Centres in Visa Lottery Boom," *P.M. News*, October 3, 2000, http://allafrica.com/stories/200010130258.html.

28. Avwode, "Mad Rush to America."

29. Tunde Asaju, "The Lucky Ones: More Than 5000 Nigerians Were among the 89,746 Applicants Who Were Successful in the 1997 United States of America Visa Lottery," *Newswatch Magazine (Ikeja, Nigeria)*, July 27, 1998.

30. Enyinna Nwagwu, "NIPOST Descends on US Visa Lottery Agents," *Daily Champion*, February 6, 1997.

31. Enyinna Nwagwu, "Visa Lottery Firm Sealed Up," *Daily Champion*, March 8, 1996.

32. Enyinna Nwagwu, "NIPOST Creates Special U.S. Visa Lottery Bags," *Daily Champion*, January 15, 1997.

33. Taye Olaniyi, a spokesperson for the Nigerian postal service, denied the rumor, arguing that the postal service had mailed ninety-two bags of applications daily to the United States from the Lagos district alone. Yusuph Olaniyonu, "Rough Road to Dreamland," *TheWeek*, February 10, 1997.

34. "2.5m Nigerians Apply for US Visa," *Sunday Champion*, October 25, 1997.

35. Nnuji Uzoamaka, "Cartoon: U.S. Visa Lottery Bonanza," *Daily Champion*, February 27, 1996.

36. Falola and Heaton, *History of Nigeria*, 234.

37. Falola and Heaton, *History of Nigeria*, 219.

38. "U.S. Postal Workers Frustrate Nigerians," *P.M. News*, August 26, 1999.

39. "U.S. Diversity Visa Lottery Generates Controversy in Ghana," *Ghana Focus*, November 18, 1997, http://allafrica.com/stories/199711180090.html.

40. Ghana Postal Services Corporation Accra, "Letter to the Editor: Burning of Visa Forms Accusation Is No News," *Ghanaian Chronicle*, November 21, 1997.

41. Akilu Sayibus, "Letter to the Editor: Clarify Situation on Diversity Visa Forms," *Ghanaian Chronicle*, November 12, 1997.

42. U.S. Department of State, Statement by James B. Foley, Deputy Spokesman, "Results of the Diversity Immigrant Visa Program (DV-99)," May 6, 1998.

43. Makuchi Nfah-Abbenyi, *Your Madness, Not Mine*, 93.

44. Makuchi Nfah-Abbenyi, *Your Madness, Not Mine*, 93.

45. Makuchi Nfah-Abbenyi, *Your Madness, Not Mine*, 93.

46. Roy-Macaulay, "Protesters Riot over Dumped U.S. Immigration Forms."

47. "Lottery Fever in Freetown," *West Africa*, March 2, 1997.

48. "Sierra Leone: Police Guard Post Office after Visa Forms Dumped," *Agence France Presse*, February 12, 1997.

49. "U.S. Visa Lottery: Post Office Mobbed," *Daily Champion* (Nigeria), February 14, 1997.

50. Clarence Roy-Macaulay, "Protesters Riot over Dumped U.S. Immigration Forms," Associated Press, February 12, 1997; "Hospital: One Killed in Visa Riot," Associated Press, February 13, 1997.

51. Howard W. French, "U.S. Marines Evacuate 900 in Freetown," *New York Times*, May 31, 1997, http://www.nytimes.com/1997/05/31/world/us-marines-evacuate-900-in-freetown.html.

52. U.S. Department of State, "Diversity Immigrant Visa Lottery Results Released," news release, September 11, 1997.

53. Consular Section of the U.S. Embassy in Freetown, Sierra Leone, "General Consular Information on Visas and Applications," May 27, 2005, https://web.archive.org/web/20100527095238/http://freetown.usembassy.gov/wi052705.html.

54. "Sierra Leone: US Explain Visa Lottery to Sierra Leoneans," *The Progress*, May 13, 1999, http://allafrica.com/stories/199905130156.html.

55. "Hundreds of U.S. Visa Lottery Winners Pour into Accra," *Ghana Focus*, October 14, 1997, http://allafrica.com/stories/199710140080.html.

56. Henrietta Blankson and Juliet Amoah, "American Lottery Winner Threatens: 'I Will Bomb U.S. Embassy,'" *The Independent*, October 9, 1997, http://allafrica.com/stories/199710090085.html.

57. "Hundreds of U.S. Visa Lottery Winners Pour into Accra."

58. "Diversity Visa Programme Ended," *Free Press*, October 29, 1997.

59. Panafrican News Agency, "Sierra Leonean Refugees Sent to Sanzule, Ghana," *Panapress*, February 27, 1998, http://allafrica.com/stories/199802270190.html. See also Sierra Leone Embassy in Washington, D.C., "Press Release March 3, 1998."

60. Charles Neequaye, "Embassy in Dubious Visa Deals . . . over Influx of S. Leone Refugees," *Ghanaian Times*, October 17, 1997.

61. Dr. Edmund Delle, president of the Africa Commission of Health and Human Rights Promotion, was reported to have taken the refugees into his care, and he was quoted as their representative.

62. "The Tell-Tale Influx," editorial, *Ghanaian Times*, October 20, 1997.

63. Daly, "Ghana Must Go," 2.

Chapter 13

1. On the forgotten armed struggle in Cameroon, see Deltombe, Domergue, and Tatsitsa, *Kamerun!*. The British embassy estimated that the war caused 60,000–76,000 civilian deaths. Other estimates are even higher. Deltombe, "Forgotten Cameroon War."

2. DeLancey and DeLancey, *Historical Dictionary of the Republic of Cameroon*.

3. Ahidjo, *Contribution à la Construction Nationale*, 44.

4. Torrent, *Diplomacy and Nation-Building in Africa*, 99–114.

5. Torrent, *Diplomacy and Nation-Building in Africa*, 37. See also Roitman, *Fiscal Disobedience*.

6. The Central African CFA franc is the currency of six countries: Cameroon, Central African Republic, Chad, Republic of Congo, Equatorial Guinea, and Gabon. Its value is equivalent to the West African CFA franc used by eight countries: Benin, Burkina Faso, Guinea-Bissau, Côte d'Ivoire, Mali, Niger, Senegal, and Togo.

7. Ngwane, *Cameroon Condition*.

8. Takougang, "Post-Ahidjo Era in Cameroon."

9. Takougang, *Cameroonian Immigrants in the United States*, 18.

10. Takougang, *Cameroonian Immigrants in the United States*, 18–21.

11. Clovis Atatah, "A Propos de Bushfalling," *Post News Magazine*, September 2006, https://web.archive.org/web/20070326142333/http://www.postnewsmagazine.com/pages/editor03.htm.

12. "Cameroon: A Transition in Crisis."

13. Nugent, *Africa Since Independence*, 397; Roitman, *Fiscal Disobedience*, 23–24; Roitman "Right to Tax"; Kenneth Noble, "Strike Aims to Bleed Cameroon's Economy to Force President's Fall," *New York Times*, August 5, 1991, https://www.nytimes.com/1991/08/05/world/strike-aims-to-bleed-cameroon-s-economy-to-force-president-s-fall.html.

14. Hopkins-Hayakawa, "Cameroonians General Strike for Democratic Elections."

15. Nugent, *Africa Since Independence*, 397.

16. Awasom, "Language and Citizenship in Anglophone Cameroon," 150–152, 154–157; U.S. Bureau of Citizenship and Immigration Services Resource Information Center, *Relationship between the Anglophone and Francophone Communities*.

17. Pelican, "International Migration," 241.

18. Konings and Nyamnjoh, "Anglophone Problem in Cameroon."

19. "L'Etat Vend Le Pays Aux Français," *Le Messager*, December 16, 1998, National Archives of Cameroon, Yaoundé.

20. Cable, Cameroon Yaoundé to Secretary of State, "Cameroon Scenesetter for General Ward's February 21-22, 2008 Visit," February 20, 2008, Canonical ID: 08YAOUNDÉ164_a. Confidential. Wikileaks: https://search.wikileaks.org/plusd/cables /08YAOUNDÉ164_a.html.

21. Alpes, "Bushfalling at All Cost," 105. And, as Takougang describes, Cameroon's economy and prospects were so strong between the 1960s and the 1980s that most emigrants generally wanted to return home. Takougang, *Cameroonian Immigrants in the United States*. Pelican also describes the term "American Wanda," which denotes the first generation of Cameroonian migrants to the United States, many of whom went temporarily to study but opted to remain in the United States. Pelican, "International Migration," 242.

22. Takougang, *Cameroonian Immigrants in the United States*, 19.

23. Pelican, "International Migration," 242.

24. Nyamnjoh and Page, "Whiteman Kontri," 611–612.

25. Alpes, "Bushfalling at All Cost," 95.

26. Bengha Innocent, interview by the author, October 29, 2015, Yaoundé, Cameroon.

27. Pelican, "International Migration," 242.

28. Atatah, "A Propos de Bushfalling."

29. Godlove Song, interview by the author, November 11, 2015, Bamenda, Cameroon.

30. Nyamnjoh, "Cameroonian Bushfailing," 706.

31. Pelican, "International Migration," 241.

32. Pelican, "International Migration," 241.

33. Henri Okele Mazimba, "Consultats de France au Cameroun: S'humilier Pour Un Visa," *Le Messager*, June 13, 1994.

34. "Paul Biya: Cameroon's 'Absentee President,'" *BBC.com*, October 5, 2018, https://www.bbc.com/news/world-africa-43469758.

35. Takougang, *Cameroonian Immigrants in the United States*, 23–29.

36. Nyamnjoh and Page, "Whiteman Kontri," 619–620.

37. U.S. Department of Justice, *1996 Statistical Yearbook of the Immigration and Naturalization Service*.

38. Amin, *Peace Corps in Cameroon*.

39. Torrent, *Diplomacy and Nation-Building in Africa*, 109.

40. Fru Desmond Awah, interview by the author, November 7, 2015, Bamenda, Cameroon.

41. Atabe Nzunse, interview by the author, November 7, 2015, Bamenda, Cameroon.

42. Ambe Mola Valentine Anyele, interview by the author, October 28, 2015, Yaoundé, Cameroon.

43. Department of State, "Table VII, Immigrant Number Use for Visa Issuances and Adjustments of Status in the Diversity Immigrant Category Fiscal Years 1995-2010," previously available at travel.state.gov, archived online here in part: https://web.archive.org/web/20210612000645/https://travel.state.gov/content/dam/visas/Statistics/FY2000%20table%20VII.pdf.

44. Nyamnjoh and Page, "Whiteman Kontri," 612.

Chapter 14

1. Bengha Innocent, interview by the author, October 29, 2015, Yaoundé, Cameroon.

2. U.S. Government Accountability Office, *Fraud Risks Complicate State's Ability to Manage Diversity Visa Program.*

3. Mergo, "Effects of International Migration on Migrant-Source Households," 72.

4. Registration dates for the electronic diversity visa were as follows:

FY 05: November 1, 2003–December 30, 2003 (Beginning of the electronic lottery)

FY 06: November 5, 2004–January 7, 2005

FY 07: October 5, 2005–December 4, 2005

FY 08: October 4, 2006–December 3, 2006

FY 09: October 3, 2007–December 2, 2007

FY 10: October 2, 2008–December 1, 2008

FY 11: October 2, 2009–November 30, 2009

FY 12: October 5, 2010–November 3, 2010 (there was a technical problem during this visa lottery)

FY 13: October 4, 2011–November 5, 2011

FY 14: October 2, 2012–November 3, 2012

FY 15: October 1, 2013–November 2, 2013

FY 16: October 1, 2014–November 3, 2014

FY 17: October 1, 2015–November 3, 2015

FY 18: October 4, 2016–November 7, 2016

FY 19: October 18, 2017–November 22, 2017 (Original dates were October 3, 2017–November 7, 2017, but due to technical problems entries received before October 10 were discarded and dates were revised)

FY 20: October 3, 2018–November 6, 2018

FY 21: October 2, 2019–November 5, 2019

FY 22: October 7, 2020–November 10, 2020

FY 23: October 6, 2021–November 9, 2021. During the Trump presidency, thousands of people selected as winners in the lottery were unable to receive visas to come to the United States because of different versions of the Muslim bans. In 2020–21, many selectees' visa applications went unprocessed due to COVID-19 and lack of urgency by the State Department.

5. Marcel Teko, interview by the author, November 13, 2015, Buea, Cameroon; Kinga Albert Wirayen, interview by the author, November 9, 2015, Bamenda, Cameroon; and Chuo Julius, interview by the author, November 9, 2015, Bamenda, Cameroon.

6. U.S. Agency for International Development, *Leland Initiative*.

7. U.S. Agency for International Development, "USAID Leland Initiative: Africa Global Information Infrastructure Project."

8. Federal Communications Commission, "FCC Launches New Initiative."

9. Zachary, "Ghana, Information Technology and Development in Africa."

10. Holderness, "Who Are the World's Information Poor?"

11. Hegener, "Telecommunications in Africa."

12. "BusyInternet Celebrates Internet's 33rd Birthday," *Ghanaian Times*, September 28, 2002. BusyInternet was launched by three partners, including Welsh entrepreneur Mark Davies, who saw investment in network technology as a means of empowering Ghanaians. See also Burrell, *Invisible Users*, 50.

13. Mohammed Abass, interview by the author, April 20, 2013, Pacthouse Internet Café, Cape Coast, Ghana; Cornelius Ayensu Noonoo, interview by the author, May 16, 2013, Cornel Internet Café, Cape Coast, Ghana.

14. Foster et al., "Global Diffusion of the Internet IV."

15. Zachary, "Ghana, Information Technology and Development in Africa."

16. Jua, "Differential Responses to Disappearing Transitional Pathways," 28.

17. Allomonwing Joseph Ngochi, interview by the author, November 4, 2015, Yaoundé, Cameroon.

18. Burrell, *Invisible Users*, 29.

19. Alpes, "Bushfalling at All Cost," 112.

20. Totimeh S. K. Richard, interview by the author, March 12, 2013, Tamale, Ghana; Hassan Saeed, interview by the author, March 12, 2013, Tamale, Ghana.

21. Mabel Sarpong, interview by the author, May 21, 2013, Accra, Ghana.

22. Alpes, "Law and the Credibility of Migration Brokers."

23. Isaac Asakora, interview by the author, April 20, 2013, Cape Coast, Ghana.

24. Bernard Gyasi, interview by the author, April 8, 2013, Kumasi, Ghana.

25. Saeed, interview.

26. Advertisement for SUP Internet Telecom Provider and Courses in Douala, *La Nouvelle Expression*, November 1, 1996.

27. "Computer School Brings New Opportunities to Locals," *Rotarian Magazine*, July 2005, 15–16, https://books.google.com/books?id=DjMEAAAAMBAJ&lpg =PA15&dq=computer%20school%20brings%20new%20opportunities%20to%20 locals%2orotarian&pg=PA15#v=onepage&q&f=false; Statement by Rep. Mark Pocan (D-WI), "Recognizing Paul Mickelson," *Congressional Record* 163, no. 9 (January 13, 2017), https://www.congress.gov/congressional-record/2017/01/13/extensions -of-remarks-section/article/E67-4?q=%7B%22search%22%3A%5B%22PL109 -13%22%5D%7D.

28. Frei, *Sociality Revisited?*, 18.

29. Siwe, Daho, and Houssou, *Report: Cameroon.*

30. Siyam and Daho, "Stammering of Cameroon's Communications Surveillance"; "Cameroon Internet Usage and Population Statistics," source: World Bank & International Telecommunications Union, UN agency, found at Internet World Stats, http://internetworldstats.com/af/cm.htm.

31. G. Pascal Zachary, "How France Lost Africa to the U.S.," *The Atlantic*, May 21, 2011, http://www.theatlantic.com/international/archive/2011/05/how-france-lost-africa-to-the-us/239646/.

32. Batema and Piot, *Visa Lottery Chronicles.*

33. "En effet, dans nombre de cybercafé à Yaoundé, des affiches invitent au jeu. Jules Bodo, gérant d'un 'cyber' au lieu dit carrefour Mvan explique que cette loterie est un bon moyen pour d'arrondir les fins de mois. Selon lui, 'il y a beaucoup de candidats mais tous ne comprennent pas comment ça marche. On les aide à faire des photos et à remplir la fiche d'inscription en ligne. Et il paie 1.000 F pour l'opération', affirme-t-il. Pourtant, la soumission d'une demande d'inscription est gratuite. Mais comme beaucoup de postulants ont du mal avec Internet, les gérants se font de beurre." Feliciet Bahane N., "Plus de 1.400 Camerounais Gagnent l'Amerique a La Loterie," *Cameroon Tribune*, October 27, 2010, http://fr.allafrica.com/stories/201010280326.html.

34. Mirabel Azamgeh Tandafor, "US Lottery Fever Grips Yaoundé as the Rush Increases," *L'Effort Camerounais*, December 11, 2005, https://web.archive.org/web/20061030022454/http://www.leffortcamerounais.com/2005/12/us_lottery_feve.html.

35. Mireille, pseud, interview by the author, October 30, 2015, Yaoundé, Cameroon (French).

36. Tandafor, "US Lottery Fever Grips Yaoundé as the Rush Increases."

37. Takougang, *Cameroonian Immigrants in the United States*, 29.

38. Takougang, *Cameroonian Immigrants in the United States*, 23–29.

39. Emily Brady, "The Year of Living Nervously," *New York Times*, December 5, 2008, http://www.nytimes.com/2008/12/07/nyregion/thecity/07asyl.html.

40. As Kanna Landry, a photographer from Yaoundé, told me, "Anglophones jouent plus longues que les francophones." Kanna Landry, interview by the author, October 28, 2015, Obili neighborhood, Yaoundé, Cameroon (French).

41. Henri Okele Mazimba, "Consultats de France au Cameroun: S'humilier Pour Un Visa," *Le Messager*, June 13, 1994, National Archives of Cameroon, Yaoundé; Hamilton, Simon, and Veniard, "Challenge of French Diversity"; and O'Connell, "Plight of France's *Sans-Papiers.*"

42. The phrases in French include "La loterie du rêve américain" and "au pays de l'oncle Sam, en toute légalité." "La Loterie du Rêve Américain," *Afrik.com*, July 18, 2001, http://www.afrik.com/article3061.html.

43. "On a plus de chance ainsi. Les Européens nous ferment déjà leurs portes. Avec cette carte, nous ne sommes pas dans l'illégalité." Dorine Ekwè, "Le Boom de La Lotterie Américaine au Cameroun," *Mutations*, November 2, 2005, http://www.bonaberi.com/article.php?aid=1390.

44. "Les Camerounais se bousculent déjà pour cette nouvelle édition et des business sont nés en marge." Feliciet Bahane N., "Plus de 1.400 Camerounais Gagnent l'Amerique a La Loterie." See also Austin Avwode, "Mad Rush to America," *The Week*, March 11, 1996.

45. A woman who helped her husband run a visa shop discussed how important it was to be able to go in "le manier legal" (the legal manner). "Mireille," interview.

46. Nkongho Walters Mbu, interview by the author, October 29, 2015, Yaoundé, Cameroon.

47. As Chief David Awa Jideofor told me about the early years of the lottery, "We didn't take it much serious like now." Chief David Awa Jideofor, interview by the author, November 9, 2015, Bamenda, Cameroon.

48. Ngochi, interview.

49. Menkan Kari, interview by the author, October 30, 2015, Yaoundé, Cameroon.

50. Yerima Kini Nsom, "Carrefour Obili: Savouring the Citadel of Anglophone Euphoria," *Cameroon Post Online*, September 10, 2010, https://web.archive.org/web /20180326025556/http://www.cameroonpostline.com/carrefour-obili-savouring -the-citadel-of-anglophone-euphoria/.

51. Wirayen, interview.

52. "Les Camerounais Se Ruent Sur La Loterie des Visas des Etats-Unis," *Panapress.com*, November 25, 2006, http://www.panapress.com/Les-Camerounais-se -ruent-sur-la-loterie-des-visas-des-Etats-Unis—13-641139-17-lang4-index.html. See also Wilfried Joël Tankeu, "Loterie Américaine: Bousculades Aux Portes du Pays d'Obama," *Cameroon-info.net*, November 10, 2008, https://web.archive.org/web /20110203073706/http://www.cameroon-info.net/stories/0,23925,@,loterie -americaine-bousculades-aux-portes-du-pays-d-obama.html.

53. "Nous avons l'habitude d'aider nos clients à jouer à la loterie américaine et ils nous consultent souvent lorsqu'ils reçoivent des messages suspects. En temps normal, les postulants à la carte verte ne doivent pas recevoir de message de notification." Louis Clovis Ketcha, quoted in Hugues Marcel Tchoua, "Des Arnaqueurs Aux Trousses des Postulants de La Loterie Américaine," *Cameroon Tribune*, November 27, 2011, http://fr.allafrica.com/stories/201111230433.html.

54. "Veuillez noter qu'il n'y a aucun frais à payer pour participer au Programme de Visa Diversité." Georges Ndenga, "La Loterie Américaine Accessible à Tous," *Africa Info—Cameroun*, October 14, 2012, http://fr.allafrica.com/stories /201210130672.html.

55. Cable, Cameroon Yaoundé to Secretary of State, "Cameroon Scensetter for General Ward's February 21-22, 2008 Visit," February 20, 2008, Canonical ID: 08YAOUNDÉ164_a. Confidential. Wikileaks: https://search.wikileaks.org/plusd /cables/08YAOUNDE164_a.html.

56. Cable, Cameroon Yaoundé to Secretary of State, "Which Visa Lottery? Consular Outreach in Cameroon," November 2, 2007, accessed at Canonical ID: 07YAOUNDÉ1304_a, Unclassified. Wikileaks: https://search.wikileaks.org/plusd /cables/07YAOUNDÉ1304_a.html.

57. Tandafor, "US Lottery Fever Grips Yaoundé as the Rush Increases."

58. Tandafor, "US Lottery Fever Grips Yaoundé as the Rush Increases."

59. "Presque toutes les rues arborent des banderoles annonçant la DV Lottery. Les cybercafés où l'inscription et autres renseignements s'obtiennent ne désemplissent pas non plus. L'effervescence est perceptible." Dorothee Ndoumbe, "Le Rêve Américain Séduit Toujours Les Camerounais," *Afrik.com*, November 19, 2010, http://www.afrik.com/article21179.html.

60. "Avant ces deux dernières années, c'était davantage les gens de la zone anglophone du pays qui postulaient. En plus, c'était plus difficile à gérer parce qu'il fallait le faire par la poste. L'avènement de l'Internet a facilité la découverte de ce moyen par les camerounais francophones." Ekwè, "Le Boom de La Lotterie Américaine au Cameroun."

61. Ambe Mola Valentine Anyele, interview by the author, October 28, 2015, Yaoundé, Cameroon.

62. "Table 3, Immigrants Admitted by Region and Country of Birth, 1986-1996," in U.S. Department of Justice, *1996 Statistical Yearbook of the Immigration and Naturalization Service*.

63. Takougang, *Cameroonian Immigrants in the United States*.

64. Eulalia Amabo Nchang, "15,000 Cameroonians in US on DV Lottery Tickets—Consul: Interview with Vice Consul Connor O'Steen," *Cameroon Post*, October 12, 2015.

Chapter 15

1. Adichie, *Thing around Your Neck*, 115.

2. Adichie, *Thing around Your Neck*, 119.

3. Chuo Julius, interview by the author, November 9, 2015, Bamenda, Cameroon.

4. Julius, interview.

5. Borstelmann, *Apartheid's Reluctant Uncle*.

6. Gleijeses, *Conflicting Missions*; Gleijeses, *Visions of Freedom*.

7. Nzongola-Ntalaja, *Congo from Leopold to Kabila*; Williams, *White Malice*.

8. Bell, "Developing a 'Sense of Community'"; Grubbs, *Secular Missionaries*.

9. Von Eschen, "Duke Ellington Plays Baghdad."

10. Von Eschen, *Satchmo Blows Up the World*; Jesse Shipley, "Part 1: Pan Africanism and Hiplife," interview, *Afropop Worldwide*, 2014, https://afropop.org/articles/jesse-shipley-part-1-pan-africanism-and-hiplife.

11. Talton, *In This Land of Plenty*, 160.

12. Talton, *In This Land of Plenty*, 161.

13. Schmidt, *Foreign Intervention in Africa*, 197.

14. Talton, *In This Land of Plenty*, 162.

15. Bowden, *Black Hawk Down*; Richard W. Stewart, "The United States Army in Somalia, 1992-1994," U.S. Army Center of Military History, 2003, https://history.army.mil/brochures/Somalia/Somalia.htm.

16. Most famously during Rwanda's genocide in 1994, which Clinton named as the top regret of his presidency. Power, *Problem from Hell*.

17. Lindsay, "State Department Complex after the Cold War."

18. Jones, "Foreign Policy Bureaucracy in a New Era," 64.

19. Sablosky, "Reinvention, Reorganization, Retreat."

20. U.S. Department of State, *Public Diplomacy for the 21st Century.*

21. Thomas L. Friedman, "The End of Something," *New York Times*, July 26, 1995.

22. Advertisement, "The Oprah Winfrey Show Highlights, 5.00pm Daily!," *Free Press*, February 13, 1996.

23. Nye, *Bound to Lead*, 193. See also Nye, *Soft Power.*

24. Akilu Sayibus, "Clarify Situation on Diversity Visa Forms," letter to the editor, *Ghanaian Chronicle*, November 12, 1997.

25. "Visa Lottery Is Simple," *The Mirror*, December 2, 1995.

26. Advertisement, "America!!! America!!! Boon to Students," *Daily Graphic*, February 6, 1996.

27. Ambe Mola Valentine Anyele, interview by the author, October 28, 2015, Yaoundé, Cameroon.

28. Bengha Innocent, interview by the author, October 29, 2015, Yaoundé, Cameroon.

29. Kinga Albert Wirayen, interview by the author, November 9, 2015, Bamenda, Cameroon.

30. Ibrahim, interview by the author, April 11, 2014, Philadelphia, PA.

31. Joseph Appiah-Nkrumah, interview by the author, February 19, 2013, Kumasi, Ghana.

32. "Extreme Act of Desperation," editorial, *The Mirror*, September 25, 1999, KNUST.

33. Makuchi Nfah-Abbenyi, *Your Madness, Not Mine*, 92.

34. King Hussain Mohammed, interview by the author, April 12, 2013, Accra, Ghana; "Mustafa," interview by the author, April 12, 2013, Accra, Ghana. See also Miescher, *Making Men in Ghana*; Hart, *Ghana on the Go.*

35. Hart, *Ghana on the Go*, 152.

36. Henry Nti Antwi, interview by the author, April 24, 2013, Kumasi, Ghana; Cornelius Ayensu Noonoo (Kwesi), interview by the author, May 16, 2013, Cape Coast, Ghana.

37. Makuchi Nfah-Abbenyi, *Your Madness, Not Mine*, 92.

38. On consumer citizenship, see Cohen, *Consumers' Republic*; Jacobs, *Pocketbook Politics.*

39. Advertisement, "America! 1995-96 Lottery Green Card," *The Mirror*, December 2, 1995.

40. Advertisement, "USA to Give 55,000 Green Cards," *The Pioneer*, February 7, 1996.

41. Advertisement, "USA Green Card," *Daily Graphic*, May 22, 2001.

42. Pemamtou Pewing Jude, interview by the author, November 9, 2015, Bamenda, Cameroon.

43. Nugent, *Big Men, Small Boys, and Politics in Ghana.*

44. Bernard Gyasi, interview by the author, April 8, 2013, Kumasi, Ghana.

45. Gyasi, interview.

46. Innocent, interview.

47. Chukwudi Nwabuko, "Going to America," *Sunday Champion* (Nigeria), March 10, 1996.

48. Anima Adjepong, *Afropolitan Projects*, 4.

49. "Mais aussi, après les etats unis je me suis aller a la lune." Donal Kago, interview by the author, October 29, 2015, Yaoundé, Cameroon (French).

50. Yusuph Olaniyonu, "Rough Road to Dreamland," *TheWeek*, February 10, 1997.

51. Innocent, interview.

52. Innocent, interview.

53. Anyele, interview.

54. Isaac Asakora, interview by the author, April 20, 2013, Cape Coast, Ghana; Mohammed Abass, interview by the author, April 20, 2013, Cape Coast, Ghana; Prince Nyarko, interview by the author, May 13, 2013, Kumasi, Ghana.

55. Antwi, interview.

56. Saeed, interview.

57. Mbi Paddy E. K., interview by the author, November 14, 2015, Buea, Cameroon.

58. Atabe Nzunse, interview by the author, November 7, 2015, Bamenda, Cameroon.

59. Walisu Alhassan, interview by the author, March 12, 2013, Tamale, Ghana.

60. Victor Mbah, "The DV Lottery: A Path to Modern Slavery," in Ngwa and Ngwa, *From Dust to Snow*, 118.

61. "C'est inévitable pour le monde puisque d'habitude des États-Unis c'est un pays de rêve, non? Ca c'est une manière une autre un rêve chaque jour de quelque chose de meilleure, quelque chose de lendemain plus bien, plus tout, et les États-Unis c'est un miroir pour nous, donc, on dit bon, aller la bas une autre vie changée d'une manière ou d'autre." Donal Kago, interview by the author, October 29, 2015, Yaoundé, Cameroon (French).

62. Morrison, "Reflecting on the Immigration Act of 1990."

63. Phillip Connor, "Applications for U.S. Visa Lottery More Than Doubled Since 2007," Pew Research Center Fact Tank, March 24, 2017, http://www .pewresearch.org/fact-tank/2017/03/24/applications-for-u-s-visa-lottery-more -than-doubled-since-2007/ updated at https://web.archive.org/web/20190308142706 /http://www.pewresearch.org/fact-tank/2018/08/23/applications-for-u-s-visa -lottery-more-than-doubled-since-2007/.

Chapter 16

1. Ambe Mola Valentine Anyele, interview by the author, October 28, 2015, Yaoundé, Cameroon.

2. Walisu Alhassan, interview by the author, March 12, 2013, Tamale, Ghana; Bernard Gyasi, interview by the author, April 8, 2013, Kumasi, Ghana; and Hassan Saeed, interview by the author, March 12, 2013, Tamale, Ghana.

3. Manuh, Asante, and Djangmah, "Brain Drain in the Higher Education Sector in Ghana."

4. Adepoju, "Patterns of Migration in West Africa," 33.

5. Much of the academic literature on migration uses the terms "high skilled" and "low skilled" to delineate types of workers. But all workers have and use a variety of skills. I prefer to differentiate between high and low *wage* work. Sako, "Brain Drain and Africa's Development."

6. Tebeje, "Brain Drain and Capacity Building in Africa."

7. Nyonator and Dovlo, "Health of the Nation and the Brain Drain in the Health Sector," 231.

8. Sankore, "Africa Killing Us Softly."

9. Kweku Tsen, "Brain Drain Is Undermining Govt.'s Efforts—President," *Daily Graphic*, May 9, 1998.

10. "Those Unpatriotic Ghanaians," *The Spectator*, November 20, 1999.

11. "Let's Check This Exodus," *Daily Graphic*, October 5, 2001.

12. Victor Mbah, "The DV Lottery," in Ngwa and Ngwa, *From Dust to Snow*, 123.

13. Anazodo O. Nwakanma, "LTE: The Green Card trap," *Daily Champion (Nigeria)*, May 28, 1994.

14. U.S. Congress, House, Committee on Ways and Means, *U.S. Trade with Sub-Saharan Africa*, August 1, 1996 (statement of H. E. Ekwow Spio-Garbrah, Ghana's Ambassador to the United States), 198–206.

15. Allomonwing Joseph Ngochi, interview by the author, November 4, 2015, Yaoundé, Cameroon.

16. John Tanton, Memorandum to: Those concerned with the population problem, Re: Amendments to the United States Immigration and Nationality Act, May 3, 1973, including "Statement by Zero Population Growth on H.R. 981, A Bill to Amend the Immigration and Nationality Act," "Brain Drain" folder, box 3, John Tanton Papers, Bentley Historical Library, University of Michigan.

17. "I've always been interested in the 'brain drain,' but I've never been able to get much going on it." Discussion between John Tanton, Board Chairman, and Linda Platt, FAIR's newly hired development director, at the FAIR Office, Washington, DC, July 26, 1985, "Folder July-Dec 1985-1986 Correspondence," box 1, Tanton Papers.

18. Memo from Patrick [Burns] Re: Possible legal immigrant selections systems, April 22, 1987, folder 7 Internal Memos 1987, box 137, Tanton Papers.

19. Joseph, "At Home Abroad," 286.

20. Exceptions are for children not "subject to the jurisdiction" of the United States, such as those born to foreign diplomats.

21. Getachew, *Worldmaking after Empire*.

22. Herbst, *States and Power in Africa*, 252–253.

23. Daly, "Ghana Must Go," 33.

24. Brown, *Walled States*.

25. Cooper, *Africa in the World*, 89.

26. Young, *Postcolonial State in Africa*. See also Cooper, *Africa Since 1940*.

27. Cooper, *Africa in the World*, 97.

28. Cooper, *Africa in the World*, 98.

29. "2.5m Nigerians Apply for US Visa," *Sunday Champion*, October 25, 1997.

30. Chukwudi Nwabuko, "Going to America," *Sunday Champion (Nigeria)*, March 10, 1996.

31. Young, "Nation, Ethnicity, and Citizenship," 241.

32. Vidacs, "Banal Nationalism"; Billig, *Banal Nationalism*.

33. Nugent, Hammett, and Dorman, "Introduction," 5.

34. Eriksen, "Place, Kinship and the Case for Non-ethnic Nations."

35. Nugent, *Smugglers, Secessionists & Loyal Citizens*.

36. Vidacs, "Banal Nationalism," 29.

37. Geschiere, *Perils of Belonging*, 21.

38. Mohammed Affum, "When the Slave Ship Returns," *Ghanaian Chronicle*, October 20, 1999, http://allafrica.com/stories/199910200214.html.

39. Spiro, "Dual Citizenship as Human Right," 116; Spiro, "Dual Nationality and the Meaning of Citizenship"; Spiro, *Beyond Citizenship*.

40. In Beys Afroyim v. Dean Rusk, Secretary of State, 387 U.S. 253 (1967), the Supreme Court ruled that citizens of the United States could not be deprived involuntarily of their citizenship (the case had to do with a naturalized citizen voting in an Israeli election). The Carter administration later abandoned the Bancroft Treaties, agreements that had limited mutual recognition of dual citizenship. In 1990, the State Department adopted further guidelines, making it almost impossible for a U.S. citizen to lose their citizenship when they acquire a second citizenship. See Spiro, "Vaunting Citizenship, Presaging Transnationality."

41. Miescher and Ashbaugh, "Been-to Visions."

42. Whitaker, "Politics of Home."

43. Leblang, "Harnessing the Diaspora."

44. Spiro, "Dual Citizenship as Human Right," 117.

45. Leblang, "Harnessing the Diaspora."

46. Faist and Gerdes, "Dual Citizenship in an Age of Mobility."

47. Alison Hird, "Ghana's Wanlov, Truant, Vagabond and Committed Outsider," *RFI English*, December 17, 2015, http://www.english.rfi.fr/africa/20151217-wanlov-kubolor-african-gypsy.

48. Wanlov the Kubolor, "Green Card."

49. Image available at the Bandcamp page for Wanlov: https://wanlov.bandcamp.com/.

50. Geraldine Ayiehfor, "Europe: Heaven on Earth?," in Ngwa and Ngwa, *From Dust to Snow*, 4.

51. Chief David Awa Jideofor, interview by the author, November 9, 2015, Bamenda, Cameroon.

52. Omoh Gabriel, "Remittances to Nigeria to Hit $21bn by Year End," *Vanguard Nigeria*, October 9, 2014, http://www.vanguardngr.com/2014/10/remittances-nigeria-hit-21bn-year-end/.

53. Nwabuko, "Going to America."

54. Kinga Albert Wirayen, interview by the author, November 9, 2015, Bamenda, Cameroon.

55. Ambe Mola Valentine Anyele, interview by the author, October 28, 2015, Yaoundé, Cameroon.

56. Ratha et al., *Leveraging Migration*, 48.

57. Ratha et al., *Leveraging Migration*, 47–108.

58. Alhassan, interview.

59. Ratha, "Lifeline for Development."

60. Mergo, "Effects of International Migration on Migrant-Source Households," 69–81.

61. Mergo, "America's Best Aid Program?"

62. Whitaker, "Politics of Home," 759.

63. Consensus around remittance-driven development has obscured gender-specific consequences for this approach. Remittances have also served to entrench neoliberal welfare practices. Kunz, *Political Economy of Global Remittances*.

64. James Ferguson, interview, "Rethinking Neoliberalism," *Humanity blog*, June 10, 2014, http://humanityjournal.org/blog/humanity-interview-with-james-ferguson-pt-2-rethinking-neoliberalism/.

65. Kofi Owusu-Daaku, interview by the author, January 30, 2013, Kumasi, Ghana.

66. Asiedu and Arku, "Rise of Gated Housing Estates in Ghana," 238. See also Grant, "Emergence of Gated Communities in a West African Context"; Fourchard, "Between World History and State Formation."

67. Owusu-Ansah and O'Connor, "Housing Demand."

68. Joseph Berger, "American Dream Is a Ghana Home: Mark of Immigrant Success to the Folks Back in Accra," *New York Times*, August 21, 2002, http://www.nytimes.com/2002/08/21/nyregion/american-dream-ghana-home-mark-immigrant-success-folks-back-accra.html.

69. Berger, "American Dream Is a Ghana Home: Mark of Immigrant Success to the Folks Back in Accra."

70. Isaac Asakora, interview by the author, April 20, 2013, Cape Coast, Ghana.

71. Fru Desmond Awah, interview by the author, November 7, 2015, Bamenda, Cameroon.

72. Nkongho Walters Mbu, interview by the author, October 29, 2015, Yaoundé, Cameroon.

73. Makuchi Nfah-Abbenyi, *Your Madness, Not Mine*, 81–82.

74. "2.5m Nigerians Apply for US Visa," *Sunday Champion*, October 25, 1997.

75. "They used to tell me that the U.S. is fine, but you need to work hard." Chuo Julius, interview by the author, November 9, 2015, Bamenda, Cameroon. "Your brother's experience might be unique. He could also be paranoid." Makuchi Nfah-Abbenyi, *Your Madness, Not Mine*, 83.

76. Chief David Awa Jideofor, interview by the author, November 9, 2015, Bamenda, Cameroon.

Chapter 17

1. Stoller, *Money Has No Smell*.

2. Ginger Thompson with Garry Pierre-Pierre, "Portrait of Slain Immigrant: Big Dreams and a Big Heart," *New York Times*, February 12, 1999, https://www.nytimes.com/1999/02/12/nyregion/portrait-of-slain-immigrant-big-dreams-and-a-big-heart.html.

3. Elkins, "Origins of Stop-and-Frisk.".

4. Ginger Thompson, "1,000 Rally to Condemn Shooting of Unarmed Man by Police," *New York Times*, February 8, 1999, https://www.nytimes.com/1999/02/08/nyregion/1000-rally-to-condemn-shooting-of-unarmed-man-by-police.html.

5. Thompson with Pierre-Pierre, "Portrait of Slain Immigrant."

6. Johnson, "When Blackness Stings," 31.

7. Johnson, "When Blackness Stings," 50.

8. Pierre, "Black Immigrants in the United States," 142.

9. Wu, *Color of Success*, 3.

10. Pierre, "Black Immigrants in the United States," 142.

11. Greer, *Black Ethnics*, 11–37.

12. Toni Morrison, "On the Backs of Blacks," *Time Magazine*, December 2, 1993, http://content.time.com/time/subscriber/article/0,33009,979736-1,00.html.

13. Treitler, *Ethnic Project*.

14. Adjepong, *Afropolitan Projects*, 149.

15. Amy Waldman, "Shooting in the Bronx: The Immigrants; Killing Heightens Unease Felt by Africans in New York," *New York Times*, February 14, 1999, https://www.nytimes.com/1999/02/14/nyregion/shooting-bronx-immigrants-killing-heightens-unease-felt-africans-new-york.html.

16. Marcel Teko, interview by the author, November 13, 2015, Buea, Cameroon.

17. Violet Showers Johnson warns us about what is lost when we place a premium on numbers. Johnson, "Black Presence in U.S. Immigration History."

18. Migration Policy Institute (MPI) tabulation of data from the U.S. Census Bureau, 2010 and 2019 American Community Surveys (ACSs), and 2000 Decennial Census; data for 1960 to 1990 are from Campbell J. Gibson and Emily Lennon, "Historical Census Statistics on the Foreign-Born Population of the United States: 1850 to 1990" (working paper no. 29, U.S. Census Bureau, Washington, DC, 1999), https://www.migrationpolicy.org/programs/data-hub/charts/largest-immigrant-groups-over-time.

19. Carlos Echeverria-Estrada and Jeanne Batalova, "Sub-Saharan African Immigrants in the United States," *Migration Information Source*, November 6, 2019, https://www.migrationpolicy.org/article/sub-saharan-african-immigrants-united-states-2018.

20. Population data on Black immigrants are inexact. The U.S. Citizenship and Immigration Services does not track immigration by race, so nationality is often used as a stand-in. Many institutions that create statistics about Africa and African migration use the term "sub-Saharan" to refer to a large part of Africa. The term both divides—to differentiate between North Africa and the rest—and lumps together vastly different peoples and countries across western, eastern, central, and

southern Africa and the Horn of Africa. Many of the assumptions in this categorization should give us pause, and critics have long objected to the use of the term "sub-Saharan" on the grounds that it is a racial category claiming the authority of geography, that it funnels too many people together under one umbrella that doesn't make sense, and that it is degrading. Max de Haldevang, "Why Do We Still Use the Term 'Sub-Saharan Africa?' *Quartz Africa*, September 1, 2016, https://qz.com /africa/770350/why-do-we-still-say-subsaharan-africa/; Emi Eleode, "It's Time to Drop 'Sub-Saharan Africa' from Our Vocabulary," *Readcultured.com*, April 25, 2021, https://readcultured.com/its-time-to-drop-sub-saharan-africa-from-our-vocabulary -3cc0561a57cb; Tatenda Chinondidyachii Mashanda, "Rethinking the Term 'Sub Saharan Africa,'" *African Exponent*, April 5, 2016, https://www.africanexponent.com /bpost/rethinking-the-term-sub-saharan-africa-36; Herbert Ekwe-Ekwe, "What Exactly Does 'Sub-Sahara Africa' Mean?," *Pambazuka News*, January 18, 2012, https:// www.pambazuka.org/governance/what-exactly-does-%E2%80%98sub-sahara -africa%E2%80%99-mean.

21. Morgan-Trostle and Zheng, *State of Black Immigrants*.

22. Refugee Processing Center, "Refugee Admissions by Region Since 1975 as of 10 J 18," Worldwide Refugee Admissions Processing System, operated by the U.S. Department of State (DOS) Bureau of Population, Refugees, and Migration (PRM), https://www.wrapsnet.org/documents/Refugee%20Admissions%20by%20 Region%20since%201975%20as%20of%2010-5-20.pdf; U.S. Department of Justice, Immigration and Naturalization Service, "Annual Report, Refugees, Fiscal Year 1997," No. 4, July 1999, https://www.dhs.gov/sites/default/files/publications /INS_AnnualReport_Refugees_1997_0.pdf; Wong, "Emerging Patterns."

23. "Table C: Percent of Immigrants Admitted by Region and Period: Fiscal Years 1955-96," 21, and "Table 3: Immigrants Admitted by Region and Country of Birth, Fiscal Years 1986-96," 30–33, in U.S. Department of Justice, *1996 Statistical Yearbook of the Immigration and Naturalization Service*.

24. "Table 5: Immigrants Admitted by Region of Birth and Type and Class of Admission, Fiscal Year 1996," 35–41, in U.S. Department of Justice, *1996 Statistical Yearbook of the Immigration and Naturalization Service*.

25. "Table 8: Immigrants Admitted by Selected Class of Admission and Region and Selected Country of Birth, Fiscal Year 1996," 46–47, in U.S. Department of Justice, *1996 Statistical Yearbook of the Immigration and Naturalization Service*.

26. Several editions of the *Yearbooks of Immigration Statistics*.

27. Morgan-Trostle and Zheng, *State of Black Immigrants*.

28. "Table 10: Persons Obtaining Lawful Permanent Resident Status by Broad Class of Admission and Region and Country of Birth: Fiscal Year 2019," in U.S. Department of Homeland Security, *2019 Yearbook of Immigration Statistics*, https:// www.dhs.gov/immigration-statistics/yearbook/2019/table10.

29. Courtland Milloy, "Cultural Plus: Ethiopians Have Brought Washington More Than New Restaurants," *Washington Post*, April 10, 1983; Vic Sussman, "Adams Morgan Is . . . ," *Washington Post*, October 9, 1988.

30. Ken Ringle, "Adams-Morgan Day '84: A Dance of Diversity," *Washington Post*, September 9, 1984.

31. Erin J. Aubry, "Culture Clash: African Americans and African Immigrants Seek a Path to Common Ground, but Misconceptions, Stereotypes Clutter the Way," *Los Angeles Times*, July 10, 1994.

32. Joel Millman, "Out of Africa—into America," *Washington Post*, October 9, 1994.

33. Ringle, "Adams-Morgan Day '84."

34. Sandra Sugawara and Elizabeth Tucker, "New Firms Backed by Family, Friends," *Washington Post*, December 16, 1987.

35. Millman, "Out of Africa—into America."

36. Sommers, "I Believe in the City," 21.

37. Asch and Musgrove, *Chocolate City*, 287.

38. Treitler, *Ethnic Project*.

39. Pierre, "Black Immigrants in the United States and the 'Cultural Narrative' of Ethnicity."

40. Chikanda and Morris, "Assessing the Integration Outcomes of African Immigrants in the United States."

41. Capps, McCabe, and Fix, *Diverse Streams*.

42. Lundberg, "Tiger Parenting and American Inequality," 946.

43. Suketu Mehta, "The 'Tiger Mom' Superiority Complex," *Time Magazine*, January 23, 2014, https://time.com/1567/the-tiger-mom-superiority-complex/.

44. Robinson Mukwanka, "Every Coin Has Its Reverse Side," in Ngwa and Ngwa, *From Dust to Snow*, 57.

45. Germaine Mbongue and Joe Mbongue, "From Dust to Snow," in Ngwa and Ngwa, *From Dust to Snow*, 75.

Chapter 18

1. Alexander M. Stephens, "Reagan's War on Drugs Also Waged War on Immigrants," *Washington Post*, October 27, 2021, https://www.washingtonpost.com/outlook/2021/10/27/reagans-war-drugs-also-waged-war-immigrants/.

2. Veney, "Effects of Immigration and Refugee Policies."

3. Ackerman, *Reign of Terror*, 16.

4. Ackerman, *Reign of Terror*, 27.

5. Belew, *Bring the War Home*.

6. American Civil Liberties Union, "Analysis of Immigration Detention Policies," https://www.aclu.org/other/analysis-immigration-detention-policies, accessed July 29, 2022.

7. Ackerman, *Reign of Terror*, 12.

8. Nguyen, *We Are All Suspects Now*, xvii.

9. Nguyen, *We Are All Suspects Now*; Jodi Wilgoren, "Swept Up in a Dragnet, Hundreds Sit in Custody and Ask, 'Why?,'" *New York Times*, November 25, 2001, https://www.nytimes.com/2001/11/25/national/swept-up-in-a-dragnet-hundreds-sit-in-custody-and-ask-why.html; Eric Lichtblau, "U.S. Report Faults the Roundup of Illegal Immigrants after 9/11," *New York Times*, June 2, 2003, https://www.nytimes

.com/2003/06/02/politics/us-report-faults-the-roundup-of-illegal-immigrants
-after-911.html.

10. Jeannette Catsoulis, "Movie Review: 'The Citizen': Alienated, from His First Day in the U.S.A.," *New York Times*, September 26, 2013, https://www.nytimes .com/2013/09/27/movies/the-citizen-directed-by-sam-kadi.html.

11. Uniting and Strengthening America by Providing Appropriate Tools Required to Intercept and Obstruct Terrorism Act (USA PATRIOT Act) of 2001, Pub. L. No. 107-56, 115 Stat. 272 (2001).

12. Researchers found that changes to airport security procedures were associated with increased risk of death in a car accident. Blalock, Kadiyali, and Simon, "Impact of 9/11 on Road Fatalities."

13. Waslin, "Counterterrorism and the Latino Community."

14. Kaplan, "Homeland Insecurities," 92.

15. Alison Mitchell, "A Nation Challenged: The Borders; Official Urges Combining Several Agencies to Create One That Protects Borders," *New York Times*, January 12, 2002, https://www.nytimes.com/2002/01/12/us/nation-challenged -borders-official-urges-combining-several-agencies-create-one.html.

16. David Stout, "Bush Proposes Restructuring of Homeland Security," *New York Times*, June 6, 2002, https://www.nytimes.com/2002/06/06/politics/bush-proposes -restructuring-of-homeland-security.html.

17. Homeland Security Act of 2002, Pub. L. No. 107-296, 116 Stat. 2135, to establish the Department of Homeland Security, https://www.dhs.gov/sites/default/files /publications/hr_5005_enr.pdf. It began operations in 2003 and absorbed INS as of March 1, 2003.

18. Countries included Iran, Iraq, Libya, Sudan, Syria, Afghanistan, Algeria, Bahrain, Eritrea, Lebanon, Morocco, North Korea, Oman, Qatar, Somalia, Tunisia, the United Arab Emirates, Yemen, Pakistan, Saudi Arabia, Bangladesh, Egypt, Indonesia, Jordan, and Kuwait.

19. Nguyen, *We Are All Suspects Now*, xviii; Rights Working Group, Penn State Law, *NSEERS Effect*.

20. While Hesham Mohamed Hadayet's name was spelled differently ("Hedayet") in a congressional hearing, most media coverage used the spelling ("Hadayet") that I have adopted here.

21. Previously the subcommittee was known as the Subcommittee on Immigration, Refugees, and International Law. In the 1990s it was renamed the Subcommittee on Immigration and Claims.

22. Department of State, "Table VII, Immigrant Number Use for Visa Issuances and Adjustments of Status in the Diversity Immigrant Category Fiscal Years 1995-2010," previously available at travel.state.gov, archived here in part: https://web.archive .org/web/20210612000645/https://travel.state.gov/content/dam/visas/Statistics /FY2000%20table%20VII.pdf.

23. U.S. Congress, House, Committee on the Judiciary, *Immigration and Naturalization Service's (INS's) Interactions with Hesham Mohamed Ali Hedayet*, October 9, 2002 (statement of Steven A. Camarota, Center for Immigration Studies), 13.

24. U.S. Congress, House, Committee on the Judiciary, *Immigration and Naturalization Service's (INS's) Interactions with Hesham Mohamed Ali Hedayet*, October 9, 2002 (statement of Paul Virtue, Hogan and Hartson, Former General Counsel, Immigration and Naturalization Service),18.

25. U.S. Congress, House, Committee on Government Reform, *Federal Interagency Data-Sharing and National Security*, July 24, 2001, 37.

26. U.S. Congress, Senate, Committee on Foreign Relations, *Post-9/11 Visa Reforms and New Technology*, October 23, 2003, "Additional Information Submitted for the Record by Janice L. Jacobs, Changes to the Visa Application Process Since September 11, 2001," 65–70.

27. Dow, *American Gulag*.

28. Rachel L. Swarns, "Illegal Aliens Can Be Held Indefinitely, Ashcroft Says," *New York Times*, April 26, 2003, https://www.nytimes.com/2003/04/26/us /aftereffects-immigrants-illegal-aliens-can-be-held-indefinitely-ashcroft-says.html.

29. Edwidge Danticat, foreword to Nguyen, *We Are All Suspects Now*.

30. Corey Robin, "Forget about It," *Harper's*, April 2018, https://harpers.org /archive/2018/04/forget-about-it/.

31. Peggy Noonan, "Rudy's Duty," *Wall Street Journal*, June 14, 2002, https:// www.wsj.com/articles/SB122418750653241949; James Traub, "The Dark History of Defending the 'Homeland,'" *New York Times Magazine*, April 5, 2016, https://www .nytimes.com/2016/04/10/magazine/the-dark-history-of-defending-the-homeland .html.

32. Kaplan, "Homeland Insecurities," 85.

33. U.S. National Defense Panel, *Transforming Defense*, ii. Bush linked the term to the study when he announced the intention to create DHS in late September 2001. Philip Bump, "How 'Homeland' Became Part of Our American Lexicon," *Washington Post*, September 11, 2014, https://www.washingtonpost.com/news/the -fix/wp/2014/09/11/how-homeland-became-part-of-our-american-lexicon/.

34. Kaplan, "Homeland Insecurities," 86.

35. Kaplan, "Homeland Insecurities," 87.

36. Nguyen, *We Are All Suspects Now*, 99.

37. Chavez, *Latino Threat*, 135–156.

38. Ackerman, *Reign of Terror*, 45.

39. Vine, *United States of War*, 247, 289.

40. "America's Image Slips, but Allies Share U.S. Concerns over Iran, Hamas," Pew Research Center, June 13, 2006, https://www.pewresearch.org/global/2006 /06/13/americas-image-slips-but-allies-share-us-concerns-over-iran-hamas/.

41. Berschinski, "AFRICOM'S Dilemma."

42. Sheryl Gay Stolberg, "Bush Confronts Hard Questions in Ghana," *New York Times*, February 21, 2008, https://www.nytimes.com/2008/02/21/world/africa /21prexy.html; "In Africa, Bush Denies Intent to Build Bases," *New York Times*, February 20, 2008. https://www.nytimes.com/2008/02/20/world/africa/20iht -prexy.2.10227196.html.

43. Vine, *United States of War*, 289.

44. Schmidt, *Foreign Intervention in Africa*, 216.

45. Cable, Morocco Rabat to Secretary of State, "Favorable Views of U.S. Surge Upward in Arab/Muslim Morocco. What Went Right?," September 23, 2005, Canonical ID: 05RABAT2004_a, Unclassified. Wikileaks: https://wikileaks.org/plusd/cables/05RABAT2004_a.html.

Chapter 19

1. Holsey, "Black Atlantic Visions."

2. Jake Tapper, Karen Travers, and Sunlen Miller, "President Obama Delivers Tough Love, Pledges Partnership in Ghana," *ABC News*, July 11, 2009, https://abcnews.go.com/Politics/story?id=8058837&page=1.

3. Imakhüs, "Return through the Door of No Return," 381.

4. "Barack Obama's Speech on Race," *New York Times*, March 18, 2008, https://www.nytimes.com/2008/03/18/us/politics/18text-obama.html.

5. Euell A. Nielsen, "Barack Hussein Obama, Sr. (1936-1982)," *Black Past*, September 12, 2020, https://www.blackpast.org/global-african-history/barack-hussein-obama-sr-1936-1982/; Schachtman, *Airlift to America*.

6. "Obama Recalls His First Visit to Kenya in 1987," video, *Washington Post*, July 16, 2018, https://www.washingtonpost.com/video/world/wirereuters/obama-recalls-his-first-visit-to-kenya-in-1987/2018/07/16/71aaba60-891e-11e8-9d59-dccc2cocabcf_video.html.

7. Hartman, *Lose Your Mother*.

8. Jacqueline Woodson, "Jacqueline Woodson on Africa, America and Slavery's Fierce Undertow," *New York Times*, December 9, 2019, https://www.nytimes.com/2019/12/09/travel/ghana-african-slave-trade-jacqueline-woodson.html.

9. Holsey, "Slavery and the Making of Black Atlantic History."

10. Pierre, *Predicament of Blackness*, 126.

11. Pierre, *Predicament of Blackness*, 135.

12. Akurang-Parry, "Obama's Visit as a Signifier of Ghanaians' 'Colonial Mentality,'" 441.

13. Adebajo, "U.S. and Africa."

14. Sylvanus, *Patterns in Circulation*, 2.

15. Barack Obama, "Remarks by the President to the Ghanaian Parliament," July 11, 2009, Accra, Ghana, Transcript, The White House, The United States Government, https://obamawhitehouse.archives.gov/the-press-office/remarks-president-ghanaian-parliament.

16. Richard Wike, "5 Charts on America's (Very Positive) Image in Africa," Pew Research Center, July 23, 2015, https://www.pewresearch.org/fact-tank/2015/07/23/5-charts-on-americas-very-positive-image-in-africa/.

17. Max Fisher, "This Map Shows That Obama Is Really, Really Popular in Africa," *Washington Post*, June 28, 2013, https://www.washingtonpost.com/news/worldviews/wp/2013/06/28/this-map-shows-that-obama-is-really-really-popular-in-africa/; Sudarsan Raghavan, "Kenya Cools on Obama," *Washington Post*, November 6, 2012, https://www.washingtonpost.com/news/worldviews/wp/2012/11/06/kenya-cools-on-obama/.

18. Benjamin Talton, "Obama Could Have Done More for Africa by Supporting Pro-democracy Protests," *The Conversation*, January 25, 2017, https://theconversation.com/obama-could-have-done-more-for-africa-by-supporting-pro-democracy-protests-71096.

19. Thomas Carothers, "Why Is the United States Shortchanging Its Commitment to Democracy?," *Washington Post*, December 22, 2014, https://www.washingtonpost.com/opinions/falling-usaid-spending-shows-a-lack-of-commitment-to-fostering-democracy/2014/12/22/86b72d58-89f4-11e4-a085-34e9b9f09a58_story.html?utm_term=.d9fef6dfdc30.

20. Ackerman, *Reign of Terror*, 114.

21. David Johnston and Charlie Savage, "Obama Reluctant to Look into Bush Programs," *New York Times*, January 11, 2009, https://www.nytimes.com/2009/01/12/us/politics/12inquire.html.

22. Vine, *United States of War*, 299.

23. Craig Whitlock, "U.S. Expands Secret Intelligence Operations in Africa," *Washington Post*, June 13, 2012, https://www.washingtonpost.com/world/national-security/us-expands-secret-intelligence-operations-in-africa/2012/06/13/gJQAHyvAbV_story.html.

24. Adam Taylor, "Map: The U.S. Military Currently Has Troops in These African Countries," *Washington Post*, May 21, 2014, https://www.washingtonpost.com/news/worldviews/wp/2014/05/21/map-the-u-s-currently-has-troops-in-these-african-countries/.

25. Frère and Englebert, "Burkina Faso—the Fall of Blaise Compaoré."

26. Nick Turse, "How One of the Most Stable Nations in West Africa Descended into Mayhem," *New York Times*, October 15, 2020.

27. Ruth Maclean, "When the Soldiers Meant to Protect You Instead Come to Kill," *New York Times*, June 22, 2020, https://www.nytimes.com/2020/06/22/world/africa/burkina-faso-terrorism.html.

28. Nick Turse, "How One of the Most Stable Nations in West Africa Descended into Mayhem," *New York Times*, October 15, 2020.

29. Eric Schmitt, "Where Terrorism Is Rising in Africa and the U.S. Is Leaving," *New York Times*, March 1, 2019, https://www.nytimes.com/2019/03/01/world/africa/africa-terror-attacks.html.

30. Savell, "Costs of United States' Post-9/11 'Security Assistance.'"

31. Vine, *United States of War*, 304.

32. Vine, *United States of War*, 306.

33. The U.S. military sought internet services at the base for its personnel. Amnesty International, *Cameroon's Secret Torture Chambers: Human Rights Violations and War Crimes in the Fight against Boko Haram*, 2017, https://www.amnesty.org/en/wp-content/uploads/2021/05/AFR1765362017ENGLISH.pdf.

34. Kathryn Watson, "Where Does the U.S. Have Troops in Africa, and Why?," *CBS News*, October 23, 2017, https://www.cbsnews.com/news/where-does-the-u-s-have-troops-in-africa-and-why/; Dan Gettinger, "The American Drone Base in Cameroon," Center for the Study of the Drone at Bard College, February 21, 2016, https://dronecenter.bard.edu/drone-base-cameroon/.

35. Amnesty International, *Cameroon's Secret Torture Chambers.*

36. Amnesty International, *Cameroon's Secret Torture Chambers,* 7.

37. Amnesty International, *Cameroon's Secret Torture Chambers,* 7.

38. Pommerolle and De Marie Heungoup, "Tale of the Cameroonian Postcolony."

39. "Cameroon," International Crisis Group, https://www.crisisgroup.org/africa/central-africa/cameroon.

40. Turse, "Soldiers in Cameroon."

41. Fahy, "America's 'Train, Advise, and Assist' Missions."

42. "US-Deported Cameroonians Suffered Serious Rights Violations: HRW," *Al Jazeera,* February 11, 2022, https://www.aljazeera.com/news/2022/2/11/us-deported-cameroonians-suffered-serious-rights-violations-hrw.

43. "Lofgren, Johnson Introduce Bill to Designate Cameroon for Temporary Protected Status," press release, October 12, 2021, https://lofgren.house.gov/media/press-releases/lofgren-johnson-introduce-bill-designate-cameroon-temporary-protected-status; "Secretary Mayorkas Designates Cameroon for Temporary Protected Status for 18 Months," news release, April 15, 2022, https://www.uscis.gov/newsroom/news-releases/secretary-mayorkas-designates-cameroon-for-temporary-protected-status-for-18-months.

44. Letter to President Biden and DHS Secretary Mayorkas from bicameral congressional coalition urging TPS for Cameroon, November 2, 2021, https://www.vanhollen.senate.gov/news/press-releases/van-hollen-bass-lead-bicameral-letter-urging-the-administration-to-provide-protections-to-cameroonians-fleeing-violence-humanitarian-crisis.

45. Vine, *United States of War,* 307.

46. Steven Feldstein, "Do Terrorist Trends in Africa Justify the U.S. Military's Expansion?," Carnegie Endowment for International Peace, February 9, 2018, https://carnegieendowment.org/2018/02/09/do-terrorist-trends-in-africa-justify-u.s.-military-s-expansion-pub-75476.

47. Vine, *United States of War,* 287.

48. The White House, Office of the Press Secretary, "Remarks of President Barack Obama—State of the Union Address As Delivered," press release, January 13, 2016, https://obamawhitehouse.archives.gov/the-press-office/2016/01/12/remarks-president-barack-obama-%E2%80%93-prepared-delivery-state-union-address.

49. Adam Serwer, "Birtherism of a Nation."

50. Barack Obama, Race Speech at the Constitution Center, March 18, 2008, National Constitution Center, https://constitutioncenter.org/amoreperfectunion/.

51. "Transcript: Read Michelle Obama's Full Speech from the 2016 DNC," *Washington Post,* July 26, 2016, https://www.washingtonpost.com/news/post-politics/wp/2016/07/26/transcript-read-michelle-obamas-full-speech-from-the-2016-dnc/.

52. Nikole Hannah-Jones, "The End of the Postracial Myth," *New York Times,* November 15, 2016, https://www.nytimes.com/interactive/2016/11/20/magazine/donald-trumps-america-iowa-race.html.

Chapter 20

1. U.S. Congress, House, Committee on the Judiciary, *Diversity Visa Program and Its Susceptibility to Fraud and Abuse*, April 29, 2004, 3–4.

2. Philip Bump, "Rep. Steve King Warns That 'Our Civilization' Can't Be Restored with 'Somebody Else's Babies,'" *Washington Post*, March 12, 2017, https://www.washingtonpost.com/news/politics/wp/2017/03/12/rep-steve-king-warns-that-our-civilization-cant-be-restored-with-somebody-elses-babies/.

3. H.R. 775—SAFE for America Act, 108th Congress, introduced February 13, 2003; U.S. Congress, House, Committee on the Judiciary, *Diversity Visa Program and Its Susceptibility to Fraud and Abuse*, April 29, 2004, 2.

4. U.S. Department of State and the Broadcasting Board of Governors, Office of Inspector General, "Diversity Visa Program, Report Number ISP-CA-03-52."

5. U.S. Congress, House, Committee on the Judiciary, *Diversity Visa Program and Its Susceptibility to Fraud and Abuse*, April 29, 2004 (statement of Steven A. Camarota, Center for Immigration Studies), 31.

6. U.S. Congress, House, Committee on the Judiciary, *Diversity Visa Program and Its Susceptibility to Fraud and Abuse*, April 29, 2004 (statement of Steven A. Camarota, Center for Immigration Studies), 31.

7. U.S. Congress, House, Committee on the Judiciary, *Diversity Visa Program and Its Susceptibility to Fraud and Abuse*, April 29, 2004 (statement of Professor Jan Ting, Temple University James E. Beasley School of Law), 52.

8. U.S. Congress, House, Committee on the Judiciary, *Diversity Visa Program and Its Susceptibility to Fraud and Abuse*, April 29, 2004 (statement of Professor Jan Ting, Temple University James E. Beasley School of Law), 16.

9. U.S. Congress, House, Committee on the Judiciary, *Diversity Visa Program and Its Susceptibility to Fraud and Abuse*, April 29, 2004 (statement of Professor Jan Ting, Temple University James E. Beasley School of Law), 17.

10. U.S. Congress, House, Committee on the Judiciary, *Diversity Visa Program and Its Susceptibility to Fraud and Abuse*, April 29, 2004 (statement of Rep. Steve King), 55.

11. Rachel Weiner, "How Immigration Reform Failed," *Washington Post*, January 30, 2013, https://www.washingtonpost.com/news/the-fix/wp/2013/01/30/how-immigration-reform-failed-over-and-over/.

12. U.S. Congress, House, Committee on the Judiciary, *Diversity Visa Program: Hearing Before the House Subcommittee on Immigration, Border Security, and Claims*, June 15, 2005 (statement of Mark Krikorian, Center for Immigration Studies), 17–22.

13. U.S. Congress, House, Committee on the Judiciary, *Diversity Visa Program*, June 15, 2005, 49.

14. U.S. Congress, House, Committee on the Judiciary, *Diversity Visa Program*, June 15, 2005 (statement of Bruce A. Morrison, former member of Congress), 5.

15. U.S. Congress, House, Committee on the Judiciary, *Diversity Visa Program*, June 15, 2005, (statement of Bruce A. Morrison, former member of Congress), 7.

16. The White House, Office of the Press Secretary, "President Bush Addresses the Nation on Immigration Reform," press release, May 15, 2006, Transcript, https://web

.archive.org/web/20220728080045/https://georgewbush-whitehouse.archives.gov
/news/releases/2006/05/20060515-8.html.

17. Transcript, "President Bush Addresses the Nation on Immigration Reform."

18. Louis Gohmert chimed in to agree with Goodlatte in one hearing: "I think the Diversity Visa Lottery Program is something that has got to go. It's an abdication of Federal responsibility that we let people get a visa by drawing at a lottery." U.S. Congress, House, Committee on the Judiciary, *Should Congress Raise the H-1B Cap?*, March 30, 2006, 73.

19. Bada, Fox, and Guskin, "Immigrant Rights Protests—Spring 2006."

20. Tancredo, "Tough Immigration Reform Essential to Maintain U.S. Identity."

21. Jonathan Weisman, "Immigrant Bill Fallout May Hurt House GOP," *Washington Post*, April 12, 2006, https://www.washingtonpost.com/wp-dyn/content/article/2006/04/11/AR2006041101643.html?itid=lk_inline_manual_20.

22. Migration Policy Institute, "Side-by-Side Comparison of 2013 Senate Immigration Bill with 2006 and 2007 Senate Legislation," Issue Brief No. 4, April 2013, http://www.migrationpolicy.org/research/side-side-comparison-2013-senate-immigration-bill-2006-and-2007-senate-legislation.

23. "Mixed Views on Immigration Bill," Pew Research Center, June 7, 2007, https://www.pewresearch.org/politics/2007/06/07/mixed-views-on-immigration-bill/.

24. Robert Pear, "Little-Known Group Claims a Win on Immigration," *New York Times*, July 15, 2007, https://www.nytimes.com/2007/07/15/us/politics/15immig.html.

25. The Development, Relief, and Education for Alien Minors Act was introduced in the Senate as S. 1291 by Sen. Dick Durbin (D-IL) and Sen. Orrin Hatch (R-UT) on April 25, 2001.

26. Goodman, *Deportation Machine*; Skrentny and López, "Obama's Immigration Reform."

27. Napolitano, "Prepared Remarks by Secretary Napolitano on Immigration Reform at the Center for American Progress."

28. Chishti, Pierce, and Bolter, "Obama Record on Deportations."

29. The phrase came in a 2014 speech, but his emphasis on shifting priorities was evident in earlier policies and speeches, for example: The White House, Office of the Press Secretary, "Remarks by the President on Comprehensive Immigration Reform in El Paso, Texas"; Thompson, "Deporting 'Felons, Not Families.'"

30. Security and Fairness Enhancement for America Act of 2011, H.R. 704, 112th Cong., 1 (2011).

31. U.S. Congress, House, Committee on the Judiciary, *Safe for America Act*, April 5, 2011 (statement of Rep. Elton Gallegly), 2.

32. U.S. Congress, House, Committee on the Judiciary, *Safe for America Act*, April 5, 2011 (statement of Janice L. Kephart, Center for Immigration Studies), 35–36.

33. U.S. Congress, House, Committee on the Judiciary, *Safe for America Act*, April 5, 2011 (statement of Rep. John Conyers), 23.

34. U.S. Congress, House, Committee on the Judiciary, *Safe for America Act*, April 5, 2011 (statement of Rep. John Conyers), 24.

35. Susan Sachs, "As New York City Immigration Thrives, Diversity Broadens," *New York Times*, November 8, 1999, https://www.nytimes.com/1999/11/08/nyregion/as-new-york-city-immigration-thrives-diversity-broadens.html.

36. U.S. Congress, House, Committee on the Judiciary, *Safe for America Act*, April 5, 2011 (statement of Ambassador Johnny Young on behalf of U.S. Conference of Catholic Bishops), 45.

37. U.S. Congress, House, Committee on the Judiciary, *Safe for America Act*, April 5, 2011 (statement of Ambassador Johnny Young), 45.

38. U.S. Congress, House, Committee on the Judiciary, *Safe for America Act*, April 5, 2011 (statement of Ambassador Johnny Young), 51.

39. U.S. Congress, House, Committee on the Judiciary, *Safe for America Act*, April 5, 2011 (statement of Ambassador Johnny Young), 126.

40. Johnny Young, interviewed by Charles Stuart Kennedy, October 21, 2005, Transcript, Foreign Affairs Oral History Project, Association for Diplomatic Studies & Training, https://adst.org/OH%20TOCs/Young,%20Johnny.toc.pdf.

41. U.S. Congress, House, Committee on the Judiciary, *Safe for America Act*, April 5, 2011 (statement of Pedro Pierluisi, Resident Commissioner of Puerto Rico), 128.

42. U.S. Congress, House, Committee on the Judiciary, *Safe for America Act*, April 5, 2011, (statement of Rep. Bob Goodlatte), 28.

43. Migration Policy Institute, "Side-by-Side Comparison of 2013 Senate Immigration Bill with 2006 and 2007 Senate Legislation."

44. Congressional Research Service, "Comprehensive Immigration Reform in the 113th Congress."

45. SKILLS Visa Act, H.R. 2131, 113th Cong. (2013-2014); Garcia, "Making Sense of the Senate and House's Visions of Immigration Reform"; American Immigration Council, "A Guide to S.744."

46. The White House, Office of the Press Secretary, "President Obama Launches 'Educate to Innovate' Campaign for Excellence in Science, Technology, Engineering & Math (Stem) Education."

47. Law, "Diversity Visa Lottery," 29.

48. Julianne Malveaux, "Blacks Underrepresented in Immigration Debate," *Louisiana Weekly*, May 2013; Cynthia Gordy, "Black Immigrants Join the Debate," *Louisiana Weekly*, June 2011.

49. "Black Lawmakers Missing from Immigration Debate," *Philadelphia Tribune*, May 5, 2013, https://www.phillytrib.com/news/black-lawmakers-missing-from-immigration-debate/article_0050d316-92a0-54ab-8524-316f38523f11.html.

50. Zong and Batalova, "Sub-Saharan African Immigrants in the United States."

51. Carol Hills and Jason Margolis, "Senate's Immigration Bill Quietly Curtails African Flows," *PRI's The World*, June 25, 2013, http://www.pri.org/stories/2013-06-25/senates-immigration-bill-quietly-curtails-african-flows.

52. Hills and Margolis, "Senate's Immigration Bill Quietly Curtails African Flows."

53. Hills and Margolis, "Senate's Immigration Bill Quietly Curtails African Flows." Song can be streamed on Mayja Money's Facebook page, https://www.facebook.com/permalink.php?storyfbid=734652466576473&id=562971710411217.

54. Kevin Bogardus, "NAACP Pushes for 'Diversity' Visas," *The Hill*, April 4, 2013, http://thehill.com/business-a-lobbying/291765-naacp-pushes-for-diversity-visas; Kevin Bogardus and Russell Berman, "Black Caucus Troubled by Senate Plan to Replace 'Diversity' Visas," *The Hill*, April 19, 2013, https://web.archive.org/web/20210811031903/https://thehill.com/homenews/house/294853-black-caucus-concerned-by-end-of-diversity-visas-in-senate-immigration-bill; Naeesa Aziz, "NAACP Lobbies for African, Caribbean 'Diversity' Visas," BET.com, April 5, 2013, https://www.bet.com/article/o5l1tk/naacp-lobbies-for-african-caribbean-diversity-visas.

55. Congressional Black Caucus, "CBC Statement on Senate Comprehensive Immigration Reform Legislation," April 19, 2013, https://cbc.house.gov/news/documentsingle.aspx?DocumentID=93.

56. Congressional Black Caucus, "CBC Statement on Senate Comprehensive Immigration Reform Legislation."

57. Carlos Echeverria-Estrada and Jeanne Batalova, "Sub-Saharan African Immigrants in the United States," *Migration Information Source*, November 6, 2019, https://www.migrationpolicy.org/article/sub-saharan-african-immigrants-united-states-2018.

58. Monica Anderson, "A Rising Share of the U.S. Black Population Is Foreign Born," Pew Research Center, April 9, 2015, http://www.pewsocialtrends.org/2015/04/09/a-rising-share-of-the-u-s-black-population-is-foreign-born/; Teresa Wiltz, "Growing African Immigrant Population Is Underemployed," Stateline, May 14, 2015, http://www.pewtrusts.org/en/research-and-analysis/blogs/stateline/2015/5/14/growing-african-immigrant-population-is-highly-educated-underemployed; Monica Anderson, "African Immigrant Population in U.S. Steadily Climbs," Pew Research Center, February 14, 2018, https://www.pewresearch.org/fact-tank/2017/02/14/african-immigrant-population-in-u-s-steadily-climbs/; Monica Anderson and Gustavo López, "Key Facts about Black Immigrants in the U.S.," Pew Research Center, January 24, 2018, https://www.pewresearch.org/fact-tank/2018/01/24/key-facts-about-black-immigrants-in-the-u-s/.

59. Halter and Johnson, *American & African*; Grant, "Coming to America with Eyes Wide Shut"; Arthur, *African Diaspora Identities*.

60. Supplying Knowledge-Based Immigrants and Lifting Levels of STEM Visas Act, H.R. Rep. No. 113-676, 113th Cong., 2 (December 15, 2014), 142.

61. Supplying Knowledge-Based Immigrants and Lifting Levels of STEM Visas Act, 141.

62. Wolgin, "2 Years Later, Immigrants Are Still Waiting on Immigration Reform."

Chapter 21

1. Atabe Nzunse, interview by the author, November 7, 2015, Bamenda, Cameroon.

2. "Full Text: Donald Trump Announces a Presidential Bid," *Washington Post*, June 16, 2015, https://www.washingtonpost.com/news/post-politics/wp/2015/06/16/full-text-donald-trump-announces-a-presidential-bid/.

3. Bouie, "White Won."

4. Daniel Wood and Geoff Brumfiel, "Pro-Trump Counties Now Have Far Higher COVID Death Rates. Misinformation Is to Blame," *NPR Morning Edition*, December 5, 2021, https://www.npr.org/sections/health-shots/2021/12/05/1059828993/data -vaccine-misinformation-trump-counties-covid-death-rate.

5. Serwer, "Cruelty Is the Point."

6. Executive Office of the President, Proclamation 9645 "Enhancing Vetting Capabilities and Processes for Detecting Attempted Entry into the United States by Terrorists or Other Public-Safety Threats: A Proclamation," *Federal Register*, September 24, 2017, https://www.federalregister.gov/documents/2017/09/27/2017 -20899/enhancing-vetting-capabilities-and-processes-for-detecting-attempted -entry-into-the-united-states-by.

7. Dara Lind, "Exclusive: Internal Documents Show How Hard It Is for Some Immigrants to Get a Travel Ban Waiver," *Vox.com*, September 21, 2018, https://www .vox.com/2018/9/20/17622622/travel-ban-waiver-muslim-how.

8. Letter from Mary Elizabeth Taylor, Assistant Secretary, Bureau of Legislative Affairs, Department of State, to Sen. Chris Van Hollen, February 22, 2019, https:// www.vanhollen.senate.gov/imo/media/doc/State%20Dept%20Response%20 to%20Oct%20Muslim%20Ban%20Letter.pdf. More guidance here: "Revisions to Presidential Proclamation 9645 April 10, 2018," Travel.gov, https://aila.org/File /DownloadEmbeddedFile/75635.

9. Kim Barker, Joseph Goldstein, and Michael Schwirtz, "Finding a Rootless Life in U.S., Sayfullo Saipov Turned to Radicalism," *New York Times*, November 1, 2017, https://www.nytimes.com/2017/11/01/nyregion/sayfullo-saipov-truck-attack -manhattan.html.

10. U.S. Department of Justice, "Sayfullo Saipov Charged with Terrorism and Murder in Aid of Racketeering in Connection with Lower Manhattan Truck Attack."

11. Laura Nahias, "Sessions: Guantanamo an Option for Terrorism Suspects," *Politico.com*, November 2, 2017, https://www.politico.com/story/2017/11/02/guantanamo -terror-suspects-jeff-sessions-reacts-244457.

12. Benjamin Weiser, "F.B.I. Wiretap Recorded Suspect on Eve of Bike Path Terror Attack," *New York Times*, December 17, 2018, https://www.nytimes.com/2018/12 /17/nyregion/terror-attack-wiretap-saipov.html.

13. Centers for Disease Control and Prevention, "Pedestrian Safety" Fact Sheet, accessed July 29, 2022, https://www.cdc.gov/transportationsafety/pedestrian _safety/index.html.

14. Hannah Allam, "Vehicle Attacks Rise as Extremists Target Protesters," *NPR*, June 21, 2020, https://www.npr.org/2020/06/21/880963592/vehicle-attacks-rise -as-extremists-target-protesters.

15. Allam, "Vehicle Attacks Rise as Extremists Target Protesters."

16. Jen Kirby, "Trump Blasts 'Diversity Visa Lottery Program' after NYC Terror Attack," *Vox.com*, November 1, 2017, https://www.vox.com/policy-and-politics /2017/11/1/16590166/trump-tweet-diversity-visa-lottery-program. After Trump's Twitter account was suspended in January 2021, his tweets disappeared from the site. They are archived here: https://www.thetrumparchive.com/.

17. "Rep. Clarke Statement on Trump Attack on Diversity Visa Lottery," November 2, 2017, https://clarke.house.gov/rep-clarke-statement-trump-attack-diversity -visa-lottery/.

18. "Diversity Visa Recipients, Congressional Leaders, Immigration Experts, and Community Groups Defend the Importance of Protecting the Diversity Visa Program," UndocuBlack Network, November 2, 2017, https://undocublack.org /press-releases/?offset=1509810999608. See also UndocuBlack Network and the National Immigration Law Center (NILC), "Frequently Asked Questions about Diversity Visas," June 8, 2018, https://www.aila.org/infonet/undocublack-and-nilc-provide -faqs-on-the-diversity.

19. Josh Dawsey, "Trump Derides Protections for Immigrants from 'Shithole' Countries," *Washington Post*, January 12, 2018, https://www.washingtonpost.com /politics/trump-attacks-protections-for-immigrants-from-shithole-countries-in -oval-office-meeting/2018/01/11/bfc0725c-f711-11e7-91af-31ac729add94_story.html.

20. Ali Vitali, Kasie Hunt, and Frank Thorp V, "Trump Referred to Haiti and African Nations as 'Shithole' Countries," *NBC News*, January 12, 2018, https:// www.nbcnews.com/politics/white-house/trump-referred-haiti-african-countries -shithole-nations-n836946.

21. Vitali, Hunt, and Thorp, "Trump Referred to Haiti and African Nations as 'Shithole' Countries."

22. "CBC Chairman to Trump: Stop Pitting Black and Brown Immigrants against Each Other," press release, Congressional Black Caucus, February 12, 2018, https:// cbc.house.gov/news/documentsingle.aspx?DocumentID=841.

23. Letter from Cedric Richmond, Chair, Congressional Black Caucus, to President Donald J. Trump, February 12, 2018, https://cbc.house.gov/uploadedfiles/cbc _letter_to_trump_on_pitting_black_and_brown_immigrants_against_each_other.pdf.

24. David Nakamura and Mike DeBonis, "Trump Administration Assault on Bipartisan Immigration Plan Ensured Its Demise," *Washington Post*, February 17, 2018, https://www.washingtonpost.com/politics/trump-administration-assault -on-bipartisan-immigration-plan-ensured-its-demise/2018/02/17/ad1661f4-133e -11e8-9065-e55346f6de81_story.html.

25. Lomi Kriel, "Trump Moves to End 'Catch and Release,' Prosecuting Parents and Removing Children Who Cross Border," *Houston Chronicle*, November 25, 2017, https://www.houstonchronicle.com/news/houston-texas/houston/article/Trump -moves-to-end-catch-and-release-12383666.php; see also Soboroff, *Separated: Inside an American Tragedy*; Caitlin Dickerson, "An American Catastrophe: The Secret History of the U.S. government's family separation policy."

26. Abby Livingston, "U.S. House Rejects Immigration Bill That Included Pathway to Citizenship for Dreamers, Border Wall Funding," *Texas Tribune*, June 27, 2018, https://www.texastribune.org/2018/06/27/immigration-bill-House-vote-border -wall-citizenship-dreamers/.

27. Dara Lind, "How Trump's Travel Ban Became Normal," *Vox.com*, June 26, 2018, https://www.vox.com/2018/4/27/17284798/travel-ban-scotus-countries-protests.

28. Laura Muñoz Lopez, "Anti-immigrant Rhetoric Was Defeated in the 2018 Midterm Elections," Center for American Progress, December 13, 2018, https://www

.americanprogress.org/article/anti-immigrant-rhetoric-defeated-2018-midterm
-elections/.

29. It was known as Presidential Proclamation 9983. Zolan Kanno-Younngs, "Trump Administration Adds Six Countries to Travel Ban," *New York Times*, January 31, 2020, https://www.nytimes.com/2020/01/31/us/politics/trump-travel-ban.html.

30. Vitali, Hunt, and Thorp, "Trump Referred to Haiti and African Nations as 'Shithole' Countries."

31. Liam Knox, "Civil Rights Groups Condemn Trump's Travel-Ban Expansion to Six African Countries," *NBC News*, February 27, 2020, https://www.nbcnews.com/news/nbcblk/civil-rights-groups-condemn-trump-s-travel-ban-expansion-six-n1142231.

32. William Wan, "WHO Declares a Pandemic of Coronavirus Disease Covid-19," *Washington Post*, March 11, 2020, https://www.washingtonpost.com/health/2020/03/11/who-declares-pandemic-coronavirus-disease-covid-19/.

33. Rob Buscher, "'Reality Is Hitting Me in the Face': Asian Americans Grapple with Racism Due to COVID-19," *WHYY*, April 21, 2020, https://whyy.org/articles/reality-is-hitting-me-in-the-face-asian-americans-grapple-with-racism-due-to-covid-19/.

34. Thomas J. Bollyky and Jennifer Nuzzo, "Trump's 'Early' Travel 'Bans' Weren't Early, Weren't Bans and Didn't Work," *Washington Post*, October 1, 2020, https://www.washingtonpost.com/outlook/2020/10/01/debate-early-travel-bans-china/.

35. "A Guide to Title 42 Expulsions at the Border," American Immigration Council, October 15, 2021, https://www.americanimmigrationcouncil.org/research/guide-title-42-expulsions-border.

36. Herrera, "Black Immigrants Matter."

37. Serwer, "The Coronavirus Was an Emergency Until Trump Found out Who Was Dying."

38. Larry Buchanan, Quoctrung Bui, and Jugal K. Patel, "Black Lives Matter May Be the Largest Movement in U.S. History," *New York Times*, July 3, 2020, https://www.nytimes.com/interactive/2020/07/03/us/george-floyd-protests-crowd-size.html.

39. Lara Putnam, Erica Chenoweth, and Jeremy Pressman, "The Floyd Protests Are the Broadest in U.S. History—and Are Spreading to White, Small-Town America," *Washington Post*, June 6, 2020, https://www.washingtonpost.com/politics/2020/06/06/floyd-protests-are-broadest-us-history-are-spreading-white-small-town-america/.

40. Coates, "First White President."

41. Mallory Simon and Sara Sidner, "Decoding the Extremist Symbols and Groups at the Capitol Hill Insurrection," *CNN.com*, January 11, 2021, https://www.cnn.com/2021/01/09/us/capitol-hill-insurrection-extremist-flags-soh/index.html; Matthew Rosenberg and Ainara Tiefenthäler, "Decoding the Far-Right Symbols at the Capitol Riot," *New York Times*, January 13, 2021, https://www.nytimes.com/2021/01/13/video/extremist-signs-symbols-capitol-riot.html.

42. Robert A. Pape, "Opinion: What an Analysis of 377 Americans Arrested or Charged in the Capitol Insurrection Tells Us," *Washington Post*, April 6, 2021, https://www.washingtonpost.com/opinions/2021/04/06/capitol-insurrection -arrests-cpost-analysis/.

43. Jamelle Bouie, "Trump Had a Mob. He Also Had a Plan," *New York Times*, September 24, 2021, https://www.nytimes.com/2021/09/24/opinion/jan-6-eastman -memo.html.

Coda

1. Berry and Gross, *Black Women's History of the United States*, 208–214.

2. Bailey, *Weeping Time*.

3. Herrera, "Black Immigrants Matter."

4. Shamira Ibrahim, "Ousman Darboe Could Be Deported Any Day. His Story Is a Common One for Black Immigrants," *Vox.com*, February 5, 2020, https://www.vox .com/identities/2019/9/30/20875821/black-immigrants-school-prison-deportation -pipeline.

5. Biden, "Biden Plan for Securing Our Values as a Nation of Immigrants."

6. American Immigration Council, "A Guide to Title 42 Expulsions at the Border," Published October 15, 2021; Modified May 25, 2022, https://www .americanimmigrationcouncil.org/research/guide-title-42-expulsions-border.

7. Vásquez, "Biden Administration Has Spent Black History Month Deporting Black Immigrants."

8. Vásquez, "Biden Administration Has Spent Black History Month Deporting Black Immigrants."

9. Camilo Montoya-Galvez, "U.S. Expels Nearly 4,000 Haitians in 9 Days as Part of Deportation Blitz," *CBS News*, September 27, 2021, https://www.cbsnews.com /news/haiti-migrants-us-expels-nearly-4000-in-nine-days/; Priscilla Alvarez, "About 4,600 Haitians Have Been Expelled from the US Since September 19, DHS Says," *CNN.com*, September 29, 2021, https://www.cnn.com/2021/09/29/politics/haitians -expelled-immigration/index.html.

10. "Read: Resignation Letter from U.S. Special Envoy for Haiti, Daniel Foote," *Washington Post*, September 22, 2021, https://www.washingtonpost.com/context /read-resignation-letter-from-u-s-special-envoy-for-haiti-daniel-foote/3136ae0e -96e5-448e-9d12-0e0cabfb3c0b/.

11. Class Action Complaint for Injunctive and Declaratory Relief, Haitian Bridge Alliance v. Biden, https://innovationlawlab.org/cases/haitian-bridge-alliance-v -biden/.

12. Julia Craven, "The Ugly History behind Those Border Agents Chasing Haitian Migrants on Horseback," *Slate.com*, September 25, 2021, https://slate.com/news-and -politics/2021/09/border-patrol-horseback-haitian-migrants-del-rio.html.

13. Adam Isacson, "A Tragic Milestone: 20,000th Migrant Deported to Haiti since Biden Inauguration," WOLA, February 17, 2002, https://www.wola.org/analysis/a -tragic-milestone-20000th-migrant-deported-to-haiti-since-biden-inauguration/.

14. Eileen Sullivan, "U.S. Accelerated Expulsions of Haitian Migrants in May," *New York Times*, June 9, 2022; Updated June 11, 2022, https://www.nytimes.com /2022/06/09/us/politics/haiti-migrants-biden.html.

15. Lindskoog, *Detain and Punish*.

16. Morgan-Trostle and Zheng, *State of Black Immigrants*.

17. Ibrahim, "Ousman Darboe Could Be Deported Any Day."

18. DeArbea Walker, "The US Is Lifting Its Travel Ban against Southern African Countries, but Medical Experts Say Stigmatization Has Already Perpetuated Anti-Blackness," *Insider*, December 27, 2021, https://www.insider.com/southern-african -countries-travel-ban-anti-black-medical-experts-say-2021-12; Laura Seay and Kim Yi Dionne, "The Long and Ugly Tradition of Treating Africa as a Dirty, Diseased Place," *Washington Post*, August 25, 2014, https://www.washingtonpost.com/news/monkey -cage/wp/2014/08/25/othering-ebola-and-the-history-and-politics-of-pointing-at -immigrants-as-potential-disease-vectors/.

19. "Frequently Asked Questions about *Gomez v. Trump*," AILA, October 21, 2020, https://www.aila.org/infonet/frequently-asked-questions-about-gomez-v-trump.

20. Ijeoma Golden Kouadio, "Biden Is Still Blocking People Like Me, with Visas, from Entering the U.S.," *Washington Post*, February 17, 2021, https://www.washingtonpost .com/outlook/2021/02/17/biden-trump-immigration-order-visa-lottery/.

21. "Press Statement: Court Orders Government to Issue 9,095 Reserved 2020 Diversity Visas," AILA, August 18, 2021, https://www.aila.org/advo-media/press -releases/2021/court-orders-government-to-issue-9095-reserved.

22. Walter Ewing, "Diversity Visa Lottery Winners Might Lose Chance to Come to the U.S. Due to Delays, Trump Policies," Immigration Impact, August 25, 2021, https://immigrationimpact.com/2021/08/25/diversity-visa-lottery-delays-update -2021/#.YcpL_L3MJQ8; Stuart Anderson, "Lawsuit Tries to Save Interviews for Di-versity Visa Immigrants," *Forbes*, February 1, 2022, https://www.forbes.com/sites /stuartanderson/2022/02/01/lawsuit-tries-to-save-interviews-for-diversity-visa -immigrants/?sh=a48dd524f611.

23. Memorandum and Order, Case 21-cv-01530-APM, November 30, 2021, https://drive.google.com/file/d/1f6bQr1mywWGUXBOWpkcUzmaFHU6JZmc3 /view; Curtis Morrison (@curtisatlaw), Twitter, December 24, 2021, https://twitter .com/curtisatlaw/status/1474249982714675200?s=20.

24. David Bier, "Build Back Better Act Immigration Provisions—Summary and Analysis," *CATO at Liberty* (blog), November 30, 2021, https://www.cato.org/blog /build-back-better-act-immigration-provisions-summary-analysis.

25. Pemamtou Pewing Jude, interview by the author, November 9, 2015, Bamenda, Cameroon.

26. Ndeh Germanus Yunishe, interview by the author, November 7, 2015, Bamenda, Cameroon.

27. Allomonwing Joseph Ngochi, interview by the author, November 4, 2015, Yaoundé, Cameroon.

Bibliography

Oral Histories

Tamiment Library/Robert F. Wagner Labor Archives, New York University.
Archives of Irish America, Ireland House Oral History Collection, AIA 030.
    Sean Benson, interview, November 29, 2005.
    Mae O'Driscoll, interview, November 18, 2005.
    Patrick Hurley, interview, October 31, 1997.
    Sean Minihane, interview, October 25, 2007.
    Lisa Johnston, interview, March 16, 2009.
Edward M. Kennedy Oral History Project, Miller Center, University of Virginia.
    Michael Myers, interview, August 28, 2008.
    Niall O'Dowd, interview, November 18, 2010.
    Edward M. Kennedy, interview, October 8, 2007.
    Alan Simpson, interview, May 10, 2006.
Foreign Affairs Oral History Project, Association for Diplomatic Studies &
    Training.
    Johnny Young, interview, October 21, 2005.
John Joseph Moakley Archive and Institute, Suffolk University.
    Edmund G. Crotty, interview, April 21, 2003.
University of Massachusetts Lowell Center for Lowell History, Oral History
    Collection.
    Rita Ofori-Frimpong, interview, November 8, 2007.
Interviews by the author (recordings/transcripts in author's possession)
    Tamale, Ghana, 2013
    Kumasi, Ghana, 2013
    Accra, Ghana, 2013
    Cape Coast, Ghana, 2013
    Philadelphia, United States, 2014
    Bamenda, Cameroon, 2015
    Buea, Cameroon, 2015
    Yaoundé, Cameroon, 2015

Archives, Papers, and Manuscript Collections

United States

American Heritage Center. University of Wyoming. Laramie, Wyoming.
    Alan K. Simpson Papers, Collection 10449

Archives & Special Collections. Thomas J. Dodd Research Center. University of
   Connecticut. Storrs, Connecticut.
   Bruce A. Morrison Papers
Bentley Historical Library, University of Michigan. Ann Arbor, Michigan.
   John Tanton Papers
Cooperative Africana Materials Project (CAMP), Center for Research Libraries
Historical Society of Pennsylvania. Philadelphia, Pennsylvania.
   Robin O'Brien Hiteshew, Collection 3059
Hoover Institution Archives. Stanford University. Stanford, California.
   Polish Subject Collection
Moakley Archive and Institute. Suffolk University. Boston, Massachusetts.
   Congressman John Joseph Moakley Papers (MS 100), 1926-2001
Special Collections, George Washington University. Washington, DC.
   Federation for American Immigration Reform Records, MS2195
Tamiment Library and Robert F. Wagner Labor Archives. New York University.
   New York, New York.
   Archives of Irish America
   Ireland House Oral History Collection, AIA 030
   Irish Immigration Reform Movement Records, AIA 016

Africa

Africana Collection. Balme Library. University of Ghana, at Legon. Accra, Ghana.
National Archives of Cameroon. Yaoundé, Cameroon.
University Library. Kwame Nkrumah University of Science and Technology
   (KNUST). Kumasi, Ghana.
University Library. University of Buea. Buea, Cameroon.

Newspapers, Periodicals, and Online Publications

United States

ABC News
AILA
Associated Press
The Atlantic
Baltimore Sun
BET.com
Black Past
Boston Globe
Boston Globe Magazine
CBS News
Center for American Progress
Chicago Metro News
Chicago Tribune
Christian Science Monitor
Cnet.com

CNN.com
The Conversation
CQ Almanac 1990
CQ Weekly
C-SPAN
Forbes Magazine
Harper's
The Hill
Houston Chronicle
Immigration Impact
Irish America
Irish Echo
Los Angeles Times
Louisiana Weekly
Migration Information Source

Migration Policy Institute
New Republic
New York Times
Newsday
NPR
Pew Research Center Fact Tank
Philadelphia Daily News
Philadelphia Inquirer
Philadelphia Tribune
Politico.com

PRI's The World
Readcultured.com
Slate.com
Texas Tribune
Time Magazine
Vox.com
Wall Street Journal
Washington Post
WHYY
Wired Magazine

Global

Africa Info—Cameroun
African Exponent
Afrik.com
Agence France Presse
BBC.com
Cameroon Post Online
Cameroon Tribune
Daily Champion (Nigeria)
Daily Graphic (Ghana)
Free Press (Ghana)
The Gazette (Montreal)
Ghana Focus
Ghanaian Chronicle
Ghanaian Times
Ghanaweb.com
The Guardian
The Independent (Accra)
Irish Central.com
La Nouvelle Expression (Cameroon)

L'Effort Camerounais
Le Messager (Cameroon)
The Mirror (Ghana)
Modernghana.com
Mutations (Cameroon)
Pambazuka News
Panapress.com (Dakar)
The Pioneer (Ghana)
P.M. News (Lagos)
The Post Express (Lagos)
Post News Magazine (Cameroon)
The Progress (Freetown)
Quartz Africa
The Spectator (Ghana)
Sunday Champion (Nigeria)
Vancouver Sun
The Week (Nigeria)
West Africa

Government Publications

Reports, Fact Sheets, and Statistics

Centers for Disease Control and Prevention. "Pedestrian Safety." Fact sheet. Accessed August 10, 2022. https://www.cdc.gov/transportationsafety /pedestrian_safety/index.html.

Congressional Record Proceedings and Debates of the 101st Congress, 2nd Session.

Congressional Research Service. "Comprehensive Immigration Reform in the 113th Congress: Major Provisions in Senate-Passed S. 744," July 9, 2013. https://www.everycrsreport.com/reports/R43097.html.

Espie, Alberta J. "Bachelor from Pakistan Is First Winner in Worldwide Lottery." *State: The Newsletter of the Department of State*, January 1989. https://www .google.com/books/edition/State/xYNNAQAAMAAJ?hl=en&gbpv=1&dq=op

-1%20berman%20visa%20eligibility&pg=RA7-PA18&printsec=frontcover&bsq
=Berman.

Kolker, Abigail F. *Visa Waiver Program*, CRS Report RL32221, Congressional
Research Service, updated October 12, 2021. https://sgp.fas.org/crs/homesec
/RL32221.pdf.

Select Commission on Immigration and Refugee Policy. *U.S. Immigration Policy
and the National Interest. The Final Report and Recommendations of the Select
Commission on Immigration and Refugee Policy with Supplemental Views by
Commissioners.* March 1, 1981. https://files.eric.ed.gov/fulltext/ED211612.pdf.

———. *U.S. Immigration Policy and the National Interest: Staff Report of the Select
Commission on Immigration and Refugee Policy, Supplement to the Final Report
and Recommendations of the Select Commission on Immigration and Refugee
Policy.* April 30, 1981. https://hdl.handle.net/2027/umn.31951t00430574g.

U.S. Agency for International Development. *Leland Initiative: Africa Global
Information Infrastructure Gateway Project (Project No. 698-0565): Best
Practices for Policy Accommodation, Technology Transfer, and End-User
Applications of the Internet in the Developing World*, prepared by Jeff Bland,
Zoey Breslar, Jim Esselman, Dana Ireland, September 1996. http://pdf.usaid
.gov/pdf_docs/PNABZ059.PDF.

———. "USAID Leland Initiative: Africa Global Information Infrastructure
Project." USAID.gov, August 28, 2001. https://web.archive.org/web
/20011109164754/http://www.usaid.gov/leland/.

U.S. Bureau of Citizenship and Immigration Services Resource Information
Center. *Cameroon: Information on the Relationship between the Anglophone
and Francophone Communities.* United States Bureau of Citizenship and
Immigration Services, October 16, 2002. http://www.refworld.org/docid
/3f51eaad4.html.

U.S. Commission on Immigration Reform. *Becoming an American: Immigration
and Immigrant Policy: Report to Congress.* September 30, 1997. https://files.eric
.ed.gov/fulltext/ED424310.pdf.

———. *Legal Immigration: Setting Priorities.* June 1995. https://www.google.com
/books/edition/Legal_Immigration/Q9L_aXKrjIMC?hl=en&gbpv=0.

U.S. Department of Commerce. *Ancestry of the Population by State: 1980,
Supplementary Report PC80-S1-10.* Department of Commerce, Bureau of the
Census, April 1983. https://www.census.gov/content/dam/Census/library
/publications/1983/dec/pc80-s1-10.pdf.

U.S. Department of Homeland Security. *2019 Yearbook of Immigration Statistics.*
Washington, DC: U.S. Department of Homeland Security, Office of Immigration
Statistics, 2020. https://www.dhs.gov/immigration-statistics/yearbook/2019.

———. *Yearbook of Immigration Statistics: 2012.* Washington, DC: U.S. Department
of Homeland Security, Office of Immigration Statistics, 2013. https://www.dhs
.gov/yearbook-immigration-statistics-2012-legal-permanent-residents.

U.S. Department of Justice. *1996 Statistical Yearbook of the Immigration and
Naturalization Service.* Washington, DC: U.S. Department of Justice,
Immigration and Naturalization Service, 1997. https://www.dhs.gov/sites

/default/files/publications/immigration-statistics/yearbook/1996/ins
_yearbook_immigration_statistics_1996.pdf.

U.S. Department of State. *Public Diplomacy for the 21st Century.* U.S. Advisory
Commission on Public Diplomacy, 1995. https://web.archive.org/web
/20150715133442/http://www.state.gov/documents/organization/176339.pdf.

———. "Table VII, Immigrant Number Use for Visa Issuances and Adjustments of
Status in the Diversity Immigrant Category Fiscal Years 1995-2010." Previously
available at travel.state.gov, archived online here in part: https://web.archive
.org/web/20210612000645/https://travel.state.gov/content/dam/visas/Statistics
/FY2000%20table%20VII.pdf.

U.S. Department of State and the Broadcasting Board of Governors, Office of
Inspector General. "Memorandum Inspection Report: Diversity Visa Program,
Report Number ISP-CA-03-52," September 2003, 4. https://www.stateoig.gov
/system/files/37437.pdf.

U.S. Government Accountability Office. *Committee on Homeland Security, Report
to the Chairman, Border Security: Fraud Risks Complicate State's Ability to
Manage Diversity Visa Program,* H.R. Rep. No. 07-1174 (September 2007).
http://www.gao.gov/new.items/d071174.pdf.

U.S. National Defense Panel. *Transforming Defense: National Security in the
21st Century.* December 1997, ii. https://www.hsdl.org/?view&did=1834.

Hearings

U.S. Congress. House. Committee on Government Reform. *Federal Interagency
Data-Sharing and National Security: Hearing Before the Subcommittee on
National Security, Veterans Affairs, and International Relations.* 107th Cong.,
1st Sess. (July 24, 2001).

U.S. Congress. House. Committee on the Judiciary. *Diversity Visa Program:
Hearing Before the House Subcommittee on Immigration, Border Security, and
Claims.* 109th Cong., 1st Sess. (June 15, 2005).

———. *Diversity Visa Program and Its Susceptibility to Fraud and Abuse: Hearing
Before the Subcommittee on Immigration, Border Security, and Claims.* 108th Cong.,
2nd Sess. (April 29, 2004).

———. *Hearings Before the United States House Committee on the Judiciary,
Subcommittee No. 1.* 88th Cong., 2nd Sess. (1964).

———. *Immigration Act of 1989: Hearings Before the Subcommittee on Immigration,
Refugees, and International Law on S. 358, H.R. 672, H.R. 2448, and H.R. 2646.*
101st Cong., 1st Sess. (September 27, 1989).

———. *Immigration and Naturalization Service's (INS's) Interactions with Hesham
Mohamed Ali Hedayet: Hearing Before the Subcommittee on Immigration, Border
Security, and Claims.* 107th Cong., 2nd Sess. (October 9, 2002).

———. *Legal Immigration: Hearing Before the Subcommittee on Immigration,
Refugees, and International Law.* 99th Cong., 2nd Sess. (July 30, 1986).

———. *Legal Immigration Legislation: Hearing Before the Subcommittee on
Immigration, Refugees, and International Law.* 100th Cong., 2nd Sess. (June 21,
1988).

——. *Reform of Legal Immigration: Hearing Before the Subcommittee on Immigration, Refugees, and International Law of the Committee on the Judiciary, House of Representatives.* 100th Cong., 2nd Sess. (September 7 and September 16, 1988).

——. *Safe for America Act: Hearing Before the Subcommittee on Immigration Policy and Enforcement.* 112th Cong., 1st Sess. (April 5, 2011).

——. *Should Congress Raise the H-1B Cap? Hearing Before the Subcommittee on Immigration, Border Security, and Claims.* 109th Cong., 2nd Sess. (March 30, 2006).

U.S. Congress. House. Committee on Ways and Means. *U.S. Trade with Sub-Saharan Africa: Hearing Before the Subcommittee on Trade of the Committee on Ways and Means, House of Representatives.* 104th Cong., 2nd Sess. (August 1, 1996).

U.S. Congress. Senate. Committee on Foreign Relations. *Post-9/11 Visa Reforms and New Technology: Achieving the Necessary Security Improvements in a Global Environment: Hearing Before the Subcommittee on International Operations and Terrorism.* 108th Cong., 1st Sess. (October 23, 2003).

U.S. Congress. Senate. Committee on the Judiciary. *Legal Immigration Reforms on S.1611: Hearings Before the Subcommittee on Immigration and Refugee Affairs.* 100th Cong., 1st Sess. (October 23 and December 11, 1987).

Speeches, Correspondence, and News Releases

Clinton, Bill, National Security Council, Speechwriting Office, and Edward (Ted) Widmer. "Africa—Ghana [POTUS Address to the People of Ghana, March 23, 1998]." Clinton Digital Library. https://clinton.presidentiallibraries.us/items /show/11361.

Congressional Black Caucus. "CBC Chairman to Trump: Stop Pitting Black and Brown Immigrants against Each Other." News release, February 12, 2018. https://cbc.house.gov/news/documentsingle.aspx?DocumentID=841.

——. "CBC Statement on Senate Comprehensive Immigration Reform Legislation." April 19, 2013, https://cbc.house.gov/news/documentsingle.aspx ?DocumentID=93.

——. Letter from Cedric Richmond, Chair, to President Donald J. Trump. February 12, 2018, https://cbc.house.gov/uploadedfiles/cbc_letter_to_trump_on _pitting_black_and_brown_immigrants_against_each_other.pdf.

Department of State. Letter from Mary Elizabeth Taylor, Assistant Secretary, Bureau of Legislative Affairs, to Sen. Chris Van Hollen. February 22, 2019. https:// www.vanhollen.senate.gov/imo/media/doc/State%20Dept%20Response%20 to%20Oct%20Muslim%20Ban%20Letter.pdf.

Federal Communications Commission. "FCC Launches New Initiative to Promote Pro-Competitive Regulatory Policies in Developing Countries." News release, June 2, 1999. https://web.archive.org/web/20030802084255/http://www.fcc .gov/Bureaus/Miscellaneous/News_Releases/1999/nrmc9038.html.

Foote, Daniel. Resignation letter from U.S. special envoy for Haiti. September 22, 2021. https://www.washingtonpost.com/context/read-resignation-letter-from

-u-s-special-envoy-for-haiti-daniel-foote/3136ae0e-96e5-448e-9d12
-0e0cabfb3c0b/.

Gore, Al. Remarks. The Superhighway Summit. Royce Hall, UCLA, Los Angeles, California, January 11, 1994. https://clintonwhitehouse1.archives.gov/White _House/EOP/OVP/other/superhig.html.

Johnson, Lyndon B. "Commencement Address at Howard University: 'To Fulfill These Rights.'" Teaching American History, June 4, 1965. https://teaching americanhistory.org/library/document/commencement-address-at-howard -university-to-fulfill-these-rights/.

Napolitano, Janet. "Prepared Remarks by Secretary Napolitano on Immigration Reform at the Center for American Progress." U.S. Department of Homeland Security, November 13, 2009. https://www.dhs.gov/news/2009/11/13/secretary -napolitanos-speech-immigration-reform.

Reagan, Ronald. *Public Papers of the Presidents of the United States: Ronald Reagan, 1984*, 1600. https://www.google.com/books/edition/Public_Papers_of_the _Presidents_of_the_U/V-bcAwAAQBAJ?hl=en&gbpv=0.

Sierra Leone Embassy in Washington, DC. "Press Release March 3, 1998," March 3, 1998, Item 24. http://www.sierra-leone.org/GOSL/Embassy -Statements.pdf.

U.S. Citizenship and Immigration Services. "Secretary Mayorkas Designates Cameroon for Temporary Protected Status for 18 Months." News release, April 15, 2022. https://www.uscis.gov/newsroom/news-releases/secretary -mayorkas-designates-cameroon-for-temporary-protected-status-for-18 -months.

U.S. Congress. Letter from bicameral congressional coalition to President Biden and DHS Secretary Mayorkas urging TPS for Cameroon. November 2, 2021. https://www.vanhollen.senate.gov/news/press-releases/van-hollen-bass-lead -bicameral-letter-urging-the-administration-to-provide-protections-to -cameroonians-fleeing-violence-humanitarian-crisis.

———. "Lofgren, Johnson Introduce Bill to Designate Cameroon for Temporary Protected Status." News release, October 12, 2021. https://lofgren.house.gov /media/press-releases/lofgren-johnson-introduce-bill-designate-cameroon -temporary-protected-status.

U.S. Department of Justice. "Sayfullo Saipov Charged with Terrorism and Murder in Aid of Racketeering in Connection with Lower Manhattan Truck Attack." News release, November 21, 2017. https://www.justice.gov/opa/pr/sayfullo -saipov-charged-terrorism-and-murder-aid-racketeering-connection-lower -manhattan.

U.S. Department of State. "Diversity Immigrant Visa Lottery Results Released." News release, September 11, 1997.

U.S. Embassy in Freetown Sierra Leone. Consular Section. "General Consular Information on Visas and Applications." June 27, 2005. https://web.archive.org /web/20100527095238/http://freetown.usembassy.gov/wi052705.html.

The White House, Office of the Press Secretary. "President Obama Launches 'Educate to Innovate' Campaign for Excellence in Science, Technology,

Engineering & Math (Stem) Education." November 23, 2009. https://
obamawhitehouse.archives.gov/the-press-office/president-obama-launches
-educate-innovate-campaign-excellence-science-technology-en.

———. "Remarks by the President to the Ghanaian Parliament," July 11, 2009,
Accra, Ghana, https://obamawhitehouse.archives.gov/the-press-office/remarks
-president-ghanaian-parliament.

———. "Remarks by the President on Comprehensive Immigration Reform in El
Paso, Texas." May 10, 2011. https://obamawhitehouse.archives.gov/the-press
-office/2011/05/10/remarks-president-comprehensive-immigration-reform-el
-paso-texas.

———. "Remarks of President Barack Obama—State of the Union Address As
Delivered." January 13, 2016. https://obamawhitehouse.archives.gov/the-press
-office/2016/01/12/remarks-president-barack-obama-%E2%80%93-prepared
-delivery-state-union-address.

Other Primary Sources

Clinton Digital Library. "Kente Robe." https://clinton.presidentiallibraries.us
/items/show/101784.

Ahidjo, Ahmadou. *Contribution à la Construction Nationale.* Paris: Présence
Africaine, 1964.

Ahmed, Syed Riaz. *The Lottery.* Denver, CO: Outskirts Press, 2016.

Annan, James. *My U.S. Adventure.* Self-published, Accra, Ghana, 2012.

AP Archive. "Ghana: Thousands Turn Out to Welcome U.S. President Clinton."
March 23, 1998. Posted July 21, 2015. YouTube video, 2:52. https://www
.youtube.com/watch?v=5RW8IDf3N4s.

Biden, Joe R. Campaign Website. 2020 Election. "The Biden Plan for Securing Our
Values as a Nation of Immigrants." https://joebiden.com/immigration/.

Campbell, K. K. "A Net.Conspiracy So Immense . . ." October 1, 1994. https://web
.archive.org/web/20210615070247/http://bella.media.mit.edu/people/foner
/Yenta/green-card-lawyers.html.

Computer History Museum Collections, https://www.computerhistory.org
/collections/search/.

Green Card. Directed by Peter Weir. 1990; Burbank, CA: Touchstone Pictures,
2003. DVD.

Jones, Clinton J. *Enter & Win the Green Card Lottery.* Middletown, DE: BookSurge,
LLC, 2005.

Kananda, John K. *Green Card Lottery and the American Dream.* Bloomington, IN:
AuthorHouse, 2007.

King, Martin Luther, Jr. "The Birth of a New Nation." Sermon delivered at Dexter
Avenue Baptist Church, April 7, 1957. https://kinginstitute.stanford.edu/king-papers
/documents/birth-new-nation-sermon-delivered-dexter-avenue-baptist-church.

Lord Kitchener. "Birth of Ghana." In *The Ghana Reader: History, Culture, Politics*,
edited by Kwasi Konadu and Clifford C. Campbell, 295–297. Durham, NC: Duke
University Press, 2016.

Lumumba, Patrice. "Speech at the Ceremony of the Proclamation of the Congo's Independence." June 30, 1960. https://www.marxists.org/subject/africa /lumumba/1960/06/independence.htm.

Mayja Money Facebook Page. https://www.facebook.com/permalink.php ?storyfbid=734652466576473&id=562971710411217.

Modenine, feat. Sage Hasson. "Green Passport." *Yes We Can—Songs about Leaving Africa*. Germany: Out Here Records, 2010. https://outhererecords.bandcamp .com/track/green-passport-modenine-feat-sage-hasson.

Nkem Owoh. "I Go Chop Your Dollar." 2005. https://genius.com/Nkem-owoh-i-go -chop-your-dollar-lyrics.

Nkrumah, Kwame. "I Speak of Freedom." 1961. Modern History Sourcebook. https://sourcebooks.fordham.edu/mod/1961nkrumah.asp.

Obama, Barack. Race Speech at the Constitution Center. March 18, 2008. https:// constitutioncenter.org/amoreperfectunion/.

Richards, Paul J. Photograph of Bill Clinton and Jerry John Rawlings, March 23, 1998. https://www.gettyimages.com/detail/news-photo/president-bill-clinton-is -shown-some-highlighted-dancers-by-news-photo/510599320?adppopup=true.

TRAC Immigration. "ICE Detainees." https://trac.syr.edu/immigration/detentionstats /pop_agen_table.html.

Trump, President Donald J. Twitter Archive, https://www.thetrumparchive.com/.

Usenet Archive, Google Groups

Uwadiae, Deba. *Coming to America: Early Life in America and Citizenship*. Self-published, 2020.

Wanlov the Kubolor. "Green Card." *Green Card*. November 15, 2007. Pidgen Music. https://wanlov.bandcamp.com/.

Wikileaks Cables.

Books, Articles, and Reports

Ackerman, Spencer. *Reign of Terror: How the 9/11 Era Destabilized America and Produced Trump*. New York: Penguin Publishing, 2021.

Adebajo, Adekeye. "The U.S. and Africa: The Rise and Fall of Obamamania." *Great Decisions* (2015): 55–64. https://www.jstor.org/stable/44214794.

Adedze, Agbenyega. "Nigeria: A Philatelic Essay." *Journal of West African History* 7, no. 1 (2021): 101–135. muse.jhu.edu/article/802211.

Adepoju, Aderanti. "Patterns of Migration in West Africa." In *At Home in the World? International Migration and Development in Contemporary Ghana and West Africa*, edited by Takyiwaa Manuh, 24–54. Accra, Ghana: Sub-Saharan Publishers, 2005.

Adichie, Chimamanda Ngozi. *The Thing around Your Neck*. New York: First Anchor Books, 2009.

Adjepong, Anima. *Afropolitan Projects: Redefining Blackness, Sexualities, and Culture from Houston to Accra*. Chapel Hill, NC: UNC Press, 2021.

Ahlman, Jeffrey. *Kwame Nkrumah: Visions of Liberation*. Athens: Ohio University Press, 2021.

Aidoo, Kobina, and Ryan C. Briggs. "Underpowered: Rolling Blackouts in Africa Disproportionately Hurt the Poor." *African Studies Review* 62, no. 3 (September 2019): 112–131.

Akalou, Wolde-Michael. "Ethiopians and Afghans in the United States: A Comparative Perspective." *Northeast African Studies* 11, no. 1 (1989): 55–73. http://www.jstor.org/stable/43660262.

Akurang-Parry, Kwabena. "Obama's Visit as a Signifier of Ghanaians' 'Colonial Mentality.'" In *The Ghana Reader: History, Culture, Politics,* edited by Kwasi Konadu and Clifford C. Campbell, 440–446. Durham, NC: Duke University Press, 2016.

Akyeampong, Emmanuel. "Africans in the Diaspora: The Diaspora and Africa." *African Affairs* 99 (2000): 183–215.

Almeida, Linda Dowling. *Irish Immigrants in New York City, 1945-1995.* Bloomington: Indiana University Press, 2001.

Alpes, Maybritt Jill. "Bushfalling at All Cost: The Economy of Migratory Knowledge in Anglophone Cameroon African Diaspora." *African Diaspora* 5 (2012): 90–115.

———. "Law and the Credibility of Migration Brokers: The Case of Emigration Dynamics in Cameroon." International Migration Institute Working Papers, Paper 80, December 2013.

American Civil Liberties Union. "Analysis of Immigration Detention Policies." Accessed August 10, 2022. https://www.aclu.org/other/analysis-immigration -detention-policies.

American Immigration Council. "A Guide to S.744: Understanding the 2013 Immigration Bill." July 10, 2013. https://www.americanimmigrationcouncil .org/research/guide-s744-understanding-2013-senate-immigration-bill.

———. "A Guide to Title 42 Expulsions at the Border." October 15, 2021. https:// www.americanimmigrationcouncil.org/research/guide-title-42-expulsions -border.

Amin, Julius A. *The Peace Corps in Cameroon.* Kent, OH: Kent State University Press, 1992.

Amnesty International. *Cameroon's Secret Torture Chambers: Human Rights Violations and War Crimes in the Fight against Boko Haram.* 2017. https://www .amnesty.org/en/wp-content/uploads/2021/05/AFR1765362017ENGLISH.pdf.

Andreas, Peter. "The Escalation of U.S. Immigration Control in the Post-NAFTA Era." *Political Science Quarterly* 113, no. 4 (Winter 1998–1999): 561–615.

Apter, Andrew. "IBB=419: Nigerian Democracy and the Politics of Illusion." In *Civil Society and the Political Imagination in Africa: Critical Perspectives,* edited by J. Comaroff and J. Comaroff, 267–307. Chicago: University of Chicago Press, 1999.

Arthur, John A. *African Diaspora Identities: Negotiating Culture in Transnational Migration.* Lanham, MD: Lexington Books, 2010.

Arthur, Peter. "The State, Private Sector Development, and Ghana's 'Golden Age of Business.'" *African Studies Review* 49, no. 1 (April 2006): 31–50.

Asch, Chris Myers, and George Derek Musgrove. *Chocolate City: A History of Race and Democracy in the Nation's Capital.* Chapel Hill: University of North Carolina Press, 2017.

Asiedu, Alex Boakye, and Godwin Arku. "The Rise of Gated Housing Estates in Ghana: Empirical Insights from Three Communities in Metropolitan Accra." *Journal of Housing and the Built Environment* 24, no. 3 (September 2009): 227–247.

Assan, Joseph Kweku, and Dinar D. Kharisma. "Political Economy of Internal Migration and Labor-Seeking Behavior of Poor Youth in Ghana." *Ghana Studies* 22 (2019): 3–35. https://doi.org/10.1353/ghs.2019.0001.

Association for Diplomatic Studies & Training. "Johnny Young—from Abject Poverty to Chief of Mission." Accessed August 10, 2022. https://adst.org/oral -history/fascinating-figures/johnny-young-from-abject-poverty-to-chief-of -mission/.

Awasom, Nico Fru. "Language and Citizenship in Anglophone Cameroon." In *Making Nations, Creating Strangers: States and Citizenship in Africa,* edited by Paul Nugent, Daniel Hammett, and Sara Dorman, 143–160. Leiden: Brill, 2007.

Ayee, Joseph RA. "The December 1996 General Elections in Ghana." *Electoral Studies* 16, no. 3 (1997): 416–427. https://doi.org/10.1016/S0261-3794(97)84379-X.

Ayelazuno, Jasper Abembia. *Neoliberal Globalisation and Resistance from Below: Why the Subalterns Resist in Bolivia and Not in Ghana.* London: Taylor & Francis, 2018.

Bada, Xóchitl, Jonathan Fox, and Jane Guskin. "Immigrant Rights Protests— Spring 2006." Mapping American Social Movements Project, University of Washington. Accessed August 10, 2022. https://depts.washington.edu/moves /2006_immigrant_rights.shtml.

Bailey, Anne C. *The Weeping Time: Memory and the Largest Slave Auction in American History.* New York: Cambridge University Press, 2017.

Baker, Pauline H., and John J. Stremlau. "Nigeria: U.S.-European Stakes in Africa's Largest State." In *Transatlantic Tensions: The United States, Europe, and Problem Countries,* edited by Richard Haass, 179–204. Washington, DC: Brookings Institution Press, 1999.

Batema, Kodjo Nicolas, and Charles Piot. *The Fixer: Visa Lottery Chronicles.* Durham, NC: Duke University Press, 2019.

Battisti, Danielle. *Whom We Shall Welcome: Italian Americans and Immigration Reform, 1945-1965.* New York: Fordham University Press, 2019.

Bayart, Jean-Francois. *Global Subjects: A Political Critique of Globalization.* Translated by Andrew Brown. Cambridge, UK: Polity Press, 2007.

Belew, Kathleen. *Bring the War Home: The White Power Movement and Paramilitary America.* Cambridge, MA: Harvard University Press, 2019.

Bell, Karen B. "Developing a 'Sense of Community': U.S. Cultural Diplomacy and the Place of Africa during the Early Cold War Period, 1953-64." In *The United States and West Africa,* edited by Alusine Jalloh and Toyin Falola, 125–146. Rochester, NY: University of Rochester Press, 2008.

Berry, Daina Ramey, and Kali Nicole Gross. *A Black Women's History of the United States*. Boston: Beacon Press, 2020.

Berschinski, Robert G. *AFRICOM'S Dilemma: The "Global War on Terrorism," "Capacity Building," Humanitarianism, and the Future of U.S. Security Policy in Africa*. Carlisle, PA: Strategic Studies Institute, U.S. Army War College, November 2007. https://www.hsdl.org/?view&did=481206.

Bier, David. "Build Back Better Act Immigration Provisions—Summary and Analysis." *CATO at Liberty* (blog), November 30, 2021. https://www.cato.org/blog/build-back-better-act-immigration-provisions-summary-analysis.

Billig, Michael. *Banal Nationalism*. London: Sage Publications, 1995.

Black, William K. *The Best Way to Rob a Bank Is to Own One: How Corporate Executives and Politicians Looted the S&L Industry*. Austin: University of Texas Press, 2005.

Blalock, Garrick, Vrinda Kadiyali, and Daniel H. Simon. "The Impact of 9/11 on Road Fatalities: The Other Lives Lost to Terrorism." *SSRN Working Paper Series*. February 10, 2005. doi:10.2139/ssrn.677549.

Blum, Carolyn Patty. "The Settlement of American Baptist Churches v. Thornburgh: Landmark Victory for Central American Asylum-Seekers." *International Journal of Refugee Law* 3, no. 2 (January 1991). https://lawcat.berkeley.edu/record/1114072?ln=en.

Blyden, Nemata Amelia Ibitayo. *African Americans and Africa: A New History*. New Haven, CT: Yale University Press, 2019.

Bobadilla, Eladio Benjamin. "'One People without Borders': The Lost Roots of the Immigrants' Rights Movement, 1954–2006." PhD diss., Duke University, 2019.

Bon Tempo, Carl J. *Americans at the Gate: The United States and Refugees during the Cold War*. Princeton, NJ: Princeton University Press, 2008.

Bonilla-Silva, Eduardo. *Racism without Racists: Color-Blind Racism and the Persistence of Racial Inequality in the United States*. Lanham, MD: Rowman & Littlefield, 2006.

Borstelmann, Thomas. *Apartheid's Reluctant Uncle: The United States and Southern Africa in the Early Cold War*. New York: Oxford University Press, 1993.

Bouie, Jamelle. "White Won." *Slate.com*, November 9, 2016. https://slate.com/news-and-politics/2016/11/white-won.html.

Bowden, Mark. *Black Hawk Down: A Story of Modern War*. New York: Grove Press, 1999.

Bredeloup, Sylvie. "The Migratory Adventure as Moral Experience." In *Hope and Uncertainty in Contemporary African Migration*, edited by Nauja Kleist and Dorte Thorsen, 134–153. New York: Routledge, 2017.

Brown, Wendy. *Walled States, Waning Sovereignty*. New York: Zone Books, 2010.

Brunton, Finn. *Spam: A Shadow History of the Internet*. Cambridge, MA: Massachusetts Institute of Technology Press, 2013.

Brydon, Lynne. "'With a Little Bit of Luck . . .' Coping with Adjustment in Urban Ghana, 1975-90." *Africa: Journal of the International African Institute* 69, no. 3 (1999): 366–385.

Burrell, Jenna. *Invisible Users: Youth in the Internet Cafes of Urban Ghana.* Cambridge, MA: Massachusetts Institute of Technology Press, 2012.

"Cameroon: A Transition in Crisis," *Article 19: Global Campaign for Free Expression*, October 1997. http://www.refworld.org/pdfid/4753d3aa0.pdf.

Campbell, John. *Nigeria: Dancing on the Brink.* Lanham, MD: Rowman & Littlefield, 2011.

Canter, Laurence A., and Martha S. Siegel. *How to Make a Fortune on the Information Superhighway.* New York: Harper Collins, 1994.

———. *U.S. Immigration Made Easy: The Insider's Guide.* Tucson, AZ: Sheridan Chandler, 1990.

Caplan, Lincoln. "Thurgood Marshall and the Need for Affirmative Action." *New Yorker*, December 9, 2015. https://www.newyorker.com/news/news-desk /thurgood-marshall-and-the-need-for-affirmative-action.

Capó, Julio, Jr. "The White House Used This Moment as Proof the U.S. Should Cut Immigration. Its Real History Is More Complicated." *Time*, August 4, 2017. https://time.com/4888381/immigration-act-mariel-boatlift-history/.

Capps, Randy, Kristen McCabe, and Michael Fix. *Diverse Streams: African Migration to the United States,* Migration Policy Institute, April 2012. https:// www.migrationpolicy.org/pubs/CBI-AfricanMigration.pdf.

Carter, Niambi Michele. *American While Black: African Americans, Immigration, and the Limits of Citizenship.* New York: Oxford University Press, 2019.

Chalfin, Brenda. *Neoliberal Frontiers: An Ethnography of Sovereignty in West Africa.* Chicago: University of Chicago Press, 2010.

Chavez, Leo R. *The Latino Threat: Constructing Immigrants, Citizens, and the Nation.* 2nd ed. Stanford, CA: Stanford University Press, 2013.

Chikanda, Abel, and Julie Susanne Morris. "Assessing the Integration Outcomes of African Immigrants in the United States." *African Geographical Review* 40 (2021): 1–18. doi:10.1080/19376812.2020.1744455.

Chishti, Muzaffar, Sarah Pierce, and Jessica Bolter. "The Obama Record on Deportations: Deporter in Chief or Not?" *Migration Information Source*, January 26, 2017. https://www.migrationpolicy.org/article/obama-record deportations-deporter-chief-or-not.

Clarke, Liz, and Trevor R. Getz. *Abina and the Important Men: A Graphic History.* New York: Oxford University Press, 2016.

Coates, Ta-Nehisi. "The First White President." *The Atlantic*, October 2017. https://web.archive.org/web/20220407074816/https://www.theatlantic.com /magazine/archive/2017/10/the-first-white-president-ta-nehisi-coates/537909/.

Cohen, Elizabeth F. *Illegal: How America's Lawless Immigration Regime Threatens Us All.* New York: Basic Books, 2020.

Cohen, Lizabeth. *A Consumers' Republic: The Politics of Mass Consumption in Postwar America.* New York: Alfred A. Knopf, 2003.

Coleman, Sarah. *The Walls Within: The Politics of Immigration in Modern America.* Princeton, NJ: Princeton University Press, 2021.

Conklin, Alice L. *A Mission to Civilize: The Republican Idea of Empire in France and West Africa, 1895-1930.* Stanford, CA: Stanford University Press, 1997.

Cooper, Frederick. *Africa in the World: Capitalism, Empire, Nation-State.* Cambridge, MA: Harvard University Press, 2014.

——. *Africa Since 1940: The Past of the Present.* 2nd ed. Cambridge: Cambridge University Press, 2019.

Cusack, Igor. "Tiny Transmitters of Nationalist and Colonial Ideology: The Postage Stamps of Portugal and Its Empire." *Nations and Nationalism* 11, no. 4 (October 2005): 591–612.

Daly, Samuel Fury Childs. "Ghana Must Go: Nativism and the Politics of Expulsion in West Africa, 1969–1985," *Past & Present,* 2022. doi: https://doi.org/10.1093/pastj/gtac006.

——. *A History of the Republic of Biafra: Law, Crime, and the Nigerian Civil War.* Cambridge: Cambridge University Press, 2020.

Davis, Todd M. *Open Doors, 1995-1996: Report on International Education Exchange.* New York: Institute of International Exchange, 1996. https://files.eric.ed.gov/fulltext/ED404959.pdf.

de Latour, Eliane. "Heros du Retour." *Critique Internationale* 2, no. 19 (2003): 171–189.

DeLancey, Mark W., and Mark Dike DeLancey. *Historical Dictionary of the Republic of Cameroon (Historical Dictionaries of Africa).* 3rd ed., no. 81. Lanham, MD: Scarecrow Press, 2000.

Delmont, Matthew. "Rethinking 'Busing' in Boston." Blog of the National Museum of American History, December 27, 2016. https://americanhistory.si.edu/de/blog/rethinking-busing-boston.

Deltombe, Thomas. "The Forgotten Cameroon War." *Jacobin Magazine,* December 10, 2016. https://jacobinmag.com/2016/12/cameroon-france-colonialism-war-resistance.

Deltombe, Thomas, Manuel Domergue, and Jacob Tatsitsa. *Kamerun! Une Guerre Cachée Aux Origines de La Françafrique (1948 - 1971).* Paris: La Découverte, 2011.

Deslippe, Dennis A. "'Do Whites Have Rights?' White Detroit Policemen and 'Reverse Discrimination' Protests in the 1970s." *Journal of American History* 91 (December 2004): 932–960.

Dickerson, Caitlin. "An American Catastrophe: The Secret History of the U.S. government's family separation policy," *The Atlantic,* September 2022, https://www.theatlantic.com/magazine/archive/2022/09/trump-administration-family-separation-policy-immigration/670604.

Donnelly, Brian. "Foreign Affairs, Drug Interdiction, and Immigration." *Suffolk Transnational Law Review* 21, no. 2 (1998): 269–292.

Dow, Mark. *American Gulag: Inside U.S. Immigration Prisons.* Berkeley: University of California Press, 2004.

Dudziak, Mary L. *Cold War Civil Rights: Race and the Image of American Democracy.* Princeton, NJ: Princeton University Press, 2011.

Elkins, Alex. "The Origins of Stop-and-Frisk." *Jacobin Magazine,* May 2015. https://www.jacobinmag.com/2015/05/stop-and-frisk-dragnet-ferguson-baltimore.

Ellis, Stephen. "Tuning in to Pavement Radio." *African Affairs* 88, no. 352 (July 1989): 321–330.

Eriksen, Thomas Hylland. "Place, Kinship and the Case for Non-ethnic Nations." *Nations & Nationalism* 10, nos. 1/2 (January 2004): 49–62. doi:10.1111/j.1354-5078.2004.00154.x.

Fahy, James. "The Dark Side of America's 'Train, Advise, and Assist' Missions." *Task & Purpose*, July 11, 2018. https://taskandpurpose.com/opinion/cameroon -train-advise-assist-missions/?amp.

Faist, Thomas, and Jürgen Gerdes. "Dual Citizenship in an Age of Mobility." Migration Policy Institute, Washington, DC, 2008.

Falola, Toyin, and Matthew M. Heaton. *A History of Nigeria*. Cambridge: Cambridge University Press, 2008.

Feldstein, Steven. "Do Terrorist Trends in Africa Justify the U.S. Military's Expansion?" Carnegie Endowment for International Peace, February 9, 2018. https://carnegieendowment.org/2018/02/09/do-terrorist-trends-in-africa -justify-u.s.-military-s-expansion-pub-75476.

Ferguson, James. *Global Shadows: Africa in the Neoliberal World Order*. Durham, NC: Duke University Press, 2006.

Fernández-Kelly, Patricia, and Douglas S. Massey. "Borders for Whom! The Role of NAFTA in Mexico-U.S. Migration." *Annals of the American Academy of Political and Social Science* 610 (March 2007): 98–118.

Fine, Ben, and Kwabia Boateng. "Labour & Employment under Structural Adjustment." In *Economic Reforms in Ghana: The Miracle and the Mirage*, edited by Ernest Aryeetey, Jane Harrigan, and Machiko Nissanke, 227–245. New York: Oxford University Press, 2000.

Fix, Michael E., and Jeffrey S. Passel. *Immigration and Immigrants: Setting the Record Straight*. Washington, DC: Urban Institute, 1994.

Fleegler, Robert L. *Ellis Island Nation: Immigration Policy and American Identity in the Twentieth Century*. Philadelphia: University of Pennsylvania Press, 2013.

Foster, William, Seymour Goodman, Eric Osiakwan, and Adam Bernstein. "Global Diffusion of the Internet IV: The Internet in Ghana." *Communications of the Association for Information Systems* 13, article 38 (June 2004): 1–46. http:// citeseerx.ist.psu.edu/viewdoc/download?doi=10.1.1.195.150&rep=rep1&type_pdf.

Fourchard, Laurent. "Between World History and State Formation: New Perspectives on Africa's Cities." *Journal of African History* 52, no. 2 (July 2011): 223–248.

Fraser, James, and Edward Kick. "The Interpretive Repertoires of Whites on Race-Targeted Policies: Claims Making of Reverse Discrimination." *Sociological Perspectives* 43, no. 1 (Spring 2000): 13–28.

Frei, Bettina Anja. *Sociality Revisited? The Use of the Internet and Mobile Phones in Urban Cameroon*. Cameroon: Langaa RPCIG, 2013.

Frère, Marie-Soleil, and Pierre Englebert. "Briefing: Burkina Faso—the Fall of Blaise Compaoré." *African Affairs* 114, no. 455 (2015): 295–307.

Fuller, Harcourt. *Building the Ghanaian Nation-State: Kwame Nkrumah's Symbolic Nationalism*. New York: Palgrave Macmillan, 2014.

——. "*Civitatis Ghaniensis Conditor*: Kwame Nkrumah, Symbolic Nationalism and the Iconography of Ghanaian Money, 1957—the Golden Jubilee." *Nations and Nationalism* 14, no. 3 (July 2008): 520–541.

Garcia, Ann. "Making Sense of the Senate and House's Visions of Immigration Reform." Center for American Progress, December 9, 2013. https://www.americanprogress.org/article/making-sense-of-the-senate-and-houses-visions-of-immigration-reform/.

García, María Cristina. "National (in)Security and the Immigration Act of 1996," *Modern American History* 1, no. 2 (2018): 233–236. doi: 10.1017/mah.2018.6

——. *The Refugee Challenge in Post-Cold War America*. New York: Oxford University Press, 2017.

Gerits, Frank. "'When the Bull Elephants Fight': Kwame Nkrumah, Non-alignment, and Pan-Africanism as an Interventionist Ideology in the Global Cold War (1957-66)." *International History Review* 37, no. 5 (2015): 951–969.

Geschiere, Peter. *The Perils of Belonging: Autochtony, Citizenship, and Exclusion in Africa & Europe*. Chicago: University of Chicago Press, 2009.

Getachew, Adom. *Worldmaking after Empire: The Rise and Fall of Self-Determination*. Princeton, NJ: Princeton University Press, 2019.

Gettinger, Dan. "The American Drone Base in Cameroon." Center for the Study of the Drone at Bard College, February 21, 2016. https://dronecenter.bard.edu/drone-base-cameroon/.

Getz, Trevor R. *The Long Nineteenth Century, 1750-1914: Crucible of Modernity*. London: Bloomsbury Publishing, 2018.

Gimpel, James P., and James R. Edwards Jr. *The Congressional Politics of Immigration Reform*. Boston: Allyn and Bacon, 1999.

Gleijeses, Piero. *Conflicting Missions: Havana, Washington, and Africa, 1959-1976*. Chapel Hill: University of North Carolina Press, 2002.

——. *Visions of Freedom: Havana, Washington, Pretoria, and the Struggle for Southern Africa, 1976-1991*. Chapel Hill: University of North Carolina Press, 2013.

Goodman, Adam. *The Deportation Machine: America's Long History of Expelling Immigrants*. Princeton, NJ: Princeton University Press, 2020.

Goodman, Carly. "Unmaking the Nation of Immigrants: How John Tanton's Network of Organizations Transformed Policy and Politics." In *A Field Guide to White Supremacy*, edited by Kathleen Belew and Ramón A. Gutiérrez, 203–219. Oakland, CA: University of California Press, 2021.

Grandin, Greg. *The End of the Myth: From the Frontier to the Border Wall in the Mind of America*. New York: Henry Holt, 2019.

Grant, Patrick A. "Coming to America with Eyes Wide Shut." In *Foreign-Born African Americans: Silenced Voices in the Discourse of Race*, edited by Festus E. Obiakor and Patrick A. Grant, 91–102. New York: Nova, 2005.

Grant, Richard. "The Emergence of Gated Communities in a West African Context: Evidence from Greater Accra, Ghana." *Urban Geography* 26, no. 8 (2005): 661–683. http://dx.doi.org/10.2747/0272-3638.26.8.661.

Greer, Christina M. *Black Ethnics: Race, Immigration, and the Pursuit of the American Dream.* Oxford: Oxford University Press, 2013.

Grubbs, Larry. *Secular Missionaries: Americans and African Development in the 1960s.* Amherst: University of Massachusetts Press, 2009.

Guyer, Jane. *Marginal Gains: Monetary Transactions in Atlantic Africa.* Chicago: University of Chicago Press, 2004.

Hailu, Tekleab Elos, Bernadette M. Mendoza, K. E. Maria Lahman, and Veronica M. Richard. "Lived Experiences of Diversity Visa Lottery Immigrants in the United States." *Qualitative Report* (December 2012): 1–17.

Halter, Marilyn, and Violet Showers Johnson. *American & African: West Africans in Post-Civil Rights America.* New York: New York University Press, 2014.

Hamilton, Kimberly, Patrick Simon, and Clara Veniard. "The Challenge of French Diversity." *Migration Information Source,* November 1, 2004. http://www.migrationpolicy.org/article/challenge-french-diversity.

Hamilton, Tod G. *Immigration and the Remaking of Black America.* New York: Russell Sage Foundation, 2019.

Hart, Jennifer. *Ghana on the Go: African Mobility in the Age of Motor Transportation.* Bloomington: Indiana University Press, 2016.

——. "'NIFA NIFA': Technopolitics, Mobile Workers, and the Ambivalence of Decline in Acheampong's Ghana." *African Economic History* 44 (2016): 181–201. http://www.jstor.org/stable/44329659.

Hartman, Saidiya. *Lose Your Mother: A Journey along the Atlantic Slave Route.* New York: Farrar, Straus and Giroux, 2008.

Hegener, Michiel. "Telecommunications in Africa." Published on the web, September 24, 1996. http://www.nettime.org/nettime/DOCS/1/05(1).html.

Henckaerts, Jean-Marie. *Mass Expulsion in Modern International Law and Practice.* Boston: Martinus Nijhoff, 1985.

Herbst, Jeffrey. *States and Power in Africa: Comparative Lessons in Authority and Control.* Princeton, NJ: Princeton University Press, 2000.

Herrera, Jack. "Black Immigrants Matter." *The Nation,* March 24, 2021. https://www.thenation.com/article/society/black-immigrants-asylum-deportation/.

Hirota, Hidetaka. *Expelling the Poor: Atlantic Seaboard States and the Nineteenth-Century Origins of American Immigration Policy.* New York: Oxford University Press, 2017.

Holderness, Mike. "Who Are the World's Information Poor?" In *Cyberspace Divide: Equality, Agency and Policy in the Information Society,* edited by Brian D. Loader, 35–56. London: Routledge, 1998.

Holsey, Bayo. "Black Atlantic Visions: History, Race, and Transnationalism in Ghana." *Cultural Anthropology* 28, no. 3 (2013): 504–518.

——. "Slavery and the Making of Black Atlantic History." In *The Ghana Reader: History, Culture, Politics,* edited by Kwasi Konadu and Clifford C. Campbell, 374–378. Durham, NC: Duke University Press, 2016.

Hong, Jane H. *Opening the Gates to Asia: A Transpacific History of How America Repealed Asian Exclusion.* Chapel Hill: University of North Carolina Press, 2019.

Hopkins-Hayakawa, Sachie. "Cameroonians General Strike for Democratic Elections, 1991." Global Nonviolent Action Database, February 28, 2011. https://nvdatabase.swarthmore.edu/content/cameroonians-general-strike -democratic-elections-1991.

HoSang, Daniel Martinez. *Racial Propositions: Ballot Initiatives and the Making of Postwar California*. Berkeley: University of California Press, 2010.

———. *A Wider Type of Freedom: How Struggles for Racial Justice Liberate Everyone*. Oakland: University of California Press, 2021.

Ignatiev, Noel. *How the Irish Became White*. New York: Routledge, 2008.

Imakhüs, Seestah. "The Return through the Door of No Return." In *The Ghana Reader: History, Culture, Politics*, edited by Kwasi Konadu and Clifford C. Campbell, 379–383. Durham, NC: Duke University Press, 2016.

International Crisis Group. "Cameroon." Accessed August 10, 2022. https://www .crisisgroup.org/africa/central-africa/cameroon.

Jacob, Walter P. "Diversity Visas: Muddled Thinking and Pork Barrel Politics." *Georgetown Immigration Law Review* 6 (1992): 297–343.

Jacobs, Meg. *Pocketbook Politics: Economic Citizenship in Twentieth Century America*. Princeton, NJ: Princeton University Press, 2005.

Jacobson, Matthew Frye. *Roots Too: White Ethnic Revival in Post-Civil Rights America*. Cambridge, MA: Harvard University Press, 2006.

———. *Whiteness of a Different Color*. Cambridge, MA: Harvard University Press, 1999.

Jacobson, Robin Dale. *The New Nativism: Proposition 187 and the Debate over Immigration*. Minneapolis: University of Minnesota Press, 2008.

Johnson, Matthew. *Undermining Racial Justice: How One University Embraced Inclusion and Inequality*. Ithaca, NY: Cornell University Press, 2020.

Johnson, Violet Showers. "The Black Presence in U.S. Immigration History." In *A Nation of Immigrants Reconsidered: U.S. Society in an Age of Restriction, 1924-1965*, edited by Maddalena Marinari, Madeline Y. Hsu, and Maria Cristina Garcia, 273–283. Urbana: University of Illinois Press, 2018.

———. "When Blackness Stings: African and Afro-Caribbean Immigrants, Race, and Racism in Late Twentieth-Century America." *Journal of American Ethnic History* 36, no. 1 (2016): 31–62. https://doi.org/10.5406/jamerethnhist.36.1 .0031.

Johnson, Walter. "The Largest Human Zoo in World History." *Laphrams Quarterly*, April 14, 2020. https://www.laphamsquarterly.org/roundtable/largest-human -zoo-world-history.

Jones, Christopher M. "The Foreign Policy Bureaucracy in a New Era." In *After the End: Making U.S. Foreign Policy in the Post-Cold War World*, edited by James M. Scott, 57–88. Durham, NC: Duke University Press, 1998.

Joseph, Richard. "At Home Abroad: Human Capital and Ghana's Development." In *At Home in the World? International Migration and Development in Contemporary Ghana and West Africa*, edited by Takyiwaa Manuh, 277–291. Accra, Ghana: Sub-Saharan Publishers, 2005.

Jua, Nantang. "Differential Responses to Disappearing Transitional Pathways: Redefining Possibility among Cameroonian Youths." *African Studies Review* 43, no. 2 (September 2003):13–36.

Kaplan, Amy. "Homeland Insecurities: Reflections on Language and Space." *Radical History Review* 2003, no. 85 (Winter 2003): 82–93. https://doi.org/10.1215/01636545-2003-85-82.

Katznelson, Ira. *When Affirmative Action Was White: An Untold History of Racial Inequality in Twentieth-Century America.* New York: W. W. Norton, 2006.

Kelsall, Tim. *Business, Politics, and the State in Africa: Challenging the Orthodoxies on Growth and Transformation.* London: Zed Books, 2013.

Kennedy, John F. *A Nation of Immigrants.* New York: Anti-Defamation League and Popular Library, 1964.

Keogh, Dermot, Finbar O'Shea, and Carmel Quinlan, eds. *The Lost Decade: Ireland in the 1950s.* Douglas Village, Cork, Ireland: Mercier, 2004.

Kleist, Nauja, and Dorte Thorsen, eds. *Hope and Uncertainty in Contemporary African Migration.* New York: Routledge, 2017. https://library.oapen.org/bitstream/handle/20.500.12657/48483/9781317335481.pdf;jsessionid=E25391C F3BF6748742B4972C366AFF08?sequence=1.

Kobo, Ousman. "'We Are Citizens, Too': The Politics of Citizenship in Independent Ghana." *Journal of Modern African Studies* 48, no. 1 (March 2010): 67–94.

Konings, Piet, and Francis B. Nyamnjoh. "The Anglophone Problem in Cameroon." *Journal of Modern African Studies* 35, no. 2 (June 1997): 207–229.

Kunz, Rahel. *The Political Economy of Global Remittances: Gender, Governmentality and Neoliberalism.* New York: Routledge, 2013.

Law, Anna O. "The Diversity Visa Lottery—a Cycle of Unintended Consequences in United States Immigration Policy." *Journal of American Ethnic History* 21, no. 4 (Summer 2002): 3–27.

Lears, Jackson. *Something for Nothing: Luck in America.* New York: Penguin Publishing Group, 2003.

Leblang, David. "Harnessing the Diaspora: Dual Citizenship, Migrant Return Remittances." *Comparative Political Studies.* Published ahead of print, September 29, 2015. doi:10.1177/0010414015606736.

Lee, Erika. *America for Americans: A History of Xenophobia in the United States.* New York: Basic Books, 2019.

———. *At America's Gates: Chinese Immigration during the Exclusion Era, 1882-1943.* Chapel Hill: University of North Carolina Press, 2004.

Lindsay, James M. "The State Department Complex after the Cold War." In *U.S. Foreign Policy after the Cold War,* edited by Randall B. Ripley and James M. Lindsay, 74–105. Pittsburgh, PA: University of Pittsburgh Press, 1997.

Lindskoog, Carl. *Detain and Punish: Haitian Refugees and the Rise of the World's Largest Immigration Detention System.* Gainesville: University of Florida Press, 2019.

Loescher, Gil. "State Responses to Refugees and Asylum Seekers in Europe." In *West European Immigration and Immigrant Policy in the New Century,* edited by Anthony M. Messina, 33–46. Westport, CT: Praeger, 2002.

Luckstead, Jeff, Stephen Devadoss, and Abelardo Rodriguez. "The Effects of North American Free Trade Agreement and United States Farm Policies on Illegal Immigration and Agricultural Trade." *Journal of Agricultural and Applied Economics* 44, no. 1 (February 2012): 1–19.

Lundberg, Shelly. "Tiger Parenting and American Inequality: An Essay on Chua and Rubenfeld's the Triple Package: How Three Unlikely Traits Explain the Rise and Fall of Cultural Groups in America." *Journal of Economic Literature* 53, no. 4 (2015): 945–960. doi: https://doi.org/10.1257/jel.53.4.945.

Makuchi Nfah-Abbenyi, Juliana. *Your Madness, Not Mine: Stories of Cameroon.* Athens: Ohio University Press, 1999.

Manuh, Takyiwaa, Richard Asante, and Jerome Djangmah. "The Brain Drain in the Higher Education Sector in Ghana." In *At Home in the World? International Migration and Development in Contemporary Ghana and West Africa*, edited by Takyiwaa Manuh, 268–269. Accra, Ghana: Sub-Saharan Publishers, 2005.

Marinari, Maddalena. *Unwanted: Italian and Jewish Mobilization against Restrictive Immigration Laws, 1882–1965.* Chapel Hill: University of North Carolina Press, 2019.

Massey, Douglas S. *Immigration and the Great Recession.* Stanford, CA: Russell Sage Foundation and the Stanford Center on Poverty and Inequality, 2012.

Matera, Marc. *Black London: The Imperial Metropolis and Decolonization in the Twentieth Century.* Oakland: University of California Press, 2015.

Matthews, Jane De Hart. "Arts and the People: The New Deal Quest for a Cultural Democracy." *Journal of American History* 62, no. 2 (September 1975): 316–339.

Mergo, Teferi. "America's Best Aid Program? Impacts of Green Card Lottery on Ethiopian Households." *Development Impact* (blog), World Bank Blogs, December 13, 2011. http://blogs.worldbank.org/impactevaluations/america-s-best-aid-program-impacts-of-green-card-lottery-on-ethiopian-households-guest-post-by-tefer.

———. "The Effects of International Migration on Migrant-Source Households: Evidence from Ethiopian Diversity-Visa Lottery Migrants." *World Development* 84 (2016): 69–81. https://doi.org/10.1016/j.worlddev.2016.04.001.

Miescher, Stephan F. *Making Men in Ghana.* Bloomington: Indiana University Press, 2005.

———. "'Nkrumah's Baby': The Akosombo Dam and the Dream of Development in Ghana, 1952–1966." *Water History* 6 (2014): 341–366. doi:10.1007/s12685-014-0112-8.

Miescher, Stephan F., and Leslie Ashbaugh. "Been-To Visions: Transnational Linkages among a Ghanaian Dispersed Community in the Twentieth Century." *Ghana Studies* 2 (1999): 57–76.

Miescher, Stephan F., and Dzodzi Tsikata. "Hydro-power and the Promise of Modernity and Development in Ghana: Comparing the Akosombo and Bui Dam Projects." *Ghana Studies* 12/13 (2009/2010): 15–53. https://www.history.ucsb.edu/wp-content/uploads/1-Miescher_Tsikata.pdf.

Migration Policy Institute. "The Nigerian Diaspora in the United States." June 2015. http://www.migrationpolicy.org/sites/default/files/publications/RAD-Nigeria.pdf.

Mikell, Gwendolyn, and Princeton N. Lyman. "Critical U.S. Bilateral Relations in Africa: Nigeria and South Africa." In *Africa Policy in the Clinton Years: Critical Choices for the Bush Administration*, edited by J. Stephen Morrison and Jennifer G. Cooke, 73–95. Washington, DC: CSIS Press, 2001.

Molina, Natalia. *How Race Is Made in America: Immigration, Citizenship, and the Historical Power of Racial Scripts*. Berkeley: University of California Press, 2013.

Morgan-Trostle, Juliana, and Kexin Zheng. *The State of Black Immigrants*. Black Alliance for Just Immigration and NYU School of Law Immigrant Rights Clinic. Accessed August 10, 2022. https://www.immigrationresearch.org/system/files/sobi-fullreport-jan22.pdf.

Morrison, Bruce. "Twenty Five Years Later: Reflecting on the Immigration Act of 1990." Migration Policy Institute, December 8, 2015. http://www.migrationpolicy.org/events/twenty-five-years-later-reflecting-immigration-act-1990.

Myers, Dowell. "Demographic Dynamism and Metropolitan Change: Comparing Los Angeles, New York, Chicago, and Washington, DC." *Housing Policy Debate* 10, no. 4 (1999): 919–954. doi:10.1080/10511482.1999.9521355.

Nevins, Joseph. *Operation Gatekeeper: The Rise of the "Illegal Alien" and the Making of the U.S.-Mexico Boundary*. New York: Routledge, 2002.

Ngai, Mae M. "The Architecture of Race in American Immigration Law: A Reexamination of the Immigration Act of 1924." *Journal of American History* 86, no. 1 (June 1999): 67–92.

———. *Impossible Subjects: Illegal Aliens and the Making of Modern America*. Princeton, NJ: Princeton University Press, 2004.

———. "'A Nation of Immigrants': The Cold War and Civil Rights Origins of Illegal Immigration." *Occasional Paper* 38 (2010). https://www.ias.edu/sites/default/files/sss/papers/paper38.pdf.

———. "The Strange Career of the Illegal Alien: Immigration Restriction in the United States, 1921-1965." *Law and History Review* 21 (Spring 2003): 69–107.

Nguyen, Tram. *We Are All Suspects Now: Untold Stories from Immigrant Communities after 9/11*. Boston: Beacon Press, 2005.

Ngwa, Lydia, and Wilfred Ngwa, eds. *From Dust to Snow: Bush-faller*. Princeton, NJ: Horeb Communications, 2006.

Ngwane, George. *The Cameroon Condition*. Bamenda, Cameroon: Langaa Research and Publishing Common Initiative Group, 2012.

Nieswand, Boris. "The Burgers' Paradox: Migration and the Transnationalization of Social Inequality in Southern Ghana." *Ethnography* 15, no. 4 (2014): 403–425.

Nkwi, Walter Gam, and Mirjam de Bruijn. "'Human Telephone Lines': Flag Post Mail Relay Runners in British Southern Cameroon (1916-1955) and the Establishment of a Modern Communications Network." *International Review of Social History* 59, no. S22 (December 2014): 211–235.

Nugent, Paul. *Africa Since Independence*. New York: Palgrave Macmillan, 2004.

———. *Big Men, Small Boys, and Politics in Ghana: Power, Ideology, and the Burden of History, 1982-1994*. London: Pinter Publishing Limited, 1995.

———. *Boundaries, Communities and State-Making in West Africa: The Centrality of the Margins.* New York: Cambridge University Press, 2019.

———. *Smugglers, Secessionists & Loyal Citizens on the Ghana-Togo Frontier: The Lie of the Borderlands Since 1914.* Athens: Ohio University Press, 2002.

Nugent, Paul, Daniel Hammett, and Sara Dorman. "Introduction." In *Making Nations, Creating Strangers: States and Citizenship in Africa*, edited by Paul Nugent, Daniel Hammett, and Sara Dorman, 3–26. Leiden: Brill, 2007.

Nyamnjoh, Francis B. "Cameroonian Bushfailing: Negotiation of Identity and Belonging in Fiction and Ethnography." *American Ethnologist* 38, no. 4 (2011): 701–713. http://www.jstor.org/stable/41410427.

Nyamnjoh, Francis B., and Ben Page. "Whiteman Kontri and the Enduring Allure of Modernity among Cameroonian Youth." *African Affairs* 101, no. 405 (2002): 607–634. http://www.jstor.org/stable/3518469.

Nye, Joseph S., Jr. *Bound to Lead: The Changing Nature of American Power.* New York: Basic Books, 1990.

———. *Soft Power: The Means to Success in World Politics.* New York: Public Affairs, 2004.

Nyonator, Frank, and Delanyo Dovlo. "The Health of the Nation and the Brain Drain in the Health Sector." In *At Home in the World? International Migration and Development in Contemporary Ghana and West Africa*, edited by Takyiwaa Manuh, 227–249. Accra, Ghana: Sub-Saharan Publishers, 2005.

Nzongola-Ntalaja, Georges. *The Congo from Leopold to Kabila: A People's History.* London: Zed Books, 2002.

Obeng-Odoom, Franklin. "Neoliberalism and the Urban Economy in Ghana: Urban Employment, Inequality, and Poverty." *Growth and Change* 43, no. 1 (March 2012): 85–109.

O'Connell, Christine. "Plight of France's *Sans-Papiers* Gives a Face to Struggle over Immigration Reform." *Human Rights Brief* 4, no. 1 (Fall 1996). https://digital commons.wcl.american.edu/hrbrief/vol4/iss1/1/.

Oquaye, Mike. "The Ghanaian Elections of 1992—a Dissenting View." *African Affairs* 94, no. 375 (1995): 259–275. http://www.jstor.org/stable/723781.

Osaghae, Eghosa. *Crippled Giant: Nigeria Since Independence.* London: Christopher Hurst, 1998.

Osei, Philip D. "Political Liberalisation and the Implementation of Value Added Tax in Ghana." *Journal of Modern African Studies* 38, no. 2 (July 2000): 255–278. https://www.jstor.org/stable/161651.

Overa, Ragnhild. "When Men Do Women's Work: Structural Adjustment, Unemployment and Changing Gender Relations in the Informal Economy of Accra, Ghana." *Journal of Modern African Studies* 45, no. 4 (December 2007): 539–563.

Owusu-Ansah, Justice K., and Kevin B. O'Connor. "Housing Demand in the Urban Fringe around Kumasi, Ghana." *Journal of Housing and the Built Environment* 25, no. 1 (April 2010): 1–17.

Padmore, George. *Pan-Africanism or Communism? The Coming Struggle for Africa.* London: Dobson, 1956.

Palmer, Breanne J. "The Crossroads: Being Black, Immigrant, and Undocumented in the Era of #BlackLivesMatter." *Georgetown Journal of Law & Modern Critical Race Perspectives* 9, no. 1 (Spring 2017): 99–121.

Park, Marlene, and Gerald E. Markowitz. *Democratic Vistas: Post Offices and Public Art in the New Deal.* Philadelphia, PA: Temple University Press, 1984.

Patel, Ian Sanjay. *We're Here Because You Were There: Immigration and the End of Empire.* London: Verso Books, 2021.

Pelican, Michaela. "International Migration: Virtue or Vice? Perspectives from Cameroon." *Journal of Ethnic and Migration Studies* 39, no. 2 (2013): 237–257.

Perry, Kennetta Hammond. *London Is the Place for Me: Black Britons, Citizenship, and the Politics of Race.* New York: Oxford University Press, 2015.

Pierre, Jemima. "Black Immigrants in the United States and the 'Cultural Narrative' of Ethnicity." *Identities: Global Studies in Culture and Power* 11, no. 2 (2004): 141–170.

———. *The Predicament of Blackness: Postcolonial Ghana and the Politics of Race.* Chicago: University of Chicago Press, 2012.

Piot, Charles. *Nostalgia for the Future: West Africa after the Cold War.* Chicago: University of Chicago Press, 2010.

Pommerolle, Marie-Emmanuelle, and Hans De Marie Heungoup. "The 'Anglophone Crisis': A Tale of the Cameroonian Postcolony." *African Affairs* 116, no. 464 (2017): 526–538.

Power, Samantha. *A Problem from Hell: America and the Age of Genocide.* New York: Basic Books, 2002.

Prestedge, Dudley Herbert. *Biafra: The Stamps, History & Postal History of the Rebel State During the Nigerian Civil War.* Dronfield: West Africa Study Circle, 2000.

Quinlin, Michael P. *Irish Boston: A Lively Look at Boston's Colorful Irish Past.* Guilford, CT: Globe Pequot, 2004.

Ratha, Dilip. "Remittances: A Lifeline for Development." *Finance & Development* 42, no. 4 (December 2005). https://www.imf.org/external/pubs/ft/fandd/2005 /12/basics.htm.

Ratha, Dilip, Sanket Mohapatra, Caglar Ozden, Sonia Plaza, and William Shaw. *Leveraging Migration for Africa: Remittances, Skills, and Investments.* Washington, DC: World Bank Publications, 2011.

Reavis, Dick J. *Without Documents.* New York: Condor, 1978.

Reimers, David M. "An Unintended Reform: The 1965 Immigration Act and Third World Immigration to the United States." *Journal of American Ethnic History* 3, no. 1 (Fall 1983): 9–28.

Rights Working Group, Penn State Law. *The NSEERS Effect: A Decade of Racial Profiling, Fear, and Secrecy.* May 2012. https://pennstatelaw.psu.edu/_file /clinics/NSEERS_report.pdf.

Rodgers, Daniel T. *Age of Fracture.* Cambridge, MA: Belknap Press of Harvard University Press, 2011.

Roediger, David R. *Working toward Whiteness: How America's Immigrants Became White: The Strange Journey from Ellis Island to the Suburbs.* New York: Basic Books, 2006.

Roitman, Janet. *Fiscal Disobedience: An Anthropology of Economic Regulation in Central Africa*. Princeton, NJ: Princeton University Press, 2005.

——. "The Right to Tax: Economic Citizenship in the Chad Basin." *Citizenship Studies* 11, no. 2 (2007): 187–209. doi:10.1080/13621020701262636.

Sablosky, Juliet Antunes. "Reinvention, Reorganization, Retreat: American Cultural Diplomacy at Century's End, 1978-1998." *Journal of Arts Management, Law, and Society* 29, no. 1 (1999): 30–46. doi:10.1080/10632929909597283.

Sako, Soumana. "Brain Drain and Africa's Development: A Reflection." *African Issues* 30, no. 1 (2002): 25–30.

Sánchez, George J. "Face the Nation: Race, Immigration, and the Rise of Nativism in Late Twentieth Century America." *International Migration Review* 31, no. 4 (Winter 1997): 1009–1030.

Sandoval-Strausz, A. K. *Barrio America: How Latino Immigrants Saved the American City*. New York: Basic Books, 2019.

Sankore, Rotimi. "Africa Killing Us Softly." *New African* 445 (November 2005): 8–12.

Savell, Stephanie. "The Costs of United States' Post-9/11 'Security Assistance': How Counterterrorism Intensified Conflict in Burkina Faso and around the World." *20 Years of War: A Costs of War Research Series*, March 4, 2021. https://watson.brown.edu/costsofwar/files/cow/imce/papers/2021/Costs%20of%20Counterterrorism%20in%20Burkina%20Faso_Costs%20of%20War_Savell.pdf.

Schachtman, Tom. *Airlift to America: How Barack Obama, Sr., John F. Kennedy, Tom Mboya, and 800 East African Students Changed Their World and Ours*. New York: St. Martin's Press, 2009.

Schmidt, Elizabeth. *Foreign Intervention in Africa: From the Cold War to the War on Terror. New Approaches to African History*. Cambridge: Cambridge University Press, 2013.

Schrag, Philip G. *A Well-Founded Fear: The Congressional Battle to Save Political Asylum in America*. New York: Routledge, 2000.

Schrag, Zachary M. *The Fires of Philadelphia: Citizen-Soldiers, Nativists, and the1844 Riots over the Soul of a Nation*. New York: Pegasus Books, 2021.

Self, Robert O. *All in the Family: The Realignment of American Democracy Since the 1960s*. New York: Hill and Wang, 2012.

Serwer, Adam. "Birtherism of a Nation," *The Atlantic*, May 13, 2020. https://www.theatlantic.com/ideas/archive/2020/05/birtherism-and-trump/610978/

——. "The Coronavirus Was an Emergency Until Trump Found out Who Was Dying," *The Atlantic*, May 8, 2020, https://www.theatlantic.com/ideas/archive/2020/05/americas-racial-contract-showing/611389/.

——. "The Cruelty Is the Point." *The Atlantic*, October 3, 2018. https://www.theatlantic.com/ideas/archive/2018/10/the-cruelty-is-the-point/572104/.

Shillington, Kevin. *History of Africa*. 4th ed. London: Red Globe Press, Macmillan Education Limited, 2019.

Shulman, Peter A. "Ben Franklin's Ghost: World Peace, American Slavery, and the Global Politics of Information before the Universal Postal Union." *Journal of Global History* 10, no. 2 (July 2015): 212–234.

Siyam, Sylvie, and Serge Daho. "Cameroon: The Stammering of Cameroon's Communications Surveillance." In *Global Information Society Watch 2014: Communications Surveillance in the Digital Age, GISWatch*. 2014. https://www.giswatch.org/sites/default/files/gw2014-cameroon.pdf.

Siyam Siwe, Sylvie, Serge Daho, and Laurence Houssou. *Report: Cameroon*. GISWatch, 2008. https://www.giswatch.org/sites/default/files/Cameroon_0.pdf.

Skrentny, John D., and Jane Lilly López. "Obama's Immigration Reform: The Triumph of Executive Action." *Indiana Journal of Law and Social Equality* 2, no. 1, article 3 (2013). https://www.repository.law.indiana.edu/ijlse/vol2/iss1/3.

Smith, Andrew. "Nigerian Scam E-mails and the Charms of Capital." *Cultural Studies* 23, no. 1 (2009): 27–47. http://eprints.gla.ac.uk/6581/1/6581.pdf.

Smith, Daniel Jordan. *A Culture of Corruption: Everyday Deception and Popular Discontent in Nigeria*. Princeton, NJ: Princeton University Press, 2007.

Soboroff, Jacob. *Separated: Inside an American Tragedy*. New York: Custom House, 2020.

Sommers, Kyla. "'I Believe in the City': The Black Freedom Struggle and the 1968 Civil Disturbances in Washington, D.C." PhD diss., George Washington University, 2019. ProQuest Number: 13423649.

Soyinka, Wole. *The Open Sore of a Continent: A Personal Narrative of the Nigerian Crisis*. New York: Oxford University Press, 1996.

Spiro, Peter J. "Afroyim: Vaunting Citizenship, Presaging Transnationality." In *Immigration Stories*, edited by David Martin and Peter Schuck, 147–168. New York: Foundation Press, 2005.

——. *Beyond Citizenship: American Identity after Globalization*. New York: Oxford University Press, 2008.

——. "Dual Citizenship as Human Right." *International Journal of Constitutional Law* 8, no. 1 (January 2010):111–130.

——. "Dual Nationality and the Meaning of Citizenship." *Emory Law Journal* 46, no. 4 (Fall 1997): 1411–1486.

Starosielski, Nicole. *The Undersea Network*. Durham, NC: Duke University Press, 2015.

Steger, Manfred B., and Ravi K. Roy. *Neoliberalism: A Very Short Introduction*. New York: Oxford University Press, 2010.

Stoller, Paul. *Money Has No Smell: The Africanization of New York City*. Chicago: University of Chicago Press, 2010.

Stovall, Tyler. *White Freedom: The Racial History of an Idea*. Princeton, NJ: Princeton University Press, 2021.

Strange, Susan. *Casino Capitalism: With an Introduction by Matthew Watson*. Manchester: Manchester University Press, 2015.

Sylvanus, Nina. *Patterns in Circulation: Cloth, Gender, and Materiality in West Africa*. Chicago: University of Chicago Press, 2016.

Takougang, Joseph. *Cameroonian Immigrants in the United States: Between the Homeland and the Diaspora*. Lanham, MD: Lexington Books, 2014.

——. "The Post-Ahidjo Era in Cameroon: Continuity and Change." *Journal of Third World Studies* 10, no. 2 (1993): 268–302. http://www.jstor.org/stable/45193445.

Talton, Benjamin. *In This Land of Plenty: Mickey Leland and Africa in American Politics*. Philadelphia: University of Pennsylvania Press, 2019.

Tancredo, Tom. "Tancredo: Tough Immigration Reform Essential to Maintain U.S. Identity." Interview by Robert McMahon, Council on Foreign Relations, July 24, 2006. https://www.cfr.org/interview/tancredo-tough-immigration-reform-essential-maintain-us-identity.

Tankus, Nathan. "Jackpot: For Colonial Slaves, Playing the Lottery Was a Chance at Freedom." JSTOR Daily, February 2, 2016. https://daily.jstor.org/jackpot-for-colonial-slaves-playing-the-lottery-was-a-chance-at-freedom/.

Tarnoff, Ben. *Internet for the People: The Fight for Our Digital Future*. London and Brooklyn, NY: Verso, 2022.

Tebeje, Ainalem. "Brain Drain and Capacity Building in Africa." International Development Research Centre, February 22, 2005. https://idl-bnc-idrc.dspacedirect.org/bitstream/handle/10625/34566/126237.pdf.

Teske, Steen. "Cuban Refugee Crisis." *Encyclopedia of Arkansas*. Updated March 12, 2015. https://encyclopediaofarkansas.net/entries/cuban-refugee-crisis-4248/.

Thompson, Christie. "Deporting 'Felons, Not Families.'" *Marshall Project*, November 21, 2014. https://www.themarshallproject.org/2014/11/21/deporting-felons-not-families.

Thompson, Dennis F. "Mediated Corruption: The Case of the Keating Five." *American Political Science Review* 87, no. 2 (June 1993): 369–381.

Tichenor, Daniel J. *Dividing Lines: The Politics of Immigration Control in America*. Princeton, NJ: Princeton University Press, 2009.

Torrent, Mélanie. *Diplomacy and Nation-Building in Africa: Franco-British Relations and Cameroon at the End of Empire*. London: I.B. Tauris, 2012.

Townsend, Sarah L. "Undocumented Irish Need Apply: Ethnic Whiteness, Immigrant Rights, and the Campaign for US Diversity Visas in the 1980s." *Radical History Review*, no. 143 (May 2022): 125–140.

Treitler, Vilna Bashi. *The Ethnic Project: Transforming Racial Fiction into Ethnic Factions*. Stanford, CA: Stanford University Press, 2013.

Turse, Nick. "Soldiers in Cameroon, a Close U.S. Ally, Commit Mass Rape, Report Says." *The Intercept*, February 26, 2021. https://theintercept.com/2021/02/26/cameroon-soldiers-mass-rape-report/.

van Wyk, Ilana. "Postcolonial Africa and its Lotteries." *Critical Gambling Studies* (blog). 2021. doi: https://doi.org/10.29173/cgs117

Vásquez, Tina. "Q&A: The Biden Administration Has Spent Black History Month Deporting Black Immigrants. Why Aren't People in the Streets?" *PRISM Reports*, February 11, 2021. https://prismreports.org/2021/02/11/qa-the-biden-administration-has-spent-black-history-month-deporting-black-immigrants/.

Veney, Cassandra R. "The Effects of Immigration and Refugee Policies on Africans in the United States: From the Civil Rights Movement to the War on Terrorism." In *The New African Diaspora*, edited by Isidore Okpewho and Nkiru Nzegwu, 196–214. Bloomington: Indiana University Press, 2009.

Vidacs, Bea. "Banal Nationalism, Football, and Discourse Community in Africa." *Studies in Ethnicity and Nationalism* 11, no. 1 (April 2011): 25–41.

Vine, David. *The United States of War: A Global History of America's Endless Conflicts, from Columbus to the Islamic State*. Oakland: University of California Press, 2020.

Von Eschen, Penny M. "Duke Ellington Plays Baghdad: Rethinking Hard and Soft Power from the Outside In." In *Contested Democracy: Freedom, Race, and Power in American History*, edited by Penny Von Eschen and Manisha Sinha, 279–300. New York: Columbia University Press, 2007.

———. *Satchmo Blows Up the World: Jazz Ambassadors Play the Cold War*. Cambridge, MA: Harvard University Press, 2004.

Walia, Harsha. *Border and Rule: Global Migration, Capitalism, and the Rise of Racist Nationalism*. New York: Haymarket Books, 2021.

Wardle, Jonathan H. "The Strategic Use of Mexico to Restrict South American Access to the Diversity Visa Lottery." *Vanderbilt Law Review* 58, no. 6 (November 2005): 1963–1999.

Warren, Robert, and Jeffrey S. Passel. "A Count of the Uncountable: Estimates of Undocumented Aliens Counted in the 1980 United States Census." *Demography* 24, no. 3 (August 1987): 375–393.

Waslin, Michelle. "Counterterrorism and the Latino Community Since September 11th." *In Defense of the Alien* 26 (2003): 83–99. http://www.jstor.org /stable/23142816.

Whitaker, Beth Elise. "The Politics of Home: Dual Citizenship and the African Diaspora." *International Migration Review* 45, no. 4 (Winter 2011): 755–783.

White, Luise. *Speaking with Vampires: Rumor and History in Colonial Africa*. Berkeley: University of California Press, 2000.

Williams, Justin. "The 'Rawlings Revolution' and Rediscovery of the African Diaspora in Ghana (1983–2015)." *African Studies* 74, no. 3 (2015): 366–387. doi:1 0.1080/00020184.2015.1015313.

Williams, Susan. *White Malice: The CIA and the Covert Recolonization of Africa*. New York: Public Affairs, 2021.

Wolgin, Philip E. "Beyond National Origins: The Development of Modern Immigration Policymaking, 1948-1968." PhD diss., UC Berkeley, 2011.

———. "2 Years Later, Immigrants Are Still Waiting on Immigration Reform." Center for American Progress, June 24, 2015. https://www.americanprogress .org/issues/immigration/news/2015/06/24/115835/2-years-later-immigrants -are-still-waiting-on-immigration-reform/.

Wong, Madeleine. "Emerging Patterns of African Refugee Resettlement in the United States." Master's thesis, Department of Geography, Florida Atlantic University, 1995. http://fau.digital.flvc.org/islandora/object/fau%3A11941 /datastream/OBJ/view/Emerging_patterns_of_African_refugee_resettlement _in_the_United_States.pdf.

Worsop, Richard L. "Gambling Boom: Will the Gaming Industry's Growth Hurt Society?" *Congressional Quarterly Press* 4, no. 11 (March 18, 1994): 241–264.

Wu, Ellen D. *The Color of Success: Asian Americans and the Origins of the Model Minority*. Princeton, NJ: Princeton University Press, 2015.

Wybiral, Leslie. "The Ethiopian Committee on Immigration, Inc.: Social Justice in Action." Hidden Heritage Collections, April 28, 2016. http://hiddenheritage collections.org/2016/04/the-ethiopian-committee-on-immigration-inc-social -justice-in-action/.

Young, Crawford. "Nation, Ethnicity, and Citizenship: Dilemmas of Democracy and Civil Order in Africa." In *Making Nations, Creating Strangers: States and Citizenship in Africa*, edited by Paul Nugent, Daniel Hammett, and Sara Dorman, 241–264. Leiden: Brill, 2007.

———. *The Postcolonial State in Africa: Fifty Years of Independence, 1960-2010*. Madison: University of Wisconsin Press, 2012.

Zachary, G. Pascal. "Ghana, Information Technology and Development in Africa" *First Monday* 9, no. 3 (March 2004). http://firstmonday.org/ojs/index.php/fm /article/view/1126/.

Zaiotti, Ruben. *Cultures of Border Control: Schengen and the Evolution of European Frontiers*. Chicago: University of Chicago Press, 2011.

Zolberg, Aristide R. "Immigration Control Policy: Law and Implementation." In *The New Americans: A Guide to Immigration since 1965*, edited by Mary C. Waters and Reed Ueda, 29–42. Cambridge, MA: Harvard University Press, 2007.

———. *A Nation by Design: Immigration Policy in the Fashioning of America*. Cambridge, MA: Harvard University Press, 2006.

Zong, Jie, and Jeanne Batalova. "Sub-Saharan African Immigrants in the United States." Migration Policy Institute, October 30, 2014. http://www.migrationpolicy .org/article/sub-saharan-african-immigrants-united-states.